RE-IMAGINING LABOUR LAW FOR DEVELOPMENT

The aim of this book is to explore labour law's conceptual and normative narrative. If labour law is informed by the wider political and economic landscape within which it operates, then given the declining prevalence of the post-war model of full employment within a formal welfare state regime, what shape does or should labour law assume in response to the transformation of the political economy in countries of the global North? Correspondingly, what is the proper role to be played by labour law and labour relations institutions in the development process within industrialising countries of the global South, where informal employment has long been, and remains, the predominant form? Drawing on the expertise of leading labour law scholars, this collection addresses those questions by examining the growth and continued prevalence of informality. Offering research that is both empirically grounded and doctrinally astute, the book explores the changing character of labour law in the global North and South.

Re-Imagining Labour Law for Development

Informal Work in the Global North and South

Edited by
Diamond Ashiagbor

•HART•
OXFORD • LONDON • NEW YORK • NEW DELHI • SYDNEY

HART PUBLISHING

Bloomsbury Publishing Plc

Kemp House, Chawley Park, Cumnor Hill, Oxford, OX2 9PH, UK

HART PUBLISHING, the Hart/Stag logo, BLOOMSBURY and the Diana logo are trademarks of Bloomsbury Publishing Plc

First published in Great Britain 2019

A catalogue record for this book is available from the British Library.

Library of Congress Cataloging-in-Publication data

Names: Society of Legal Scholars. Annual conference. (2016 : University of London, Institute of Advanced Legal Studies) | Ashiagbor, Diamond, editor.

Title: Re-imagining labour law for development : informal work in the global north and south / edited by Diamond Ashiagbor.

Description: Oxford, UK ; Chicago, Illinois : Hart Publishing, 2019. | Includes bibliographical references and index. | "The Society of Legal Scholars (SLS) awarded the conference its largest annual research grant, with the conference being badged as the SLS Annual Seminar 2016. Additional research funding which facilitated the conference organisation was provided by the SOAS School of Law and the SOAS Faculty of Law and Social Sciences. I wish to thank colleagues in the SOAS Centres & Programmes Office who provided logistical support: Jane Savory, Thomas Abbs and Yasmin Jayesimi. Many thanks also go to the Institute of Advanced Legal Studies for agreeing to host us for the two day conference."—ECIP acknowledgements.

Identifiers: LCCN 2019004516 (print) | LCCN 2019006126 (ebook) | ISBN 9781509913121 (EPub) | ISBN 9781509913152 (hardback)

Subjects: LCSH: Labor laws and legislation—Congresses. | Under-the-table employment—Congresses. | Law and economic development—Congresses. | BISAC: LAW / Labor & Employment. | LAW / Research.

Classification: LCC K1704.8 (ebook) | LCC K1704.8 .S63 2016 (print) | DDC 344.01—dc23

LC record available at https://lccn.loc.gov/2019004516

ISBN: HB: 978-1-50991-315-2
ePDF: 978-1-50991-311-4
ePub: 978-1-50991-312-1

Typeset by Compuscript Ltd, Shannon

ACKNOWLEDGEMENTS

I would like to offer my thanks to the people and organisations who made possible this edited collection, and the preceding conference from which the chapters are drawn. The Society of Legal Scholars (SLS) awarded the conference its largest annual research grant, with the conference being badged as the SLS Annual Seminar 2016. Additional research funding which facilitated the conference organisation was provided by the SOAS School of Law and the SOAS Faculty of Law and Social Sciences. I wish to thank colleagues in the SOAS Centres & Programmes Office who provided logistical support: Jane Savory, Thomas Abbs and Yasmin Jayesimi. Many thanks also go to the Institute of Advanced Legal Studies for agreeing to host us for the two-day conference.

Finally, I am very grateful for the scholarly contribution of colleagues whose chapters appear in this volume and who presented their papers at the conference, as well as those who agreed to chair the sessions and act as discussants: Pamhidzai H Bamu, Lizzie Barmes, Adelle Blackett, Nicola Countouris, Simon Deakin, Hitesh Dhorajiwala, Ruth Dukes, Colin Fenwick, Judy Fudge, Emily Grabham, John Howe, Deirdre McCann, Liam McHugh-Russell, Shelley Marshall, Petra Mahy, Richard Mitchell, Guy Mundlak, Tonia Novitz, Amanda Perry-Kessaris, Sanjay Pinto, Lorena Poblete, Kerry Rittich, Supriya Routh, Ann Stewart, Maria Azzurra Tranfaglia, and Dzodzi Tsikata.

Cover image:

Fading Cloth, by El Anatsui. Saint Louis Art Museum, purchased from October Gallery, London.

El Anatsui (born 1944) is a Ghanaian sculptor and painter. This work is part of a series which combines traditional (west) African techniques and imagery (in this case, the design of a woven Kente cloth) with abstraction. It uses found recycled African materials (drink bottle caps) which are flattened and stitched together with copper wire to form a wall-mounted installation or assemblage. The work hangs like a tapestry or large Kente cloth. The work reflects and traces a story of colonial and postcolonial economic and cultural exchange between Africa and the global North. It can be seen as representing informality: the use of found materials, repurposing of materials, and the absence of a fixed form.

Diamond Ashiagbor,
December 2018

CONTENTS

NOTES ON CONTRIBUTORS

Diamond Ashiagbor

Professor of Law at the University of Kent, and Senior Associate Research Fellow at the Institute of Advanced Legal Studies (IALS), University of London; formerly Professor of Law and Director of Research at IALS, Professor of Law at SOAS University of London, and Reader in Law at University College London. She is a graduate of the University of Oxford and has a PhD from the European University Institute in Florence. She has been Visiting Scholar at Columbia Law School, New York; Senior Fellow at Melbourne Law School; and Genest Global Faculty at Osgoode Hall Law School. She has been the recipient of a US-EU Fulbright Research Award; and a Leverhulme Trust Research Fellowship. Diamond publishes on labour/employment law; regional integration (the European Union and the African Union); law and development; economic sociology of law; human rights and equality. Publications include *The European Employment Strategy: Labour Market Regulation and New Governance*, OUP, 2005; *Towards an Economic Sociology of Law*, Wiley, 2013 (with Prabha Kotiswaran and Amanda Perry-Kessaris). She is on the Editorial Board of *Feminist Legal Studies*, and the Executive Committee of the Socio-Legal Studies Association.

Pamhidzai H. Bamu

Law Programme Coordinator for Africa, Women in Informal Employment Globalizing and Organizing (WIEGO). Pamhidzai was born and raised in Harare, Zimbabwe. She holds an LLB, LLM (Labour Law) and a PhD (Labour Law) from the University of Cape Town, and held a Post-Doctoral Research Fellowship at Stellenbosch University. She has worked as a Researcher in the Institute of Development and Labour Law at the University of Cape Town, and the Social Law Project at the University of the Western Cape and has undertaken and published research on various labour issues in South Africa and Southern Africa. She has served as a consultant to the ILO (Pretoria) on labour migration in SADC (2013–2014), a consultant to the ILO (Harare and Pretoria) on migrant domestic workers in the Zimbabwe-South Africa corridor in 2014 and to the SADC Secretariat (Gender Unit) on trafficking in persons in the SADC Region from 2014 to 2015. She has also served as a consultant to the ILO Geneva on non-standard employment in Africa in 2015. Recent publications include: 'Social regionalism in the Southern Africa Development Community: The international, regional and national interplay of labour alternative dispute resolution mechanisms' (with Rutendo Mudarikwa) in Adelle Blackett and Anne Trebilcock (eds) *Research Handbook on Transnational Labour Law*, Edward Elgar Publishing, 2015.

Simon Deakin

Professor of Law at the University of Cambridge. He specialises in labour law, private law, company law and EU law. His research is concerned, more generally, with the relationship between law and the social sciences, and he contributes regularly to the fields of law and economics, law and development, and empirical legal studies. He is Director of the Centre for Business Research, co-Chair of the University's Strategic Research Initiative in Public Policy, and a Fellow of Peterhouse. He is editor in chief of the *Industrial Law Journal* and a member of the editorial board of the *Cambridge Journal of Economics*. He was elected to a Fellowship of the British Academy in 2005 and in 2012 was awarded an Honorary Doctorate by the Catholic University of Louvain. He is currently a principal investigator on two ESRC-funded projects and has recently carried out contract research for the International Labour Organization and for the UK Government's Foresight review of the future of British manufacturing. Publications include: *The Law of the Labour Market: Industrialization, Employment, and Legal Evolution*, OUP, 2005 (with Frank Wilkinson); *Labour Law* (with Gillian Morris) Hart, 2012; *Legal Origin Theory* (with Katharina Pistor) Edward Elgar, 2012, and *Labour, Finance and Inequality: The Insecurity Cycle in British Public Policy* (with Suzanne J. Konzelmann, Marc Fovargue-Davies and Frank Wilkinson), Routledge, 2018.

Ruth Dukes

Professor of Labour Law at the University of Glasgow and Principal Investigator on the ERC-funded project *Work on Demand: Contracting for Work in a Changing Economy*. Member of the Young Academy of the Royal Society of Edinburgh. Ruth holds degrees from the University of Edinburgh (LLB), the Humboldt University in Berlin (LLM with distinction), and the London School of Economics (PhD). In 2011/12 she was an Early Career Fellow of the Arts and Humanities Research Council, and a MacCormick Fellow at the University of Edinburgh. Ruth has published widely in the fields of labour law and labour history. Her 2009 article 'Otto Kahn-Freund and Collective Laissez-Faire: an Edifice without a Keystone?', was awarded the Modern Law Review's Wedderburn Prize. Her 2014 monograph, *The Labour Constitution: the Enduring Idea of Labour Law* (OUP) was widely reviewed and formed the subject of a Symposium in the 2018 volume of *Jurisprudence*.

John Howe

Professor and Director of the University of Melbourne School of Government, and previously Co-Director of the Centre for Employment and Labour Relations Law in Melbourne Law School. John's research interests include labour market policy and regulation, regulatory theory, and corporate accountability. He has written extensively on the role of the state in regulating employment and labour markets, and on the intersection between state-based regulation and corporate governance. John is presently engaged in research concerning regulatory enforcement of minimum employment standards in Australia and the Asia-Pacific region. He is also researching how large business organisations engage in self-regulation of labour practices through internal policy and rule-making processes, and the interaction between these policies and employment laws. John is Chair of the Steering Committee of the Labour Law Research Network, and he is an Editor of the *Australian Journal of Labour Law*.

Deirdre McCann

Professor at Durham Law School. Her research is in the field of labour law and policy at the domestic, EU and international levels. It has a particular focus on the influence of flexibility discourses on labour market regulation, precarious work, the measurement and comparison of labour law regimes and the influence of state norms in low-income settings. Her publications include *Regulating Flexible Work*, OUP, 2008 and *Creative Labour Regulation*, Palgrave, 2014. A former official of the International Labour Office in Geneva, Deirdre has also acted as an independent expert to the European Commission on the revision of the EU Working Time Directive and International Labour Organization on the Domestic Workers Convention, 2011 (No 189). She is a founder of the international research Network on Regulating for Decent Work, a global interdisciplinary network of researchers and policy-makers that promotes innovative approaches to labour market regulation. She is on the editorial Board of the *Industrial Law Journal* and a member of the Advisory Committee of the Labour Law Research Network. In 2015, Deirdre was awarded a Leverhulme Research Fellowship for her project on Creative Uncertainty? Labour Market Regulation in a World of Doubt and in 2017 she led the ESRC/GCRF Strategic Network on Legal Regulation of Unacceptable Forms of Work.

Liam McHugh-Russell

Doctoral candidate in the law department at the European University Institute (Florence) and visiting researcher at the Labour Law Development Research Lab (McGill University, Montreal). Liam's research investigates how law works in combination with other techniques of governance to constitute economic relations, and how law is shaped by other forms of economic expertise. His doctoral dissertation critiques a tradition of evolutionary theories of legal change that have informed and legitimated core development practices at the World Bank, especially through the Doing Business project. His masters thesis, at McGill University, identified ways in which the discourse of informality, and the forms of work it encompasses, challenge labour law's traditional narratives and normative categories. He has been a consultant at the International Labour Organization in Geneva, and practiced union and employee side labour law in Ontario. He has presented his work at the Institute for Global Law and Policy, Harvard's Labor and Worklife Program, the Law and Society Association, and the Interuniversity Research Centre on Globalization and Work (CRIMT).

Petra Mahy

Senior Lecturer in Law in the Department of Business Law and Taxation, Monash University. Previously she was a lecturer in law at the School of Oriental and African Studies (SOAS) University of London (2015–2017), a postdoctoral research fellow at the Centre for Socio-Legal Studies, University of Oxford (2013–2015) and a research fellow at the Department of Business Law and Taxation, Monash University (2010–2013). Petra is both a lawyer and an anthropologist and her research interests fall in the disciplines of socio-legal and regulatory studies. Her current research interests are concerned with the comparative historical evolution of company law and labour law and with the formal and informal regulation of work in Southeast Asia, with a particular focus on Indonesia.

Shelley Marshall

Senior Research Fellow, Graduate School of Business and Law at RMIT University, having previously been Senior Lecturer in the Department of Business Law and Taxation at Monash University. She is a cross-disciplinary scholar whose research focusses on the disciplines of law, political science, and regulatory and development studies. Her research has informed labour law reform in several countries and the policies of the International Labour Organization regarding informal, precarious workers. She is editor, with Colin Fenwick, of *Labour Regulation and Development: Socio-Legal Perspectives* (Edward Elgar Publishing, 2016). She has been the principle investigator and co-coordinator of three large, multi-country grants. In 2016, she and her team published 19 reports on access to remedy when communities and workers experience human rights breaches at the hands of transnational business. She earned her PhD in 2015 from ANU for her research into insights from regulatory theory for transnational labour regulation. In addition, she holds a Masters in development studies from the London School of Economics and Political Science.

Richard Mitchell

Professor (part-time) in the Department of Business Law and Taxation, and a member of the Labour, Equality and Human Rights Research Group, and the Ethical Regulation Research Group, at Monash University. He was previously Director of the Centre for Employment and Labour Relations Law (CELRL), Melbourne Law School, from 1994 to 2006. He studied at the University of Melbourne and the London School of Economics and Political Science. He was an editor of the *Australian Journal of Labour Law* from 1988 to 2002. Richard's areas of specialisation include the regulation of labour markets and the role of law in the construction of employment systems; his current research focuses on labour market regulation, and varying styles of regulation in different types of economies.

Tonia Novitz

Professor of Labour Law at the University of Bristol. She first studied law at the University of Canterbury in New Zealand and qualified there as a Barrister and

Solicitor. She then studied at Balliol College, Oxford, where she was awarded the BCL and completed her doctorate. She has held visiting fellowships at the International Institute for Labour Studies (Geneva), the European University Institute (Florence), the University of Melbourne and the University of Auckland. She is a member of the editorial board of the UK *Industrial Law Journal*, with special responsibility for the Recent Legislation section. She is also a honorary member of Old Square Chambers (non-practising). She has written on UK and comparative labour law, international labour standards, EU social policy, EU external relations, and mechanisms for the protection of human rights. She was author of *International and European Protection of the Right to Strike* (Oxford University Press, 2003), and has been co-editor of a number of edited collections, including *Human Rights at Work* (with Colin Fenwick, Hart Publishing, 2010), *The Role of Labour Standards in Development* (with David Mangan, British Academy Series, Oxford University Press, 2011) and *Voices at Work* (with Alan Bogg, Oxford University Press, 2014).

Sanjay Pinto

Sanjay Pinto is a sociologist based in Brooklyn with a range of interests related to social inequality, social policy, and social movements. He has an MSc in Development Studies from the London School of Economics and a PhD in Sociology and Social Policy from Harvard. Sanjay's academic writing includes work on unions and collective bargaining institutions in the US and other economically advanced countries. He co-organised a special section of the journal *Politics & Society* on global economic governance, and co-edited a book, *New Visions for Market Governance: Crisis and Renewal*, which was published by Routledge in 2012. His current work focuses largely on understanding labour market inequality and studying and supporting efforts to build power and raise standards for low-wage workers, and on understanding the impact of efforts to improve job quality for domestic workers in New York and elsewhere. Sanjay spent two years as a post-doctoral research fellow at Columbia's Committee on Global Thought, and has been a fellow at the Rutgers School of Management and Labor Relations.

Lorena Poblete

Researcher at Centro de Investigaciones Sociales, CONICET (Argentina's National Research Council) and Associate Professor at Universidad Nacional de San Martín. Lorena has a PhD in Sociology from the École des Hautes Études en Sciences Sociales (Paris), and was a visiting scholar at Université de Lille 1, Freie Universität Berlin, Princeton University and McGill University. Her current project, 'Regulatory Innovations: The ILO Domestic-Workers Convention in Latin America', involves the analysis of the influence of the ILO Convention 189 in Latin American countries. Lorena's research focuses on labour regulations, social security regimes and social stratification.

Kerry Rittich

Professor of Law, Women and Gender Studies, and Public Policy and Governance at the University of Toronto. She has served as Associate Dean, JD Program in the Faculty of Law. She obtained an LLB from the University of Alberta in 1992, and an SJD from Harvard University in 1998. In 1992–93, she served as Law Clerk to Madame Justice Claire L'Heureux-Dubé at the Supreme Court of Canada. She writes in the areas of labour law, international institutions and global governance, law and development, and gender and critical theory. Publications include *Recharacterizing Restructuring: Law, Distribution and Gender in Market Reform* (Kluwer Law International, 2002); (with Joanne Conaghan), *Labour Law, Work and Family: Critical and Comparative Perspectives*, (OUP, 2005); 'The Future of Law and Development: Second Generation Reforms and the Incorporation of the Social' in David M. Trubek and Alvaro Santos eds, *The New Law and Economic Development: A Critical Appraisal* (CUP, 2006); 'Black Sites: Locating the Family and Family Law in Development' (*American Journal of Comparative Law*, 2010); 'The Right to Work and Labour Market Flexibility: Labour Market Governance Norms in the International Order', V. Mantouvalou, ed., *The Right to Work: Legal and Philosophical Perspectives* (Hart, 2015) and (with Guy Mundlak) 'The challenge to comparative labor law in a globalized era', M. Finkin and G. Mundlak, eds, *Comparative Labor Law* (Elgar, 2015); and 'Theorizing International Law and Development', F. Hoffman and A. Orford, eds, *Oxford Handbook of the Theory of International Law* (OUP, 2016). She has been the Mackenzie King Visiting Professor of Canadian Studies at Harvard University, Visiting Professor at the Watson Institute for International Studies at Brown University, and Professor and Academic Director of the Center for Transnational Legal Studies, London.

Supriya Routh

Assistant Professor of Law at the Faculty of Law, University of Victoria. Supriya was previously Assistant Professor at the West Bengal National University of Juridical Sciences, and has held research positions (Post-doctoral and Chair Research) at the University of Laval, Nantes Institute for Advanced Study, and Humboldt University. A Fulbright Scholar, Supriya holds a PhD in Law & Society from the University of Victoria, LLMs from the Vanderbilt University Law School and the West Bengal National University of Juridical Sciences, and BA, LLB from the University of North Bengal. Supriya is author of *Enhancing Capabilities through Labour Law: Informal Workers in India*, Routledge, 2014, and academic journal articles in the areas of labour law, informal workers, trade unionism, law and development, corporate social responsibility, right to information, and legal education. He is the co-editor (along with Vando Borghi) of *Workers and the Global Informal Economy: Interdisciplinary Perspective*, Routledge, 2016.

Maria Azzurra Tranfaglia

Maria Azzurra is finalising a PhD in comparative Labour Law, focusing on the protection of workers involved in agency work arrangements (or labour-hire) in Australia and in Italy. She has been a Teaching Fellow in Employment Law at Melbourne Law School and has lectured the subject 'Employment Relations and Legal Framework' at the Australian Catholic University. As a Research Assistant and Research Fellow at the Centre for Employment and Labour Relations Law at Melbourne Law School, she has been involved in several research projects, ranging from ownership of employees' creations, enforcement of workplace rights and labour migration in Australia. She is an employment lawyer admitted to practice in Italy and has studied and worked both in Italy and in Australia in this field. In particular, Azzurra completed a Law Degree in 2008 at LUISS Guido Carli University of Rome, with a major in Labour Law and a final dissertation thesis analysing the protection of employees during transfer of undertaking in Europe and in Australia. She worked as an employment lawyer in Milan and studied Human Resource Management in Australia. Azzurra has been the Administrator of the Labour Law Research Network (LLRN) and currently volunteers for a not-for-profit organisation that assists newly arrived Italian migrants in Melbourne (NOMIT).

Introduction: Narratives of Informality and Development

DIAMOND ASHIAGBOR

I. Introduction

This collection examines the role of law in development; more specifically, the changing role of *labour* law in industrial, post-industrial and developing countries, and the challenges which the informalisation of work poses to our understanding of labour law's functions.

The aim is to explore labour law's conceptual and normative narrative. If labour law, as Harry Arthurs puts it, 'takes its purpose, form, and content from the larger political economy from which it originates and operates',[1] what shape does or should labour law assume in response to the transformation of the political economy in countries of the global North, with the declining prevalence of the post-war model of full employment within a formal welfare state regime? Correspondingly, what is the proper role to be played by labour law and labour relations institutions in the development process within industrialising countries of the global South?

A. Rationale and Scope

Dominant narratives within labour law scholarship reflect and give legitimacy to the traditional regulatory mechanisms and institutions of labour relations, and also shape which types of employment relationships are deemed suitable for regulation. These prevailing narratives, and the scholarly framing of the discipline which have originated in the 'hegemonic' countries of the global North,[2] have in large part been transplanted to the global South. Yet these narratives are closely allied to a particular economic history of regulation of primarily Fordist productive relations; regulation which has evolved along with the protective

[1] H Arthurs, 'Labour Law After Labour' in B Langille and G Davidov (eds), *The Idea of Labour Law* (Oxford, Oxford University Press, 2011).

[2] J Fudge, 'Labour as a "Fictive Commodity": Radically Reconceptualizing Labour Law' in B Langille and G Davidov (eds), *The Idea of Labour Law* (Oxford, Oxford University Press, 2011).

capacities of industrialised states during the twentieth century. Thus, traditional regulatory frameworks for governing work relations have taken as their starting point and as their main (sometimes, only) subject of regulation, the post-war ideal type of the 'standard' employee within the 'standard employment relationship', buttressed by institutions of social citizenship.

In contrast, informal employment has long been the predominant form in the labour markets of developing countries, and predictions that work would become formalised as these economies modernised have proved incorrect. In particular, it is clear that the Polanyian trajectory predicted within economic sociology,[3] of the creation of a link between wage labour in the formal economy and social citizenship at the core of the welfare state, has not occurred in the South; industrialising states have never enjoyed the protective capacities witnessed within the North.

Further, the process of informalisation is not confined to developing countries. Indeed, it is increasingly arguable that, even in the global North, the model of formal employment, with an implicit or psychological contract, existed only for an elite group of mostly male workers and is now unravelling. Accordingly, dominant narratives, which were never particularly apt for the global South, are also becoming less relevant for the global North. A key element in this declining relevance is the pervasiveness of informal work. The contributions to this book will therefore ask what shape does or should labour law take, in light of the declining dominance of forms of labour linked to the political economy of 'hegemonic' countries of the global North? What are the challenges for labour law in both industrialised and developing countries posed by the refashioning of economies in response to trade liberalisation and the related rise of market rationality as the governing metric of economic life?

B. Objectives, Impact, Implications: Development as a Continuing Process

This collection offers a contribution to labour law scholarship, and to reappraising the discipline. Whilst there has been extensive literature on rethinking the personal scope and substantive underpinnings of labour law, much of this has taken place, first, by reference to employment contract doctrine and attempts to reconfigure that doctrine; and second, by reference to the characteristics and changing patterns of work within the global North. The scholarship within this book will build on what

[3] The argument here, following Polanyi, is that many industrialised states of the global North were able to successfully construct (a version of) a welfare state through what Polanyi refers to as a 'countermovement' of society in response to the domination by the market under capitalism, with the forces of *laissez-faire* economic liberalism offset by principles of social protection: K Polanyi, *The Great Transformation: The Political and Economic Origins of Our Time* (Boston, MA, Beacon Press, [1944] 2001); E Webster and R Lambert, 'Markets Against Society: Labor's Predicament in the Second Great Transformation' in A Denis and D Kalekin-Fishman (eds), *The ISA Handbook in Contemporary Sociology: Conflict, Competition, Cooperation* (London, SAGE Publications Ltd, 2009).

is so illuminating in that scholarship, but also address its shortcomings by providing a platform for research which is empirically grounded as well as being doctrinally astute, and which turns its attention to the global South. This focus on the South will provide the necessary level of detail for reappraising what are the most appropriate 'tools and institutions for regulating work that falls outside the traditional regulatory repertoire of labour law'.[4] Accordingly, the ambition of this book is to recast the conceptual underpinnings of labour law, through an analysis of informal work.

The topic is particularly timely. As the economic crisis in Latin America in the 1980s highlighted – and the post-2008 global financial crisis is reiterating – during periods of economic or financial crisis, employment in the informal sector increases instead of, or in addition to, the increase in unemployment. The unfolding European Union example illustrates how governmental (and supranational) responses to the current crisis, in particular the crisis in sovereign debt, have placed labour and employment law centre-stage in the array of policy responses. In particular, EU Member States receiving financial support from the 'Troika' of the European Commission, European Central Bank and International Monetary Fund have been required to undertake '[r]adical, deregulatory labour law reforms'[5] which intensify the process of informalisation. This phenomenon provides an opportunity for scholars in the North to learn from those in the South, as the EU experience mirrors the effect of structural adjustment programmes (SAPs) implemented by the International Monetary Fund and the World Bank on labour markets in developing states from the 1970s onwards.

Both 'crisis response' and 'structural adjustment' and the accompanying informalisation, present challenges to labour law and to conceptions of the role of law in economic development. In understanding development as a continuing process, which affects all countries which have undergone or are undergoing the transition to a market economy, it is the task of this book to reimagine labour law for development. This Introduction has three overlapping aims, whilst also providing an overview of the book's chapters: first, it examines what law and development thinking might mean in the context of the labour market; second, it focuses on the persistence of informality; third, on the question of formalising the informal in an era of labour market flexibility.

II. Law, Institutions and Development: The Logic of Formalisation

Labour law, formality and development are intertwined: the chapters in this collection test assumptions about the 'correct' route to economic development,

[4] Fudge, above n 2.

[5] S Deakin, 'Editorial: The Sovereign Debt Crisis and European Labour Law' (2012) *Industrial Law Journal*, 251–53.

and what this means for the role of law in general and labour law in particular. More specifically, they interrogate the question where states are located on the 'path' towards economic development, how one defines development, and indeed the very understanding of capitalist modernity or 'formality' to be aspired to.[6]

A. Development and Legal Formality

A prior question for this introductory chapter is, how convincingly does orthodox thinking about law and development explain the phenomenon of the labour market? What role is played by law in the economic development process? The adoption of formal legal institutions has so long been argued as a precondition for economic development more broadly; are formal legal institutions such as the contract of employment also a prerequisite for the proper functioning of labour markets and employment relations?

One particular concern is the extent to which labour law scholarship offers alternatives to the dominant modernisation thesis with regard to economic development. The assumption that there is a universal path towards economic development is one which has been adopted by the World Bank and other international financial institutions, which have drawn upon Max Weber's ideal type of 'logically formal rationality' as a prerequisite for economic growth and development.[7] The relationship between law, institutions and development is one which preoccupied Weber. But what one might say is a distorted version of Weberian thinking is now central to mainstream law and development thinking, as is a Hayekian conception of the rule of law.[8] Weber's observations on the central role of 'rational' legal systems in the emergence of modern capitalism and on economic development more generally have been implicitly and explicitly co-opted by the World Bank and other international financial institutions.[9] According to Weber, one of the most important preconditions for the development of market economy

[6] D Chakrabarty, *Provincialising Europe: Postcolonial Thought and Historical Difference* (Princeton, Princeton University Press, 2000). See also Rittich, this volume.

[7] M Weber in Guenther Roth and Claus Wittich (eds), *Economy and Society: An Outline of Interpretive Sociology* (Berkeley, CA, University of California Press, [1921/22] 1978); D Kennedy, 'The Disenchantment of Logically Formal Legal Rationality, or Max Weber's Sociology in the Genealogy of the Contemporary Mode of Western Legal Thought' (2004) 55 *Hastings Law Journal*, 1031–76. The following paragraph draws from D Ashiagbor, 'Theorizing the Relationship Between Social Law and Markets in Regional Integration Projects' (2018) 27: 4 *Social & Legal Studies*, 435–55.

[8] In his taxonomy of differing conceptions of the rule of law, all of which are to some extent discernible in World Bank policy prescriptions, Santos distinguishes between institutional and substantive conceptions; and within both conceptions, intrinsic and instrumental versions. A Hayekian vision would, accordingly, regard the rule of law as a system that articulates a free market economy, with the rule of law being 'the legal embodiment of freedom': A Santos, 'The World Bank's uses of the "Rule of Law" promise in economic development' in DM Trubek and A Santos (eds), *The New Law and Economic Development: A Critical Appraisal* (Cambridge, Cambridge University Press, 2006) esp at 263, 264.

[9] Santos, above n 8, 272–73; IFI Shihata, F Tschofen and AR Parra, *The World Bank in a Changing World: Selected Essays* (Dordrecht, Martinus Nijhoff, 1991).

('capitalistic enterprise') was the 'rationalization and systematization of the law in general', namely the predictability and security gained from a formal legal process.[10]

Thus, in the view of the World Bank, the key to economic development is converting the 'informal' into the 'formal'.[11] According to this approach, developing countries should adopt formal legal institutions – in particular the rule of law and protection of private property – so as to ensure the predictable and effective enforcement of 'background' rules necessary for capitalist economic growth. This approach also requires them to reject labour market institutions, which are assumed to have a largely negative impact on growth and economic development. Whilst not sharing the World Bank's view that informality arises in large part in order to avoid overly burdensome or 'rigid' labour regulation, the International Labour Organization (ILO), in its promotion of its decent work agenda, similarly advocates formalisation of the informal economy. How does or should labour law respond to these apparently incommensurable aims: of promoting formalisation whilst retaining (labour market) flexibility?[12]

Both the modernisation theory and the Washington Consensus[13] accord significant priority to private law rights, as can be seen in the focus on the formalisation of *property* rights. But what of *regulatory* law, of the sort which labour lawyers typically advocate? Neoliberal law and development thought is focused primarily on the law of the market, with regulation often presented as an unnecessary intrusion on the market, and 'relatively little concern … shown for law as a guarantor of political and civil rights or as protector of the weak and disadvantaged'.[14]

B. The Persistence of Informality

One of the most significant challenges facing work and its regulation in market economies is the persistence of informal work and the growth of informalisation. As the ILO acknowledges, there is no universally accurate or accepted definition

[10] Weber, above n 7, at 883.

[11] S Marshall, J Howe and C Fenwick, 'Labour Law and Development: Creating an Enabling Regulatory Environment and Encouraging Formalisation', Paper presented at Conference on Regulating for Decent Work: Innovative Labour Regulation in a Turbulent World, 8–10 July 2009, on file with the ILO; available at http://www.ilo.org/public/english/protection/condtrav/pdf/rdwpaper27a.pdf.

[12] K Rittich, 'Modeling Informal Labor Markets and Development: Exit, Exclusion and the Paradoxes of Labor Market Flexibility', Paper presented at Feminist Theory Workshop, Fall 2009, Columbia Law School; K Rittich, in this volume.

[13] The widespread orthodoxy, in particular shared by the international financial institutions located in Washington, as to the necessity to adopt competitive exchange rates, trade liberalisation, deregulation, privatisation, and foreign direct investment liberalisation as the route to economic development. See B Langille, 'Imagining Post "Geneva Consensus" Labor Law for Post "Washington Consensus" Development' (2010) 31 *Comparative Labor Law & Policy Journal* 523–52.

[14] DM Trubek and A Santos, 'Introduction: The Third Moment in Law and Development Theory and the Emergence of a New Critical Practice' in DM Trubek and A Santos (eds), *The New Law and Economic Development: A Critical Appraisal* (Cambridge, Cambridge University Press, 2006), 2.

of informal work or the informal economy, encompassing as it does considerable diversity in terms of workers, enterprises and entrepreneurs.[15] However, a working definition adopted by the ILO refers to all economic activities by workers and economic units that are – in law or in practice – not covered or insufficiently covered by formal arrangements.[16] Thus, informal work is understood to embrace activities either not included in the law, namely operating outside the formal reach of the law; or not covered in practice, namely where the law is not applied or not enforced or compliance is inappropriate, burdensome, or imposes excessive costs.[17] The ILO further describes the informal economy as consisting of unregistered and/or small unincorporated private enterprises engaged in the production of goods or services for sale or barter.[18]

Modernisation theory predicted that 'modernity' would replace 'traditions' as economies developed and 'evolved'.[19] The informal economy was thus a temporary phenomenon, a remnant of feudalism and agrarian production, which would be absorbed within and disappear into the urbanised, formal economy.[20] Drawing on classical economic theory and the historical experience of Western industrialised countries, mainstream development theory coalesced around a dualistic model of the development process, where the transfer of labour from the subsistence to the capitalist sector came to reflect sectoral differences in the marginal productivity of labour, eventually leading to an integrated labour market and economy.[21]

But contrary to these predictions, economic development in developing countries has not generated enough 'modern' jobs to absorb surplus labour from the traditional economy.[22] As observed above, the trajectory predicted within

[15] ILO, 'Resolution concerning decent work and the informal economy', International Labour Conference, 90th Session, Geneva, 2002, para 3.

[16] The ILO definition has evolved over the years, but owes much to the work of the International Conference of Labour Statisticians (ICLS). See *Resolution concerning statistics of employment in the informal sector, Adopted by the Fifteenth International Conference of Labour Statisticians* (January 1993) and the discussion of the ICLS 1993 and amended 2003 definitions of informal work in the chapters in this volume by Deakin, Marshall and Pinto, and by McHugh-Russell.

[17] ILO, 'Resolution concerning decent work and the informal economy'. See also International Labour Conference 90th Session 2002, Report VI, *Decent work and the informal economy*, Sixth item on the agenda, ILO 2002.

[18] An unincorporated enterprise is a production unit that is not constituted as a separate legal entity independently of the individual (or group of individuals) who owns it; an enterprise is unregistered when it is not registered under specific forms of national legislation (eg factories' or commercial acts, tax or social security laws, professional groups' regulatory acts).

[19] W Whitman Rostow, *Stages of Economic Growth: A Non-Communist Manifesto* (Cambridge, Cambridge University Press, 1960); 'The Stages of Economic Growth' (1959) *Economic History Review* 1–16. See also W Arthur Lewis, 'Economic Development with Unlimited Supplies of Labour' (1954) 23:2 *Manchester School of Economic and Social Studies* 139–91.

[20] R Agarwala, 'An Economic Sociology of Informal Work: The Case of India' in Nina Bandelj (ed), *Economic Sociology of Work* (Research in the Sociology of Work, Volume 18) (Bingley, Emerald Group Publishing, 2009) 315–42, 319.

[21] C Kirkpatrick and A Barrientos, 'The Lewis Model After Fifty Years', Development Economics and Public Policy Working Paper Series, Paper No. 9, September 2004, Institute for Development Policy and Management, University of Manchester; available at http://www.seed.manchester.ac.uk/medialibrary/IDPM/working_papers/depp/depp_wp09.pdf.

[22] See, eg, the discussion of Argentina in the chapter by Lorena Poblete in this volume.

Polanyi-inspired economic sociology of the creation of a link between wage labour in the formal economy and social citizenship at the core of the welfare state, has not occurred in the South.[23] As Nancy Fraser has noted: postcolonial states never enjoyed protective capacities equal to those of 'the core', thanks to 'long histories of colonial subjection, as well as to the continuation, after independence, of imperialist predation by other means'.[24] On the contrary, however, the informal economy has expanded in both industrialised and developing countries. Indeed, the bulk of new employment in recent years, particularly in developing and transition countries, has been in the informal economy.[25] In coining the term 'informal sector' in 1973, Hart also exposed the limits of modernisation theory, with his findings as to the crucial role played by self-employed workers in Ghana's development, as a source of employment, and of essential cheap goods and services relied on by low-wage urban workers.[26]

In industrialised (or post-industrial) states the growth of informal work (also variously known as atypical, non-standard, precarious or flexible work) has been explained in large part by reference to changing methods of production and the move by employing enterprises towards increased flexibilisation of employment relationships. Sandra Fredman explains the phenomenon of the rise in what she refers to as 'atypical' work as a result of the move from industrial mass production towards the service economy, in addition to global competition and the growth of new technology, coupled with governmental encouragement (in the UK) of the shift towards more flexible work contracts in particular through labour market deregulation.[27] Using different terminology, Martha Chen and Hugh Collins both identify a calculated process of increased informalisation within advanced capitalist economies,[28] wherein production is reorganised into 'small-scale, decentralized, and more flexible economic units'[29] as firms show a greater willingness to arrange aspects of production through subcontracting, franchising, concessions and outsourcing (with similar developments occurring in the public sector as a result of privatisation).[30] Such decentralisation of production and creation of more flexible and specialised production units – typically by formal firms in *industrialised* states – further reinforce the prevalence of informal work in

[23] Polanyi, *The Great Transformation*, above n 3; Webster and Lambert, above n 3.

[24] N Fraser, 'A Triple Movement? Parsing the Politics of Crisis after Polanyi', *New Left Review* 81 May-June 2013, 119–32, at 126.

[25] ILO, *Decent work and the informal economy*, above n 17, 1.

[26] Agarwala, above n 20, 322.

[27] S Fredman, 'Labour Law in Flux: The Changing Composition of the Workforce' (1997) *Industrial Law Journal*, 337–52.

[28] M Alter Chen, 'The Informal Economy: Definitions, Theories and Policies', Women in Informal Employment: Globalizing and Organizing (WIEGO) Working Paper No 1, August 2012, available at http://wiego.org/sites/wiego.org/files/publications/files/Chen_WIEGO_WP1.pdf; H Collins, 'Independent Contractors and the Challenge of Vertical Disintegration for Employment Protection Laws' (1990) *Oxford Journal of Legal Studies*, 353–380.

[29] Chen, above n 28, 2–3.

[30] Collins, above n 28, 353.

developing states, since such flexible specialisation is increasingly associated with cross-border commodity and value chains in which the lead enterprise is located in an industrialised country, with the final producer an own-account worker in a micro-enterprise or a homeworker in a developing or transition country.[31]

The trend, observed by Chen and Collins among others, toward 'vertical disintegration', wherein the management of large enterprises substitute commercial contracts for employment relations, places many workers in industrialised states who would previously have been within the paradigm of the 'standard employment relationship' outside this paradigm and thus beyond the range of much employment protection legislation.[32] However, in developing states, informal work has been and remains the main source of employment and income for the majority of the workforce and population.[33]

C. Formalising the Informal in an Era of Labour Market Flexibility

'[D]ecent work deficits are most pronounced in the informal economy.'[34] With this statement, the ILO has acknowledged the undeniable link between informality and substandard or precarious working conditions. If one recalls that the definition of informal work as that not covered or insufficiently covered by formal arrangements, operating outside the formal reach of the law, or where the law is not applied or not enforced, then a central feature of informal work is that it generally lacks basic social or legal protections or employment benefits.[35] As such, informal *employment* may be found in the formal *sector*, the informal sector, or within households. Informality has long been associated with exclusion from legal and regulatory frameworks designed to cover employees (and workers); but it is also very likely to be associated with vulnerability.

Whilst some workers who fall outside the standard employment relationship – for instance those at the high end of the spectrum such as 'knowledge workers',

[31] International Labour Conference, 90th Session, 2002, Report VI, *Decent work and the informal economy*, ILO 2002, above n 17, at 2. See also Chen, above n 28, 13.

[32] Collins, above n 28.

[33] Chen, above n 28, 20.

[34] ILO, 'Resolution concerning decent work and the informal economy', International Labour Conference, 90th Session, Geneva, 2002, para 9.

[35] ibid:

> Workers in the informal economy are not recognized, registered, regulated or protected under labour legislation and social protection, for example when their employment status is ambiguous, and are therefore not able to enjoy, exercise or defend their fundamental rights. Since they are normally not organized, they have little or no collective representation vis-à-vis employers or public authorities. Work in the informal economy is often characterized by small or undefined workplaces, unsafe and unhealthy working conditions, low levels of skills and productivity, low or irregular incomes, long working hours and lack of access to information, markets, finance, training and technology. Workers in the informal economy may be characterized by varying degrees of dependency and vulnerability.

associated with the rise of the 'new economy' and networked organisations – are not typically considered to be in need of labour protection,[36] at the other end of the spectrum are 'precarious' or vulnerable workers who do not enjoy a privileged social location or access to social and economic capital. The weaker social location of those engaged in the informal economy further exacerbates their vulnerability as workers and the decent work deficits. Women workers, workers from ethnic minorities and racialised groups, and workers with precarious immigration statuses, whether temporary or undocumented, are overrepresented in precarious work arrangements that fall outside the norm of the standard employment relationship.[37]

In about half of the countries surveyed by the ILO, the share of informal workers in total employment is higher for women than for men, although it notes that the gender bias in the informal economy is probably underestimated.[38] Why is this the case? With regard to developing countries, it is argued that no country has successfully industrialised via export promotion without drawing upon a pool of low-wage female workers. Similarly, most industrialised countries rely on low-wage women workers, a disproportionate number of whom are immigrants or racial and ethnic minorities, for increasing amounts of service and production work.[39] Consequently, the vast majority of the working poor are located in informal markets, and a disproportionate number of those in informal markets are women.[40] The ample empirical research showing that workers in the informal economy face higher risks of poverty than those in the formal economy has led the ILO to conclude that 'there is a significant, but not complete, overlap between working informally and being poor and vulnerable'.[41] The informal economy, according to the ILO, is marked by acute decent work deficits: individuals and enterprises may be trapped in a spiral of low productivity and poverty; informal workers are not recognised, registered, regulated or protected under labour and social protection legislation, and are not therefore able to enjoy, exercise or defend their fundamental rights; there are varying degrees of dependency and vulnerability, in particular experienced by women, young persons, migrants and older workers, including child labour and bonded labour.[42]

[36] J Fudge, 'Blurring Legal Boundaries: Regulating for Decent Work' in J Fudge, S McCrystal and K Sankaran (eds), *Challenging the Legal Boundaries of Work Regulation* (Oxford, Hart Publishing, 2012), 12.

[37] ibid, 13.

[38] ILO, *Decent work and the informal economy*, above n 17, 12.

[39] K Rittich, 'Feminization and Contingency: Regulating the Stakes of Work for Women' in J Conaghan, RM Fischl and K Klare (eds), *Labour Law in an Era of Globalization: Transformative Practices and Possibilities* (Oxford, Oxford University Press, 2002), 118.

[40] A Trebilcock, 'Using Development Approaches to Address the Challenge of the Informal Economy for Labour Law' in G Davidov and B Langille (eds), *Boundaries and Frontiers of Labour Law: Goals and Means in the Regulation of Work* (Oxford, Hart Publishing, 2006), 63.

[41] International Labour Conference, 103rd Session, 2014 Report V(1) *Transitioning from the informal to the formal economy*, ILO 2014, para 2.

[42] ibid, paras 25–26.

Accordingly, the ILO has come to see formalisation of the informal economy as an essential component of its 'decent work' agenda.[43] As Rittich notes, formalisation is itself imagined *as* development[44] and arguments for formalisation 'now sound both in the registers of better work and economic development'.[45] Indeed, the overlap between these two agendas has been articulated by the ILO itself: in its 2014 report on *Transitioning from the informal to the formal economy*, the ILO referred to the need to implement 'a range of integrated and coherent policies' to 'move economic units into the formal economy' including the extension of social protection and the promotion of labour rights.[46]

The ILO's formalisation strategy – most clearly articulated in the adoption of Recommendation No. 204, 2015 on Transition from the Informal to the Formal Economy[47] – entails promoting decent work along the entire continuum from the informal to the formal end of the economy, in particular, by ensuring that those who are currently in the informal economy are 'recognized in the law and have rights, legal and social protection and representation and voice'.[48] Thus, it is clear that the preoccupation with formalising economic activity in general similarly affects labour and employment relations. Formalisation is seen as the answer to economic development; and also to the decent work deficit arising from the persistence of informal work. Rittich, however, cautions that labour market formalisation as a development strategy may be in tension with the goal of better or 'decent' work.[49]

The stress on formalisation of working relations takes place against a backdrop which recognises the importance of law for the operation of private markets, but is sceptical about state intervention or the protection of human rights. In particular, a key part of this orthodoxy, when applied to the regulation and governance of labour markets, is a scepticism – most forcefully articulated by the OECD and the IMF – towards labour market institutions, which are perceived to be an exogenous interference, and a powerful faith in labour market flexibility. Orthodox economic thinking has long held that the systems of labour market regulation which exist(ed) in most EU Member States were the major cause of their high unemployment in the 1970s and 1980s, and that the EU would therefore do best to adopt the more flexible wage systems, employment practices and labour laws of the United States. Such 'labour market rigidities' were routinely blamed for high European unemployment, and this was certainly the conclusion of the OECD *Jobs Study*.[50]

[43] ibid. Initially articulated in ILO, *Decent work and the informal economy*, 2002, above n 17.

[44] Rittich, in this volume.

[45] Rittich, above n 12.

[46] ILO, *Transitioning from the informal to the formal economy*, above n 41, 31.

[47] Recommendation No 204, 2015: Transition from the Informal to the Formal Economy. This Recommendation codifies the definition of informal work contained in the 2002 Resolution: ILO, 'Resolution concerning decent work and the informal economy', International Labour Conference, 90th Session, Geneva, 2002, para 3.

[48] ILO, *Decent work and the informal economy*, 2002, above n 17, 5.

[49] Rittich, above n 12, 6.

[50] Organisation for Economic Co-operation and Development (OECD), *The OECD Jobs Study: Evidence and Explanations* and *Facts, Analysis, Strategies* (Paris, OECD, 1994).

Of relevance to *developing* states is that whilst the discourse and policy prescription of labour market flexibility was initially developed to remedy the perceived 'Eurosclerosis' that afflicted one region of the industrial world, it was soon deployed as a general approach to the regulation and governance of labour markets. As Rittich notes, such prescriptions soon came to be adopted by the international economic and financial institutions and incorporated as part of standard reform advice, and sometimes lending conditionality.[51] And as noted above, these 'radical deregulatory' prescriptions are now being applied to Europe.

The logic underpinning the approach to labour market regulation of the *Jobs Study*, the IMF and the World Bank's *Doing Business* reports,[52] is that since only free, unrestricted operation of market forces produces optimal results – in labour markets, as in commodity markets – state intervention through regulation serves to distort labour supply and demand, restrict job creation and increase unemployment.[53] These assumptions about the economically harmful effects of labour market institutions underpin the consensus among the international financial institutions, and the international development institutions, about the appropriateness of labour market flexibility for both industrialised and developing countries. However, a shift which Trubek and Santos identify in what they refer to as the 'new' mainstream of (law and) development thinking is a greater acceptance of regulatory law, and of the need for legal intervention to reduce transaction costs and compensate for market failures.[54] What is unclear, however, is whether this softening of neoliberal orthodoxy amounts to a new paradigm or a chastened form of neoliberalism?[55]

Two key policy instruments which may point towards a greater tolerance of (labour market) institutions is the World Bank's Comprehensive Development Framework,[56] which on the face of it represents an attempt to soften the Washington Consensus view of development and formalisation, and the more recent dilution of opposition to labour market institutions of the Doing Business reports. The then World Bank president described the CDF as an approach which 'balances good macroeconomic and financial management with sound social, structural and human policies'.[57]

The World Bank has long placed great store by measures of business and employment regulation (the '*Doing Business*' Report and 'Employing Workers

[51] Rittich, above n 12, 17.

[52] The most recent iteration is *Doing Business 2019: Training for Reform* (Washington, World Bank, 2018).

[53] N Adnett, *European Labour Markets: Analysis and Policy* (London, Longman, 1996), at 278.

[54] Trubek and Santos, above n 14, 11.

[55] ibid, 3.

[56] World Bank, A Proposal for a Comprehensive Development Framework (A Discussion Draft), 21 January 1999; http://web.worldbank.org/archive/website01013/WEB/0__CO-87.HTM.

[57] World Bank/IMF, 'The Comprehensive Development Framework (CDF) and Poverty Reduction Strategy Papers (PRSP)' Joint Note by James D Wolfensohn and Stanley Fischer, 5 April 2000; available at https://www.imf.org/external/np/prsp/pdf/cdfprsp.pdf. Wolfensohn was President of the World Bank from 1995 to 2005; Fischer was First Deputy Managing Director of the International Monetary Fund from September 1994 to August 2001.

Index')[58] which were fundamentally rooted in the classic neoliberal critique of labour market institutions outlined above. The relatively recent (2013) decline in the importance of the *Doing Business* project evidences a tentative process of 'institutional convergence and divergence' between the differing approaches to labour market regulation of the ILO and the World Bank.[59] The 2013 World Development Report[60] confirmed the diminished importance of the *Doing Business* project, as well as signalling what Deirdre McCann refers to as a 'new narrative on the scope, purpose and functioning of labour market regulation'.[61]

The 'Comprehensive Development Framework' and the incorporation of a social agenda into the policy recommendations of international development institutions,[62] in particular in the turn away from the *Doing Business* mind-set, suggest a chastened form of neoliberalism, and greater tolerance within the international development institutions of public regulation or state intervention of the sort needed to realise the ILO's formalisation agenda.

D. The Epistemology of Informality

At a broader theoretical level, as seen above, much of the orthodox law and development discourse fetishes the formal, which involves a preoccupation with the rule of law and, relatedly, a view of law that is excessively formalistic. A common problem within the rule of law orthodoxy is inattention to the evidence that the best way of implementing the law 'is not through external imposition but rather through drawing agents into the system through a process of building internal legitimacy'.[63] A similar critique of excessive legal formalism was articulated by legal realists, who questioned the assumptions that legal form determines outcome. To this might be added a critique of the 'unthinking

[58] The Employing Workers Indicator or Index (EWI), a sub-indicator of the *Doing Business* indicators developed by the World Bank, has been extensively reviewed and assessed as not being suitable for inclusion into the overall aggregate *Doing Business* indicator or for ranking countries. Following important criticism from academia, civil society, and other international organisations it underwent an independent evaluation and examination by a consultative group and a review by an independent panel: World Bank, *Independent Panel Review of the Doing Business Report*, 2013; available at: http://www.dbrpanel.org/.Bank.

[59] For a detailed analysis of a dynamic process of institutional *convergence* and *divergence*, see Deirdre McCann, 'Labour Law on the Plateau: Towards Regulatory Policy for Endogenous Norms' in Alan Bogg, Cathryn Costello, ACL Davies and Jeremias Prassl (eds), *The Autonomy of Labour Law* (Oxford, Hart Publishing, 2015). For a historical overview of the tensions between the ILO and the World Bank, see Yaraslau Kryvoi, 'The World Bank and the ILO: Two Visions of Employment Regulation' in Roger Blanpain and Clare Grant (eds), *Fixed-term Employment Contracts: A Comparative Study* (Bruges, Vanden Broele Publishers, 2009).

[60] World Bank, *World Development Report 2013: Jobs* (Washington, World Bank, 2012).

[61] McCann, above n 59, 405.

[62] K Rittich, 'The future of law and development: Second generation reforms and the incorporation of the social' in DM Trubek and A Santos (eds), *The New Law and Economic Development*, above n 8.

[63] A Haldar, 'Law and Development in Crisis: An Empirical Challenge to the Current Theoretical Frames' (2014) *Northern Ireland Legal Quarterly*, 303–21, 317.

transfer' of categories developed in the global North to the economic and social structures of developing countries.[64]

As Deakin, Marshall and Pinto note in their chapter, official statistics in different jurisdictions adopt distinct approaches and use competing measures and terms. The definitions used by international agencies, whilst not uniform, are however coalescing around an expanded definition which includes 'employment in the informal sector' as well as informal employment.[65] Throughout the literature, one finds use of competing and sometimes overlapping terms, definitions and classificatory schemes. Rather than seeking to provide a definitive account of 'the informal', I wish to instead reflect on the epistemology of 'informality', the drawing of distinctions between formal and informal, which encode other binaries: those which perpetuate colonial binaries, equating the North with progress, order and enlightenment and the South with backwardness and chaos.[66]

There has long been a strong interdisciplinary tradition within labour law scholarship, with the discipline (in the UK) in conversation with the social sciences, in particular sociology and industrial relations.[67] But with regard to the 'binary divide' and questions of classification of working relationships, there has been a tendency to adopt a predominantly doctrinal methodology, based on close textual analysis and meticulous scrutiny of doctrine. The more recent move to greater engagement with empirical method to understand working lives in an *individualised* legal environment[68] is thus to be welcomed, enabling and facilitating as it has a richer and more meaningful engagement with the particularities of jurisdictions in the global South.[69] Such a grounded approach can reveal how the simple transplant of doctrines or laws developed in the context of the global North simply does not capture the realities of a predominantly informal economy.

Guha-Khasnobis, Kanbur and Ostrom rightly question the usefulness of the formal–informal dichotomy, suggesting that 'formal and informal are better thought of as metaphors that conjure up a mental picture of whatever the user has in mind at that particular time'.[70] In particular, the tendency to associate 'informal'

[64] See K Hart, 'Informal Income Opportunities and Urban Employment in Ghana' (1973) *Journal of Modern African Studies* 61–89, 61.

[65] eg ILO, *Decent work and the informal economy*, 2002, 16; Statistical definition of informal employment: Guidelines endorsed by the Seventeenth International Conference of Labour Statisticians (2003), ILO, 2003.

[66] See Chakrabarty, above n 6.

[67] See, eg, O Kahn-Freund, 'Intergroup Conflicts and their Settlement' (1954) 5 *British Journal of Sociology* 193–227; Lizzie Barmes, *Bullying and Behavioural Conflict at Work: The Duality of Individual Rights* (Oxford, Oxford University Press, 2016), Chapter 1.

[68] See Barmes, above n 67, 4.

[69] See, eg, A Ludlow and A Blackham (eds), *New Frontiers in Empirical Labour Law Research* (Oxford, Hart Publishing, 2015); S Marshall and C Fenwick (eds), *Labour Regulation and Development: Socio-Legal Perspectives* (Cheltenham, Edward Elgar, 2016).

[70] B Guha-Khasnobis, R Kanbur, and E Ostrom, 'Beyond Formality and Informality' in B Guha-Khasnobis, R Kanbur and E Ostrom (eds), *Linking the Formal and Informal Economy: Concepts and Policies* (Oxford, Oxford University Press, 2006) 1 and 3.

with 'unstructured' and 'chaotic' is unhelpful.[71] Indeed, empirical research suggests the existence of, for instance, highly structured interactions within groups which do not interact with official governance.[72] As Hart observes, practices may 'appear to be informal because their forms are largely invisible to the bureaucratic gaze'.[73]

One value, however, of holding on to the binary – perhaps better conceptualised as the formal–informal continuum – is that it can still be a useful analytical device or heuristic 'we can fruitfully use the terminology, formal–informal to characterize a continuum of the reach of official intervention in different economic activities, especially since official statistics already use variants of such a criterion'.[74]

There is irony in that the ILO has come to the same policy conclusions as others (international financial institutions and scholars of development) more traditionally associated with a positivist account of the role of law and the rule of law; faith in the power of formal legal institutions to bring order to the informal world. In recent years, following the developmental logic of formalisation, the extension of formal legal property rights to the 'informal' sector has been advocated as a 'possible powerful policy tool to help the poor make the best of their assets'.[75] However, the reality of economic activity in developing countries belies such a simplistic transfer of models from the global North to the South.

I want to give an example from outside the world of work of the fetishisation of the formal. In her studies of land-titling in Peru and microfinance in Bangladesh, Antara Haldar illustrates the limits of the 'formalist model' or the law and economics paradigm.[76] She questions the dominant paradigm within law and development thinking – 'an amalgamation of Chicago-school law and economics, new institutional economics and the "rule of law" orthodoxy' – contrasting it with an alternative, 'law and society' perspective, which sees markets as fundamentally embedded in society. As an example of development policy heavily influenced by the law and economics approach, with its advocacy of interventions which are 'linear, procedural, instrumental and formal', Haldar offers the illustration of the land-titling programme in Peru established by Hernando De Soto, with its preoccupation with state-enforced law over more community-based regulatory mechanisms, 'vesting paramount faith in law as written down in statutory form'.[77] In contrast, the microfinance model, which exemplifies the law and society approach, is less preoccupied with a written code 'but rather adopts an informal view of the law as lived practice'.[78] The perspective that formal law is superior to

[71] ibid, 16.
[72] ibid, 6.
[73] K Hart, 'Bureaucratic Form and the Informal Economy' in B Guha-Khasnobis, R Kanbur and E Ostrom (eds), above n 70, 22.
[74] Guha-Khasnobis, Kanbur and Ostrom, above n 70, 16.
[75] ibid, 2.
[76] Haldar, above n 63.
[77] ibid, 316.
[78] ibid.

other more informal mechanisms is shown to be flawed in Haldar's empirical work, which finds that the informal, more socially rooted, model performed better than the formalist model on counts of both efficiency and equity.[79]

What lessons might this examination of the limits of the formalist model have for work relations and labour markets? The persistence of informal work requires us to think more imaginatively about informal *norms* governing informal *work*. Gains for workers may be achieved without necessarily having to resort to formal institutions such as the contract of employment.

III. Overview of the Book

Formalisation is seen as the answer to economic development, and also to the decent work deficit arising from the persistence of informal work. As mentioned earlier, the key to economic development is perceived to lie in converting the 'informal' into the 'formal'. However, whilst the discourse of formalisation gains increasing purchase, within both the ILO and the international financial institutions, the discourse and practice of flexibilisation retains its dominance. For instance, it is unlikely that the vertical disintegration of production will be reversed. So the downward pressure on workers' bargaining power will continue, as will the shift of risk from employers to workers.

This collection brings together a carefully chosen group of scholars – with different perspectives on labour, law, markets and development; from industrialised and developing countries; and at different stages in their professional formation as lawyers and social scientists – to examine one of the most significant challenges facing work and its regulation in market economies: the growth of informalisation.

The contributions to this book emerge from a conference, held at the Institute of Advanced Legal Studies (IALS), University of London, in September 2016, which was made possible through the generous support of the SOAS Faculty of Law and Social Sciences, and the Society of Legal Scholars (SLS) and IALS. The conference was badged as the SLS Annual Seminar 2016.

In chapter one, **Kerry Rittich** weaves together many of the themes in the book, in exploring continuities not only between informality in industrialised and developing countries, but also between work in the colonial era (for instance, indentured labour) and contemporary forms of labour. As Rittich makes clear, to understand contemporary projects of formalisation in both global North and South, one needs to look historically. She finds the question of labour and work relationships – the productivity and regulation of 'native' labour, the subjection of 'free' labour to market discipline, and the application of coercion in the creation of a 'free' labour market – deeply interconnected with the colonial project and to

[79] ibid.

development as a governance practice. The contemporary association of formality with modernisation, modernity, and development can be seen to have strong antecedents in the project of British colonial administration.

Rittich's analysis of informality as a category within development thinking is further developed by **Liam McHugh-Russell** in chapter two. His particular focus is on the problems for transnational governance caused by the competing conceptualisations of informality arising from the agendas of different epistemic communities, national authorities and policy actors. However, what his close reading of the evolution of official definitions of informality elaborated by the International Conference of Labour Statisticians and by the ILO reveals is that, despite the lack of analytical rigour or clear boundaries to the concept, 'informality' serves an important purpose as a heuristic: a constructed knowledge object which is a resource in struggles over development practice, and a means to articulate the problem of the relationship between labour law, development discourses and working conditions in the global South.

Deirdre McCann's chapter reviews the discourses of informality within the labour regulation literatures and transnational policy regimes of the World Bank and ILO. They key contribution of this chapter is the carefully drawn distinction between the concept of informality and the process of informalisation. It explores how recent international policy discourses convey informalisation, with a particular focus on the role of legal regulation. What emerges is the more sophisticated understanding of informality emanating from the ILO, which recognises the continuum of formality and informality and the presence of informality within formal enterprises, and encompasses informalisation. Yet, she argues, this more robust concept of informalisation is not matched by the Organization's renditions of the function and potential of labour regulation. She concludes that informalisation must be better integrated into the formalisation project, including to improve and sustain job quality in the formal economy, and calls for a new – pre-emptive – labour law aimed at preventing the unravelling of decent jobs.

In chapter four, **Supriya Routh** questions the 'labour rights as human rights' strategy, in particular with regard to its salience to the subjective experience of informal workers: the 'disembodied abstraction' of rights discourse and the rights standard arguably fails to recognise or address the distinct experience of informal workers, given its abstract generalised legal norms and its use of industrial factory-based workers' experiences as the point of reference. Routh adopts an institutional ethnography approach – an epistemology of society and social relations from the perspective of the marginalised people – to facilitate access to knowledge about the embodied/situated experience of informal workers that tends to be invisible within discourses such as that of human rights. In articulating a 'rights plus' approach, Routh thus outlines the possibility of experience-based policy making complementing a human rights strategy.

Pamhidzai H Bamu offers a case study of Zimbabwe to illustrate a broader claim as to the utility and generalisability of the dominant narratives which underpin labour regulation. She provides a sober account of how the model of formal regulation of formal employment relations developed for the Fordist workplace of the global North is so problematic when transposed to the global South, illustrating how the multiple harms of colonialisation find elements of continuity in the post-independence era. Adopting a political economy approach, which also considers Zimbabwe's labour market in historical context, Bamu surveys the conceptual and methodological challenges with framing formality and informality in a context where workers and households straddle both formal and informal sectors, challenges which are also accompanied, in the Zimbabwean context, by difficulties with obtaining accurate statistics and data with which to measure the phenomenon of informal work.

In a chapter which also pays attention to the foundational narratives of labour law whilst focusing on the industrialised world, in particular the UK, **Ruth Dukes'** study of labour market segmentation explores notions of conflicts of interest contained in the characterisation of labour market insiders and outsiders. Dukes adopts a political-economy approach to develop a case study of the agricultural sector in Scotland: in this, she explores the role of the state in configuring precariousness and low-wage labour, and the role of employer interests in such segmentation, focusing on unease about the use of precarious or informal workers as a means to 'discipline' marginally more secure workers.

Lorena Poblete in her chapter reviews, from a socio-historical perspective, the process of formalisation in Argentina – a process which in its more recent incarnation during an era of neoliberal policy making has been underpinned in particular by the perceived affinity between formality and flexibility. Poblete's study shows how labour law mechanisms (such as redefining the scope of employment protection measures) are not the only ways to ensure informal workers are included and protected by the state. Rather, taking as a starting point the prevalence of informality in the economies of Latin America (in particular, the inability of the industrial sector to absorb the growth in the workforce), Poblete traces the policy experiments within Argentina designed to integrate 'non-standard' workers – own-account workers, economic actors in micro-enterprises, unpaid workers and domestic workers – by bringing them into social security coverage by means of changes to the taxation system.

Tonia Novitz, writing on migrant labour in supply chains, captures how the new and growing patterns of temporary, circular and posted labour migration create new categories of informal worker. As Novitz shows, modern production techniques and new forms of service provision, some facilitated by technological innovation, intensify transnational trade and cross-border contracting. However, the decline of migration for permanent settlement and the growth of temporary migration – which includes circular and increasingly also posted migrant work – is at the heart of these informal workers' precariousness and vulnerability: the interaction of supply chains, trade in services and migrant labour illustrates the literal connections between the global North (where corporate entities at the top of the supply chain are predominantly located) and the global South, the usual although not invariable origin of the workers.

The importance of adopting an empirical *and* comparative approach in order to better understand informality, and the relationship between informal work and labour market regulation, is shown in the final two chapters, on 'What is Actually Regulating Work? A Study of Restaurants in Indonesia and Australia' and 'Labour Laws, Informality, and Development: Comparing India and China'.

In their empirical study of the regulation of work arrangements in one economic sector, the restaurant industry, in two locations (Yogyakarta in Indonesia and Melbourne in Australia) **Petra Mahy, Richard Mitchell, John Howe and Maria Azzurra Tranfaglia** illustrate the value of taking a regulatory pluralism approach, recognising that it is *regulation*, not solely labour, which can be formal or informal. Their dual case studies uncover a variety of norms governing the 'regulatory space' of work arrangements – a spectrum from formal regulation to work arrangements regulated almost entirely informally, with 'inter-legality' in the middle – which suggests the need for scholars and policy makers to move away from a fixation with formal labour law and its effectiveness in order to better understand the production of working conditions and to seek 'solutions' for improving worker security and well-being.

This introductory chapter began with the observation that labour law, formality and development are intertwined, and interrogated the assumption that the key to economic development lies in converting the 'informal' into the 'formal'. The book ends with a concluding analysis, by **Simon Deakin, Shelley Marshall and Sanjay Pinto**, which explores further this relationship between law, institutions and development by placing formalisation and informalisation in historical perspective, and also through a careful comparison of China and India. Appreciating the development trajectories of these two countries is essential for an understanding of formality in the development process, in particular in light of the divergence between the Indian and Chinese cases – with the persistence of informality in the former, and the emergence of a state-directed variant of the standard employment relationship in the latter – which Deakin, Marshall and Pinto's empirical study reveals. This concluding chapter also provides us with a guide for further study, especially comparative study, in its appraisal of the evolution of understandings of informality and how to navigate the multiple meanings accorded to the term given the lack of uniformity in definition and in data collection.

PART I

Theorising Informality and Informalisation: Historical and Development Perspectives

1

Historicising Labour in Development: Labour Market Formalisation through the Lens of British Colonial Administration

KERRY RITTICH

I. Introduction

Informal labour markets and work practices have long attracted the concern of development thinkers and planners. The source of this attention is not difficult to locate. Securing an adequate labour force, one that reliably serves the needs of capitalist enterprise, is invariably regarded as central to advancing economic development. Informal economic structures and arrangements often confound such ambitions, impeding the expected reallocation of resources such as labour and land, and disturbing the general vision of social progress behind the development enterprise itself.

Recasting work relationships in legal, and explicitly contractual, form has been a favoured means to advance the ends of greater productivity and economic growth, and it remains virtually definitional to development in its present market-centred forms, especially those that aim to advance human as well as economic development.[1] Yet although highly popular both within development constituencies and beyond, addressing informality at work turns out to be a complex and obstacle-ridden exercise. Formalisation never 'succeeds' in any simple way: whatever the aims of those introducing reforms, formalisation rarely if ever produces the well-functioning markets and workers that are its imagined result. Indeed, it is sometimes unclear to what extent formalisation changes how productive activity is organised. Even what it means to formalise work is, in legal terms, highly contentious and uncertain. Yet for all this uncertainty, formalisation can be highly consequential nonetheless. In context after context, formalisation not

[1] A Sen, *Development as Freedom* (New York, Alfred Knopf, 1999).

only produces outcomes quite different from those originally envisaged. It may produce distinct disadvantages rather than benefits for those who find their status formalised.[2] How and why such results might occur therefore seems of deep interest.

One way to illuminate these possibilities is to investigate the genealogy of labour market formalisation efforts, tracing the hopes and claims that have motivated its pursuit and shaped its form over time. Looking at two classic texts of British colonial administration, here I locate the conundrums of informality alongside the long-standing preoccupation among colonial administrators to create a more productive labour force. The idea is to uncover something about the character, direction and consequences of current efforts at formalisation by juxtaposing them with historical efforts to manage the problems of labour as they were then conceived. For the dilemmas of informality and the problems of native labour emanate from at least one common source and, for this reason, they can be productively viewed through a common lens: they are fundamentally about what happens when societies are set upon the trajectory towards liberal modernity, and their affiliations, institutions and activities reorganised according to market principles in the service of more efficient production and greater economic growth. Along with something about the enduring as well as changing forms of work itself, then, through this juxtaposition we might discern something about the heuristics and techniques that are common to managing labour in the colonial context and contemporary engagements with informal markets and workers.

The first text is Lord Lugard's *The Dual Mandate in British Tropical Africa*,[3] first published in 1922; the second is JS Furnivall's *Colonial Policy and Practice: A Comparative Study of Burma and Netherlands India*,[4] now Indonesia, published in 1948. Each was written in the shadow of cataclysmic global conflicts that, *inter alia*, destabilised British colonial projects and either sharply curtailed or effectively ended their ambitions. Both works can also, I suggest, be read as a species of development tract or treatise *avant la lettre*. To be clear, the claim is not that these texts can be read as providing the essential 'truth' concerning the nature and organisation of work within the colonised societies which they describe; on this and on other issues, there are multiple bases on which to differ or object. Any contemporary reader, for example, is likely to be struck by the pervasive racial bias evident throughout Lugard's analysis, as well as the open preference for furthering 'global' demands and interests or those of European powers, common to both when it comes to matters of policy and

[2] K Rittich, 'Formality and Informality in the Law of Work' in S Archer, D Drache and P Zumbansen (eds), *The Daunting Enterprise of Law: Essays in Honour of Harry W Arthurs* (Montreal, McGill-Queen's University Press, 2017).

[3] FD Lugard, *The Dual Mandate in British Tropical Africa* (Edinburgh, William Blackwood and Sons, 1922).

[4] JS Furnivall, *Colonial Policy and Practice: A Comparative Study of Burma and Netherlands India* (Cambridge, Cambridge University Press, 1948).

development strategy. Rather, reading these texts is designed to do something else: to provide a window onto the minds, observations and calculations of those who governed as they attempted to address the challenges they viewed as central to the larger economic and political purposes they were aiming to further.

Tracing the continuities as well as discontinuities, in the problems as the administrators saw them and in the projects they chose to pursue provides a vantage point for examining informality, as an empirical phenomenon and as an object of interest in respect of governance. This same exercise also reveals repeated, persistent gaps between the aims and effects of formalisation, casting doubt on claims that formalisation is ineluctably linked to greater freedom and empowerment for workers,. As Chris Tomlins trenchantly observed, '[c]olonizing's incessant demands for labor, the forms in which both the supply of labor and the work performed were organised in response, and the social and ideological practices that resulted, interrupt conventional narratives of Anglo-American modernity and the waxing formal freedoms in relations among law, economy, and society that are their marker.'[5]

II. Representing Work: Formality and Informality Reconsidered

'Your illusions are a part of you like your bones and flesh and memory'.[6]

A. Representing Informality

The larger project of which this analysis is a part is framed as an inquiry into the normative and conceptual narratives of labour law.[7] We take it as common ground, then, that these narratives themselves do important work in shaping our approach to the discipline. But this central insight extends further, to the very subject matter of the field, work itself. Put simply, work and its problems do not simply exist as facts to which we have common and unmediated access. Rather, we access the world of work through structures of representation. Normative and conceptual narratives also inform the specific problems of work with which we grapple. They provide a grammar through which we understand the world of work, a means through which its features becomes legible to us. We register certain activities *as* work, and particular aspects of those activities as salient and significant, in the context of the frame in which we make sense of the world of work as a whole.

[5] C Tomlins, *Freedom Bound: Law, Labor, and Civic Identity in Colonizing English America, 1580–1865* (Cambridge, Cambridge University Press, 2010), 342.

[6] W Faulkner, *Absalom, Absalom* (New York, Random House, 1936).

[7] D Ashiagbor, 'Introduction: Narratives of Informality and Development', this volume.

If we approach informality in this vein, as a vehicle and site of representation, we can better see the work that informality itself performs itself as a heuristic: how it frames the objects of concern, how it constitutes some features of economic life and activity as problematic, and how it impels us to address those problems in particular ways. From this standpoint, informality appears not simply a socio-legal condition: it emerges as a decision-making apparatus, a way of ordering claims, a means to make choices about what counts and what to do. As a category within development thinking, informality stands in hierarchical relation to formality. As a normative frame, it produces its own narratives of backwardness and progress, directing our attention to a pre-identified set of predicaments and channelling reform efforts and simultaneously crafting normal work and normal labour markets. Viewed through the prism of informality, we can better see how the legal rules that constitute, and reconstitute, the world of work might be ordered and chosen, how they are intended to function in the larger picture of the economy as a whole.

B. Resituating Informal Work

Pushing the representational motif further, we might effect a figure/ground reversal and imagine that informality now constitutes as much a 'normal' as an exceptional condition of work. Although informality is strongly associated with the labour markets and traditional work practices of the global South, a series of collapsing distinctions between core and periphery in the world of work make this conceptual reversal seem plausible.

The first is the spread of waged work both as empirical reality and as normative or aspirational trajectory in the global South.[8] We might understand this as a vindication of the modernisation thesis, the claim that like other markets, labour markets tend towards formalisation as they expand over time and space while work relations tend to converge around the employment relationship as economies industrialise.[9] The second move goes in the opposite direction, and involves a phenomenon unanticipated in modernisation narratives: the emergence and entrenchment of informal work and informal labour markets alongside their formal counterparts across the industrialised world.[10] The third shift is the normalisation of labour market flexibility, a complex process involving the deconsolidation of the regulatory benchmark for work in the industrialised world, the standard employment relationship, and its replacement with a rapidly proliferating

[8] S Deakin, S Marshall and S Pinto, 'Laws, Informality, and Development: Comparing India and China', this volume.

[9] D North, *Institutions, Institutional Change, and Economic Performance* (Cambridge, Cambridge University Press, 1990).

[10] A Portes, M Castells and L Benton (eds), *The Informal Economy: Studies in Advanced and Less Developed Countries* (Baltimore, John Hopkins University Press, 1989); S Sassen, *The Global City: New York, London, Tokyo* (Princeton, Princeton University Press, 1992).

set of fragmented, highly differentiated workplace relations. Although flexibility itself operates through legal rules and institutions, the process is sometimes identified as 'informalisation'[11] because of the extent to which it leaves workers shorn of the protections that labour market institutions used to provide, and because, insofar as the allocation of contractual risk is concerned, the results are increasingly difficult to distinguish from other commercial relations. Operating together, these changes help explain the last shift: growing transnational linkages across core and periphery in the world of work, and the consequent difficulty of continuing to locate particular sectors and societies within categories such as 'developed' or 'industrialising'.[12]

If informality now captures central aspects of work in the industrial and post-industrial as well as 'developing' world, there are other reasons to look beyond formal law when it comes to work. Complex and fragmented normative environments – those in which some of the legal rules typically associated with formal markets are missing; customary practices and local norms concerning access to property and resources organise much of working life; and rule enforcement tends to be either variable, privatised or simply unavailable – are characteristic of more labour markets than we conventionally acknowledge. While they are long-standing features of the world of work, they are especially important to comprehending precarious and 'fissured' forms of work.[13] Moreover, labour markets everywhere tend to be organised through social networks, and work practices and arrangements are powerfully cross-cut with ethnic, racial, gender and religious norms. Absent some knowledge of how these norms and networks function in a given locale, it may be impossible to make sense of central questions of interest – namely, who does what and under what terms – concerning work.

These continuities and categorical breakdowns suggest that informality may provide a useful vantage point from which to reflect on the general regulatory context of work, especially under conditions of vertical disintegration where work is organised through supply chains and networks of economic actors are connected through fluid, contractual relations.[14] The claim is not only that this reversal of disciplinary perspective may capture a more diverse set of work situations (although that is certainly the case). It is that it promises to bring a wider range of norms, rules and institutions, social and customary as well as legal, that operate on *all* work into view. It may even alter our perception of what constitutes a problem of work.

[11] J Fudge, 'The Legal Boundaries of the Employer, Precarious Workers, and Labour Protection' in G Davidov and B Langille (eds), *Boundaries and Frontiers of Labour Law: Goals and Means in the Regulation of Work* (Portland, OR, Hart Publishing, 2006) 295.

[12] See also D McCann, 'Informalisation in International Labour Regulation Policy: Profiles of an Unravelling'; T Novitz, 'Supply Chains and Temporary Migrant Labour: The Relevance of Trade and Sustainability Frameworks?'; and R Dukes, 'Insiders, Outsiders and Conflicts of Interest', this volume.

[13] D Weil, *The Fissured Workplace: Why Work Became So Bad for So Many and What Can Be Done to Improve It* (Cambridge, MA, Harvard University Press, 2014).

[14] See also IGLP Law and Production Working Group, 'The Role of Law in Global Value Chains: A Research Manifesto' (2016) 4 *London Review of International Law* 57.

III. Development and Formalisation

Like work, development projects, too, can be approached as works of imagination. First and foremost, they involve the projection of future states of social and economic doing and being. These projections function to orientate institutional practice. But they also serve as modes of (re)making our understanding of the present as well as the past.

The current preoccupation with informality derives from a specific set of concerns fundamental to modern conceptions of development: briefly stated, how informal arrangements – whether in labour, land, finance or simply the transfer of goods and services – might preclude the commoditisation of productive assets and/or impede their efficient allocation, thereby derailing the optimisation of economic growth as a whole. Combined with the association of formal legal institutions with modernisation, an association that can be traced at least to Weber,[15] these concerns invariably impel development practitioners to counsel formalisation; they may induce them to imagine formalisation *itself* as development.

Contemporary development is conceptually and programmatically connected to formalisation in any event; as governance projects, they lead parallel lives. Efforts at formalisation are integral to the legalisation of development, a process that envisages rights recognition and the institutionalisation of legal entitlements not simply as mechanisms necessary to transformative change but as part of the very definition of development itself.[16] Thus, to be informal now is not simply to occupy a particular socio-legal position; it is to be in a condition of deficit or 'lack'. And because informality is closely identified with underdevelopment, because development itself is so centrally conceptualised in legal and institutional terms, and because informality necessarily makes reference to its opposite, formality, to be labelled informal is to already be set up for – to require – an intervention of a specifically legal kind. Note the animating assumption: *pace* Douglass North, societies and markets do not simply evolve towards formality, adopting more and more of the indicia of legality as a function of the demands of expanded trade and commerce alone.[17] Rather, informality itself is a discrete condition, a problem with a remedy: more complete and effective institutionalisation in legal form.

[15] See D Trubek, 'Max Weber and the Role of Law in Capitalism' (1972) *Wisconsin Law Review* 720; C Thomas, 'Max Weber, Talcott Parsons and the Sociology of Legal Reform: A Reassessment with Implications for Law and Development' (2006) 15 *Minnesota Journal of International Law* 383. See also D Kennedy, 'The Disenchantment of Logically Formal Legal Rationality, or Max Weber's Sociology in the Genealogy of the Contemporary Mode of Western Legal Thought' (2004) 55 *Hastings Law Journal* 103.

[16] Sen, *Development as Freedom*, above n 1; K Rittich, 'Second Generation Reforms and the Incorporation of the Social' in D Trubek and A Santos (eds), *The New Law and Economic Development: A Critical Appraisal* (Cambridge, Cambridge University Press, 2006), 203.

[17] D North, *Institutions, Institutional Change, and Economic Performance* (Cambridge, Cambridge University Press, 1990).

Like development itself, formalisation is both an ideology and a project.[18] Formalisation comprises a constellation of ideas, institutional commitments and practices that, combining normative claims about the place of rights and the rule of law in liberal market societies with assertions about their economic consequences, links 'bringing the law in' to sectors imagined as un-, under- or dis-regulated with a host of economic and welfare gains.[19] Reforms then proceed, typically on the basis of models that have been endorsed and diffused by international institutions and transnational technocrats and policy elites.[20] For example, following an image popularised by Hernando de Soto, land titling is thought to rescue land from its status as 'dead capital',[21] while the elimination of costly regulations and burdensome administrative requirements allows the natural entrepreneurial instincts of the poor to rise up and prevail.[22] Undergirding these claims lies a conceptualisation of the subject: the purveyor of human capital who, calculating her economic prospects in response to regulatory incentives, once endowed with the powers and protections conferred by legality, increases her welfare and drives the economy as a whole toward higher levels of growth.

These projects take distinctive contemporary form, particularly insofar as they link formalisation to objectives like gender equality and the 'empowerment of the poor' via the path of entrepreneurialism.[23] However, much of the ideological/political project behind formalisation is not new. It is the perception with informality as a condition of lack that must be remedied to create a (more) productive economy that makes formalisation at once central to the project of development and somewhat continuous with colonial administration. For the general preoccupation with increasing productivity along with more specific questions about how to produce more market-responsive workers were also at the centre of the problems of native labour in the minds of British colonial administrators. While their concerns may seem to be of purely historical interest, there are reasons to resist such a conclusion, particularly if we are interested in informal workers.

[18] K Rittich, 'Theorizing International Law and Development' in Orford and Hoffman, *The Oxford Handbook of The Theory of International Law* (Oxford, Oxford University Press, 2016). See also S Pahuja, *Decolonizing International Law: Development, Economic Growth and the Politics of Universality* (Cambridge, Cambridge University Press, 2011).

[19] United Nations, *Making the Law Work for Everyone: Report of the Commission on Legal Empowerment of the Poor* (New York, United Nations, 2008).

[20] K Deininger, *Land Policies for Growth and Poverty Reduction* (Washington, D.C., World Bank and Oxford, Oxford University Press, 2003).

[21] H de Soto, *The Mystery of Capital: Why Capitalism Succeeds in the West and Fails Everywhere Else* (New York, Basic Books, 2000).

[22] H de Soto, *The Other Path: The Economic Answer to Terrorism* (New York, Basic Books, 1989); see also Perry et al, *Informality: Exit and Exclusion* (Washington, D.C, World Bank, 2007), available at: http://web.worldbank.org/WBSITE/EXTERNAL/COUNTRIES/LACEXT/0,contentMDK:21345369~pagePK:146736~piPK:146830~theSitePK:258554,00.html.

[23] World Bank, *Engendering Development: Through Gender Equality in Rights, Resources, and Voice* (Washington D.C., World Bank, 2001); United Nations, *Making the Law Work for Everyone*, above n 19.

IV. Informality, Work, and the Uses of History

William Faulkner – 'The past is never dead; it's not even past.'[24]

A. Work and History

Although there are some truly new aspirations when it comes to transforming work in developing countries, whether viewed in terms of the objectives themselves, the discourses in which they are discussed and justified, or the legal forms through which they are advanced, an astonishing amount is not.

Work arrangements have histories, histories which often remain influential even in the face of epochal changes, and the hold of old norms and ways of organising work can be powerfully retentive, even where work's formal terms have changed. Nor does legal transformation translate into social or economic change in any simple way; legal change may even function to preserve the fundamental terms of social and economic arrangements.[25] As is well understood, the law of master and servant across the Anglo-American world remained infused with feudal remnants importing obligations of obedience and faithful service into what were, under the emergent legal and political regimes, putatively free bargains among equals.[26] Similarly, forced labour didn't simply disappear upon the abolition of slavery and the decline of indentured servitude; instead, coercive work relations that effectively replicated many of their features appeared and persisted, often in new contractual forms.[27] Reflecting on these possibilities is, I suggest, a central part of thinking clearly about informality, current attempts to remedy it in the service of social and economic progress in particular.

B. Colonial Labour Market Governance: Back to the Future?

Historical inquiry into colonialism and its legacies is increasingly central to international legal scholarship, including its study of development practices. Much of this historical work might be described as work *of* and *on* representation, insofar

[24] W Faulkner, *Requiem for a Nun* (New York, Vintage, 1951).

[25] RB Siegel, 'The Rule of Love: Wife Beating as Prerogative and Privacy', 105 *Yale Law Journal* 2117, 2119 (1996).

[26] A Fox, *Work, Power and Trust Relations* (London, Faber and Faber, 1974), 181–84. Tomlins argues that rather than a move from status to contract, as master and servant law came to serve as the general law of waged work, 'over the course of the eighteenth century, "employees" become "servants," not vice versa.' Tomlins, *Freedom Bound*, above n 5, 355–56.

[27] R Steinfeld, *The Invention of Free Labor: The Employment Relation in English and American Law and Culture* (Chapel Hill, University of North Carolina Press, 1991); E Nakano Glenn, *Forced to Care: Coercion and Caregiving in America* (Cambridge, MA, Harvard University Press, 2010); DA Blackmon, *Slavery by Another Name: the Re-enslavement of Black Americans from the Civil War to World War 2* (New York, Anchor Books, 2008).

as it involves excavating, reframing, and sometimes reconstructing entirely the received narratives about colonial endeavours, along with colonialism's successor projects such as the mandate and trusteeship systems.[28] In the process, core principles and doctrines have been revealed to have striking genealogies and attachments, histories and features that both challenge central elements of the discipline of international law itself and serve to cast current legal problems, including those connected to development, in a new light.[29] Such inquiries have provided a basis on which to query the global economic and political modernisation in the (neo)liberal style, at the level of purpose, ideology and effect.

The intuition pursued here is that as integral parts of development, we can usefully perform this historical analysis on practices and ideologies connected to the formalisation of labour. The payoff, I suggest, is as follows. First, examination of colonial practices enables us to uncover continuities between older and newer forms of work, including forms of coerced and indentured work that we imagine now to be marginal and mostly of historical interest. Second, it reveals a number of connections among historical and contemporary projects to manage workers, particularly those designed to make workers more disciplined and productive, so characteristic in an era of pervasive market liberalisation. Third, it discloses enduring patterns in the allocation of risks and entitlements as between workers and those that employ them, as well as the preferred legal forms through which those risks and entitlements are secured. Fourth, it tells us something about the consequences that may follow from the emergence of markets in waged labour for the affected workers. Beyond reminding us that, whatever their benefits, interventions designed to re-constitute working arrangements have gone awry in ways that start to look predictable if not systematic, such an inquiry serves as a caution about outcomes and traps of concern to workers: cycles of indebtedness, restrictions on economic opportunities, heightened economic insecurity, etc. Finally, I suggest, it discloses the enduring centrality of labour market regulation and institutions to governance agendas themselves. Overall, it provides some useful starting points from which to trace continuities and change in the normative orientation of governance initiatives, the locations in which power and authority are to be found, and the bureaucratic and administrative forms and structures through which control is exercised.

Situating informality historically thus may provide one way to surface what lies below the standard narratives about formalisation, a means to get beyond formalisation 'on its own terms'. It may permit us to capture the risks of interventions designed to transform informal markets, and to better understand why such interventions have a mixed, unsuccessful, sometimes disastrous track record,

[28] A Anghie, *Imperialism, Sovereignty, and the Making of International Law* (Cambridge, Cambridge University Press, 2005), B Rajagopal, *International Law from Below: Development, Social Movements and Third World Resistance* (Cambridge, Cambridge University Press, 2006); S Pahuja, *Decolonizing International Law*, above n 18.

[29] Anghie, *Imperialism, Sovereignty, and the Making of International Law*, above n 28.

whether measured in terms of purely economic or broader welfare outcomes. With respect to work, it may help illustrate continuities as well as discontinuities across the labour problems in the north and south, the present and the past, continuities in the terms of work and the relationships in which they are situated that traverse slavery, indentured servitude, and low-wage labour, for example, despite the changing legal forms.

V. Lugard – The Dual Mandate in British Tropical Africa

Frederick Lugard, a colonial administrator in British West Africa, wrote what remains the *locus classicus* on administrative policy and practice in the British Empire, *The Dual Mandate in British Tropical Africa*.[30] Drawing principally on his experience in what is now Nigeria, but informed by his military service in colonial India, time in commercial affairs in the British East Africa Company and the Royal Niger Company, along with his term as the governor of Hong Kong, Lugard produced a detailed treatise containing reflections on virtually every significant dimension of colonial governance as it was practised in the late nineteenth and early twentieth centuries.

Among Lugard's most enduring contribution was his articulation of the colonial endeavour itself. As Lugard elaborated at length in normative and institutional terms in his monograph, colonialism was at heart a project of modernisation, involving the transformation of 'backward' societies, where backwardness had both economic and moral/cultural connotations. From this imperative Lugard derived the concept that remains central to its analysis nearly a century later, the 'dual mandate': on the one hand, the obligation to further the moral and material advancement of the natives while, on the other, provisioning the metropole with resources and markets crucial to its own ends and requirements.

As conceived by Lugard, each element of the mandate possessed an internal duality as well. The moral and material advancement of the colonies were themselves inextricably conjoined, insofar as the attitudinal and behavioural transformation of the native populations was seen as essential to advancing the colony's prospects for economic development. However, free trade and economic transformation were themselves touted as means to incite greater engagement in productive activity and demand for the rule of law on the part of the natives. And for Lugard and the audience to which his treatise was directed, enhanced productivity and greater propensity to rely on legality were themselves self-evident markers of moral as well as material progress for individuals as well as societies.

[30] Lugard, *The Dual Mandate in British Tropical Africa*, above n 3.

This enmeshment of the moral and the material is visible across Lugard's account of the colonial venture: from the investments and interventions undertaken by the British to the economic benefits they recouped in return, all were defended in the name of moral and cultural advances, from the suppression of the slave trade and the end of inter-tribal warfare to the elimination of barbaric practices such as human sacrifice and ordeals associated with primitive religions.[31] Nowhere was this entanglement more clearly in view than when it came to matters concerning work. Discussing the circumstances in which resort might be had to compulsory labour, for example, Lugard notes that beyond necessity, they include the 'desirability of training of natives to work, so that they shall not "live in idleness and vice"'.[32]

The moral and material development of the native population was, of course, also key to realising colonialism's benefits at home, namely access to valuable resources along with expanded markets for British goods. European powers felt entitled to freely access the resources of their colonies for both general and specific purposes, openly using language expressing that entitlement.[33] Citing the material depletions and financial burdens experienced by Britain as a consequence of World War I, for example, Lugard described colonial development as a central means by which land and resources crucial to the power and advancement, and even the survival, of imperial powers could be secured.[34]

Given the range of ambitions housed within the dual mandate, it seems hardly surprising that colonial ventures were rife with conflicts, among them tensions between the desire to exploit untapped resources for commercial gain and the demands of advancing native social welfare, and conflicts between the interests of native populations and the competing, putatively legitimate, interests of the local settlers and the global community. Indeed, conflicts surfaced within each of these aims and constituencies as well as between them.

Labour problems are arguably where the internal tensions and conflicts thrown up by the dual mandate were most clearly in view;[35] they are also where decisions about how to resolve them seem most continuous with the welfare of the population of the colony itself. How these tensions and conflicts were both conceptualised and managed remains important in itself; to the extent that they reflect continuing practices, they are also instructive when it comes to contemporary governance. For throughout Lugard's account the management

[31] ibid, 616.

[32] ibid, 411.

[33] 'The partition of Africa is, as we all recognise, due primarily to the economic necessity of increasing the supplies of raw materials and food to meet the needs of the industrialised nations of Europe.' ibid, 613.

[34] ibid, 498.

[35] The management of native labour was also a central problematique in the mandate system administered by the League of Nations during the interwar period. See A Anghie, 'Colonialism and the Birth of International Institutions: Sovereignty, Economy, and the Mandate System of the League of Nations', 34 *New York University Journal of International Law and Politics* 513 (2002), 584.

of labour problems was coterminous with the emergence of an administrative style in which the welfare and interests of native workers were both recognised yet (re)configured, to be merged with, and ultimately subordinated not just to the demands of the metropole but to the interests of the local planters, miners and industrialists as well. Once reframed in this way, many of the most pressing tensions in colonial policies could, at least at the conceptual level, be mitigated if not eliminated entirely. Thus, labour's position provides a window not only on how the dual mandate was conceptualised but on how its constituent elements were to be ordered and reconciled.

To understand how and why colonial administrators might have engaged with the policy and regulatory dilemmas around native labour in this way, adopting techniques of reconfiguration, convergence and absorption, it is useful to observe just how central native labour was to the achievement of colonial objectives. Almost no matter the subject or endeavour, managing the problems of labour emerged as a crucial concern: in Lugard's study, labour questions surface in the context of securing the defence of the colony,[36] land tenure and agricultural policy,[37] taxation and the generation of revenue,[38] economic development and the construction of infrastructure such as ports and railways,[39] and of course health and education,[40] to list only the most prominent areas. Labour's distinctly subordinated position in the colonial enterprise, however, is arguably a function of the centrality of commercial activity to the colonial venture itself. Lugard put this imperative in plain words,

> [n]ot only is the wealth and prosperity of a country dependent upon its trade, but it is obvious that it can only pay for its administration and for its development works by its exports and the result of its industry. It is manifest therefore that it is of the first importance that Government should do everything in its power to promote and encourage commerce [in the colony].[41]

The overarching imperative of advancing commerce not only ensured that transforming the labour force would be a central task, crucial to moving from a barter and subsistence economy to a more commoditised, productive and expansive market economy. It meant that commercial imperatives would frame the choices about how the transformation would occur at virtually every turn, at least in the first instance.

Throughout *The Dual Mandate*, Lugard grappled with a series of issues connected to the native labour problem: managing the legacy of slavery and the transition to a free labour market; advancing the state of native education,

[36] Lugard, above n 3, 576.
[37] ibid, chs 14 and 15.
[38] ibid, ch 13.
[39] ibid, ch 26.
[40] ibid, 411–12; chs 21 and 22.
[41] ibid, 483.

health and welfare; increasing the productivity of native labour; securing adequate labour resources for commercial ventures and the growing demands of industry; and generating a wage labour force responsive to market signals and incentives. These were not objectives, however, that all lived happily together; to the contrary, a daunting range of practical and political problems immediately manifested when they were pursued simultaneously. Indeed, an immense amount of representational and discursive labour went into the construction of a narrative in which these competing objectives and commitments *could* imaginably co-exist.

As did Furnivall later on, Lugard reflected at length on the dilemmas surrounding the creation of a labour force of workers habituated to the norms and practices of free contracting. In the colonial context, these dilemmas opened up a broader discussion of the merits of free contracting versus coerced labour.[42] The backdrop to this discussion was the end of slave labour and the status of other forms of coerced labour, live issues across colonial societies given the persistence of various forms of bonded and unfree labour across colonial societies. Discussion of the slave trade had already taken centre stage at the Berlin conference in 1885, when African territory was divided and jurisdiction over its parts assumed by European states.[43] Yet although the colonial powers were by this point unambiguously committed to the suppression of slavery (the British having abolished it in the first half of the nineteenth century), *The Dual Mandate* makes clear that managing its end still preoccupied colonial administrators almost 40 years later. One complication in the colonial context was the simultaneous interest in securing a tractable labour force to support commercial activity. Lugard devotes two chapters to the question in which he describes, inter alia, the relative merits of sudden versus gradual abolition of slavery, with particular attention to the potential adverse economic consequences of the former for the slaveholder.[44] Here, Lugard comes down unequivocally against a 'wholesale assertion' and on the side of 'gradual and permissive' freedom for slaves; however this coincided with exemptions from freedom altogether for those who were concubines.[45]

Lugard's discussion of the possible strategies to end slavery prefigures a more general labour market conundrum: fixing the degree of coercion that was compatible with a free market in labour and, more particularly, trying to prognosticate

[42] For useful analogous inquiries, see: Robert J Steinfeld, *The Invention of Free Labour: The Employment Relation in English and American Law and Culture* (Chapel Hill, NC, University of North Carolina Press, 1991); 'Caring for One's Own and Caring for a Living' in Evelyn Nakano Glenn, *Forced to Care: Coercion and Caregiving in America* (Cambridge, MA, Harvard University Press, 2010) chapter 2.

[43] For a recent analysis of the Conference of Berlin, see M Craven, 'Between Law and History: The Berlin Conference of 1884–85 and the Logic of Free Trade', 3 *London Review of International Law* 31 (2015).

[44] Lugard, above n 3, chapters 17 and 18. For a comprehensive discussion of efforts to compensate slaveholders for the losses they incurred by the end of slavery, see Catherine Hall, Nicholas Draper, Keith McClelland, Katie Donington and Rachel Lang, *Legacies of British Slave-Ownership: Colonial Slavery and the Formation of Victorian Britain* (Cambridge, Cambridge University Press, 2014).

[45] Lugard, above n 3, 370.

the consequences of adopting different forms of free and unfree work.[46] As *The Dual Mandate* makes clear, in the colonial context the European powers remained deeply ambivalent about eliminating coercive labour practices that fell short of complete enslavement. Not only were the British tolerant, indeed desirous, of subjecting 'free' labour to economic discipline; they were entirely prepared to entertain the use of compelled labour purely for its inherent virtues, 'in order to induce the African to work, solely for his own moral and material benefit and advancement'.[47]

What degree of freedom workers should possess, and precisely how much unfreedom or compulsion should be tolerated were, then, pressing questions of colonial policy. Some degree of compulsory community labour was common within the societies colonised by the British. As Lugard describes, colonial administrators had tried, successfully and not depending on the context, to leverage such traditional practices into a requirement that natives build the infrastructure needed for economic development – roads, dams, railways – in locales both near and far from their homes.[48] But such uses of forced labour on the part of public authorities turned out to raise a series of other conundrums, like whether private companies should *also* be able to avail themselves of forced labour, or whether, by contrast, forced labour for public purposes should be curtailed because it would cut into the supply of labour available for Western enterprises. Subtending these debates was the recognition that workers' freedom to leave their traditional forms of work might itself constitute an economic threat, insofar as it undermined the preservation of labour resources relied upon by colonial entrepreneurs seeking to maintain or expand their commercial enterprises. The bottom line was fairly clear: whatever its merits according to liberal theory, free labour in practice posed some degree of threat to the interests of, in Lugard's words, 'the ruling classes, whom it is our desire to support and strengthen'.[49]

The competing interests of labour and capital, then, were clearly in view within the colonial venture, and Lugard's views of the relative priority of these interests reflected what would have been a fairly standard elite position of the time, one shared, for example, by judges adjudicating labour and employment disputes at home.[50] But the debates over forced labour were also infused with recognisably modern – even contemporary – development preoccupations, such as the extent

[46] As Seinfeld and Tomlins have observed in respect of America, 'compulsion and modern free wage labor are no contradiction'. See Tomlins, *Freedom Bound*, above n 5, 56.

[47] Lugard, above n 3, 411–12.

[48] Furnivall, too, described how the imperative of road-making required compulsory labour in Burma on the part of villagers of about two months of every year. However, noting that it was 'most irksome to the people' and incoherent as a policy because it interfered with the cultivation of rice – the product the roads were designed to transport – Furnivall then linked this strategy to the importation of convict labour from India. Furnivall, above n 4, 43.

[49] Lugard, above n 3, 372.

[50] For a contemporaneous example of judicial scepticism concerning workers' collective action, see *Taff Vale Railway v Amalgamated Society of Railway Servants* [1901] AC 426.

to which workers could be expected to respond to economic incentives. Liberals had long been against forced labour on purely ideological grounds: free contract rules![51] But as Lugard observed, forced labour in practice was often inefficient while 'free' (contract) labour more productive. In short, arguments about paying for work and the merits of extending of freedom of contract to labour rested not just on normative and political justifications but on consequentialist ones: they were necessary incentives to engagement in productive work. Although elsewhere he trafficked in such stereotypes himself, on this point Lugard distanced himself from the suggestion that natives were naturally lazy or undisciplined; he 'cannot think why Europeans persist in assuming that a native lives in degrading idleness unless working for a European',[52] noting that wage labour was hardly foreign to Africans.[53]

As did Furnivall later on in his account of British colonial practice in Burma, Lugard described the techniques classically employed by the colonial powers to induce or compel engagement in waged work and thereby normalise participation in markets for labour. One key proved to be the requirement that taxes be paid in cash rather than in kind.[54] But a powerful incentive was provided simply by opening markets and flooding them with new foreign goods to purchase, something only possible for the vast majority by working for wages.[55] These direct inducements to waged work were further supported by initiatives such as the creation of an educational system that, organised according to the British model, placed immense stress on the formation of good character and habits of discipline thought to be conducive to productive labour.[56]

Lugard himself was, in theory, opposed to compulsory labour in all its forms but for the most limited exceptions. Yet while he repeatedly made the case for a free market in labour, Lugard was also wary of the effects on development of the rising wages that such a free market in labour might produce.[57] Faced with wage demands from workers who were free to move if those demands were not satisfied, Lugard appeared to find it entirely expected, even describing it as a 'perfect right', that employers would act to prevent workers from exercising their bargaining power in the market, by '"settling" among themselves' – that is, colluding over – the prevailing wage rate in an industry.[58] He also canvassed strategies, like the introduction of piece-work[59] and the importation of alien labour,[60] that might

[51] For a recent discussion of these debates, see M Fakhri, *Sugar and the Making of International Trade Law*, (Cambridge, Cambridge University Press, 2014).
[52] Lugard, above n 3, 401.
[53] ibid, 402.
[54] ibid, 415.
[55] ibid, 403.
[56] ibid, 431–32.
[57] ibid, 404.
[58] ibid.
[59] ibid, 421.
[60] ibid, 405.

be adopted to positively reduce wage rates in a free labour market. At the end of the day, he described the importation of indentured labour as the 'only solution' to the problem of securing the labour supply in some situations, including to support private enterprise.[61]

Two issues relevant to contemporary efforts to commodify work and formalise labour markets emerge from Lugard's discussion of compulsory labour, raising questions of classification in addition to normative concerns. One is the very uncertain border between different forms of work: how different *was* contract labour, increasingly common and thought necessary to secure adequate labour resources for development of the colony, from the discredited forms of indentured labour of old?[62] The other is the uncertain payoff in moving from one form of labour to another: in what senses could sharecropping and tenancy arrangements, for example, be regarded as per se better or more 'free' than practices like formal indenture to the land?

Second, Lugard identified two groups of workers whose presence created particular difficulties, complicating still further the move toward free, commodified labour that was imagined as definitional to successful economic modernisation. For reasons that Lugard would have recognised well, these workers remain both troubling and troublesome categories in the context of contemporary labour market policy and transformation.

One was women, whose status as workers was shaped and constrained by the gendered identities, norms and duties arising from marriage, concubinage and customary household and family arrangements.[63] Lugard did not even attempt to grapple with the questions of work enmeshed in these norms and practices, for example by considering how the tasks traditionally performed by women might be part of, related to, or simply affected by, the general commodification of labour. Instead, he simply accepted the existing roles and their constraints on women as given by custom and tradition. As was conventional British colonial practice, such norms and practices were consigned to the private, household sphere that, in the characteristic division of jurisdiction and subject matter competence of indirect rule, fell outside the purview of colonial administrators.[64] But Lugard was assisted here in his conclusions by external events: by this time, across the Anglo-American world, the household labour of women was simply no longer recognised as economically valuable work, an event conterminous with the normalisation of waged labour among men.[65] Thus, in British colonial administration as in British society itself was the position and the labour of women further exceptionalised – this, in a domain, work, that was already subject to exceptional characterisation and treatment when it came to market practices and logics.

[61] ibid, 416; 424.

[62] ibid, 415–16.

[63] ibid 364; 375.

[64] K Rittich, 'Black Sites: Locating the Family and Family Law in Development', 58 *American Journal of Comparative Law* 1023 (2010)

[65] N Folbre, 'The Unproductive Housewife: Her Evolution in 19th Century Economic Thought' (1991) 16 *Signs: Journal of Women in Culture and Society* 463.

The other problematic category was migrant workers – more specifically, imported 'Asiatic' workers.[66] The difficulties that British colonial administrators encountered in inducing native workers to perform their imagined roles as reliably productive labourers meant that the presence of contract workers, often in the form of indentured labour, soon came to be regarded as essential to supporting Western enterprise and British settlers and realising other colonial economic objectives.[67] Yet Lugard recognised full well that however crucial such workers were to supporting economic development in the colonies, contract labour raised innumerable difficulties, including routine abuses of workers by contractors and violations of local labour norms and standards.[68]

In all of his discussion of labour issues, Lugard traversed related and remote matters of colonial policy, from the requirement of settlers for access to native labour in order to survive, to the importance of transport and education policy to make the market for labour actually function. In so doing he repeatedly drew attention to the many complexities that attend efforts to introduce fundamental changes to labour practices on the ground. Among them included very basic issues around disruption to land and social structure, from the need to allow time to permit labourers to return home to cultivate their crops and secure the food supply to the importance of ensuring that labourers working far from home could bring their wives if 'order' was to be maintained. Whether intentionally or not, Lugard demonstrated the far-reaching, often disruptive, effects of any effort to generate, or import, a labour force responsive to the demands of commerce.

Furnivall, too, devoted considerable thought to the implications of reliance on contract labour for citizenship and national cohesion.[69] For Furnivall, these predicaments provided a revealing window onto not only the problems of labour in the colony, but onto a more general concern of which they are an essential part: the fraught relationship between the promotion of a market-centred economy and social or welfare considerations.

VI. Furnivall – Colonial Policy and Practice

> 'Naturally, colonial policy is framed with reference to the interest, real or imagined, of the colonial power. But modern colonization is an affair of capital and not of men, and capital knows no country.'[70]

Furnivall would have to be described as an atypical colonial administrator in at least two respects. First, Furnivall's insights into colonial policy and governance

[66] Lugard, above n 3, 417–18.

[67] ibid, 416–18.

[68] ibid, 422–24.

[69] Furnivall is most famous for his thesis on the 'plural society' in which he identified the corrosive effects of ethnic fissuring on efforts at national self-determination; in Furnivall's view, this was a product of the importation of contract labour and the resulting stratification of labour and living arrangements along ethnic lines. See Furnivall 303 ff.

[70] Furnivall, above n 4, 5.

come at a very late period in time, on the very eve of decolonisation. Second, his personal circumstances were unusual: he married a Burmese woman early on in his long tenure in Burma and they had children together, with the result that he became deeply immersed in Burmese life at multiple levels.[71] Yet if Furnivall was unusually well positioned to observe at close quarters not just the aims but the effects of colonial interventions over the *longue durée*, including as perceived by the Burmese themselves, he nonetheless retained some of the classic sentiments of a colonial administrator. Coming to Burma with a background in the Indian Civil Service, Furnivall was sharply critical of British colonial policy in many respects. Yet even when the end of the imperial era was clearly in view, voicing the prevailing metropolitan elite consensus Furnivall wrote that 'it is a matter of common sense that backward regions should contribute as fully as possible to the resources of the world or, at least, to the resources of the colonial power'.[72] Believing that '[t]he primary function of any Government is to comply with the requirements of the outer world',[73] he placed his ultimate hopes in the transformation of Burmese society through contact with the western world.[74]

Notwithstanding such, general pronouncements, Furnivall's actual analysis constantly subverts any easy conclusion that colonial policy reliably engendered beneficial outcomes for the colonised population. Perhaps because of his doubled position – as someone within the colonial administration who was also unusually invested in its effects on the subject population – Furnivall demonstrates how little of colonial policy and practice could be described as a matter of common sense, and how much, *au contraire*, it both shifted over time and was riven with internal contradictions at the levels of design and implementation. And despite his apparent faith in the beneficent effects of the 'requirements of the outer world', over and over again Furnivall saw fit to point out the ways in which those requirements operated to subvert the welfare of the native peoples themselves. Thus, Furnivall can be read in two modes: as colonial administrator and as critic.

In tracing the path of British colonialism in Burma, Furnivall divides the history into two main periods, giving significant emphasis to the move from simple *laissez-faire* in the earlier period to what he terms 'efficiency' or constructivism in the latter. This is a shift he attributed to the opening of the Suez Canal in 1869 and the realisation of the immense economic potential of expanded trade that it enabled.[75] At the heart of this shift was the recognition by the colonial powers that

[71] RH Taylor, 'Disaster or Release? JS Furnivall and the Bankruptcy of Burma' (1995) 29 *Modern Asian Studies* 45.

[72] Furnivall, above n 4, 513.

[73] ibid, 488

[74] ibid, 177.

[75] ibid, 112. The canal changed Burma's economic as well as geographic relation to Europe, as it did Africa's, facilitating an expansion in trade which shortly led to the generalised scramble for Africa. See M Craven, 'Between Law and History: The Berlin Conference of 1884–85 and the Logic of Free Trade' (2015) 3 *London Review of International Law* 31.

it was not enough simply to promote the values and policies of free trade if the full range of benefits of colonialism were to be realised. Rather, a new 'impartial' balance was required between the interests of Western enterprise and the people;[76] as Furnivall identified, here lay the essence of 'the White Man's Burden'.[77]

Furnivall had an immense amount to say about the importance of these shifting ideologies, both their role in organising colonial ventures and enterprises in the first place and their subsequent part in transforming colonial policy in the latter half of the nineteenth century. Perhaps because of his long attachment to Fabian Socialism,[78] Furnivall was deeply attentive to how the ideology of *laissez-faire* that initially animated colonial policy was ultimately displaced by a more complex set of objectives and governance practices associated with the social turn in twentieth-century European law and politics. Here Furnivall drew a relatively straight line between the expanding range of functions assumed by the state as part of the normalisation of welfare considerations within metropolitan politics and governance, what we now call the shift to biopolitics,[79] and the transformed scope and objectives of colonial policy, a process that he labelled 'efficiency'.[80] Here's how he put the shifting logics of governance; note the links in the colonial context to the objective of self-determination, as well as the explicit reference to development. Initially under liberal colonial policy,

> Economic freedom was the key to progress, and economic progress an automatic and sufficient guarantee of welfare, which would in due course lead to political independence; it aimed accordingly at restricting State activities to an unavoidable minimum. The modern constructive policy advocates State intervention in promoting development, so as to provide funds for economic and social services intended to enhance native welfare and thereby lay the foundations of autonomy. Liberals regarded economic development as a cause of welfare and, therefore, a means of political advancement; modern colonial policy regards it as a condition of welfare and a condition, therefore, of political advancement.[81]

Furnivall was also unusually attentive to the discontinuities, even outright conflicts, that pervaded colonial objectives and governance practices. As against

[76] Furnivall, above n 4, 62–64.

[77] ibid, 63; 227.

[78] J Pham, 'JS Furnivall and Fabianism: Reinterpreting the "Plural Society" in Burma', 39 *Modern Asian Studies* 321 (2005).

[79] M Foucault, *The Birth of Biopolitics: Lectures at the Collège de France, 1978–79* (New York, Picador, 2010).

[80] Descriptions of the turn to the social can be found across a range of disciplines: in the social welfare literature, see TH Marshall, *Citizenship and Social Class: and other essays* (Cambridge, Cambridge University Press, 1950); in international law, see WG Grewe, *The Epochs of International Law* trans. M Byers (New York, Walter de Gruyter, 2000); in philosophy and social theory, see M Foucault, *Security, Territory, Population: Lectures at the Collège de France, 1977–78* (New York, Picador, 2010); and Foucault, above n 4; and in comparative law and legal theory, see D Kennedy, 'The Three Globalizations of Legal Thought', in D Trubek and A Santos (eds), *The New Law and Economic Development*, above n 16.

[81] Furnivall, above n 4, 313.

the claim that the colonial project reliably delivered benefits to both parties, Furnivall unearthed the tenuous – and often inverted – relationship between policy designed to promote commerce and native welfare gains simultaneously. For Furnivall flagged early that what is good for 'world development' – read imperial interests – might be at odds with advancing the welfare of the natives.[82] And if we were tempted to forget, Furnivall reminds us that market opening and expanded trade typically have momentous, disruptive effects, many of which are ambiguous if not simply bad for colonial societies and their inhabitants. Yet what is perhaps most useful for contemporary purposes is Furnivall's detailed engagement with the problems and perversities routinely generated by colonial policies, whatever the motivation for their introduction. In tracing the legal technologies by which colonial ends were furthered, Furnivall exhibited a commitment to the rule of law, albeit one made ambivalent because of its often-devastating effects in practice. Yet he also demonstrated an abiding interest in digging below the surface, to trace what legal rules and institutions actually did in practice. It is Furnivall in his coolly analytic mode, asking 'how did this go wrong or just *differently* than planned?' that seems most pertinent to current development interventions, including those designed to promote entrepreneurialism and render labour more efficient. Indeed, reading Furnivall now produces the uncanny sense that contemporary critics of development policy are merely echoing many of the observations already made, with a fine degree of attention to detail, by colonial administrators themselves.

Furnivall attended to the relation between the economic and the social with particular care, and he was unsparing in voicing the threat posed by expanded trade to the social fabric. Furnivall began his account by identifying 'five notorious evils' all of which he traced to a common cause: 'the inadequacy of law to control the working of anti-social economic forces'.[83] Much of his treatise could be read as an extended explication of the fissiparous effects of those forces when introduced into traditional societies, as well as the discontinuities between welfare gains and 'mere growth' which they reliably produced.[84] Furnivall argued strenuously that, absent adequate countervailing policies, the end point of market liberalisation was predictably disastrous: once society was reorganised to respond to economic forces, all non-economic values would be eliminated;[85] indeed anything beyond the struggle for existence, what we might call 'bare life', became impossible.[86]

Echoing the observations of his contemporary, Karl Polanyi,[87] Furnivall took it as simply given that unbridled economic forces were destined to disorganise

[82] ibid, 322.
[83] ibid, Preface.
[84] ibid, 321–22.
[85] ibid, 299.
[86] ibid, 298–300.
[87] K Polanyi, *The Great Transformation: The political and economic origins of our time* (Boston, Beacon, 2001).

pre-existing social structures, and that protection against these forces was necessary if social life is not to be destroyed. Refusing the tendency to conflate economic with social progress, he noted:

> Public works are instruments of economic progress, of world welfare, not of native welfare; sometimes in some ways they may improve the common lot, but they extend and intensify the action of economic forces and, without protection against these, they do not promote native welfare but enhance the need of measures to protect welfare.[88]

Furnivall could be equally sceptical of the relationship between legal and social progress and was entirely capable of waxing on about the superiority of the western principle of the rule of law, particularly in contrast with what he saw as local administrative corruption.[89] Yet when it came to the actual uses of the rule of law, Furnivall often cast a gimlet eye. Although Furnivall recognised that the promotion of local enterprise depended on the rule of law, he was equally cognisant that the rule of law could, and likely would, lead to a host of outcomes at odds with enhanced popular welfare, from economic inefficiency to increased litigation and the breakdown of traditional sources of authority.[90]

Furnivall was especially alert to the damage to local industry and, by extension, to popular welfare that could result from the introduction of contract-based commercial practices into societies organised on the basis of custom and religious authority. He flagged the fact that once backed by the rule of law, economic forces routinely, indeed predictably, led to land dispossession and widespread indebtedness, as well as to an increase in migrant labour and the attendant problems of labour contracting and social differentiation. Moreover, he explained exactly how and why these outcomes recurred. As he recounted, when new trading goods are introduced and Western enterprise begins to take root, native industries tend to decline, as labour is diverted to new ventures and existing industries are starved of traditional sources of labour at the same time as their customer base is eroded. Commodification for export, which Furnivall tells mainly through the prism of the rice trade and the evolution of industrial agriculture, turns out to be a perfect recipe for increased debt and land 'grabbing' and consolidation, leading to widespread economic insecurity and inequality among the native population.[91] For in the process of ensuring continuous supplies of produce for sale in foreign markets, common lands are likely to end up in the hands of individuals, and complex traditional user rights such as rights of pasturage, rights of way and access to fuel, extinguished.[92] At the same time, attracted by the lure and immediate promise of hard currency, people could be expected to engage in unwise and unsustainable practices. Through the combined effects of the commodification

[88] Furnivall, above n 4, 322.
[89] ibid, 175–78.
[90] ibid, 299.
[91] ibid, 89 ff.
[92] ibid, 299.

of agricultural labour and the introduction of new enterprises from abroad that drive out local production, a pattern begins to emerge: people start to engage in fewer, less diverse economic activities and at the same time become increasingly dependent on wage labour, labour that turns out to be both intermittent and less remunerative as access to work declines. What was most striking to Furnivall is that despite the promise of welfare gains through increased trade, what seemed to be happening was the opposite: 'it is difficult to resist the conclusion that over Lower Burma as a whole the great mass of the people were steadily growing poorer'.[93] As Furnivall described, the rise of industrialised agriculture for export 'impoverished the agricultural labourer and left him without work, wages or maintenance for a great part of the year, and compelled him to be continually on the move in search for work'.[94] Economic transformation, in turn, provoked social and political upheaval, as the importation of convict and migrant labourers, 'coolies' from India, who arrived in numbers to take jobs that Burmese would not,[95] led not just to deep and enduring ethnic and racial stratification of the emerging labour markets but to permanent communal fissures that, at the point of decolonisation, threatened the possibility of national solidarity itself.[96]

At least some of the systemic disadvantage experienced by the local population could, in Furnivall's assessment, be attributed to the introduction of contractual forms and relations into economic life and the enforcement of contractual rights by colonial courts. As the practice of contracting took hold and markets for land and labour became more pervasive and entrenched, foreigners were often able to successfully exploit ignorance about contractual terms on the part of natives, as well as arbitrage any differences between contractual rights and settled local norms and expectations concerning land use, labour and other economic arrangements, norms and expectations which, not surprisingly, natives continued to both invoke and rely upon.[97] Assisted by British judges who had little interest in, and no inclination to apply, local norms, it begins to seem predictable rather than surprising that, as Furnivall noted, foreigners would routinely reap a disproportionate amount of the gains from the underlying economic transactions.[98]

Attending to the range of risks posed by commercial life, Furnivall helpfully distinguished native from western enterprise, noting that each form of enterprise gives rise to the need for specific forms of legal protection. It is western enterprise that generates the classic problems of labour as we know them – low wages and bad working conditions produced by vast disparities in contractual power between the parties – as its primary requirement in the colonial context is simply cheap labour.[99] The promotion of native enterprise, by contrast, reliably

[93] ibid, 103–04.
[94] ibid, 91.
[95] ibid, 89.
[96] ibid, 46.
[97] See Furnivall's discussion of the conditional nature of any sale of land, above n 4, 134.
[98] ibid.
[99] ibid, 300.

generates predicaments centred around land use and land transfer, debt and access to credit. Indeed, Furnivall thought that the entire economic system in colonies such as Burma and Indonesia rested on 'indebtedness among the cultivators and labourers'.[100]

Furnivall's practice of thinking both within and across economic activities turns out to be immensely helpful to the present day analysis of markets classified as informal. For example, he noticed that the economically insecure and impoverished might well be independent operators or 'contractors' rather than those, such as employees, in formally subordinate relationships. And whether it concerned welfare gains or exposure to risk, Furnivall observed that the specific roles occupied by economic actors – labourer versus tenant, for example – matters less than we might think; in some circumstances, labourers might be better off than the tenants that employ them. Individuals themselves might occupy a variety of positions over time in any event. As a result, it wasn't safe to identify the class of economically vulnerable parties – the losers as distinct from the winners – on the basis of their legal status or position alone.

What *did* matter, according to Furnivall, was the parties' ability to extract rents. Furnivall was acutely aware of the problems of debt that attended the commoditisation of economic life, describing the condition of widespread agricultural indebtedness as 'almost inevitable' once production was cultivated for the market.[101] He described both the likelihood that and the mechanisms by which – from easy credit to unscrupulous moneylenders – people would assume large amounts of debt, often more than they needed for the task at hand. He also recounted how they would just as predictably find themselves unable to pay it off, typically for reasons completely beyond their control, such as variation in economic cycles or climate. The typical result of these cycles of indebtedness was land consolidation and rack-renting.[102] For closely related reasons, Furnivall also documented massive, recurring problems around the distribution of profits, even within the ventures and enterprises that ended up flourishing. Reprising the theme of uncertain and disparate benefits from trade as between natives and others, Furnivall observed that any increase went mostly to foreigners.[103]

Yet beyond his observations about the variable benefits of commoditisation and the introduction of the rule of law, surely one of Furnivall's most enduring insights is simply that, '[e]verywhere production is a social function', although he thought that in Europe this is mostly overlooked.[104] Throughout his analysis, Furnivall carried an acute consciousness of the degree to which economic activity is supported by social norms and practices, many of which are so far receded into the background that they are taken entirely for granted. Over and over,

[100] ibid, 389.
[101] ibid, 335.
[102] ibid, 335–36.
[103] ibid, 333
[104] ibid, 238.

he noted that the failure to attend to this 'social' dimension of economic life led to overestimates of the benefits of introducing alien norms and practices, underestimates of the functionality and viability of existing ones, and sheer surprise at the far-ranging consequences of both new and alterations to old economic arrangements.

Furnivall's other enduring insight concerns the intricate linkages *among* economic dilemmas themselves, particularly for those who routinely find themselves in a subordinate position in market exchanges. In the colonial context, the problems that beset labour turned out to be the consequences of *other* economic decisions, processes and problems. Because all were manifestations of a general economisation of society, in Furnivall's judgement, there was no point in dealing with them on their own. Instead, it was necessary to grapple with the more fundamental transformation in its totality.

VII. Formalisation for Development Revisited

The interventions in aid of the colonial endeavour described by Lugard and Furnivall do not map on to contemporary development policy and practice in any simple way. Yet there are visible continuities in the aims, the subjects and the societies on whom transformation is visited, as well the legal technologies and institutional forms that are employed. As has been observed before, family resemblances among them abound so much as to suggest a common genealogy; they may even indicate a continuing project.[105]

While the precise nature of these continuities and discontinuities in the realm of work deserve much lengthier exploration, some initial observations nonetheless seem possible.

The first is the most basic: in the present as in the past, a core governance objective is the expansion and normalisation of market relations within economies organised partly, even substantially, around competing principles and values. The underlying claim – that following this path is the key to increases in both wealth and welfare – and the animating vision – the global commoditisation of economic life, especially rural life, in the service of economic growth – is recognisably shared. As Sven Beckert has observed, 'much of the emergence of the modern world occurred in the countryside – by the often violent turning of rural people into the creators and consumers of commodities made or used elsewhere.'[106] This process continues. Indeed it is tempting to read contemporary claims that social welfare is best secured by the commoditisation of labour and consumption and the universalisation of 'higher-value' market participation *as* an updated version of the dual mandate.

[105] Anghie, 'Colonialism and the Birth of International Institutions', above n 35.
[106] Sven Beckert, *Empire of Cotton: A Global History* (New York, Alfred A Knopf, 2014), 441.

State-enabled, legal transformation of labour practices so as to more reliably serve private-sector commercial purposes lies at the heart of both. Indeed, in both eras, the reorganisation of work and workers stand at the centre of an imagined vast transformation in productive life.

Still, when it comes to market logics and market norms, labour remains subject to exceptional treatment. As Lugard makes clear, the market for labour within British colonies operated at variance from the general defence of free markets and free trade. Labour contracts were cross-cut with terms and conditions that are impossible to account for by the move to wage labour alone. But contracts for work still routinely exhibit forms of market exceptionalism, including special powers for employers and correlative liabilities for employees. Social norms – 'informal' norms – complicate their operation in a myriad different ways; outright deviations from contractual terms remain common. Both reflect accreted assumptions about 'normal' work relations, what employers may do and what workers can be compelled to accept, that have endured over time.

When it comes to the crafting of law and policy, the force of commercial considerations in the face of the countervailing interests of labour is as hard to miss now as it is in Lugard's treatise. The compulsion to work is still promoted as sound economic policy, even if some of the tools at hand – 'making work pay' by keeping baseline levels of social protection low and weakening the power of unions – differ from those available to colonial administrators.[107] Even the focus on capacitating individuals to perform at higher levels of productivity, the animating vision of contemporary labour market governance, has a nineteenth century predecessor.[108]

References to the rule of law are as ubiquitous in contemporary development policy as they were in colonial administration; in both, the benefits of legally secure entitlements are axiomatic. Open reference to the superiority of Western or European institutions and legal forms has, for the most part, been displaced; the language of civilisation and barbarism, freely expressed in Lugard and already receded in Furnivall, has now disappeared. But as the now ubiquitous references to 'good governance', along with the many indices created by international institutions purporting to measure the state of legality across states attest,[109] when it comes to the design of legal rules and institutions, belief in the salutary role of external actors and market pressure continues, as does the investment in an economy governed by global rather than local norms.

Furnivall described the dual mandate as a mechanism that professed the reconciliation of economic progress with native welfare, yet took native interests

[107] OECD, *Jobs Survey* (Paris, OECD, 1994); OECD, *Boosting Jobs and Income* (Paris, OECD, 2006)

[108] Prefiguring Amartya Sen's concept of 'development as freedom', John Stuart Mill already imagined a future in which people acted as developers and enjoyers of their capacities. See Model II, 'developmental democracy', in CB Macpherson, *The Life and Times of Liberal Democracy* (New York, Oxford University Press, 1977).

[109] World Bank, *Doing Business* (various years); World Justice Project, *Rule of Law Index* (various years).

as paramount.[110] As colonial administrators before them, development technocrats now exhibit a pronounced tendency to imagine market-centred economic transformation as congruent – even coterminous – with the advancement of popular welfare, however discontinuous their realisation might appear in practice. Both present economic progress and social welfare as conjoined dimensions of a general process of modernisation, and having staked out this fundamental alliance, tend to then read their demands in compatible, even convergent, ways. In their most advanced incarnations, economic and social progress become not just complementary aims but mutually referential elements of an integrated project of legal and institutional reform; as per the dual mandate, the economic not only ends up aiding the social and vice versa, one informs and ultimately becomes the other.[111]

Life on the ground, however, often confounds such narratives. The resulting predicaments for the local population also seem familiar. Growing economic insecurity combined with a high degree of economic coercion are salient features of work in 'free markets' for labour in the contemporary as in the historical context.[112] As before, economic coercion in labour markets continues to be sharply distinguished from the unfreedom for workers that matters.[113]

Yet this possibility of bad, rather than good, labour market outcomes can be more difficult to bring to the surface now than before. Despite the convergence of aims and ends evident in both the colonial and contemporary eras, at least within elite discourse, the effective fusion of the economic and the social is arguably now more complete. Like colonial policies, contemporary development policies are infused with the reigning ideologies of the day. But in comparison to their colonial counterparts, contemporary development technocrats now often appear less forthright about the competing interests at stake, global versus local, capital versus labour, for example; they are also less open about any failures, or even the costs of their 'successes' to those on the losing end. They are far less likely to foreground a core impulse, one frankly admitted in colonial policy: the desire to diffuse normative commercial practices so that resources and markets can be easily accessed and products moved across borders with minimal costs to the traders themselves. Nor do they identify the source of that demand – politically connected and economically powerful constituencies, often with external links and interests – or disclose that in crucial contests, law and policy may be expressly intended to benefit those constituencies as well. Instead, development interventions are presented simply as an anodyne process of legal and policy reform and rationalisation from which all stand to benefit.

[110] Furnivall, above n 4, 313.

[111] Kerry Rittich, Clive Schmitthoff Lecture, 'Convergence and Fragmentation: The Evolving Social in the International Order', Kent Law School, 10 June 2014.

[112] Guy Standing, *The Precariat: The New Dangerous Class* (London, Bloomsbury, 2011).

[113] For a discussion of economic coercion in the context of trafficking, see ILO, *Profits and Poverty: The Economics of Forced Labour* (Geneva, International Labour Office, 2014).

Set against colonial administrative treatises, current development policy analysis also seems less sociologically and institutionally informed. Anyone reading Lugard or Furnivall in parallel is sure to be struck by the very different views then and now about what matters to observe or to know, along with very different decisions about how to allocate analytic time and space. In current policy work, much effort goes into explaining model reforms and their putative benefits; as compared to Lugard and Furnivall, relatively little is devoted to evaluating the specific terrain – institutional, geographic, political and cultural – into which reforms are to be introduced. There is comparatively scant interest in studying the phenomenon and complexities of intervention itself: the disparate outcomes reforms might produce in the encounter with existing norms and practices; modifications or even alternative strategies that might be devised in response; calculation of political and social consequences – or even the full range of economic consequences; and strategies to mitigate adverse effects.

Writing during World War II, Furnivall announced simply that '*laissez-faire* is dead'; now, colonial policy is 'permeated by the idea of social justice which gathered force in Europe with the reaction against the impoverishment due to unbridled competition'.[114] Yet Furnivall's announcement turned out to be premature, at least if, after Polanyi, we recall that the road to *laissez-faire* invariably is kept open by a process of state intervention.[115] Understood as a style of governing privileging a particular subset of legally constituted economic relations, *laissez-faire* returned in revamped form at the end of the post-war Golden Age, this time buttressed by a prescriptive regulatory model travelling under the name of 'good governance'.[116] Although good governance, too, now includes the social, facilitating economic integration stands first in the order of priorities,[117] and it profoundly shapes the aims and forms that the social now takes. Like colonial policy, contemporary development policy followed a trajectory from devotion to an imagined liberal ideal in the first phase to a reformed agenda which merges social concerns into the policy and institutional matrix, all the while ensuring that the initial project of economic reform continues, now in the name of human rights as well as economic progress.[118] Furnivall's plaintive observation seems as apposite now as when he uttered it: '[l]aissez-faire is dead, but economic forces still remain active, everywhere, unceasingly'.[119] The order of interventions – from

[114] Furnivall, above n 4, 312–13.

[115] Polanyi, *The Great Transformation*, above n 87, chapter 12, 'The Birth of the Liberal Creed'.

[116] The first use of the term appears to be in World Bank, *From crisis to sustainable growth – Sub-Saharan Africa: a longterm perspective* (Washington, DC, World Bank, 1989); it is now ubiquitous within international policy documents.

[117] Parallel observations about the relative priority of market building over the social have been made concerning the project of European integration as well. See D Ashiagbor, *The European Employment Strategy: Labour Market Regulation and New Governance* (Oxford, Oxford University Press, 2005).

[118] Rittich, 'Second Generation Reforms and the Incorporation of the Social', above n 16; J Stiglitz, 'Is There a Post-post Washington Consensus?' in N Serra and J Stiglitz (eds), *The Washington Consensus Reconsidered: Towards a New Global Governance* (Oxford, Oxford University Press, 2008).

[119] Furnivall, above n 4, 313.

market liberalisation to social protection in response – tends to repeat, as does the unsynthesised amalgam of programmatic elements into which law and policy ultimately tend to settle.[120]

Standing back, two features stand out viewed through the lens of colonial administration.

The first is that a productive labour force is a work of imagination. It must be conjured up before it can exist 'in fact', indeed before it can become a project of law and policy. Second, the process of subject-formation is a central element of 'creating labour'. Under the colonial imaginary, the objective was to inculcate the right character and habits of discipline and industriousness among peoples who were thought to lack such attributes. Open processes of racialisation and attributions of natural or cultural difference, moreover, vested populations with specific characteristics and propensities; to the extent that those characteristics impaired the colonial project, law and policy were intended to remedy, mitigate or, if necessary, simply circumvent them.

Whether in analyses of informal markets[121] or discussions of labour market governance in general,[122] the subject of labour now has shed such particularities; people are represented as simply naturally or essentially entrepreneurial. Even – especially – women workers are depicted as calculating, industrious agents who are responsive to that universal imperative, market incentives.[123] Indeed, the exemplary female entrepreneur figures at the centre of narratives about formalisation and related development initiatives like microcredit and financial inclusion.[124]

And yet, current labour policy itself belies the claim, revealing the entrepreneurial worker of today to be no more a fact of nature and no less a work of imagination than the native worker of Lugard's time. Whatever the force of economic incentives, it turns out to take effort to inculcate a disposition towards entrepreneurialism, at least as an overriding orientation toward people's use of their time and labour. The many policy and regulatory interventions designed to compel greater individual and household economic activity and self-reliance suggest that the entrepreneurial spirit is not, in fact, sufficiently present to satisfy current governance norms and, paradoxically, that it is anything but natural. Despite their new status as central actors in the labour market, women continue to trouble the image of the fungible market actor, their non-market desires, duties and practices revealing a persistent, non-trivial gap between actuality and ideal. Vestiges of the native worker remain in circulation as well, visible in the degraded treatment of migrant workers as well as punitive policies that discipline

[120] Kennedy, 'Three Globalizations of Legal Thought', above n 80.

[121] Commission on Legal Empowerment of the Poor, *Making the Law Work for Everyone* (New York, United Nations, 2008).

[122] World Bank, *World Development Report 2013: Jobs* (Washington, DC, World Bank, 2012).

[123] K Rittich, 'Engendering Development/Marketing Equality' (2003) 67 *Albany Law Review* 575.

[124] See D Roodman, *Due Diligence: An Impertinent Inquiry into Microfinance* (Washington, DC, Center for Global Development, 2012).

(often racialised) workers to accept work, sometimes under conditions that approach the slavery and indenture of old.[125] As before, workers continue to resist or ignore the world that is imagined for them, even as they must work within it.

The second is that the fetishisation of the formal is unwarranted. After Furnivall's extended survey of work arrangements in late colonial Burma, there can be no easy assumption that 'bringing in the rule of law' confers unmitigated benefits to those seen as legally disenfranchised. Formalisation – 'legal empowerment' as it is now called – remains an agent of economic disruption, one that, if colonial past is prologue, can easily lead to the concentration of economic gains and may serve just as well as an engine of insecurity as an antidote to it. In the colonial context, wage labour and contractualised work relations emerge *not* as superior to informal work arrangements per se, whether measured on welfare grounds or even by the metric of efficiency. As Furnivall describes, informal workers can expect to receive the sharp end of any differences between legal and informal norms as well as suffer the usual disabilities that come from lack of capital, as more powerful actors deploy their superior knowledge, bargaining power and resources to their advantage. And as Lugard's discussion makes clear, contracts for labour are subject to norms and practices that confer burdens on workers and correlative extraordinary powers on employers; in the name of supporting commerce and advancing growth, myriad other policies may be adopted that, by design or effect, suppress wages and thus workers' ability to gain from their labour as well.

None of these possibilities has disappeared; to the contrary, all have contemporary analogues.[126] Like the native workers in British colonies, the informal workers of today, particularly those in developing countries some of whom of course were their direct forebears, are often engaged in a mix of economic activities, including directly productive activities of their own. As before, formalisation designed to provoke development through commoditisation may close off some avenues of economic engagement, even while opening up others. Whether, on balance, the result is beneficial for such workers remains a question; for example, the constant indebtedness of producers growing for export continues today.[127]

Formalisation may even produce more informal workers. Whatever their activities, the actual powers workers possess within economic relationships will be only loosely connected to their legal status; whether as employees or as independent contractors, for example, they may be deeply dependent in fact, with no actual ability to influence the terms on which they work. As before, workers' concerns and fates invariably will be interconnected with other decisions of law and policy.

[125] N Zatz et al, *Get to Work or Go to Jail* (Los Angeles, CA, UCLA Institute for Research on Labor and Employment, 2016); N Zatz, 'Is "the Market" the Enemy? Racial Exploitation in *Bailey v Alabama*', see https://lpeblog.org/2018/01/17/is-the-market-the-enemy-racial-exploitation-in-bailey-v-alabama/.

[126] A Lewis, 'Economic Development with Unlimited Supplies of Labour' (1954) 22 *The Manchester School* 139–91; P Temin, *The Vanishing Middle Class: Prejudice and Power in a Dual Economy* (Cambridge, MA, MIT Press, 2018).

[127] Beckert, *Empire of Cotton*, above n 106, 432.

This suggests, on the one hand, caution against any reification of the categories of workers and, on the other, close attention to the impact of *many* regulatory and policy decisions on the terms, conditions and even the possibility of work.

Lugard's and Furnivall's accounts put the spotlight on the power of social norms and practices, indicating the different ways in which they may frustrate the ambitions of those who govern. Like those introduced by their colonial predecessors, interventions to formalise and commodify markets now are destined to intersect with pre-existing norms and practices. But while those norms and practices will surely influence the operation of new ones, their combined effects are difficult to project: ultimately, the old may serve to legitimate or empower the new; sometimes they may have a moderating effect; sometimes they may defeat the new entirely.[128] Just as pressing is the question, what in the ways of entitlements and obligations, burdens and benefits will formalisation confer, and on whom? The range of possibilities on both counts makes general assertions about formalisation difficult to maintain. As Lugard's discussion of compulsory and forced labour reveals, a fixation on legal form may cloak more basic issues of stasis and change in the nature of work itself. Given this history and these possibilities, those concerned with the fate of workers would be well advised to ask more precise questions, not only about formalisation but also about the larger project of which it is a part: 'what makes it work, and what had to be done to make it so'.[129]

As Furnivall underscored, a host of social and political problems could be traced to a single root, the release of economic forces. Processes of commodification are expected to alter informal activities, and sometimes to eliminate them altogether. If the insecurity and disempowerment commonly faced by informal workers in the course of market reform and economic integration – interruptions to livelihood, loss of access to resources, competition from savvier, better-endowed market actors, for example – are inextricably connected to basic decisions and practices around market opening and resource commodification, and if the manner in which legal entitlements are set down – or even the introduction of the rule of law itself – appears to enable or aggravate these predicaments just as easily as it ameliorates them, then the basic narrative about formalisation's contribution to development, and to work itself, seems ripe for retelling.[130] Like the native workers before them, informal workers stand at the centre of some of the largest governance questions of our time, shouldering significant risks in the name of a greater 'global' economic good whose benefits, for them, remain uncertain at best.[131]

[128] See D Kennedy, *A Critique of Adjudication (fin de siècle)* (Cambridge, MA, Harvard University Press, 1997) for a discussion of these effects in the context of judicial decision making.

[129] S Jasanoff, 'Subjects of reason: goods, markets, and competing imaginaries of global governance' (2016) 4 *London Review of International Law* 361, 371.

[130] For an argument for the recognition of a general law of economic disadvantage, see H Arthurs, 'Labor Law as the Law of Economic Subordination and Resistance' (2013) 34 *Comparative Labor Law and Policy Journal* 585.

[131] B Milanovic, *Global Inequality: A New Approach for the Age of Globalization* (Cambridge, MA, Harvard University Press, 2016).

2

Labour Law, Development Discourse and the Uses of Informality

LIAM McHUGH-RUSSELL[1]

What are we to do with 'informality?' Rather than being a label for a definite but poorly understood collection of economic practices or a term whose loose usage muddles a multiplicity of referents,[2] informality is an essentially contested concept.[3] It is not simply that disagreements exist about the nature or meaning of informality. Rather, like other keywords of transnational governance, contests over the concept's meaning are entangled with struggles over socio-economic policy, institutional design, and administrative process – struggles, that is, over how power is to be exercised, and by whom. More precisely, disagreements about how to conceptualise informality interface with theoretical debates about the legitimate ends, means, agents and beneficiaries of development, as well as with processes that determine development practice.

Development researchers had already by the 1970s identified informality's semantic entanglements with competing agendas.[4] Subsequent research has noted how competing conceptualisations of informality are shaped by differences over task (measurement, analysis, policy design), approach (legal, economic, statistical), policy concern (decent work, public order, economic growth) and regulatory perspective.[5] Yet research on informality usually simply notes contradictions

[1] I thank participants of the September 2016 conference on Re-Imagining Labour Law for Development: Informal Work in the global North and South, as well as Przemysław Pałka, Sofie Møller, Vivian Kube and Nicola Hargreaves for their feedback on earlier drafts, and Genevieve Painter, Leila Kawar and Diamond Ashiagbor for extensive commentary. Remaining errors are mine.

[2] The ILO stresses that informality has 'no universally … accepted description' and 'accommodates considerable diversity'. ILO, *Conclusions Concerning Decent Work and the Informal Economy*, International Labour Conference, 90th Session (Geneva, International Labour Office, 2002) para 3.

[3] WB Gallie, 'Essentially Contested Concepts' (1955) 56 *Proceedings of the Aristotelian Society* 167.

[4] Notably Caroline Moser and Lisa Peattie, discussed below, text to nn 73–84.

[5] Claire La Hovary, 'The Informal Economy and the ILO: A Legal Perspective' (2014) 30 *International Journal of Comparative Labour Law and Industrial Relations* 391, 391–92, 396, 410; Anne Trebilcock, 'International Labour Standards and the Informal Economy' in Jean-Claude Javillier et al (eds), *Les normes internationales du travail, un patrimoine pour l'avenir: mélanges en l'honneur de Nicolas Valticos* (Geneva, International Labour Office, 2004) 585–86; Anne Trebilcock, 'Using Development Approaches to Address the Challenge of the Informal Economy for Labour Law' in Guy Davidov and Brian Langille (eds), *Boundaries and Frontiers of Labour Law: Goals and Means in the*

between the resulting applications of the concept before moving to deploy a preferred conceptualisation. The resulting discussions are somewhat aware that the concept's semantic troubles have political undertones. Arguments over informality's meaning tacitly (and sometimes overtly) present an 'operative definition' as a prerequisite of addressing some governance problem. Unfortunately, the relation between 'meaning' and 'politics' in transnational governance is not so one-dimensional.[6] The meaning and significance of such concepts emerge out of an encounter among competing national traditions, epistemic communities, bureaucratic groupings, and other groups of 'people with projects',[7] each using the term in line with their respective methodological tactics.[8]

In this context, making an argument for any particular use of informality is not only a contribution to a debate about the concept's (true/proper) meaning or (real) nature, but an intervention in contentious processes that determine the concept's semantic force, and its practical consequences. Indeed, *every* use of informality (and every time it is passed over in favour of an alternative) constitutes such an intervention, albeit to greater or lesser effect. Therefore, the use of informality is, at least potentially, both a pragmatic decision that takes into account the consequences of using a concept in a particular way[9] and a strategic

Regulation of Work (Portland, OR, Hart Publishing, 2006) 67–76; Martha Alter Chen, 'Rethinking the Informal Economy: Linkages with the Formal Economy and the Formal Regulatory Environment' in Basudeb Guha-Khasnobis et al (eds), *Linking the Formal and Informal Economy: Concepts and Policies* (Oxford, Oxford University Press, 2006) 90; Alice Sindzingre, 'The Relevance of the Concepts of Formality and Informality: A Theoretical Appraisal' in Basudeb Guha-Khasnobis et al (eds), *Linking the Formal and Informal Economy: Concepts and Policies* (Oxford, Oxford University Press, 2006) 63.

6 Annelise Riles, '[Deadlines]: Removing the Brackets on Politics in Bureaucratic and Anthropological Analysis' in Annelise Riles (ed), *Documents: Artifacts of Modern Knowledge* (Ann Arbor, University of Michigan Press, 2006) 71–72.

7 See, for interactions with national practices, Nikolas M Rajkovic et al (eds), *The Power of Legality: Practices of International Law and Their Politics* (Cambridge, Cambridge University Press, 2016); with bureaucratic groupings: Alvaro Santos, 'The World Bank's Uses of the "Rule of Law" Promise in Economic Development' in David M Trubek and Alvaro Santos (eds), *The New Law and Economic Development: A Critical Appraisal* (New York, Cambridge University Press, 2006); with disciplinary formations: Galit A Sarfaty, *Values in Translation: Human Rights and the Culture of the World Bank* (Stanford, CA, Stanford University Press, 2012) 75–105; between 'academics' and 'activists': Riles, above n 6; see generally David Kennedy, *A World of Struggle: How Power, Law, and Expertise Shape Global Political Economy* (Princeton, Princeton University Press, 2016) for the role of 'people with projects' in constituting global order.

8 My use of 'tactics' corresponds to what Bourdieu has called 'strategy' or 'feel for the game': the repertoire of techniques or dispositions that together comprise the practical sense or tacit knowledge of how to select a course of action in familiar but never identical situations. Bourdieu carefully distinguishes such 'strategy' both from rational, calculated choice and from internal motivations that determine action. My use of tactics rather than strategies follows Fleur Johns, *Non-Legality in International Law: Unruly Law* (Cambridge, Cambridge University Press, 2013) 26–29.

9 Compare the work on the pragmatics of using 'human rights', especially Martti Koskenniemi, 'Human Rights, Politics, and Love' (2004) 13 *Finnish Yearbook of International Law* 79; David Kennedy, 'International Human Rights Movement: Part of the Problem?' (2002) 15 *Harvard Human Rights Journal* 101.

one, guided by reflection on how those outcomes may be influenced by other actors.[10]

I deliberately pose the question not as 'what is to be done…' but rather as 'what are *we* to do…' because the latter question depends on the situation of the group or individual asking the question. As such, this chapter considers the strategic context in which decisions about the use of informality are made, from the position of scholars concerned with how labour regulation can contribute to the promotion of decent work in the twenty-first century.[11] An important part of that context is the role that informality might play in the quotidian tactics – that is, the methodological dispositions – of labour law.[12] Section I uses an historical review of controversies about the meaning of the term and a close reading of official definitions of informality to develop a critical restatement of the methodological problem the concept raises for labour law. I show that, contrary to concerns that the concept is vague or contradictory, the key issue is its poor fit with labour law's way of tying together epistemology with governance. Section II broadens the view, taking into account how the uses of informality interact in the production of development thought and development practice. Reading with and against research that has engaged with the relation between the uses of informality and the countervailing agendas of its users, I conclude that a focus on methodological fit misses important aspects of how 'informality' works. Having established that the significance of informality is not reducible to its semantics, and that its meaning is not reducible to its propositional sense, section III concludes by discussing some of the risks and opportunities labour lawyers confront in deciding whether and how to use informality.

I. Informality as Methodological Misfit

It has become something of a common creed among those interested in promoting decent work that addressing informality is essential to that mission. Yet experts in both labour law and development have found that studying informality or responding to it demands clarifying a set of persistent ambiguities in and divergent perspectives on the concept of the informal. Some have described the

[10] On this sense of strategy, central to game theory, see eg Avinash K Dixit and Barry Nalebuff, *Thinking Strategically: The Competitive Edge in Business, Politics, and Everyday Life* 1st edn (New York, Norton, 1991). Contrast Bourdieu's sense of strategy, above n 8.

[11] Rather than indicating a specific position in debates about how to properly understand the normative ends of labour law, *decent work* is invoked here as a term capacious enough to encompass any one of many competing positions in those debates.

[12] In accord with Bourdieu's idea of tactics as dispositions or techniques (above n 8), he and his co-authors identify disciplinary methodology as a 'system of intellectual habits' or *habitus* that embodies a researcher's theory of knowledge. Pierre Bourdieu et al, *The Craft of Sociology: Epistemological Preliminaries*, Beate Krais (ed), Richard Nice (tr) (Berlin, W de Gruyter, 1991) 2, 5.

consequences for labour law as epistemological: because informality is vague or ambiguous, it is hard to determine what is being ascribed to situations, relations or contexts labelled as informal or, vice versa, hard to know which attributes make it appropriate to use the concept.[13] Yet, as elaborated below, a close reading of official definitions elaborated under International Labour Organization (ILO) auspices shows that that even a rigorous, precise and authoritative definition 'sits uneasily in law'.[14] The issue is not simply a lack of conceptual precision, but a poor fit with the ways that labour law draws together epistemology and governance.

A. A Controversial Concept

Informality has been always a controversial concept. Keith Hart, often credited with first applying the term, introduced 'informal income opportunities' as a way of discussing the diversity and idiosyncrasies of non-employment income earned by workers in the global South.[15] He also floated the idea that the formal and the informal might be understood as separate sectors.[16] The idea of an 'informal sector' became the primary use of the term for at least the next two decades.[17]

Debates about informality's nature and etiology were almost coeval with the first uses of the concept. Analyses have explained informality as a product of survival activities cut off from market production,[18] of small-scale, market-based production,[19] and of subordination in global production chains.[20] Scholars interested in working conditions in the global South have identified informality with precarious work,[21] with flexibility of work relations,[22] with a lack of official

[13] See respectively, Sindzingre, above n 5, 59; Ravi Kanbur, *Conceptualising Informality: Regulation and Enforcement*, IZA Discussion Paper DP 4186 (Bonn, Institute for the Study of Labor, 2009) 2; Guy Davidov, 'Enforcement Problems in Informal Labor Markets: A View from Israel' (2005) 27 *Comparative Labor Law & Policy Journal* 3, 5; La Hovary, above n 5, 392.

[14] Trebilcock, 'Development Approaches', above n 5, 65.

[15] Most accounts date first usage of the term to Keith Hart, 'Informal Income Opportunities and Urban Employment in Ghana' (1973) 11 *Journal of Modern African Studies* 61; ILO, *Employment, Incomes and Equality: A Strategy for Increasing Productive Employment in Kenya* (Geneva, ILO, 1972).

[16] See Hart, 'Informal Income', above n 15, 85.

[17] It remains in vogue in many circles. See Guillermo E Perry et al, *Informality: Exit and Exclusion* (Washington, DC, World Bank, 2007).

[18] Hart, 'Informal Income', above n 15.

[19] William F Maloney, *The Structure of Labor Markets in Developing Countries: Time Series Evidence on Competing Views*, World Bank Policy Research Working Paper 1940 (Washington DC, World Bank, Policy Research Dissemination Centre, 1994).

[20] Francie Lund and Jillian Nicholson (eds), *Chains of Production, Ladders of Protection: Social Protection for Workers in the Informal Economy* (Durban, School of Development Studies, University of Natal, 2003); Tonia Novitz, 'Supply Chains and Temporary Migrant Labour: The Relevance of Trade and Sustainability Frameworks?' (this volume).

[21] Elizabeth Hill, *Worker Identity, Agency and Economic Development: Women's Empowerment in the Indian Informal Economy* (New York, Routledge, 2010) 21–22.

[22] Guy Standing, 'Global Feminization Through Flexible Labor: A Theme Revisited' (1999) 27 *World Development* 583, 585, 587.

registration with tax and administrative authorities,[23] and with regulatory non-compliance (especially non-compliance with official labour standards).[24] So is informality an economic, or a social characteristic? A legal issue? An administrative category? Some combination of the above?

The controversies did not end there. A more recent strand of thinking deployed what is intended to be a broader concept – the informal economy – to stress that formal and informal activities are often intermingled in practice, that activities often lie along a continuum between formal and informal, and that informal practices are themselves heterogeneous. Some insist that 'informal economy' still evokes an image of two discrete spheres of economic activity.[25] For that reason, many opt to speak of 'informality'[26] or the 'informalisation'[27] of economic practices. So is informality a *category* that groups together some specific set of cases, or a *quality* applicable in varying degrees to all cases?

These slack analytical boundaries have been loosened by growing attention to informality. For one, the original focus on the organisation of work and production has been softened, with contrasts between 'formal and informal' applied to a broader set of governance challenges.[28] Moreover, while earlier literature used informality exclusively to discuss socio-economic realities in developing economies, the end of the 1980s saw the introduction of studies on the 'informal economy' in the industrialised, global North.[29]

B. Elaborating Official Definitions of Informality

To understand informality's fraught meaning, it will be useful to have a handle on official definitions, elaborated both by the International Conference of Labour Statisticians (ICLS)[30] and by the ILO in its 2015 Formalisation Recommendation.[31]

[23] Hernando de Soto, *The Mystery of Capital: Why Capitalism Triumphs in the West and Fails Everywhere Else* (New York, Basic Books, 2000).

[24] In Chen's typology of four schools of thought on informality, administrative non-registration and regulatory non-compliance are particularly relevant in 'legalist' and 'voluntarist' approaches. Martha Alter Chen, *The Informal Economy: Definitions, Theories and Policies*, WIEGO Working Paper No 1 (Cambridge, MA, WIEGO, 2012) 4–6.

[25] Trebilcock, 'Labour Standards', above n 5, 64–65.

[26] See eg Basudeb Guha-Khasnobis et al, 'Beyond Formality and Informality' in Basudeb Guha-Khasnobis et al (eds), *Linking the Formal and Informal Economy: Concepts and Policies* (Oxford, Oxford University Press, 2006).

[27] Alejandro Portes et al (eds), *The Informal Economy: Studies in Advanced and Less Developed Countries* (Baltimore, Johns Hopkins University Press, 1989).

[28] See chapters by Andersson and Pacheco, Guha-Khasnobis and Ahuja, Lensink, McGillivray and Pham, and Sawyer in Basudeb Guha-Khasnobis et al (eds), *Linking the Formal and Informal Economy: Concepts and Policies* (Oxford, Oxford University Press, 2006).

[29] Notably Portes et al, above n 27.

[30] The ICLS meets under the auspices of the ILO; its work is supported by the ILO's permanent secretariat, the International Labour Office.

[31] International Labour Conference, 95th Session, 'Recommendation (No 204) Concerning Transition from the Informal to the Formal Economy' (12 June 2015).

In the 1993 *Resolution Concerning Statistics of Employment in the Informal Sector*, the ICLS set out an operational definition that above all identifies the 'informal sector' as a subset of 'unincorporated enterprises owned by households'.[32] Drawing on the System of National Accounts (SNA),[33] the resulting conceptualisation turns primarily on the lack of a formal legal separation between the revenue streams of a business and of its owner(s), and on the absence of any formal record-keeping for 'the business' proper.[34] The Resolution distinguishes *informal* enterprises from this broader category using a collection of protean conceptual characteristics,[35] along with a set of factors identified as potentially relevant 'for operational purposes'. Whether the informal sector is limited to firms under a certain size,[36] whether agricultural production and domestic workers are to be included,[37] whether it comprises only firms that are unregistered[38] or non-compliant with law (along with which regulatory frameworks might set the standard of compliance[39]) – these issues are left to the discretion of those using the standard. Being 'employed in the informal sector' is defined to include anyone who (usually) does work for an 'informal enterprise', whether for wage or salary, profit or family gain.[40]

[32] ILO, 'Resolution Concerning Statistics of Employment in the Informal Sector' in *Fifteenth International Conference of Labour Statistics, Report of the Conference*, ICLS/15/D.6 (Rev. 1) (Geneva, International Labour Office, 1993) paras 6(1)–6(2).

[33] The SNA is a global compendium of guidelines on the collection of economic statistics, compiled and approved by a coalition of international institutions. See Inter-Secretariat Working Group on National Accounts, *System of National Accounts* (Washington DC, Commission of the European Communities, International Monetary Fund, Organisation for Economic Co-operation and Development, United Nations and World Bank, 1993).

[34] ILO, '1993 Resolution', above n 32, para 7.

[35] ibid, paras 8(1), 9(1); ibid, para 5(1), describing informal sector in terms of various factors couched in the language 'may', 'mostly', or 'typically'; ibid, para 5(2), listing practices typical of (ie not decisive of) 'household enterprises'.

[36] ILO, '1993 Resolution', above n 32, paras 9(2)(i), 9(3)–9(4).

[37] ibid, paras 14, 16, 19.

[38] ibid, paras 8(2), 9(2)(ii).

[39] The Resolution's distinction between informal activities and the 'underground' economy suggests that regulatory non-compliance, while a possible incident of informality, is not a *defining* characteristic: ibid, s 5(3). Yet the language of 'non-registration' – ascertained 'under factories or commercial acts, tax or social security laws, professional groups' regulatory acts, or similar acts, laws, or regulations established by national legislative bodies' – does not distinguish being exempt from a particular legislative regime (and thus from any ancillary registration requirement) from operating in violation of a legal regime (in part by violating a de jure registration requirement). There is thus some sense that non-compliance with law may be a defining characteristic. This conflation between non-registration under a regime and non-compliance with that regime is clearest in the case of employees: ibid, paras 8(3), 9(6).

[40] International Labour Organization, '1993 Resolution', above n 32, para 11(1); ILO, 'Resolution Concerning Statistics of the Economically Active Population, Employment, Unemployment and Underemployment' in *Thirteenth International Conference of Labour Statistics, Report of the Conference*, 18–29 October 1982 (Geneva, International Labour Office, 1983) paras 9(1)(a)–(b).

In 2003 the ICLS returned to questions of informality to address critiques that the earlier, top-down focus on informal production had drawn an incomplete picture of informal work.[41] The *Guidelines Concerning a Statistical Definition of Informal Employment* (2003 Guidelines) advance a more comprehensive definition of 'informal employment,' which complements 'employment in the informal sector'.[42] The result is an exhaustive, 15-part map of all (or almost all) working relationships.[43] As summarised in a diagrammatic 'Conceptual Framework' (see Figure 2.1),[44] the cragged borders of informal work are drawn, at various moments, by combining considerations of market orientation,[45] what is being produced,[46] who the work is done for,[47] whether the work counts as 'production,'[48]

[41] Chen, *The Informal Economy*, above n 24, 7.

[42] ILO, 'Guidelines Concerning a Statistical Definition of Informal Employment' in *Seventeenth International Conference of Labour Statistics, Report of the Conference*, ICLS/17/2003/4 (Geneva, ILO, 2003), paras 5–6 of the preamble. Note that neither 'informal employment' nor 'employment in the informal sector' is limited to employees.

[43] In addition to excluding some work that lies outside the 'production boundary' (see below, n 48), the Guidelines have an awkward relationship with crime. Some readers understand informal employment to exclude work in the production of illegal goods and services. Sindzingre, above n 5, 63; International Labour Office, *Women and Men in the Informal Economy: A Statistical Picture* (Geneva, ILO, 2002) 12. Yet the Guidelines go no further than distinguishing the two concepts. Preamble to ILO, '2003 ICLS Guidelines', above n 42, para 3.

[44] ILO, '2003 ICLS Guidelines', above n 42, 15. The chart as it appears in the official ICLS record seems to have been incorrectly copied from the version (reproduced here) in International Labour Office, *Decent Work and the Informal Economy*, International Labour Conference, 90th Session. Report VI (Geneva, ILO, 2002) 123.

[45] Contrary to the deliberate exclusion of 'non-market production' (ie subsistence activities) from the 1993 definition of the informal sector, the 2003 Guidelines include 'the production of goods exclusively for own final use by [the] household' in the definition of informal employment, so long as 'such production comprises an important contribution to the total consumption of the household'. ILO, '2003 ICLS Guidelines', above n 42, para 3(2)(vi); ILO, 'Resolution on Economically Active Population', above n 40, para 9(6); ILO, '1993 Resolution', above n 32, para 14.

[46] The 2003 Guidelines do not speak directly to whether agricultural work is to be included under the category of informal employment. Given the extent of subsistence agriculture in the global South, the inclusion of non-market production (above, n 45) would seem to weigh in favour of inclusion. Yet the discretionary exclusion of all agricultural production from the informal sector (per the 1993 Resolution, see above, n 37) potentially implies different accounting standards for informal employment in agricultural and non-agricultural production. Whereas informal employees are always to be counted, for agricultural production, own-account, subsistence and family work might be left out – not just excluded from the category of informal employment, but left uncounted and invisible as work. In practice the standard has often been applied so as to wholly exclude agricultural work – both formal and informal – from labour statistics. See eg International Labour Office, above n 43, 19–25. The 2003 Guidelines acknowledge this issue without offering a solution. ILO, '2003 ICLS Guidelines', above n 42, para 7.

[47] The 2003 Guidelines characterise all work contributed to a family enterprise as informal, regardless of working conditions or compliance with legal norms: ILO, '2003 ICLS Guidelines', above n 42, para 3(3)(iii).

[48] The 1993 Resolution leaves the inclusion or exclusion of domestic work from the informal sector up to local discretion (above n 37); the 2003 Guidelines count domestic work as informal employment *if and only if* such workers are not given adequate protection as employees (above n 42, paras 2, 3(2)(v), 5(i)). Thus where there is a market relation, the distinction between production and social reproduction becomes irrelevant – all such work counts, and counts as informal on the basis of the application of labour standards (see below, n 50). Outside market relations, the distinction between productive work and care work, is the difference between work that counts as informal employment (see above n 45) and work that does not count at all.

Figure 2.1 Matrix: A conceptual framework for the informal economy

Production units by type	Jobs by status in employment								
	Own-account workers		Employers		Contributing family workers	Employees		Members of producers' cooperatives	
	Informal	Formal	Informal	Formal	Informal	Informal	Formal	Informal	Formal
Formal sector enterprises					1	2			
Informal sector enterprises[a]	3		4		5	6	7	8	
Households[b]	9					10			

Notes: [a]As defined by the Fifteenth International Conference of Labour Statisticians in 1993. [b]Households producing goods for their own final use and households employing domestic workers.

Dark grey cells refer to jobs that by definition do not exist in the type of production unit in question.
Light grey cells refer to jobs which exist in the type of production unit in question but which are not relevant to our concerns.
The unshaded cells are the focus of our concern – they refer to types of jobs that represent the different segments of the informal economy.

Cells 1 and 5: Contributing family workers: no contract of employment and no legal or social protection arising from the job, in formal entrprises (cell 1) or informal enterprises (cell 5). (Contributing family workers with a contract of employment, wage, social protection, etc. would be considered employees in formal employment.)
Cells 2, 6 and 10: Employees who have informal jobs, whether employed by formal enterprises (cell 2) or informal enterprises (cell 6) or as paid domestic workers by households (cell 10).
Cells 3 and 4: Own-account workers (cell 3) and employers (cell 4) who have their own informal enterprises. The informal nature of their jobs follows directly from the characteristics of the enterprise they own.
Cell 7: Employees working in informal enterprises but having formal jobs. (This may occur, for example, when enterprises are defined as informal using size as the only criterion.)
Cell 8: Members of informal producers' cooperatives.
Cell 9: Producers of goods for own final use by their household (e.g. subsistence farming).

Source: International Labour Office, *Decent Work and the Informal Economy*, International Labour Conference, 90th Session. Report VI (Geneva, ILO, 2002) 123.

enterprise ownership structure,[49] and, perhaps most saliently, whether labour laws are applied and employment benefits provided.[50]

The ILO has also crafted definitions of informality as part of ongoing efforts to develop a normative response to informality at work. That project is not wholly distinct from the work of the ICLS on the issue: the conceptual schema of the 2003 Guidelines had been finalised over a year earlier, and used in background material for discussions at the International Labour Conference that led to the adoption of the 2002 *Conclusions on Decent Work and the Informal Economy*.[51] While the goal was to provide guidance on promoting decent work for all workers,[52] the *Conclusions* adopted the 'informal economy' as an umbrella term for both work- and production-related informality.[53] The Formalisation Recommendation, adopted in 2015, embraced formalisation as the rubric for responding to informality at work, and adapted text from the 2002 Conclusions as a free-standing definition of the informal economy: 'all economic activities by workers and economic units that are – in law or in practice – not covered or insufficiently covered by formal arrangements'.[54]

C. Framing Informality as an Epistemological Problem for Labour Law

Where efforts to understand informality in the abstract had long wrestled with a myriad of competing definitions and occasionally slipshod meanings, the ILO texts offered concrete, coherent textual standards, and the authority of official sanction. Considering the critiques levelled against even these definitions makes

[49] The 2003 Guidelines stress that informal employment should include members of 'informal producers' cooperatives': ibid, paras 3(2)(iv), 3(3)–3(4). This distinction seems no more than a trifling distinction between types of (own-account) employment in the informal sector. Yet the category draws attention to an otherwise-obscured dividing line: co-operative enterprises that contribute to market production are given new attention, while the work of social reproduction through 'voluntary', co-operative community work – largely performed by women – is left unrecognised and (still) unaccounted for. On the prevalence of such community work, see Tzehainesh Teklè, 'Labour Law and Worker Protection in the South: An Evolving Tension Between Models and Reality' in Tzehainesh Teklè (ed), *Labour Law and Worker Protection in Developing Countries* (Portland, Hart Publishing, 2010) 15–16.

[50] Whereas the definition of the informal sector in the 1993 Resolution can, by discretion, be based on the (non)-application of labour legislation to employees (above n 39), the 2003 Guidelines place access to labour legislation, social protection and employment at the core of the definition of informal employment: ILO, '2003 ICLS Guidelines', above n 42, paras 3(2)(v), 3(5).

[51] International Labour Office, above n 44; International Labour Office, above n 43; ILO, *Informal Economy Conclusions*, above n 2.

[52] ILO, *Informal Economy Conclusions*, above n 2, 25/52.

[53] International Labour Office, above n 44, 121–27; ILO, '2003 ICLS Guidelines', above n 42, Preamble, paras 3, 8.

[54] International Labour Conference, 95th Session, above n 31; compare ILO, *Informal Economy Conclusions*, above n 2, para 3.

it possible to fully appreciate the structure of the conceptual problem informality presents to labour lawyers. The facets of that problem can be discerned by placing those critiques against a robust articulation of how concepts function in the techniques and dispositions – the methodological tactics – central to labour law.[55] The juxtaposition makes clear that informality 'sits uneasily in law' because it traverses boundaries that underpin the analytical apparatus of labour regulation.

Modern, western law depends on a 'cognitive map', a set of operative categories. As Deakin and Wilkinson state, '[w]ithout classification, the law cannot be mobilised'.[56] Classification has two legally relevant meanings. Those charged with administering law perform classification as slotting-in: subsuming situations to the appropriate legal categories. While many legal concepts themselves express conformity with or violation of a norm, more complex instances knit together a framework of obligations, authorisations, and allocations of authority with a model of the situation which engenders those norms. Some such categories, like marriage, property or the corporation, are conventions that crystallise a structure of mutual expectations about patterns of behaviour.[57] Other categories function as an index for regulatory interventions aimed at redressing narrow policy issues or fulfilling more fundamental social functions.[58] Many categories, like the employment contract long central to labour law, clearly combine the two. Both types compose a corpus of peremptory, enforceable norms with a model of the situations for which those norms are appropriate. Such categories articulate a *form* – a way that things are (to be) done under certain circumstances – which, though in one sense 'normative', is distinct from the norms qua obligations and authorities occasioned when situations are found to sufficiently correspond to that form. Conversely, the categories serve a diagnostic function, inasmuch as relative congruence with the form suggests some need that makes the applicability of those norms necessary.

The second, taxonomical aspect of classification entails developing and refining the catalogue of available categories (forms-cum-norms). The forms are subject to a variety of lapses, failures or infelicities, many of which are at the centre of the current crisis of labour law.[59] A particular body of positive law may have gaps or

[55] See above, n 12. Such study of 'ways of doing legal knowledge' has been described as ethnographic or quasi-ethnographic: Annelise Riles, 'A New Agenda for the Cultural Study of Law: Taking on the Technicalities' (2005) 53 *Buffalo Law Review* 973; Leila Kawar, 'Making the Machine Work: Technocratic Engineering of Rights for Domestic Workers at the ILO' (2014) 21 *Indiana Journal of Global Legal Studies* 483; Johns, above n 8, 21–22.

[56] Simon Deakin and Frank Wilkinson, *The Law of the Labour Market: Industrialization, Employment, and Legal Evolution* (New York, Oxford University Press, 2005) 4.

[57] This claim accords with but is not unique to the approach of the new institutional economics. See ibid, 7–9, especially sources in fns 20–21.

[58] A good example is the concept of a 'security' in investment regulation in the United States and Canada. *Ontario Securities Commission v Tiffin*, 2016 ONCJ 543, 133 OR (3d) 341 shows how much the term's definition is bound up with regulatory purpose.

[59] Michel Coutu et al, 'Broken Paradigms: Labor Law in the Wake of Globalization and the Economic Crisis' (2013) 34 *Comparative Labor Law & Policy Journal* 565.

exceptions, where the form fits but the norms are not de jure applicable.[60] There may be conceptual and administrative difficulties applying the law to situations at the boundary of the form.[61] The taxonomy may lack for juridical categories that are sufficiently responsive to the needs and challenges of a particular type of situation.[62] The success of a regulatory intervention may depend on a form being more or less prevalent than it actually is.[63] The goal of refining law's categories is the production of a taxonomy where norms are de jure applicable to appropriate situations, and where the de facto application of those norms engenders a proper order of things – an appropriate practice, or a desirable outcome.

With those preliminaries about law and classification in place, one way of understanding the problem with informality is that the heterogeneity of its referents undermines the diagnostic function.[64] Even the meticulous definition of informal employment in the 2003 Guidelines does not pick out a distinct kind of work relationship. The primary issue is not the vagueness of the category. It offers a relatively determinate standard, with some margin of appreciation, by which to classify particular work as informal or not. Adjudicators and administrators overcome such indeterminacy all the time. The issue is that its selection follows no single rationale. The jumbling together of subsistence farming, work in a family enterprise, and unprotected work for an employer means that the situations covered by the definition have nothing in common on which to base a regulatory analysis or normative response. The standard offered by the Formalisation Recommendation – though it is determinate, relatively authoritative and compatible with the 2003 Guidelines – provides even less analytical specificity, because of the even greater diversity of situations it covers.[65]

That is only one aspect of the confusion, however. The reference in the Formalisation Recommendation to insufficient or absent coverage of activities 'in law or in practice' analytically commingles situations where a norm is not applicable as a matter of positive law with situations that violate an applicable norm.[66] Though this commingling is not at the centre of 'informal employment', it is still there in the 2003 Guidelines, in the delineation of employees with informal jobs as those 'in law or in practice, not subject to national labour legislation, income taxation, social protection or entitlement to certain employment benefits'.[67] There is a more profound

[60] This was the situation adjudicated, for agricultural workers excluded de jure from protections extended to other employees in *Ontario (Attorney General) v Fraser*, 2011 SCC 20, [2011] 2 SCR 3.

[61] Martha Alter Chen et al, 'Counting the Invisible Workforce: The Case of Homebased Workers' (1999) 27 *World Development* 603.

[62] Adelle Blackett, 'Introduction: Regulating Decent Work for Domestic Workers' (2011) 23 *Canadian Journal of Women and the Law* 1.

[63] Harry Arthurs, 'Labour Law After Labour' in Guy Davidov and Brian Langille (eds), *The Idea of Labour Law* (New York, Oxford University Press, 2011).

[64] Sindzingre, above n 5, 59–60.

[65] La Hovary, above n 5, 402–03; Trebilcock, 'Development Approaches', above n 5, 65.

[66] ibid, 403–04; Davidov, above n 13, 3–4; Kanbur, above n 13.

[67] ILO, '2003 ICLS Guidelines', above n 42, para 3(5).

issue. A cursory reading of 'activities...insufficiently covered...by formal arrangements' suggests a mismatch between the content of the practice and the form set out in (official, legal, sanctioned) 'formal arrangements'. Such a mismatch need not be occasioned either by an applicable norm not being obeyed or by an appropriate norm not being applied. As emphasised above, a mismatch may also arise where the confluence of factors that seem relevant in a given situation is inadequately captured or addressed by any of the available 'formal' categories. Informality thus evokes any and all of the ways that the prevailing regulatory taxonomy can fail: applicable norms not followed, appropriate norms not applicable, nominally compatible categories carrying inappropriate norms, and the absence of any truly fitting category.

Some have suggested that informality signals a poorness of fit between the favoured forms of economic life and the reality of economic practice.[68] While that conceptualisation draws together much of the existing usage, it maintains all the concept's analytical weaknesses. Labour law's current existential problem is driven not just by the factual gap between regulatory form and actual practice, but by doubts and disagreements about how to properly understand that mismatch. Where does the problem lie – in norm-violating practices? In the de jure scope of the law? In its de facto application and enforcement? Or in its basic forms, categories and narratives? The dangers of using informality lie not in indeterminacy but in the ways that the term unsystematically groups together these 'failures of form,' ignores the differences between them, and, most dangerously, encourages users to mistake them for one another.

Scholars and policy makers have tried in various ways to overcome the concept's analytical deficiencies. Some have suggested that existing concepts are sufficient to labour law's purposes, and that informality can be retired without further ado.[69] Others have urged precise stipulation of what is intended by any particular use of the term.[70] Taking that advice, some have adopted whatever definition best serves their own study. Others have embraced a preferred conceptualisation and pressed others to follow suit.[71] Martha Alter Chen and her collaborators have suggested that informality is not one thing, and argued that the informal economy is best understood as an agglomeration of four or five different 'segments', each raising a distinct regulatory challenge.[72] Though these approaches each have advantages and disadvantages, a question hangs over all of them (save abandonment): if analytical coherence depends on elaborating discrete subtypes, stipulated definitions or excluding a sizeable portion of the target domain, why bother using informality at all? Why not opt for bespoke, less capacious categories that serve the intended analytical purpose, without risking the confusions that informality engenders?

[68] Supriya Routh, 'Informal Workers' Aggregation and Law' (2016) 17 *Theoretical Inquiries in Law*, 286.
[69] Davidov, above n 13.
[70] Kanbur, above n 13, 6.
[71] eg William F Maloney, 'Informality Revisited' (2004) 32 *World Development* 1159.
[72] Chen, above n 24, 11.

II. 'Conceptualising Informality' as Strategic Context

We might look for answers to that question in research that addresses the use of informality as a strategic matter, rather than as a technical one. In this section, I review four studies that have engaged with how competing agendas have shaped the concept of informality and integrated reflection on those dynamics into their reasoning about how the concept should be used. Those studies present a cross-section of rigorous engagement with the context that shapes the use of informality, yet they all conclude that we should 'go beyond' formality and informality. By integrating critiques of the reasoning in those studies with findings about how concepts interact with the politics of transnational governance and how words function as part of language, I show that, if informality is worth using, it is because a concept's significance is not exhausted by its meaning, nor its meaning reducible to its analytical content.

A. Engaging with Informality as Contested Concept: Key Studies

Caroline Moser's criticisms of the informality concept were part and parcel of her discomfort with a prominent analytical apparatus that, throughout the 1970s, had conceived of informal activities as part of a distinct, separate sector.[73] Though the macroeconomic, multi-sectoral model in that approach did not deny that formal and informal might have interfaces, it assumed the two could be separately analysed and independently targeted for policy measures. Moser instead endorsed what has been characterised as a distinct 'structuralist' approach to understanding informality. The crux of this approach is attention to the linkages between a formal economy, composed of dominant, capitalist firms, and the workers and firms in the informal economy.[74] The diagnosis is subordination; the prescription, regulation. Yet Moser aimed for more than a replacement of one dualism, rooted in neoclassical macroeconomics, with another drawn from Marxist analysis of forms of production.[75] Her primary concern was with the diversity of subordinate relations that existed between large, dominant (and generally government-favoured) firms and those working outside this 'capitalist' mode of production.[76] Analysis of informal activities as an economic aggregate, she argued, is no substitute for

[73] Caroline Moser, 'Informal Sector or Petty Commodity Production: Dualism or Dependence in Urban Development?' (1978) 6 *World Development* 1041, 1056.

[74] On 'schools of thought' on informality, see above, above n 24.

[75] There is a tension between the traditional Marxist sense of 'modes of production' intended to characterise whole economies, and Moser's deployment of the concept to discuss the diverse forms of economic relations within a single economy. Moser, above n 73, 1056–57.

[76] Compare Hill, above n 21, 19; Victor E Tokman, 'An Exploration into the Nature of Informal–Formal Sector Relationships' (1978) 6 *World Development* 1065, 1071.

attending to 'the complexities of relationships...which fit inadequately into a wage/self-employment or formal/informal sector dichotomy' – subcontracting, agency agreements, outwork, apprenticeship, and family work.[77] The problems of poverty, unemployment and exploitation required analysis that considered the economy as a whole, but that also accounted for the social structures of economic relationships in all their diversity (not just the existence of different economic activities).[78] Ultimately, Moser was unconvinced that the discourse of informality could rise to that task.[79]

Where Moser hedged on whether 'informality' could be salvaged from its prior analytical entanglements, Lisa Peattie was unequivocal. Her repudiation of the concept was interwoven with an explanation of its success in development circles, despite its perennial difficulties of conceptualisation. Her explanation lay not only in the concept's aspiration to fill gaps in the analytical picture of developing economies but in its versatility as a 'banner' for divergent tendencies in the development community. For those with more radical, less mainstream analytical perspectives, the concept lent credence to their critiques. For those engaged with sector-based macro-economic analysis and planning, the concept promised a more comprehensive picture of the economy. In a moment when macro-economic planning dominated development policy, the concept created an opening for more qualitative, institutionally nuanced research. Finally, against the myopic focus on economic growth promoted through large, dominant firms, the concept amplified the voices of those concerned with social justice, by casting welfare and growth as equal partners in effective, balanced development.[80] No matter her sympathy for many of these goals, Peattie concluded that the concept was useless for economic analysis or development policy making. A hard-to-define and even harder-to-measure category would impede fruitful economic accounting. Using the informal sector as a proxy for the worst off paradoxically validated the idea that welfare improvements would march in lockstep with the expansion of mass production in large corporate firms. For those concerned with tracking relations of production, documenting the structure of those relations, and critiquing their consequences, starting with a focus on a particular group of firms and workers got the analysis the wrong way round.[81] Ultimately, for Peattie, thinking in terms of a strict division between formal and informal sectors obstructed understanding of the dynamics and relations that condition the accessibility of goods, work and markets – and thus the relative prices – for various groups of producers cum workers cum consumers.[82] Peattie was thus concerned, like Moser, with

[77] Moser, above n 73, 1056.
[78] ibid, 1061.
[79] ibid, 1062.
[80] Lisa Peattie, 'An Idea in Good Currency and How it Grew: The Informal Sector' (1987) 15 *World Development* 851, 855–57.
[81] ibid, 857–58.
[82] ibid, 858.

the 'relationship between different elements of the ensemble'.[83] In her view, the real task for anyone interested in development policy, the welfare of the poor, or economic planning, is to understand how the impact of even macro-economic policy choices would be mediated through the micro-economics of institutions and their interactions.[84]

Though recommending analysis attentive to the diversity of institutional forms and interactions, Peattie did not specify what such analysis might look like. That issue was addressed in a seminal chapter by Basudeb Guha-Khasnobis, Ravi Kanbur and Elinor Ostrom. Guha-Khasnobis and his co-authors mooted the idea that the formal–informal dichotomy is nothing more than 'metaphors that conjure up a mental picture of whatever the user has in mind at that particular time'.[85] Yet their primary target was the concept's complicity in a conflation of two different traits of economic practices: on the one hand, formlessness or lack of structure; on the other, distance from the reach of official governance mechanisms.[86] Guha-Khasnobis and his co-authors demonstrated not only that these are empirically independent qualities, but that the two had often been confounded in policy making, with disastrous consequences.[87] By discarding the presumption that practices labelled as informal are characterised by a lack of structure or normativity, Guha-Khasnobis and his co-authors concluded that one-size-fits-all, centralised policy models should be abandoned in favour of an institutionalist approach to analysis and policy making sensitive to 'informality' – understood as the distance between pre-existing local practices and the forms of top-down governance.[88]

The understanding of informality in the Formalisation Recommendation seems to coincide rather well with the approach proposed by Guha-Khasnobis and his co-authors.[89] Yet a study of this definition and the process leading to its adoption led Claire La Hovary to conclude that labour lawyers should abandon the concept. La Hovary enumerated several reservations about the definition adopted by the Recommendation that applied to the concept of informality more generally.[90] Her primary concerns, however, were with the political consequences of the concept's flexibility. In a context where 'typical' working relationships no longer guarantee decent work, the push to formalise threatens to become a project to universalise, and legally sanction, precarious or insecure forms of work.[91] This is more than just a hypothetical concern, as demonstrated by her close reading of the discussions leading up to the Formalisation Recommendation. For as much as the Workers group within the ILO saw formalisation as a

[83] Moser, above n 73, 1055–56.
[84] Peattie, above n 80, 858.
[85] Guha-Khasnobis et al, above n 26, 3.
[86] ibid, 4–7.
[87] ibid, 5–6.
[88] ibid, 7–8, 10–12, 12–13, 16.
[89] Above n 54.
[90] See above, nn 64–70.
[91] La Hovary, above n 5, 404–05.

stand-in for increased compliance with labour regulations, the Employers group filled in the concept with an ideal of a level playing field between formal and informal firms – constituted as much by a retrenchment of the regulatory corpus as by improved enforcement and compliance.[92] For La Hovary, the amenability of 'the formal' to deregulatory projects casts doubt on the desirability of making formalisation part of the ILO's decent work strategy. What matters is not formality *qua* correspondence with legally mandated form, but the degree of precarity or level of protection. Those concerned with promoting decent work are liable to be led astray by the opposition between formality and informality. It may be better to focus analysis and action on the situations of workers doing particular kinds of work.[93]

Though these four studies broke new ground in contextualising the challenges posed by informality, their conclusions did not take full advantage of the critical threads their observations made available. Drawing those threads out, and weaving them together with insights on the politics of transnational governance and philosophy of language, produces a richer image of the strategic context in which informality is being deployed.

B. Informality's Entanglements with the Practice and Politics of Governance

These four strategic critiques, first of all, did not fully reckon with how concepts enter into the politics and practice of governance. Each tried to shift the focus away from 'informality' toward what might be called 'what is actually going on'. But, as Peattie emphasised, informality, as concept, is an important part what is actually going on.[94] Concepts like informality 'do work' (in the world) even when they do not 'work' (as analytical categories).[95]

The arguments in the strategic critiques drive toward the conclusion that the concept of informality is flawed or even dangerous. From there, the shared aspiration is to go beyond the concept or to leave it behind.[96] If we care about inequality, decent work, effective policy, etc. then (they suggest) discussions of informality are a 'conceptual swamp'.[97] We should (they say) 'bypass' that terrain for 'something

[92] ibid, 405–09. La Hovary emphasises that the ILO Employers' group was first to support the idea of an international labour standard concerning the informal economy.

[93] ibid, 393, 405, 410–11.

[94] Peattie, above n 80, 851.

[95] Compare Bernard E Harcourt, *The Illusion of Free Markets: Punishment and the Myth of Natural Order* (Cambridge, MA, Harvard University Press, 2011) 45–46.

[96] Even Moser, who framed her analysis in terms of the ideological priors that necessarily condition policy analysis, claimed her tools offered superior 'explanatory power and relative utility … for understanding and providing solutions'. Moser, above n 73, 1042.

[97] Peattie, above n 80, 851.

more interesting'.[98] Note that this proposed course of action depends on the invocation of an implicit 'we', united by an open-minded curiosity about 'what works', and a good-faith commitment to implement it.[99] The appeal to such a 'we', however, jars against another observation made in the strategic critiques, that informality is imbricated in countervailing agendas informed by diverse disciplinary traditions, policy priorities and analytical toolkits.

What are the consequences of informality's interactions with these competing agendas? Once endowed with the prestige of policy relevance, a concept can be conscripted into the service of disparate projects.[100] Constructive ambiguity – deliberate use of unclear, indeterminate terminology – has long served, in labour negotiations and in international relations, as a way for parties to defer difficult questions (or implicitly delegate them to adjudicators).[101] La Hovary's account of the negotiations leading to the Formalisation Recommendation saw these dynamics playing out in real time. Internal, bureaucratic power struggles can manifest as disputes about the relative prominence of various concepts in an institutional agenda.[102] The introduction of a new concept can work to rationalise and extend the governing authority of international actors.[103] Or it may become bound up with organisational behaviour, labelling and lending legitimacy to particular ways of distributing internal resources and authority.[104] So it went with informality, which rose to prominence largely through a deliberate strategy to bolster the ILO's relevance in development circles.[105]

These interactions give governance keywords a real-world significance that exceeds the content assigned to them by any particular 'we'. Their significance instead emerges from those interactions. The concept of informality, in the sense advanced by actor-network theory, thus counts as an actor in its own right.[106] As a 'constructed knowledge-object', it enters into a network of effects, and acts in those networks in ways not reducible to some other substance, factor or agenda.[107]

[98] ibid, 858.

[99] Compare the invocation of 'well-meaning legal professionals' and 'people of good heart' in Kennedy, 'International Human Rights Movement', above n 9, 102, 104.

[100] Santos, above n 7.

[101] For example, during the Cold War, a shared commitment to 'social justice' worked at the ILO as a way to avoid explicit conflict between industrial pluralism, proletarian authoritarianism, and the right to development various actors associated it with: Francis Maupain, *The Future of the International Labour Organization in the Global Economy* (Oxford, Hart Publishing, 2013) 24–25.

[102] Sarfaty, above n 7, 75–105.

[103] Anne Orford, 'In Praise of Description' (2012) 25 *Leiden Journal of International Law* 609.

[104] Riles, above n 6, 76–78; Santos, above n 7.

[105] Peattie, above n 80, 853–54. See generally Liam McHugh-Russell, *Under Development: Informality's Past and Labour Law's Future* [unpublished manuscript], 39–41.

[106] Bruno Latour, *Reassembling the Social: An Introduction to Actor-Network-Theory* (Oxford, Oxford University Press, 2005).

[107] See Nehal Bhuta, 'Governmentalizing Sovereignty: Indexes of State Fragility and the Calculability of Political Order' in Kevin E Davis et al (eds), *Governance by Indicators: Global Power Through Quantification and Rankings* (Oxford, Oxford University Press, 2012) 135, especially sources cited at fn 17.

Part of this is common sense. After all, the strategic critiques were acutely concerned with the real consequences of actors ascribing to informality a coherence it lacks: flawed analysis, bad advice, failed policy. But its continuing use is not just a mistake. Peattie, especially, noted that informality works the way it does in part because it serves a purpose for various development communities, even in the absence of a rigorous, analytically coherent usage. Beyond working as a broad tent that accommodates loosely connected projects,[108] informality lends legitimacy and credibility to ways of acting and governing.[109] What Nehal Bhuta concludes about state fragility applies in equal measure to informality:

> To criticize the notion…as lacking analytical rigor or clear boundaries is in a certain sense to misunderstand how it acts: it provides a heuristic and vocabulary for organizing, describing, interpreting, and classifying, which then becomes a basis for acting in and on a complex reality.[110]

The ICLS definitions illustrate this vividly. Informality has been shaped by the politics of measuring the economy; at the same time, it has also been useful to those interested in counting what was previously counted differently, or not counted at all.[111] Though it may be hard to say what statistics on informality measure,[112] those definitions make informality accessory to the whole bureaucratic apparatus that allows us to say, credulously, that 'informal employment comprises one half to three-quarters of non-agricultural employment in developing countries'.[113]

Informality's emergent effects means no one group has control over its significance. So long as the concept remains useful to various groups, they are unlikely to stop using it or trying to shape its meaning. In that context, were some narrow 'we' to follow Peattie, Moser and La Hovary's advice to adopt an alternative conceptual toolkit, they might increase the salience of that alternative. But using that alternative will not stop others from continuing to use informality. Formal and informal cannot be 'suppressed'.[114] Adoption of an alternative term by one 'we' will instead leave in place informality's current web of significance, while ceding influence over its future to other actors. The broader lesson is that, even were the development community to suddenly and unanimously abandon informality, any replacement would face similar entanglements.

[108] It serves for example as a cognitive anchor to rationalise the work of groups like WIEGO (Women in Informal Employment: Globalizing and Organizing). www.wiego.org.

[109] La Hovary, above n 5, 392.

[110] Bhuta, above n 107, 136.

[111] Sindzingre, above n 5, 62–63; see especially the guidelines on 'informal aspects of the economy' including reference to the 2003 definitions of informal employment, in European Commission et al, *System of National Accounts 2008*, ST/ESA/STAT/SER.F/2/Rev.5 (New York, Published jointly by Commission of the European Communities, International Monetary Fund, Organisation for Economic Co-operation and Development, United Nations and World Bank, 2009) 471–82.

[112] La Hovary, above n 5, 401–02; Sindzingre, above n 5.

[113] International Labour Office, above n 43, 7, 19.

[114] Guha-Khasnobis et al, above n 26, 7.

C. Informality's Semantic Resources

If the strategic critiques did not fully reckon with how concepts act in struggles over development practice, neither did they engage sufficiently with why those struggles draw on particular concepts and not others. The habitual use of a concept like informality may work in development circles to validate, substantiate and coordinate narrowly favoured practices, shared enterprises or institutional settlements. Yet its power to do so is not the arbitrary result of an a priori entente between its users. Informality, rather, acquired and maintains its salience (its *agency* as a constructed knowledge object), by dint of its linguistic meaning. This may seem strange given how much has been said about the concept's apparent semantic weaknesses. But this apparent strangeness recedes if one overcomes the tendency, evident in the strategic critiques, to mistake a word's 'sense and reference' for its whole meaning.

'The meaning of a word' is a slippery notion, made more tractable by philosophy of language. Wittgenstein tells us that the meaning of a word is in its use.[115] To some degree, Wittgenstein meant that a word's polysemy could be overcome by attending to the context in which it is deployed. His more profound point was that understanding the meaning of a word is not like possessing something – 'as if the meaning were an aura the word brings along with it'[116] – but is instead a matter of knowing how the word is used, and how to use it, in various language games.[117] Austin averts us to what actions a speaker intends to undertake *in* making an utterance, and what they hope to achieve *by* making an utterance; the use of a word, in his parlance, carries illocutionary force, and may underwrite a perlocutionary act.[118] A word is situated in a semantic field, including its relations to synonyms, antonyms, and subordinate and superordinate concepts.[119] Skinner notes that the semantic field apportions associations among its members, meaning that the use of a word invokes, and implicitly validates, a way of 'approaching…a large tract of our cultural experience' rather than just the slice of reality that the word might denote.[120] In broad strokes, this literature tells us that to use a word is to do more than just say what it means. A word may also evoke, invoke or imply, advert or emphasise, distinguish or draw together, associate or ascribe, commend or condemn.

[115] Ludwig Wittgenstein, *Philosophische Untersuchungen/Philosophical Investigations*, PMS Hacker and Joachim Schulte (eds), GEM Anscombe et al (trs) 4th edn (Chichester, Wiley-Blackwell, 2009) paras 43, 197.

[116] ibid, para 117.

[117] ibid, para 43.

[118] JL Austin, *How To Do Things With Words* (London, Oxford University Press, 1975).

[119] John Gerring, *Social Science Methodology: A Criterial Framework* (Cambridge, Cambridge University Press, 2001) 50–51.

[120] Quentin Skinner, *Visions of Politics* (Cambridge, Cambridge University Press, 2002) 163–65.

Literature that has addressed informality's meaning, including the strategic critiques, shows that the word is used so as to:

- **Contrast:** References to informality suggest a duality or opposition:[121] things in a domain are cast as either formal or informal;[122] or, to be more of one is necessarily to be less of the other.[123] Beyond this, informality is, like state fragility or corruption, a 'contrastive concept'.[124] As a negation of 'the formal', informality invokes a distance from regulatory power; an incompatibility with 'the bureaucratic gaze'.[125]
- **Venerate the formal:** In accordance with ordinary language, the formal–informal dichotomy will generally colour the formal not just as typical or standard, but as conforming to a *norm*.[126] Informality by contrast will connote the *failure* of some form.[127] Especially when tied to a push for formalisation, the dichotomy may commend the 'standard' form almost as an end in itself.[128] Yet when used in sufficiently vague ways, informality averts any confrontation over which conceptions of the form are to be encouraged.[129]
- **Make visible:** Unlike state fragility, informality's associations are not so universally negative. Even acknowledging 'informal' economic activities gives 'standing' and visibility to those activities, drawing attention to what was not previously considered or counted.[130] This broadened outlook puts in question the boundaries conventionally drawn around 'the economy'[131] or what counts as (legitimate) work.[132]
- **Shift emphasis:** Whether or not it favours one or the other, informality, like cognate concepts (underground, hidden etc), highlights the gap between norm and practice, bringing it to mind or putting it in question. Though informality can convey an absence (illegality, formlessness), it can also intimate the presence of something that does not fit.[133] Thus, by contrast to other

[121] Moser, above n 73, 1052–55; Peattie, above n 80, 852; Keith Hart, 'Bureaucratic Form and the Informal Economy' in Basudeb Guha-Khasnobis et al (eds), *Linking the Formal and Informal Economy: Concepts and Policies* (Oxford, Oxford University Press, 2006) 30–31, 33.
[122] Sindzingre, above n 5, 62.
[123] See Guha-Khasnobis et al, above n 26.
[124] Bhuta, above n 107, 134; compare Hart, 'Bureaucratic Form', above n 121, 28; Sindzingre, above n 5, 61.
[125] See text to above n 86; Hart, 'Bureaucratic Form', above n 121, 22.
[126] ibid 22, 29.
[127] Simon Deakin, Shelley Marshall and Sanjay Pinto, 'Labour Laws, Informality, and Development: Comparing India and China' (this volume).
[128] La Hovary, above n 5, 404–05; compare Guha-Khasnobis et al, above n 26, 6–7.
[129] ibid, 410; Guha-Khasnobis et al, above n 26, 3.
[130] Peattie, above n 80, 855–57.
[131] Hill, above n 21, 8–9.
[132] Chen et al, above n 61; compare Prabha Kotiswaran, 'Abject Labors, Informal Markets: Revisiting the Law's (Re)Production Boundary' (2014) 18 *Employee Rights and Employment Journal* 111.
[133] Guha-Khasnobis et al, above n 26, 4–7.

dichotomies – employment and unemployment, for example[134] – informality invites closer engagement with the qualitative detail of what lies beyond 'the formal'.[135] In a different vein, informality evokes and implies the relevance of the precarious, the vulnerable, or the worst off.[136] Yet in associating poverty and unprotected work with infelicities of form, we may divert focus from the former.[137]

- **Revalue**: By contrast to underground, illegal, or non-compliant, informal has less judgemental undertones, expressing a relative value-neutrality about the gap between norm and practice.[138] Yet by putting practice and norm on equal footing, the term may raise doubts about the adequacy of the formal, and put in question its universality, relevance or fairness.[139] For sceptics of bureaucracy, regulation or conformity, the term draws on the esteem of flexibility, self-organisation and freedom.[140]
- **Lump together:** The formal–informal dichotomy operates to present each side as a unity.[141] Thus, despite continuing emphasis on the diversity of the informal economy, 'the informal' suggests a homogenous whole, spurring the mind toward abstractions defined in terms of what is common.[142] In a related way, references to informality can reinforce associations between the characteristics it brings to mind.[143]

As this list makes clear, philosophy of language generates no claims about informality's meaning not already explicit in the literature. It does, however, offer a way to organise those claims, by rephrasing questions about meaning as inquiries into how concepts are actually used. Neither knowing how words are used nor knowing how to use them, it turns out, prevents us from misunderstanding 'the meaning of a word'. Armed with the insights of philosophy of language, we may resist illusions about language and meaning built into our intuitive accounts of epistemic keywords and the relations between them.[144]

[134] Hart, 'Informal Income', above n 15, 61, 77, 82–87; Hart, 'Bureaucratic Form', above n 121, 24–26.
[135] Peattie, above n 80, 857; Hart, 'Informal Income', above n 15, 68.
[136] La Hovary, above n 5, 393; Peattie, above n 80, 857; see eg ILO, *Informal Economy Conclusions*, above n 2, paras 1–2, 9–11, associating informality with 'most pronounced' decent work deficits.
[137] La Hovary, above n 5, 405, 410, 411.
[138] ibid, 404.
[139] Peattie, above n 80, 853–54; Guha-Khasnobis et al, above n 26, 10–13; ILO, *Informal Economy Conclusions*, above n 2, para 3, discussing law as 'inappropriate, burdensome'; especially Hernando de Soto, *The Other Path: The Invisible Revolution in the Third World*, June Abbott (tr) 1st edn (New York, Harper & Row, 1989).
[140] Hart, 'Bureaucratic Form', above n 121, 28.
[141] ibid, 33.
[142] ibid, 28.
[143] Guha-Khasnobis et al, above n 26, 6–7.
[144] Wittgenstein, above n 115, paras 5, 115. Compare Barbara Herrnstein Smith, 'Reply to an Analytic Philosopher' (2002) 101 *South Atlantic Quarterly* 229, 230.

The strategic critiques demonstrated how seductive those illusions can be. Despite tacit awareness of the semantic resources showcased above, their *explicit* accounts of a word's 'meaning' drew exclusively from that intuitive understanding of language, knowledge and thought. In their accounts, a concept is either *applied* to the world, or mediates the application of a broader framework (or model, theory, etc).[145] Concepts and frameworks are *analytical* tools;[146] they break up the world. A concept *identifies* or *refers to* elements or aspects of the world that correspond to features of, sites in, or variables from the framework.[147] A concept selects cases based on their *characteristics*, or *characterises* cases in a given domain.[148] Its *meaning* is what it selects or how it characterises.[149] What *belongs to* and *constitutes* the term are the elements, aspects or characteristics of the world that are *encompassed by* its meaning.[150] Knowing a term's meaning is like having an unformulated definition;[151] a term's *definition*, conversely, is like a recipe for doing the selection, demarcation or characterisation.[152]

Proceeding on the basis of such an incomplete account of how words mean sustains a mischaracterisation of how words and their uses are chosen. Though the strategic critiques each ascribed a different failing to informality – that its reference is unclear (due to uncertainty or controversy about what it picks out),[153] that its sense is imprecise or inconsistent,[154] or that it draws phenomena into an unhelpful picture[155] – those failures were all measured against the same epistemological standard. Operating in the background is a model of fit, with concepts that establish a tidy congruence among a term, its meaning and the aspects of the world it picks out, and an overall framework whose structure and constituent concepts provides a relevant, useful map of relationships among phenomena in the

[145] Guha-Khasnobis et al, above n 26, 2, 3, 7.

[146] Peattie, above n 80, 857–58; Guha-Khasnobis et al, above n 26, 6. Moser framed her entire discussion as a comparison of analytical frameworks.

[147] Moser, above n 73, 1052; Peattie, above n 80, 851; Guha-Khasnobis et al, above n 26, 4; La Hovary, above n 5, 396, 397, 398.

[148] Moser, above n 73, 1052–53; Guha-Khasnobis et al, above n 26, 3, 5–6, 16.

[149] La Hovary, above n 5, 395, 398; Guha-Khasnobis et al, above n 26, 7; Moser, above n 73, 1051–52.

[150] ibid, 397; Moser, above n 73, 1051, 1057; Guha-Khasnobis et al, above n 26, 16.

[151] Compare Wittgenstein, above n 115, para 75.

[152] Moser, above n 73; Guha-Khasnobis et al, above n 26, 2–3; La Hovary, above n 5, 391, 395, 397–98, 401–05.

[153] It may have no uniformly or generally accepted, or consistently applied, definition; or there may be an overabundance of (incompatible) *conceptualisations*; or it may mean different things to different people: La Hovary, above n 5, 396, 395, 397, 410; Guha-Khasnobis et al, above n 28, 2–3; Moser, above n 73, 1052–55; Peattie, above n 80, 852.

[154] It may, that is, be *fuzzy*, or *too broad*, or *imprecise* or *not well spelt out*: Peattie, above n 80, 851, 856; La Hovary, above n 5, 401, 402, 403; Guha-Khasnobis et al, above n 26, 3, 5.

[155] The framework may *neglect* what is important, *focus* on the wrong thing, or be *misleading, unsound or crude*: Moser, above n 73, 1056, 1060; La Hovary, above n 5, 410–11; Guha-Khasnobis et al, above n 26, 6, 16; Peattie, above n 80, 858.

real world.[156] Though they may or may not 'carve nature at the joints',[157] concepts are to be compared by the *usefulness* of their mapping of the world.[158]

Such an approach misses the mark because we decide between concepts by accounting both for their analytical strength and for what might be called their rhetorical force. Familiar vocabulary lightens the cognitive load and, among development professionals at least, informality 'resonates'.[159] Informality, too, lends users the cachet of addressing a topic widely believed to be relevant.[160] Yet saying 'rhetorical force' may miss the mark as well, inasmuch as it evokes a cynical, one-dimensional trade-off between clarity and persuasion – as if certain keywords did no more than smuggle in more tractable, but less appealing thoughts.[161] The calculus is not a maximisation of fit nor an effort to balance the advancement of an argument against the expression of a thought.

It is better to say that in choosing among concepts, we balance what they make possible against how they hinder and constrain. Indeed, we not only choose among concepts, but among uses of words, and not just among words, but among combinations of them. As emphasised by Wittgenstein's discussion of grammar and Austin's attention to convention, making use of a concept's semantic resources draws us into constraints on how the word can be combined with others.[162] And the constraints on how words can be combined means that we cannot deploy semantic resources à la carte, so that we always may mean both more and less than we strictly intend. Informality may allow its users to do things with words they could not do as well otherwise, but no words allow us to say or do exactly what we want with language.

There is an additional layer of strategy involved. Though a concept's meaning cannot be controlled, usages (and arguments in favour of a particular usage) can still shift its semantic centre of gravity. We can foster innovation in how elements

[156] Legal classification (see above, section I.C) offers only one approach to drawing such a map. Positivist social science does it rather differently. See Gerring, above n 119, 35–60.

[157] On debates between nominalist and realists about how concepts relate to our experience of the world, see Ian Hacking, *The Social Construction of What?* (Cambridge, MA, Harvard University Press, 1999) 82–84.

[158] *cf* Pickering's 'representational idiom', which frames science as an effort 'to produce knowledge that maps, mirrors, or corresponds to how the world really is'. Andrew Pickering, *The Mangle of Practice: Time, Agency, and Science* (Chicago, University of Chicago Press, 1995) 5.

[159] La Hovary, above n 5, 392; compare Guha-Khasnobis et al, above n 28, 7.

[160] Kanbur, above n 13, 2.

[161] Bruno Latour, 'Why Has Critique Run out of Steam? From Matters of Fact to Matters of Concern' (2004) 30 *Critical Inquiry* 225; compare Duncan Kennedy, 'The Hermeneutic of Suspicion in Contemporary American Legal Thought' (2014) 25 *Law and Critique* 91.

[162] See Constantin Fasolt, 'Respect for the Word: What Calvin and Wittgenstein Had against Images' in Amy Nelson Burnett (ed), *John Calvin, Myth and Reality: Images and Impact of Geneva's Reformer* (Eugene, OR, Cascade Books, 2011) for a lucid account of Wittgenstein's idea of 'grammar'. For the role of convention in Austin's account of speech acts: Marianne Constable, *Our Word Is Our Bond: How Legal Speech Acts*, Cultural Lives of Law (Stanford, Stanford University Press, 2014). Inherent to Austin and Wittgenstein's approach is a fundamental scepticism about common sense distinctions among syntax, semantics and pragmatics.

of our shared lexicon draw together denotations, connotations and evaluations.[163] The last 40 years are filled with such considered efforts to give informality new meaning.[164] Of course, linguistic innovation has unpredictable results: it might fail to achieve uptake, or transform the lexicon in unintended ways.[165] Still, the use of a word not only draws on, but is also an intervention in, a semantic network.

III. Conclusions: Using Informality Strategically

Where does this leave us? Uses of informality are moves in a contest over what comes to mind when people think of work, poverty, regulation or development. They are, more profoundly, manoeuvres in a struggle that determines what gets done and how – especially what is done in the name of development. Informality acts in those processes by serving as a nexus for argument about the organisation of regulatory practices, but also by furnishing a store of semantic resources in those arguments and by lending legitimacy, validity and prestige to existing administrative practices, bureaucratic formations and political coalitions. That struggle is not a winner-takes-all competition. Informality's meaning and significance never correspond to any one usage, but emerge from an interaction of those uses with the world.

Being strategic means weighing informality's analytical shortcomings together with the semantic resources it makes available, its incidental semantic effects, and its sociological by-products. Realising decent work no doubt requires the kind of conceptual-analytical-taxonomical groundwork that labour jurists are wont to do. But we should not confuse means with ends. Thinking through how to structure and regulate work – as part of a larger strategy of growth and poverty reduction, or as a way to address challenges faced by discrete groups of workers – is one thing. *Realising* those structures and regulations is another. Labour law scholarship implicitly invites judges, legislators or regulators to adopt a particular conceptual schema, with the hope is that the resulting conceptual innovations will 'stick'.[166] Yet the uptake of a conceptual innovation is not determined by how well it works in bringing together form, norm and practice. For that reason, we can and do choose our repertoire of terms and concepts not only for their place in a grid that orders our experience of the world, but also for how they might materially influence the competitive, open-ended processes that lie between competing development agendas and what ends up being done in the name of development.

[163] Skinner, above n 120, chs 8–9.
[164] See eg Peattie, above n 80, 854, discussing the ILO's early transformation of the term.
[165] Skinner, above n 120, 167–69.
[166] Compare Raymond Geuss, *Philosophy and Real Politics* (Princeton, Princeton University Press, 2008) 42–50.

So what are we to do with informality? I have my own views, largely informed by the insights of Moser, Peattie, Guha-Khasnobis, Ostrom and Kanbur, and La Hovary. I think that using informality is worth the risk for labour lawyers, but that we should leverage usages that draw attention to the diverse ways that power shapes the experience of workers in the global South while resisting those that reinforce folk images of work and production based on economic forms privileged in the global North during the twentieth century. The invocation of informality can fetishise or reify – lending credibility and an air of reality to forms that are less relevant than they are made out to be, and an illusory coherence to departures from those forms[167] – and I side with those who think the term should be used so as to interrogate those forms, rather than treating them as standard. Yet I would not presume to offer a universal, once-and-for-all answer to the question. Uncertainty, contingency and the strategising of other actors means we quickly run up against the limits of our capacities to account for the probable consequences of the concepts we use. Language is just one of many factors that intervene between the articulation of a regulatory problem and the ordering of the world. And across the span of time and space, pursuing the project of labour law may not only require a flexible strategy, but also demand a more fundamental re-imagination of what pursuing that project entails.[168] I would only insist that, while recognising the concept's analytical weaknesses, we not overlook or take for granted all the uses that informality has in the agendas of development – including our own.

[167] Adelle Blackett, 'Decolonizing Labour Law' in D'Arcy du Toit (ed), *Labour Law and Social Progress: Holding the Line or Shifting the Boundaries?*, Bulletin for Comparative Labour Relations 92 (The Hague, Kluwer Law International, 2016) 96; Judy Fudge, 'Blurring Legal Boundaries: Regulating for Decent Work' in Judy Fudge et al (eds), *Challenging the Legal Boundaries of Work Regulation* (Oxford, Hart Publishing, 2012) 9.

[168] Blackett, above n 167, 89–90.

3

Informalisation in International Labour Regulation Policy: Profiles of an Unravelling

DEIRDRE McCANN[1]

I. Introduction

The ILO Transition from the Informal to the Formal Economy Recommendation 2015 (No 204) introduced a novel objective to international-level policy on informal work: that states should, as a key element of formalisation policies, prevent informalisation. Awareness of informality, as Ashiagbor points out,[2] and as the contributions to this volume testify, is invigorating the debates on the role, form, and future of labour regulation. Yet informalisation as a discrete process has tended to be neglected in informality policy. It is therefore crucial to single out informalisation as a distinct element of the evolving growth in informality, and to reflect on the demands that it imposes on law and policy.

This chapter is the first scholarly investigation of informalisation in global labour regulation policy. It explores how recent regulatory discourses absorb and convey the processes of informalisation, with a particular focus on the role of legal regulation. Section II highlights anxiety about the expansion of informal work, including in middle- and high-income countries, situating the problem within the 'unacceptable forms of work' framework. Section III explores the academic literature on the regulatory dimension of informality, highlighting two crucial insights – that informality exists on a continuum and that legal regulation mediates the shifting boundaries between the formal and the informal. Section Four examines informalisation in international regulatory policy. The regulatory sites examined are the pivotal transnational spheres of the World Bank

[1] Durham Law School, deirdre.mccann@durham.ac.uk. Research towards this chapter was conducted with the support of a Leverhulme Research Fellowship, Project on *Creative Uncertainty?: Labour Market Regulation in a World of Doubt* (RF-2015-547).

[2] Diamond Ashiagbor, this volume. 'Introduction: Narratives of Informality and Development'.

and the International Labour Organization (ILO). Section V concludes that a shift in ILO informality discourses to embrace informalisation is significant, but has not been absorbed in the Organization's conception of the functioning or potential of labour regulation. It argues that informalisation must be better integrated into the formalisation project, including as an objective of improving and sustaining job quality in the formal economy. As a crucial element of this project, the chapter concludes by calling for a new approach to labour law – a pre-emptive approach – that is aimed at preventing the unravelling of decent jobs.

II. Post-crisis Informality and the Unacceptable Forms of Work Paradigm

Prominent in analyses of the enduring fallout of the global financial and economic crisis are signs of the expansion of informal economies, including in middle- and high-income countries.[3] Disproportionately associated with poverty, poor job quality and insecurity,[4] any growth in informal work poses a formidable risk to efforts to reduce work-centred poverty and is therefore a broader challenge to social and economic development.[5] The outcomes embrace a range of deficient labour practices, including the delay or non-payment of wages, excessive hours, unpaid overtime, high earnings volatility, risky health and safety conditions and the denial of collective rights.[6] It is also clear that deficient manifestations of informal work are disproportionately concentrated among historically disadvantaged groups, including women and young workers.[7]

For these reasons, this chapter situates the problem of informality, and its expansion, in the presence of unacceptable forms of work (UFW).[8] This notion

[3] Johannes Jütting and Juan R de Laiglesia (eds), *Is Informal Normal? Towards More and Better Jobs in Developing Countries* (Paris, OECD, 2009). See also Henrik Huitfeldt and Johannes Jütting, 'Informality and Informal Employment' in OECD, *Promoting Pro-Poor Growth: Employment and Social Protection* (Paris, OECD, 2009), 95–108; M Anne Visser, 'A Floor to Exploitation? Social Economy Organizations at the Edge of a Restructuring Economy' (2016) 31 *Work, Employment and Society* 782. On the evolving affinities between global North and South, see Kerry Rittich, in this volume, 'Historicising Labour in Development: Labour Market Formalisation through the Lens of British Colonial Administration'.

[4] eg Martha Chen, 'Rethinking the Informal Economy: Linkages with the Formal Economy and the Formal Regulatory Environment' in Basudeb Guha-Khasnobis, Ravi Kanbur and Elinor Ostrom (eds), *Linking the Formal and Informal Economy: Concepts and Policies* (Oxford, Oxford University Press, 2006); David Kucera and Theodora Xenogiani, 'Persisting Informal Employment: What Explains It?' in Jütting and de Laiglesia, above n 3.

[5] Jütting and de Laiglesia, above n 3, 13.

[6] Martha Alter Chen, 'The Informal Economy: Recent Trends, Future Directions' (2016) 26(2) *New Solutions* 155; OECD, *Employment Outlook 2015* (Paris, OECD, 2015), ch 5; Françoise Carré and James Heintz, 'Toward a Common Framework for Informal Employment across Developed and Developing Countries,' WIEGO Working Paper (Statistics) No 26 May 2009 (revised March 2013), 9.

[7] ILO, *World of Work* (Geneva, ILO, 2014); on Africa, James Heintz and Imraan Valodia, 'Informality in Africa: A Review', WIEGO Working Paper No 3, September 2008, 8.

[8] See further Deirdre McCann and Judy Fudge, 'Unacceptable Forms of Work: A Multidimensional Model' (2017) 156 *International Labour Review* 147.

is derived from a recently emerging ILO policy discourse that singles out UFW as a site of urgent action, defining these working relations as jobs in 'conditions that deny fundamental principles and rights at work, put at risk the lives, health, freedom, human dignity and security of workers or keep households in conditions of extreme poverty'.[9] An associated research project has since generated a conceptual framework – a Multidimensional Model – to identify and address UFW, designed as a diagnostic tool for local actors in economies at a range of levels of development.[10] A premise of the Multidimensional Model is that informal work is not inevitably unacceptable, yet, given its association with UFW, a site that is ripe for regulatory intervention.[11]

III. Informalisation: Towards the Regulatory Conduits

The global crisis propelled informalisation to the forefront of the debates on rising informality.[12] This notion has been attached to a range of definitions in the policy and scholarly literatures, pointing to a risk of a conceptual incoherence.[13] Some definitions are insufficient to anchor a robust conception of informalisation. The term periodically functions, for example, to denote expanding informality: the broader trend towards labour markets that are significantly characterised by the presence of informal work.[14] Sharper imagery of informalisation, however, has been associated with the shift in the international policy realm from an enterprise-centred notion of informal work to a job-centred model.[15] This shift

[9] In the 2013 report to the International Labour Conference, the ILO Director-General included UFW among Areas of Critical Importance for the Organization: ILO, *Towards the ILO Centenary: Realities, Renewal and Tripartite Commitment Geneva* (Geneva, ILO, 2013), para 148. Action on UFW has since been incorporated as an objective of the ILO's contribution to the UN 2030 Agenda and the Sustainable Development Goals. See www.ilo.org/global/topics/dw4sd/lang--en/index.htm.

[10] McCann and Fudge, 'Unacceptable Forms of Work', above n 8; McCann and Fudge, 'A Strategic Approach to Regulating Unacceptable Forms of Work' *Journal of Law and Society*, forthcoming 2019. See further Project on *Legal Regulation of Unacceptable Work*, supported by the UK Economic and Social Research Council (ESRC) through the Global Challenges Research Fund [Grant No ES/P00746/1] https://www.dur.ac.uk/law/policyengagement/ufw/ufw/.

[11] McCann and Fudge, 'Unacceptable Forms of Work', above n 8.

[12] eg Jütting and de Laiglesia, *Is Informal Normal?*, above n 3.

[13] Kanbur has raised a similar objection to the notion of informality: Ravi Kanbur, 'Conceptualising Informality: Regulation and Enforcement' 2009 52(1) *The Indian Journal of Labour Economics* 33, 33.

[14] eg James Heintz and Robert Pollin, 'Informalization, Economic Growth and the Challenge of Creating Viable Labor Standards in Developing Countries', Political Economy Research Institute, Working Paper Series 60, June 2003.

[15] On this shift, see Carré and Heintz, 'Common Framework', above n 6; Elizabeth Hill, *Worker Identity, Agency and Economic Development: Women's Empowerment in the Indian Informal Economy* (London, Routledge, 2010); Supriya Routh, 'Building Informal Workers Agenda: Imagining 'Informal Employment' in Conceptual Resolution of 'Informality' (2011) 2(3) *Global Labour Journal* 3; Martha Chen, 'The Informal Economy: Definitions, Theories and Policies' WIEGO Working Paper No 1, 2012); Colin Williams and Mark Lansky, 'Informal Employment in Developed and Developing

in the models of informality has embraced a more refined account of processes of informalisation within the formal economy. The earlier enterprise-centred conceptions – hinging on enterprise-size and legal status – neglected key manifestations of informal work, and in particular excluded the formal sector, missing the dynamics of informalisation.[16] More recent models, underpinned by the job-centred rendition of informality ('all economic activities by workers and economic units that are – in law or in practice – not covered or insufficiently covered by formal arrangements'[17]) capture the diversity of informal employment across countries at different levels of development.[18] These models encompass informal jobs in the formal sector: that a 'growing proportion of jobs possess what may be called informal characteristics, ie without regular wages, benefits, employment protection, and so on.'[19]

The evolution towards job-centred conceptions of informality has crystallised informalisation as a distinct dynamic of informality of increasing significance. As Standing has pointed out, traditionally informal economic activities were taken mainly to encompass the means of survival of the rural and urban poor.[20] In more recent decades – in both industrialised and industrialising countries – there has been a trend towards enterprises informalising their labour processes. Standing and others have linked the rise in flexible labour relationships from the 1980s to informalisation across the world, including through formal firms in the global North that sub-contract production to workers in developing countries.[21]

Informalisation has long been recognised in low-income settings. In this regard, Theron, on the South African experience, offers contrasting notions of informalisation 'from above' and 'from below'.[22] The latter captures the conceptions

Economies: Perspectives and Policy Responses' (2013) 152 *International Labour Review* 355, and the discussion in McCann and Fudge, 'Unacceptable Forms of Work', above n 8, pp 165–66. See further below, section IV.B.

[16] International Conference of Labour Statisticians 'Resolution Concerning Statistics of Employment in the Informal Sector,' in Report of the Fifteenth International Conference of Labour Statisticians (Geneva, ILO, 1993) 51–64.

[17] ILO *Resolution concerning Decent Work and the Informal Economy* (Geneva, ILO, 2002) para 3. See below, section IV.B.

[18] ibid; International Conference of Labour Statisticians (ICLS) 'Guidelines concerning a Statistical Definition of Informal Employment,' in *Report of the Seventeenth International Conference of Labour Statisticians* (Geneva, ILO, 2003) 12–15; Chen, 'Rethinking the Informal Economy', above n 4; Chen, 'The Informal Economy', above n 6; ILO, *Statistical Update on Employment in the Informal Economy* (Geneva, ILO, 2012).

[19] Guy Standing, 'Global Feminisation Through Flexible Labor: A Theme Revisited' (1999) 27 *World Development* 583, 585.

[20] ibid, 587.

[21] ibid, 585. See also Martha Alter Chen, 'Rethinking the Informal Economy: Linkages with the Formal Economy and the Formal Regulatory Environment,' DESA Working Paper No 46 ST/ESA/2007/DWP/46, July 2007, 9, citing Michael Piore and Charles Sabel, *The Second Industrial Divide* (New York, Basic Books, 1984).

[22] Jan Theron, 'Informalization from Above, Informalization from Below: The Options for Organization' (2010) 11 (2 & 3) *African Studies Quarterly* 87.

of informality that are familiar from the literatures on the global South: individual workers devising survivalist strategies in response to job losses.[23] 'Informalisation from above', more pertinently for present purposes, equates with the notion of informalisation pursued in this chapter: it unfurls through the capacity to bypass labour laws by resorting to either outsourcing or retrenchment.[24] This process has been identified in recent years, for example, in the signs from India and a number of African countries that growing numbers of workers in the small formal sectors are not protected by labour law, including through outsourcing and sub-contracting.[25]

Awareness of comparable trends in higher-income settings is more recent. Early in the post-crisis era, for example, Jütting and de Laiglesia spotted a growing trend towards informalisation in OECD countries, which they attributed to heightened international competition in the course of globalisation, offering as an example the phenomenon of false self-employment.[26] Visser has also pointed to an expansion of the informal economy in industrialised economies that is limiting access to benefits, training opportunities, access to social services, security, and the right to organise.[27]

An intriguing element of the more recent academic work, in this regard, is that it is beginning to engage much more energetically with the regulatory conduits to informalisation. The informality literature has often been received, with justification, as adrift from the preoccupations of legal scholarship: identified and

[23] ibid.

[24] ibid. Drawing on this model, Webster et al have recently analysed the South African private security industry as engaging in 'informalisation from above', as employers gradually increase outsourcing to labour-brokers and workers are de facto excluded from the operation of many labour laws. Edward Webster, Katherine Joynt and Thabang Sefalafala, 'Informalization and Decent Work: Labour's Challenge' (2016) 16(2) *Progress in Development Studies* 203, citing T Sefalafala, *Precarious Work: A Case Study of Security Guards in Johannesburg* (Johannesburg, University of Witwatersrand, 2012).

[25] Heintz and Valodia, 'Informality in Africa', above n 7; Paul Benjamin (assisted by Urmilla Bhoola), 'Subordination, Parasubordination and Self-Employment: A Comparative Study of Selected African Countries' in Giuseppe Casale (ed), *The Employment Relationship: A Comparative Overview* (London, Palgrave Macmillan, 2011); Kamala Sankaran, 'Flexibility and Informalisation of Employment Relationships' in Judy Fudge, Kamala Sankaran and Shae McCrystal (eds), *Regulating Work: Challenging Legal Boundaries* (Oxford, Hart Publishing, 2012); R Agarwala, *Informal Labour, Formal Politics and Dignified Discontent in India* (Cambridge, Cambridge University Press, 2013); Dibyendu Maiti, 'Precarious Work in India: Trends and Emerging Issues' (2013) 57 *American Behavioral Scientist* 507.

[26] Jütting and de Laiglesia, *Is Informal Normal?*, above n 3.

[27] Visser, 'A Floor to Exploitation?', above n 3 at 5, citing Visser, *Race, Poverty, and State Intervention in the Informal Economy: Evidence from South Africa* (New York, New School University, 2011). On informalisation in the global North, see further Colin C Williams and Frédéric Lapeyre, 'Dependent Self-Employment: Trends, Challenges and Policy Responses in the EU', International Labour Office, Employment Policy Department, Working Paper No 228, 2017. On Japan and South Korea, see Fang Lee Cooke and Yumei Jiang, 'The Growth of Non-Standard Employment in Japan and South Korea: The Role of Institutional Actors and Impact on Workers and the Labour Market' (2017) 55 *Asia Pacific Journal of Human Resources* 155. On Norway, see John Fredrik Rye, 'Negotiating Neoliberalism: Informalisation and Reformalisation of Industrial Relations in Norway's Agricultural Industry in the 21st Century' (2017) 32 *Population, Space and Place*. On the UK, see Sam Scott, 'Informalisation in Low-wage Labour Markets: A Case Study of the UK Food Industry' (2017) *Population, Space and Place*.

elaborated primarily by economists; ill-suited and neglectful of the intricacies, objectives, and structures of labour regulation.[28] La Hovary, centrally, has voiced dissatisfaction with the concept of the informal economy and cast doubt on its promise for effective policy intervention.[29] Yet the evolution of the informality narrative has the potential to illuminate the present regulatory era, precisely because it is approaching with more rigour and precision the relationship between formality and informality and the channels that link them. Two insights from the literature are particularly useful for conceptualising informalisation: that informality exists on a continuum, and that legal regulation mediates the shifting boundaries between the formal and informal.

A. Informality as a Continuum

The trajectory in the informality literature is towards an extended, more probing, destabilisation of the dichotomy of the formal and informal. The resultant imagery is of informality as existing on a continuum in which working relationships are compliant with certain legal sub-fields, or specific obligations, but not others.[30] Along this continuum, there is an increasingly restricted engagement with regulatory obligations and requirements and an increasingly inhibited access to a range of legal protections and entitlements – in the labour dimension, protection from arbitrary dismissal, for example, work/family entitlements, rights to equality, to organise and collectively to bargain, social security benefits, training opportunities etc.[31]

These observations may appear fairly mundane, at first glance, from the vantage point of labour law scholarship. The uneven protection offered by labour and social protection frameworks has long been highlighted in the literatures on non-standard work and precariousness. This literature has unfurled, at least in part, as 'gap analyses' that have mapped uneven coverage, exiled workers, and lost protections in higher-income countries.[32] The informality literature, however, has

[28] Claire La Hovary, 'The Informal Economy and the ILO: A Legal Perspective' (2014) 4 *International Journal of Comparative Labour Law and Industrial Relations* 391.

[29] ibid.

[30] Visser, 'A Floor to Exploitation?', above n 3 at 5, citing Jamie Peck and Nik Theodore, 'Politicizing Contingent Work: Countering Neoliberal Labour-Market Regulation … From the Bottom Up?' (2012) 111(4) *South Atlantic Quarterly* 741.

[31] Williams et al have applied this model to an investigation of South-East European countries by drawing on data from a 2007 Eurobarometer survey: Colin C Williams, Abbi Kedir, Sara Nadin and Tim Vorley, 'Evaluating the Extent and Nature of the Informalization of Employment Relations in South-East Europe' (2013) 19(2) *European Journal of Industrial Relations* 91. This framework, however, is centred primarily on the extent of firm declaration to regulatory authorities, therefore capturing primarily the overlap of formality and informality in which workers are paid two distinct wages (the officially declared wage and an undeclared counterpart) (at 94).

[32] eg Sandra Fredman, 'Labour Law in Flux: The Changing Composition of the Workforce' (1997) 26(4) *Industrial Law Journal* 337; Leah Vosko (ed), *Precarious Employment: Understanding Labour*

a particular vigour in unveiling the complex dependencies between the realms of formality and informality, their dynamic interaction, and the repercussions for legal standards and worker protection across the economy as a whole.[33] Visser's recent analysis is particularly adept:

> [T]hese "economies" are not distinct separate spheres of economic activity. Rather, they are engaged in a complex dialectical relationship through which a structural dependency is continuously constructed and reinforced by labour and material supply chains facilitated under policy and market practices that promote deregulation in the formal economy. The formation of these supply chains, in turn, induce the expansion of the informal economy which manifests in increased levels of employment "informality" or "precarity" in the formal labour market and results in the embedding of informal labour markets and economic activity within the formal economy.[34]

B. Legal Regulation as Mediating the Informality Boundary

Relatedly, as Sassen noted comparatively early in the debates, 'the informal economy can only be understood in its relation to the formal economy'.[35] Informality can be identified, that is, only because there exists an institutional framework for economic activity through which the state regulates working relations.[36] Sassen's observation serves, first, further to reinforce that informal economies are not distinct economic spheres: they are 'deeply embedded within the formal economy and are socially and legally regulated by a battery of social institutions'.[37] Second, this analysis emphasises that it is legal regulation, including labour law frameworks, that mediate the ragged boundary between the informal and formal dimensions of working relationships.

The latter insight is particularly valuable for conceptualising the mechanisms of informalisation that channel workers from formality to informality, which need to be identified in detail and with precision. Lacunae or deficiencies in regulatory regimes and institutions shape the formality/informality boundary. Legislation permits, facilitates, or neglects paths to worker protection, and formal employers devise strategies that respond to these regulatory prompts. The scholarship points in particular to externalisation strategies – in their myriad forms – as a

Market Insecurity in Canada (Montreal, McGill-Queen's University Press, 2000); Judy Fudge and Rosemary Owens (eds), *Precarious Work, Women and the New Economy: The Challenge to Legal Norms* (Oxford, Hart Publishing, 2006); Deirdre McCann, *Regulating Flexible Work* (Oxford, Oxford University Press, 2008); Vosko, *Managing the Margins: Gender, Citizenship and the International Regulation of Precarious Employment* (Oxford, Oxford University Press, 2010).

[33] Visser, 'A Floor to Exploitation', above n 3.

[34] ibid, 4.

[35] Saskia Sassen, 'Informalization in Advanced Market Economies', Issues in Development Discussion Paper 20, ILO 1999, 2.

[36] ibid.

[37] Visser (n 3) 4.

central conduit to informalisation: hiring on a casual basis, for example, outsourcing or sub-contracting to small firms or home-based workers, securing labour through temporary agency or labour-hire arrangements, or tolerating or facilitating false self-employment.[38] Relatedly, the scope of coverage of protective labour legislation, and in particular fealty to traditional conceptions of the employment relationship, deprive workers of legal recognition or protection where the employment relationship is either disguised or an ill-fit with conventional models.[39] Other conduits include the failure of legislative frameworks adequately to incorporate dispersion of the responsibilities of employment among multiple entities, the punitive intersection of regulatory fields, notably labour and immigration laws,[40] and ineffective enforcement regimes.[41]

The guiding contemporary notion of informality, then, loops together the regulatory dimensions of precariousness, in particular where it manifests in non-standard work, deficiencies in the implementation and enforcement of labour laws, and the intersection of regulatory regimes. The research on informality is therefore paralleling advances in the labour regulation literatures in producing a holistic picture of labour law's uncertain or deficient outcomes. Most notably, the notion of 'regulatory indeterminacy'[42] is playing a parallel role, including as it has been elaborated to identify and to link key drivers of the indeterminate protective impacts of labour regulation, identified as fragmentation, institutional interactions, and enforcement efficacy.[43] This complexity renders the concept of informality inevitably challenging to operationalise for statistical measurement and comparison, as Deakin et al argue in this volume.[44] Yet the notion is nonetheless valuable at the conceptual and policy levels, to clarify the regulatory conduits to informality and to fashion suitably expansive and coherent policy responses.

Towards such policy interventions, these insights are revealing how legal frameworks shape the incidence and texture of informality. Yet they also suggest

[38] M Vanamala, 'Informalisation and Feminisation of a Formal Sector Industry: A Case Study' (2001) 36(2) *Economic and Political Weekly* 2378–83 and 2385–89; Standing, *Global Feminisation*, above n 19; Theron, 'Informalisation from Above', above n 22; Peck and Theodore, 'Politicizing Contingent Work', above n 30; Webster et al, 'Informalization and Decent Work', above n 24.

[39] Chen, 'Rethinking the Informal Economy', above note 21 at 8.

[40] Peck and Theodore, 'Politicizing Contingent Work', above n 30 at 753.

[41] See eg Leah F Vosko, John Grundy and Mark P Thomas, 'Challenging New Governance: Evaluating New Approaches to Employment Standards Enforcement in Common Law Jurisdictions' (2016) 37(2) *Economic and Industrial Democracy* 373.

[42] Simon Deakin and Prabirjit Sarkar, 'Assessing the Long-Run Economic Impact of Labour Law Systems: A Theoretical Reappraisal and Analysis of New Time Series Data' (2008) *Industrial Relations Journal* 453.

[43] Sangheon Lee and Deirdre McCann, 'Regulatory Indeterminacy and Protection in Contemporary Labour Markets: Innovation in Research and Policy' in Deirdre McCann, Sangheon Lee, Patrick Belser, Colin Fenwick, John Howe and Malte Luebker (eds), *Creative Labour Regulation: Indeterminacy and Protection in an Uncertain World* (Geneva, ILO/Palgrave, 2014) 3.

[44] Simon Deakin, Shelley Marshall, and Sanjay Pinto, 'Labour Laws, Informality, and Development: Comparing India and China', this volume.

that legal regimes can be designed to curb or to alleviate the detrimental outcomes that are associated with informal work. It is evident, for example, that countries at similar income levels exhibit significant variations in the incidence of informality.[45] These varying outcomes suggest the need for an attentiveness to the policy mix, including to the role of the state in generating and preventing informalisation. In this regard, informalisation can be conceived of as a process, often in flux, and channelled through diverse conduits. This process is not inevitable, but can be shaped, tempered, or reversed by regulatory intervention. It is crucial, then, to track the regulatory and institutional activity that engineers informalisation, and to craft policy measures that adequately respond. It is with this objective in mind that the key international regulatory policy responses – by the World Bank and ILO – are evaluated in the following section.

IV. Informalisation in International Regulatory Policy

Given the evolving conceptions of informality traced in the previous section, it is worth investigating how the regulatory supports for informalisation are reflected in key policy discourses. To that end, this section examines the most significant renditions of informalisation that are conveyed in international policy discourses. In this regard, the international is understood as a crucial site in which informality is conceptualised and the mechanisms to tackle it are constructed. The regulatory policy sites under consideration are the pivotal international spheres of the World Bank and the ILO. This section builds on earlier work that has argued that the relationship between these institutions should be understood as a dynamic process of institutional convergence and divergence that is generating a conversation about the objectives, format and tenor of labour market regulation.[46] The objective is to trace evolving notions of informalisation within broader narratives of informality; to investigate how these discourses capture and convey the nature and dynamics of informalisation; and in particular to highlight how each conveys the role of legal regulation. The section is based on a review of the recent outputs of each of these transnational actors, with a particular focus on the evolving influence of the 'plateau model' of labour regulation developed

[45] Sangheon Lee and Deirdre McCann, 'Measuring Labour Market Institutions: Conceptual and Methodological Questions on "Working Hours Rigidity"' in Janine Berg and David Kucera (eds), *In Defence of Labour Market Institutions: Cultivating Justice in the Developing World* (Geneva, ILO and Palgrave Macmillan, 2008).

[46] Deirdre McCann, 'Labour Law on the Plateau: Towards Regulatory Policy for Endogenous Norms' in Alan Bogg, Anne Davies, and Jeremias Prassl (eds), *The Autonomy of Labour Law* (Oxford, Hart Publishing, 2015).

in the World Bank's *World Development 2013*, in particular in the Bank's *Doing Business* project, and on ILO Recommendation No 204 and the formalisation strategy that it embodies.

A. Informalisation on the Regulatory Plateau: The World Bank

Until recently, World Bank discourses on labour regulation strictly adhered to a dualist model of formal and informal work. The Bank's regulatory policy has in recent decades primarily been associated with the *Doing Business* initiative – a set of indicators that measure and compare various elements of 'business regulation' in 190 countries, the results of which have been disseminated through a series of annual reports since 2003.[47] The project engages with labour regulation through a Labour Regulation Index – previously the Employing Workers Index – which measures and compares select labour protections (eg hiring, working hours, redundancy). Conventionally, as has been elaborated elsewhere, the policy discourse associated with *Doing Business* has conveyed labour regulation to float adrift from a discrete informal economy.[48] A pessimistic account of labour law's promise relayed a clear-cut dichotomy between 'formal' and 'informal' economies.[49] One consequence was the characterisation of rigid labour regulation as driving workers into the informal economy; another, the assumption that labour standards are unknown or entirely irrelevant to informal workers.[50] Informalisation within formal settings was therefore largely overlooked: an 'informal sector' was assumed and the informal workforce identified with that domain.

The World Bank's imagery of labour regulation has been refined since the limitations of the *Doing Business* initiative prompted reform of the project.[51] With the Employing Workers Index (EWI) widely discredited for its conceptual and methodological limitations, the Bank showcased a new approach. A 'plateau' imagery was pioneered in the 2013 *World Development Report* (*WDR2013*).[52] The

[47] World Bank, *Doing Business 2004: Understanding Regulations* (Washington DC, World Bank, 2003).

[48] Janine Berg and Sandrine Cazes, 'Policymaking Gone Awry: The Labor Market Regulations of the Doing Business Indicators' (2008) 29(4) *Comparative Labor Law & Policy Journal* 349–81; Sangheon Lee and Deirdre McCann, 'The Impact of Labour Regulations: Measuring the Effectiveness of Legal Norms in a Developing Country' in Lee and McCann (eds), *Regulating for Decent Work: New Directions in Labour Market Regulation* (Geneva, Palgrave Macmillan/International Labour Office, 2011); McCann 'Labour Law on the Plateau', above n 46.

[49] See, eg, World Bank, *Doing Business 2006* (Washington, DC, World Bank, 2005); see further Lee and McCann, 'The Impact of Labour Regulations', above n 48.

[50] World Bank, above n 49.

[51] See McCann, 'Labour Law on the Plateau', above n 46.

[52] World Bank, *World Development Report 2013: Jobs* (Washington DC, World Bank, 2012).

Report identified twin risks – that labour regulations may be either too rigid or too lax – and contended that both can have detrimental effects.[53] An appropriate level of labour regulation is, instead, situated on a 'plateau' between excessive and lax labour regulation: '[l]abour policies that are not to undermine job creation, while maximizing development payoffs from jobs, must remain on this plateau.' The plateau model was an important reset of the Bank's frequently hostile engagement with labour regulation.[54] *WDR2013* acknowledged research findings that labour laws do not inhibit job creation, entertained alternative explanations for poor employment outcomes, and acknowledged the benefits of legal regulation, including social objectives such as improved living standards and social cohesion.[55] The outcry about the *Doing Business* methodology also prompted the Bank to rebrand the EWI as the Labour Regulation Index (LRI) and to incorporate questions on protective regulations ('job quality'): on equal remuneration for work of equal value, measures to combat gender discrimination in hiring, maternity leave, paid sick leave, and unemployment protection.[56] Insofar as 'balance' is a proxy for effective regulation, the quest for the regulatory plateau is welcome and has potential to illuminate efforts to conceptualise the regulatory dimensions of informalisation. In this respect, the Bank's policy discourse parallels a central objective of the recent labour regulation literature: properly to conceptualise and to gauge the effectiveness of regulatory frameworks, including their role in generating and sustaining informality.[57] Yet the plateau model has not been absorbed uniformly across the Bank's labour regulation policy discourses.

In the *Doing Business* project, at the rhetorical level the language of 'balance' is sustained: '[t]he challenge in developing labour policies is to avoid the extremes of over and under-regulation by reaching a balance between worker protection and flexibility.'[58] An examination of the post-*WDR2013* era evolution of this project, however, shows its fidelity to the plateau model to be uneven and poorly absorbed into the LRI methodology, including in relation to informality. Most fundamentally, there is no recognition that informality spans a continuum: the rendition of dichotomous informality and formality remains strikingly intact.[59] A central role

[53] ibid, p 258.

[54] See further McCann, 'Labour Law on the Plateau', above n 46.

[55] World Bank, *World Development Report 2013*, above n 52 at 22.

[56] World Bank, *Doing Business 2016* (Washington DC, World Bank, 2015), 159–60, *Doing Business 2017* (Washington DC, World Bank 2016), 161–62. *Doing Business 2016* included four questions that are not present in the 2017 report, on the availability of on-the-job training; whether an employee can create or join a union; the availability of administrative or judicial relief where there has been infringement of employees' rights; and the availability of a labour inspection system: *Doing Business 2016*, at 160.

[57] eg Sangheon Lee and Deirdre McCann, 'New Directions in Labour Regulation Research,' in Lee and McCann, *Regulating for Decent Work: New Directions in Labour Market Regulation* (Geneva, Palgrave Macmillan/ILO, 2011); McCann and Fudge, 'Strategic Regulation', above n 10.

[58] World Bank, *Doing Business 2017*, above note 56 at 87.

[59] See the discussion of employment protection legislation on p 87, ibid, referring to 'dual labour markets, whereby a labour force becomes segmented into formal versus informal sector workers (in developing economies)'.

for regulation in generating informality, further, is present, but it is 'rigid' labour regulation that continues to be identified as the culprit. Employment protection laws in particular are conveyed almost exclusively as drivers of labour market segmentation, relying on a small number of studies.[60]

On the methodological level, the LRI is not attuned to capturing either the dynamics of informalisation or the legal mechanisms that are being tested to reorient these processes. Legal frameworks in fields other than labour law and social protection, are beyond the Index's scope. It cannot, therefore, capture the diversity of legal regimes that regulate labour markets. Inevitably missing, in particular, is the harsh logic of the immigration frameworks that channel migrant workers into informal work.[61] Even within the conventional parameters of labour law, however, the *Doing Business* methodology does not capture the regulatory supports of informalisation. The 2017 Report reverts to the evaluation of national labour regulation frameworks, following a post-reform hiatus in which the LRI findings were relayed without comment.[62] The Report's – laudable – conclusion is that regulation should be tailored to national circumstances and designed in collaboration with the social partners.[63] The return to an evaluative strategy, however, purports to demonstrate the association of labour regulation with informal employment and unregistered firms[64] (including through a reversion to the original nomenclature of a 'rigidity of employment regulation' index).[65] This outcome is realised through a scoring system that has presumably been in abeyance since the reform of *Doing Business*, although it is not elaborated in detail in the Report.

Yet despite the tenor of these conclusions, the LRI and the associated literature miss much of how regulation sustains informality, and, most pertinently for present purposes, channels informalisation. Elements can be singled out that are both central to the deficiencies of this project and of broader significance for the exploration of the regulatory dimensions of informalisation in international labour policy. First, the LRI is orientated towards substantive standards – hours limits, rest periods, annual leave, redundancy protections, equal pay, maternity leave etc.[66]

[60] ibid, citing Simeon Djankov and Rita Ramalho, 'Employment Laws in Developing Countries,' Centre for Economic Policy Research (CEPR) Discussion Paper No DP7097, December 2008; Siddharth Sharma, 'Entry Regulation, Labor Laws and Informality', Working Paper 48927, World Bank, 2009; Norman V Loayza, Ana Maria Oviedo and Luis Serven, 'The Impact of Regulation on Growth and Informality – Cross-Country Evidence,' Policy Research Working Paper, WPS 3623, World Bank, 2005.

[61] eg Working Lives Research Institute, 'Study on Precarious Work and Social Rights. Study carried out for the European Commission,' VT/2010/084 (Working Lives Research Institute, London Metropolitan University, 2012).

[62] World Bank, *Doing Business 2017*, above n 56, Annex: Labour Market Regulation, pp 87–95.

[63] ibid, 87.

[64] ibid, Figures 10.1, 10.2, pp 88–89.

[65] Defined as the average of four sub-indices: hiring; working hours; redundancy rules; and cost. See ibid, eg Figure 10.1, p 88.

[66] The key exception is in the treatment of redundancy, which captures procedural requirements, but not exclusions from protection; *Doing Business 2016*, above n 56 at 161.

The Index therefore misses central features of labour regulation frameworks, highlighted in section III.B, that are associated with informalisation. These tend to be found in the minutiae of labour law texts, rather than in their flagship protections. The LRI does not, for example, capture exclusions from protection, explicit or implicit. Nor does it, centrally, capture the personal scope of legal measures, typically tied to the presence of a judicially endorsed 'contract of employment' and therefore elusive for many workers.[67]

Second, and linked to the project's tilt towards the substantive, *Doing Business* is unable to capture the crucial role of non-standard work regulation in propelling workers towards the informality continuum. In this regard, the Bank's thin rendition of informality hosts a supplementary dichotomy: between formal and informal workers in developing countries and 'permanent' and 'contingent' workers in high-income economies.[68] This account inevitably misses the parallel processes of informalisation in lower- and higher-income countries, and the degree to which informality manifests as non-standard work in both.

This deficiency crystallises in *Doing Business*'s treatment of fixed-term contracts, the only non-standard work-form that is tracked by the LRI. The hiring sub-index captures (1) the extent to which employers can hire workers on a fixed-term basis to perform permanent tasks, and (2) the maximum duration of fixed-term contracts (including renewals).[69] The Index is again taken to capture rigidity; the merits of widespread fixed-term contracting are assumed.[70] The 2017 *Report* asserts the potential of fixed-term contracts to enhance the employability of labour market entrants, particularly young workers, through providing experience and access to professional networks.[71] There is little effort to convey the downside of short-term work,[72] or to quantify or compare the protections increasingly available to fixed-term workers in countries across the world: mandated maximum durations/renewals, for example, equal treatment, or conversion rights to open-ended contracts.

Doing Business also continues to miss the actual strength of labour regulation, thus remaining open to the criticisms that have endured from the outset of the project about the Index's failure to accommodate the observance of legal standards.[73] In particular, the LRI does not capture enforcement – an enduring omission, long noted,[74] central to the *Doing Business* reforms and touching on

[67] That the worker subject to legal rules is an employee is a feature of the project's 'assumptions about the worker', *Doing Business 2017*, above n 56 at 160.

[68] ibid, 87.

[69] ibid, 161.

[70] ibid, 88.

[71] ibid, 88–89, citing OECD *Employment Outlook 2014* (Paris, OECD, 2014).

[72] *cf* Arvo Kuddo, David Robalino and Michael Weber, *Balancing Regulations to Promote Jobs: From Employment Contracts to Unemployment Benefits* (Washington, DC, World Bank, 2015), 2–3.

[73] Lee and McCann, 'Measuring Labour Market Institutions', above n 45.

[74] ibid.

key elements of informality. Questions, further, that might offer some insight into informality channels were dropped in the 2017 report, on the availability of administrative/judicial relief where employees' rights have been infringed and the presence of a labour inspection system.[75] As a result, the Index risks inaccurate conclusions about the impacts of labour laws, including on informal work.

While the extensive and punctual annual outputs of the *Doing Business* project tend to overshadow alternative narratives of labour regulation that emanate from the Bank, these periodically surface. The key comparator is *WDR2013* and the literature that takes it as a point of departure. One is the 2015 report on *Balancing Regulations to Promote Jobs* ('the *Balancing* report'), which emanates from the Bank's Social Protection, Labor and Jobs realm and was produced in consultation with the ILO, International Trade Union Confederation and International Organization of Employers.[76] The analyses that characterise this line of the Bank's work have a more refined and expansive grasp of the regulatory dynamics of informalisation. *WDR2013*, for example, catches the *de jure* routes to informality, listing the features of legal frameworks that preclude protected status: exceptions – of domestic workers, small enterprises, export zones; the complexities of regulating multilateral working relationships; and limited access to adjudication mechanisms.[77] The *Balancing* report also recognises the significance of non-standard work regulation, capturing key regulatory conduits and certain of the measures that are being trialled to reorder them.[78] The report advocates protective regulatory frameworks for non-standard workers:[79] legislation that entitles temporary and part-time workers to protections equivalent to full-time workers,[80] restrictions on the use of fixed-term contracts (citing ILO Convention No 166 on preventing abusive recourse to fixed-term work),[81] legislation to combat disguised employment,[82] and requirements that employees receive written employment contracts.[83]

[75] Both were included in *Doing Business 2016*; above n 56.

[76] Kuddo et al, above n 72.

[77] World Bank, *World Development Report 2013*, above n 52, 156.

[78] Kuddo et al, above n 72, ch 1. *WDR2013* was weaker on non-standard work, offering few suggestions, for example, on the regulation of multipartite relationships; see McCann, 'Labour Regulation on the Plateau', above n 46.

[79] Kuddo et al, above n 46, at 4, citing ILO Employment Relationship Recommendation, 2006 (No 198).

[80] ibid.

[81] The illustrations are limiting recourse to a specified period to cases in which, owing to nature of work or circumstances under which it is to be effected, or the interests of worker, the employment relationship cannot be of indeterminate duration; deeming contracts for a specified period to be contracts of employment of indeterminate duration; deeming contracts for a specified period that are renewed on one or more occasions to be contracts of employment (ibid).

[82] Although with a curious definition that is confined to trilateral relationships; ibid, note 23.

[83] ibid.

B. The Formalisation Paradigm: The ILO

ILO policy discourses on the informal economy have been attuned to the presence of informality in formal enterprises since the language of the 'informal sector' was replaced by the 'informal economy' at the turn of the century.[84] As discussed in section III, a job-centred definition of informality was enshrined in the ILO's 2002 *Resolution concerning decent work and the informal economy* and since incorporated into the International Conference of Labour Statisticians (ICLS) 2003 *Guidelines concerning a statistical definition of informal employment*[85] and, ultimately, the Transition from the Informal to the Formal Economy Recommendation 2015 (No 204). This job-centred model, capturing economic activities that are insufficiently covered by formal arrangements in law or practice,[86] always implicitly extended to formal-site informality, made explicit in the Recommendation's coverage of 'employees holding informal jobs in or for formal enterprises'.[87]

Evaluating the ILO instruments by drawing on the insights on the regulatory dimension of informality elaborated in section III confirms their value in transmitting sophisticated conceptions of informality to the international labour policy arena. The ILO policy discourses embody the two insights highlighted in section III. First, they are alive to the continuum between the formal and the informal. Most strikingly, in the 2002 *Resolution* even the more expansive job-centred concept of the informal economy is conveyed as tending 'to downplay the linkages, grey areas and interdependencies between formal and informal activities'.[88] Second, legal frameworks are recognised to govern the uneven boundary between formal and informal work, emphasising the crucial role of domestic legal regimes.[89]

The ILO policy discourses are explicit in recognising informality as a problem of governance:

> Informality is principally a governance issue. The growth of the informal economy can often be traced to inappropriate, ineffective, misguided or badly implemented macroeconomic and social policies, often developed without tripartite consultation; the lack of conducive legal and institutional frameworks; and the lack of good governance for proper and effective implementation of policies and laws.[90]

[84] Above, section III.

[85] ICLS 2003 (n 18).

[86] Transition from the Informal to the Formal Economy Recommendation 2015 (No 204), para 2(a).

[87] ibid, para 4(c) (also in the 2003 *Guidelines*, above n 16), para 5(i)).

[88] ILO, *Resolution concerning Decent Work and the Informal Economy*, above n 17, para 3.

[89] '[S]ince a defining characteristic of workers and enterprises in the informal economy is that they often are not recognised, regulated or protected by law, the legal and institutional frameworks of a country are key': ibid, para 16.

[90] The 2015 Recommendation is less assertive, noting informality 'has multiple causes, including governance and structural issues' (Preamble).

The ILO instruments also capture the diversity of the modes and forms of regulatory escape that are generated at this boundary. The 2003 *Guidelines* are most elaborate, incorporating a list that includes non-declaration of jobs or employees, casual and temporary employment, working hours or wages below legal thresholds, work at home or beyond the premises of the employer, and jobs to which labour laws 'are not applied, not enforced, or not complied with for any other reason'.[91] The Recommendation's scope provisions add explicit references to both individuals in subcontracting and supply chains[92] and workers in 'unrecognized or unregulated' employment relationships.[93] The 2002 Resolution, most expansively, alludes to 'grey areas' in which the economic activity involves characteristics of both the formal and informal economy, such as workers in formal enterprises whose wages and working conditions are typical of those in informal work.[94]

Processes of informalisation, however, were not central to the 2002 *Resolution*. Recommendation No 204 is therefore pioneering in including preventing the informalisation of formal economy jobs among its key objectives.[95] Embracing the prevention of informalisation as an integral element of the formalisation project is a key contribution of the Recommendation that should not be understated. The preventive objective strengthens research and policy conceptualisations of the nature and dynamics of informality and is available to shape global renditions of formalisation. Given its far-reaching potential, it is not surprising that the inclusion of this objective in the Recommendation was contested. The preparatory documents reveal that the objective was incorporated through an amendment to the International Labour Office proposed Conclusions that were deliberated upon by the Committee on Transitioning from the Informal Economy at its first discussion in 2014. Proposed by the Worker Vice-Chairperson, the amendment was opposed by the Employer counterpart on the grounds that the existing text was sufficient,[96] highlighting that the stance of the international employer lobby would have precluded informalisation as an element of domestic formalisation policies.[97]

[91] ICLS (n 18), para 3(5).

[92] Recommendation No 204, above n 86, para 4(c).

[93] ibid, para 4(d).

[94] ILO *Resolution concerning Decent Work and the Informal Economy*, above n 17, para 5.

[95] This aim is enshrined among a trilogy of key objectives in para 1(c), 'Objectives and Scope', together with facilitating the transition of workers and economic units from the informal to the formal economy 'while respecting workers' fundamental rights and ensuring opportunities for income security, livelihoods and entrepreneurship' (1 (a)); and promoting enterprises and decent jobs in the formal economy and the coherence of macroeconomic, employment, and social policies (1(b)).

[96] It was also opposed by the Africa Group of governments, see *Report of the Committee on the Transition from the Informal to the Formal Economy: summary of proceedings* (International Labour Conference, 103rd Session, Geneva, May–June 2014), available at https://www.ilo.org/wcmsp5/groups/public/---ed_norm/---relconf/documents/meetingdocument/wcms_246193.pdf, paras 734–41, and below.

[97] The International Organization for Employers (IOE) had earlier objected to the inclusion of the 'informal in the formal' in the standard-setting exercise. See La Hovary, 'The Informal Economy and the ILO', above n 28 at 407–08, citing IOE *Proposed New ILO Standard(s) – Informal Economy* (Geneva, IOE, 2013), 6.

The Recommendation is also robust on the breadth and mix of the policy response to informality, including to informalisation. In this regard, labour regulation can only be an element in a range of policy arenas that must be engaged to improve or discourage informal working relations. The Recommendation stresses the need for coherence and coordination across a wide range of policy fora including macroeconomic, employment, and social protection policies.[98] Related ILO literature has also captured the role of formalisation strategies and legal regulation in a crafted policy mix that embraces macro-economic, monetary, financial sector, exchange rate, and public investment policies and favours job creation in the formal economy, structural shifts to higher productivity activities, and labour markets polices and institutions that enable transitions to formality.[99]

Labour regulation initiatives that have the potential to curb informalisation are included in the Recommendation. These respond to the legislative mechanisms and employer strategies that generate and sustain pockets of informality. Governments, first, are called upon to ensure that workers are covered by labour laws. The Recommendation prompts ILO members to adopt, review, and enforce legal measures to ensure appropriate coverage and protection of all workers and economic units.[100] Second, effective enforcement – part-constitutive of the parameters of informality in the job-centred model – is also extensively treated. States are encouraged to address avoidance of labour laws,[101] to ensure recognition and enforcement of employment relationships,[102] to strengthen inspection,[103] to provide information and assistance on legal compliance,[104] and to establish efficient and accessible complaint procedures.[105] The Recommendation, third, calls for states to realise the fundamental principles and rights[106] and ensure health and safety protections in informal work,[107] progressively extend social security, maternity protection, decent working conditions and a minimum wage to informal workers,[108] and encourage the provision of affordable childcare and other care services.[109] These recommendations are relevant to tackling

[98] paras 1, 7(d). It also calls for an 'integrated policy framework … included in national development strategies … as well as in poverty reduction strategies and budgets', para 10.

[99] eg ILO 'Informality and the Quality of Employment in G20 Countries,' Report prepared for the G20 Labour and Employment Ministerial Meeting, Melbourne, Australia, 10–11 September 2014, available at https://www.ilo.org/wcmsp5/groups/public/---dgreports/---dcomm/---publ/documents/publication/wcms_305425.pdf, 8–9.

[100] Recommendation No 204, above n 86, para 9. As part of ensuring compliance with national laws and regulations, states are also encouraged to ensure the recognition and enforcement of employment relationships, para 26.

[101] ibid, para 22. The Recommendation also highlights a need to prevent and sanction deliberate avoidance of, or exit from, the formal economy to evade taxation and labour laws, para 7(l).

[102] ibid, para 26.

[103] ibid, para 27.

[104] ibid, paras 28.

[105] ibid, para 29.

[106] ibid, para 16.

[107] ibid, para 17.

[108] ibid, para 18.

[109] ibid, para 21.

informalisation, since parity of entitlements would curb the incentives associated with resorting to precarious forms of work.

The Recommendation, further, does not betray the hesitancy about the international labour standards that has become characteristic of the ILO's flagship policy discourses during the last decade. Recommendation No 204 has a fairly robust embrace of the ILO standards, requesting Member States to take into account a range of instruments that are listed in an Annex.[110] Particularly useful, in this regard, is the presence of 'non-standard work' standards: the Private Employment Agencies Convention, 1997 (No 181), which requires a degree of protection – albeit unambitious – for temporary agency workers;[111] the Employment Relationship Recommendation (2006) No 198 – again flawed, but nonetheless a source of some guidance on the regulatory dimension of the formalisation project;[112] and the Home Work Convention, 1996 (No 177) and Domestic Workers standards,[113] both essential references for formalisation policies that target crucial harbours of protective frailty in the global economy.[114]

The Recommendation is not equally convincing, however, on what can be achieved by using such legal frameworks and techniques to combat informalisation. While preventing the unravelling of formal jobs is among the Recommendation's objectives, the mechanisms that might stem the slide into informality are sparsely elaborated. Yet the regulatory options are numerous, diverse, and available for testing at local levels:[115] equal treatment mandates, specific allocation of legal obligations in multilateral relationships, explicit distribution of responsibilities across value chains, restricting outsourcing or mandating protections for the outsourced workforce, working time techniques that limit fragmentation or that promote certainty in scheduling and wages, and specific protections for the range of forms of temporary, casual or multilateral work.

To some degree, this limitation reflects that the Recommendation references the non-standard work standards without fully absorbing the regulatory strategies that these instruments demand. The equal treatment model is a case in point. It has

[110] para 7(g). These standards do not include the Hours of Work Conventions.

[111] Convention No 181 primarily preserves the rights to freedom of association and to bargain collectively (Art 4), prohibits discrimination (Art 5(1)), and requires signatories to provide 'adequate protection' in relation to a list of entitlements (Art 11).

[112] The most convincing aspect of the Recommendation is the suggestion that governments mandate a legal presumption that an employment relationship exists where one or more indicators is present, para 11(b).

[113] Domestic Workers Convention, 2011 (No 189) and Recommendation (No 201). Both home work and domestic work are classified as 'specific categories of workers' in the Annex to Recommendation No 204. On the potential for legal frameworks on domestic work to offer lessons for labour-protective formalisation strategies, see Deirdre McCann and Jillian Murray, 'Prompting Formalisation Through Labour Market Regulation: A "Framed Flexibility" Model for Domestic Work' (2014) 43(3) *Industrial Law Journal* 319.

[114] McCann and Murray, ibid.

[115] On testing as a strategy, see Lee and McCann, 'New Directions in Labour Regulation Research', above n 57.

been observed that the Recommendation encourages the progressive extension of decent working conditions to informal economy workers.[116] Yet one obvious route to this goal is an equality mandate that demands parity of treatment between non-standard and standard workers. One of the key models developed to ensure that non-standard working relationships – part-time, fixed-term, temporary agency – match the quality of standard-form jobs, the equality model, is being tested in legal frameworks across the world.[117] This approach, further, is particularly apt for the dual-track complexion of formal-site informality, in which the differential treatment is accented by proximity. As the international spearhead of the equal treatment model,[118] the Home Work Convention could have been drawn on to support a more expansive endorsement of the equal treatment model. This opportunity was neglected, however. Nor is the Part-Time Work Convention 1994 (No 175) included in the Recommendation's Annex, although it elevated the equality approach to an economy-wide model and targets a core mode of fragmentation, through shortened hours.[119]

In this regard and more broadly, Recommendation No 204 parallels the World Bank literature by assuming the centrality of substantive protections. This point is further illustrated by section IV of the Recommendation (*Employment Policies*), which calls for measures to help low-income households to escape poverty, and includes wages policies such as the minimum wage.[120] Wages policies, however, cannot adequately respond to the regulatory conduits to informalisation; in this case, legal structures that facilitate, or do not impede, casualisation. Fragmented work-forms, captured in equally splintered terminology (casual work, zero hours contracts, day labour etc), are characterised by the absence of guaranteed hours and have harsh repercussions for the level and predictability of incomes. Yet these outcomes cannot be tempered by conventional wage policies.[121] Necessary instead are novel – and at present only nascent – mechanisms designed specifically to regulate casual work. Other elements of the Recommendation are an equally poor match for the dynamics of informalisation. Section V (*Rights and Social Protection*) calls for measures to prevent avoidance of labour, tax, and social security laws. Yet the proposed strategies are exclusively configured

[116] para 18.

[117] On the UK, for example, see McCann *Regulating Flexible Work*, above n 32, Lisa Rodgers, *Labour Law, Vulnerability and the Regulation of Precarious Work* (Cheltenham, Edward Elgar, 2016); on Korea, see JooHee Lee, 'More Protection, Still Gendered: The Effects of Non-standard Employment Protection Acts on South Korean Women Workers' (2017) 47(1) *Journal of Contemporary Asia* 46.

[118] Art 4.

[119] This omission may indicate a broader oversight, which fails to associate casualisation with working time arrangements rather than exclusively with contractual status; see further Deirdre McCann, 'New Frontiers of Regulation: Domestic Work, Working Conditions, and the Holistic Assessment of Nonstandard Work Norms' (2012) 34(1) *Comparative Labour Law and Policy Journal* 167; McCann and Murray, 'Prompting Formalisation', above n 113: McCann, 'Travel Time as Working Time: Tyco, the Unitary Model, and the Route to Casualization' (2016) 45(2) *Industrial Law Journal* 244.

[120] para 15(d), mentioning also social protection schemes and public employment programmes.

[121] These policies are recommended in para 15(d).

towards smoothing the transition from informal to formal.[122] The level of detail, most strikingly, on the routes to formalisation for micro and small economic units,[123] while immensely helpful, is not matched by any comparable blueprint on preventing informalisation.

These limitations are significant, not only because they weaken Recommendation No 204, but because they expose the centre of gravity of the international formalisation project. The project is tethered, that is, to a preoccupation with informal firms and settings. Informalisation is an adjunct. This outcome can be read as path dependence associated with the origins of the informality project, which also accounts for the late, and contested, entry of the preventive objective into the Recommendation. The assumed direction of travel is perhaps most stark in the objection of the Africa group of governments to the inclusion of the preventive objective, that 'the subject of the [Recommendation is] the transition from the informal to the formal economy, not the other way around'.[124] This objection crystallises an assumption about the orientation of the formalisation project, both within key ILO policy-making bodies and across the international and national policy realms. This focus neglects the expansive imagery of informality, its emergence, and its potential solutions of the kind pursued in this volume. It exposes a broader threat to the rapidly evolving formalisation project that is of particular risk to its legal architecture and impedes a vigorous role for this policy realm in combatting the informalisation of formal jobs. Emphasising cure over prevention, the outcome is that the key international policy discourse on informality does not grasp the symbiotic relationship between formalisation and prevention of informalisation. It therefore does not hold these targets in the sensitive balance that is needed to underpin sophisticated policy making and effectively to allocate resources between the twin objectives.

V. Conclusions: Towards a Refined Conception of Informalisation in Global Regulatory Policy

This chapter has investigated the regulatory dimension of informality in global policy discourses with a focus on informalisation. It therefore responds to the relative neglect of informalisation within the policy debates on informal work. The chapter has observed that labour regulation literatures are devising refined conceptions of informality, which have a firmer grasp of the role of legal regulation in generating, shaping and sustaining informal work. Particularly crucial contributions from this literature were identified: the linked insights that informality is a

[122] para 22.
[123] para 25.
[124] See *Report of the Committee on the Transition from the Informal to the Formal Economy* (n 96), at paras 734–741.

continuum and that legal regulation governs a shifting boundary between formal and informal work. These notions are revealing when deployed to interrogate policy discourses. In this chapter, they have been drawn on to elaborate and to assess a recent turn in international labour policy towards the regulatory dimensions of informality. To this end, the chapter has examined policy discourses from the two most significant sites of global labour regulation policy, the World Bank and the ILO.

This analysis has revealed an unsurprising divergence in the policy narratives that emanate from the World Bank and the ILO, accompanied by some revealing convergences. World Bank policy streams have unevenly absorbed the plateau model that was unveiled in the 2013 *World Development Report*, thereby sustaining a slippery grasp of informality that eschews the continuum model and, in the recent literature, has reverted to identifying 'rigid' protective regulation as the cause of informality. An examination of the Bank's flagship *Doing Business* project has found these notions to be conveyed through a focus on substantive standards, a lack of attention to the regulatory conduits to informalisation, and an enduring neglect of labour regulation's de facto influence on working relations, including the efficacy of state enforcement. Alternative narratives within the Bank are both less prominent and more promising, including in that they highlight legal measures that have been engineered to improve the treatment of workers in non-standard working arrangements.

Recent discourses from the ILO are particularly significant, given the Organization's status as the key global host of the formalisation project, the home of the sole international standard, and the most prominent international policy forum in which trade unions play an integral role. The ILO has long recognised informality that resides in formal settings and the Organization's policy discourses are alive to certain of the associated regulatory dynamics. Yet informalisation was not a central preoccupation of the ILO until the inclusion of the preventive objective in Recommendation No 204. The repercussions of this shift, further, have not been fully absorbed. Labour regulation mechanisms that can curb informalisation feature in the Recommendation, and it cites most of the pertinent international labour standards. Yet the Recommendation is deficient at the level of regulatory strategy. It is not as robust on what can be achieved, and how, by legal frameworks and techniques. Partially, this is because the Recommendation adopts, like the World Bank literature, a focus on the substantive standards that are enshrined in legal instruments, rather than on the intricacies of their scope, exceptions, distribution of legal obligations etc. It was concluded that the formalisation project is primarily preoccupied with informal settings, rather than with informalisation of formal working relations or the balance that should be struck in regulatory policy between formalising and preventing further informalisation.

A more robust conception of informalisation, then, must be demanded from international policy makers, which better captures the contemporary dynamics of this phenomena and in particular the associated regulatory supports. Informality narratives are significantly driving the debates on poor quality work, prominently at the global level. Informality policy is therefore a site with which it is vital for labour law scholars to engage and where the promise and risks of labour regulation can be explored. Formalisation, in particular, is a potential gateway to incorporating legal regulation into flagship global policy discourses, including towards the UN Sustainable Development Goals. This notion would, ideally, be fashioned to embrace sophisticated conceptions of informalisation, and of legal regulation, thus marrying the formalisation project with the objective of improving – or sustaining – job quality in the formal sector. In this regard, earlier contributions have called for a *reconstructive* labour law, which builds coherent jobs from fragmented working relations.[125] This reflection on informalisation suggests a parallel *pre-emptive* labour law, which should be integrated into formalisation policies and is targeted at preventing the unravelling of decent jobs. To some degree, this is a call for an alertness to, and defence of, the architecture of the mundane. In recent decades – perhaps unexpectedly – labour regulation scholars have been called on to produce refined typologies of the mechanisms and institutions that have supported, and can extend and surpass, the standard employment model. Intensified endeavours of this type are now vital if high-quality work is to be sustained – as aspiration and reality – in the face of the increasingly intense pressures towards informalisation.

[125] McCann and Murray (n 113).

PART II

Interdisciplinary Approaches: Historical, Institutional and Political Economy

4

Do Human Rights Work for Informal Workers?

SUPRIYA ROUTH[1]

I. Introduction

In this chapter, by taking note of unique experiences of informal workers in their innumerable activities, I contend that treating labour rights as human rights is no sure recipe for improving the conditions of such workers. Based on the epistemological foundation of institutional ethnography (IE), I argue that law and policy need to accept embodied experiences of informal workers at work as the informational basis for conceptualising such workers' justified claims. Informal workers' justified claims – because of their heterogeneous *sui generis* experiences – may not always neatly fit the legally safeguarded human rights standards. The claims that go beyond the human rights standards need to be legally institutionalised if informal workers' aspirations are to be promoted.

Taking cognisance of non-human rights claims does not mean that the human rights discourse is completely useless for informal workers. Under certain circumstances human rights standards are useful for informal workers. However, workers' human rights standards, which were developed against the backdrop of industrial mass production, are generally not appropriately suited to take account of the diverse and unique needs and concerns of informal workers. Accordingly, I propose a human rights-plus approach to promoting the aspirations of informal workers. While there are certain limited human rights standards that might

[1] Assistant Professor, Faculty of Law, University of Victoria, Canada. This chapter has greatly benefited from conversations at the Society of Legal Scholars Annual Seminar 2016, titled 'Re-imagining labour law for development: Informal work in the global North and global South' at SOAS University of London. I thank the participants at the seminar, in particular Judy Fudge, Guy Mundlak, Tonia Novitz and Diamond Ashiagbor, for their comments on an earlier version of the chapter. Remaining errors are my responsibility. Some ideas pursued in this chapter were first introduced in a brief article: Supriya Routh, 'Explorer une approche axée sur l'expérience pour les travailleurs informels' in Isabelle Daugareilh and Maryse Badel (eds), *La Sécurité Sociale: 70 ans d'age, une idée neuve* (Paris: Dalloz, forthcoming).

be useful for certain categories of informal workers, for other justified claims, workers' experiences at work need to constitute the basis of an entitlement framework.

The chapter has five sections. Following this Introduction, I begin by discussing the debate on labour rights as human rights (which I also call the human rights strategy) in section II. Visualising labour rights as human rights was originally advanced as a strategy to promote the labour rights of industrial employees. While this strategy did not go unchallenged, several scholars argue that the human rights strategy would be more useful for informal workers, the majority of whom are non-unionised. Having discussed this proposal and its counter-arguments, in section III I indicate some of the problems with the human rights strategy and, more specifically, with the human rights discourse for informal workers. I do not undertake an extensive critique of the human rights discourse. I discuss only those concerns that fail to account for the unique and varied circumstances of informal work and concerns of informal workers. In section IV, following fundamental tenets of IE and, more importantly, their underlying epistemological foundation, I argue that disembodied abstraction of the rights standards is ill-suited to address localised specific experiences of informal workers. Accordingly, I propose, informal workers' specific embodied experiences be mainstreamed in devising any entitlement policy that hopes to promote their aspirations. I conclude the chapter in section V by proposing a human rights-plus approach to promoting informal workers' aspirations.

II. Labour Rights as Human Rights

In a recent intervention Judy Fudge notes that workers are increasingly adopting the strategy of formulating their demands as human rights claims and are successfully moving the constitutional and human rights courts in realising their claims.[2] Her observation is premised on her survey of Canadian and European Union developments. From her survey of these two jurisdictions, Fudge concludes that we are witnessing a process of shift in the source of political legitimacy – from direct participatory democracy to human rights-based discourses. What this shift means for workers is that instead of relying on their collective power to influence industrial relations outcomes and facilitate their well-being, they are invoking the human rights vocabulary and engaging the judiciary to win their victories.[3]

It is this political legitimacy along with the universal appeal and hegemonic nature of the human rights language that draw scholars to adopt a human rights

[2] Judy Fudge, 'Constitutionalizing Labour Rights in Canada and Europe: Freedom of Association, Collective Bargaining, and Strikes' (2015) 68 *Current Legal Problems*, 267–305.

[3] ibid; see also Judy Fudge, 'The New Discourse of Labor Rights: From Social to Fundamental Rights?' (2007) 29: 1 *Comparative Labor Law and Policy Journal*, 29–66.

strategy to promote labour rights.[4] It is argued that although there are disagreements about the 'existence, source, nature, and scope of human rights and worker rights', human rights offer an enduring emancipatory idea accepted by the global community.[5] This strategy of treating labour rights as human rights is a defensive strategy and is articulated as a last resort for workers. Although not everyone agrees with it, there seems to be a consensus amongst labour and industrial relations scholars that workers' power has diminished globally.[6] The deteriorating density and political insignificance of trade unions are indicators of this diminished worker power. Since workers' power and political significance have diminished, they cannot rely on their collective capacity to negotiate their justified claims.

Accordingly, their claims should be couched in human rights vocabulary and enforced through the judiciary. While workers cannot force employers (capital in general) to realise their claims any more, it is argued that the judiciary is able to compel employers to promote workers' claims as human rights. Although human rights-based strategies could range from integration of the rights language in political discourse to lobbying of governments and corporations on the basis of human rights, in this chapter, by human rights strategy I mean workers' litigation-based strategy employing the human rights language, which legal scholars have mainly been concerned with.

In any case, in this strategic move by labour (mostly legal) scholars they seek to convert private contract-based labour rights into public state-centred human rights.[7] Particularly in the context of the United States and other advanced industrial capitalist countries, where labour rights emanate from freedom of commerce,

[4] See James A Gross, 'A Long Overdue Beginning: The Promotion and Protection of Workers' Rights as Human Rights' in James A Gross (ed), *Workers' Rights as Human Rights* (Ithaca, NY, ILR Press, 2003) 1; Lance Compa, 'Workers' Freedom of Association in the United States: The Gap between Ideals and Practice' in Gross (ed), *Workers' Rights as Human Rights*, above, 23. Also see generally the collection of different essays in Gross (ed), *Workers' Rights as Human Rights*, above; Judy Fudge, 'Labour Rights as Human Rights: Turning Slogans into Legal Claims' (2014) 37: 2 *The Dalhousie Law Journal* 601; Virginia A Leary, 'The Paradox of Workers' Rights as Human Rights' in Lance A Compa and Stephen F Diamond (eds), *Human Rights, Labor Rights, and International Trade* (Philadelphia, University of Pennsylvania Press, 1996) 22; Simon Deakin, 'Social Rights in a Globalized Economy' in Philip Alston (ed), *Labour Rights as Human Rights* (Oxford, Oxford University Press, 2005) 25.

[5] Gross, 'A Long Overdue Beginning', above n 4, 6–8; also Edward E Potter, 'A Pragmatic Assessment from the Employers' Perspective' in Gross (ed), *Workers' Rights as Human Rights*, above n 4, 118, 120.

[6] See Walter Galenson, *Trade Union Growth and Decline: An International Study* (Westport, CT, Praeger 1994); Manuel Castells, *The Information Age: Economy, Society and Culture, Volume I: The Rise of the Network Society* 2nd edn (Oxford, Blackwell, 2000) 135, 165–67, 224; Anil Verma and Thomas A Kochan, 'Unions in the 21st Century: Prospects for Renewal' in Anil Verma and Thomas A Kochan (eds), *Unions in the 21st Century: An International Perspective* (Basingstoke, Palgrave Macmillan, 2004) 1; but see Beverly J Silver, *Forces of Labor: Workers' Movements and Globalization Since 1870* (Cambridge, Cambridge University Press, 2003). Silver argues that worker power has not diminished; it has, instead, dispersed across the globe.

[7] Kevin Kolben, 'Labor Rights as Human Rights?' (2009–2010) 50: 2 *Virginia Journal of International Law* 449; also see Virginia Mantouvalou, 'Servitude and Forced Labour in the 21st Century: The Human Rights of Domestic Workers' (2006) 35: 4 *Industrial Law Journal*, 395–414.

Lance Compa notes that the human rights strategy is capable of upholding labour rights independently of the logic of market exchange.[8] The argument goes, since human rights violations are taken more seriously and are politically sensitive, violations of labour rights have better possibilities of remedy if pitched as human rights.[9] The human rights vocabulary is particularly useful, argues Compa, in claiming workers' living wages, safe and healthy conditions at work, safeguards for migrant workers, workers' compensations, health insurances, provision for pensions, paid vacations and other social protections, equality in pay, non-discrimination, prohibition on child labour, and determinate maximum working hours.[10] Virginia Leary, however, sees workers' freedom of association and claims against forced labour as proper human rights claims.[11]

In jurisdictions such as the United States, where trade unionism is under specific threat from employers, a human rights claim to association might be useful in framing the demand as citizens' political claim against the state.[12] The cost associated with this strategy, however, is that workers' legitimate claims would become citizens' rights claims. If workers' right to organise becomes citizens' right to association it is doubtful whether citizens can still demand bargaining (with the employer) as a right, as a constituent of their associational right. In any case, the human rights strategy could be useful in realising workers' individual claims to a living wage, safe conditions at work, health insurance, paid vacations, or equality and non-discrimination as citizens' claims to be established through the judiciary.

This possibility of judicial promotion of human rights, in contrast to the bargained vindication of labour rights, makes scholars advocate for constitutionalisation of workers' human rights.[13] Constitutional integration of international human rights standards endows such standards with legitimacy and places labour rights on a higher pedestal. However, the problem with this approach is that it concedes that labour cannot win its battle with capital/employers any more. Accordingly, workers' best hope lies with the judiciary outside the purview of industrial democracy. Even in this way of thinking about promotion of workers' rights, scholars narrowly focus on how the judiciary may realise constitutional

[8] Lance Compa, 'Solidarity and Rights: Two to Tango – A Response to Joseph A McCartin' (2011) 80 *International Labor and Working-Class History* 161, 163–64; also see Lance Compa, 'Labor's New Opening to International Human Rights Standards' (2008) 11 *Working USA: The Journal of Labor and Society* 99–123, 102.

[9] See generally Lance Compa, 'Legal Protection of Workers' Human Rights: Regulatory Changes and Challenges – The United States' in Colin Fenwick and Tonia Novitz (eds), *Human Rights at Work: Perspectives on Law and Regulation* (Oxford, Hart Publishing, 2010) 293.

[10] Lance Compa, 'Solidarity and Human Rights: A Response to Youngdahl' (2009) 18: 1 *New Labor Forum* 38, 42.

[11] See Leary, above n 4, 38.

[12] See Leary, ibid; also see generally Compa, 'Workers' Freedom of Association in the United States', above n 4.

[13] Ruth Dukes, *The Labour Constitution: The Enduring Idea of Labour Law* (Oxford, Oxford University Press, 2014); Fudge, 'Constitutionalizing Labour Rights in Canada and Europe', above n 2.

rights, which is by taking cognisance of violation of rights and ordering responsible parties to recognise the violated right. What they do not consider is how effective judicial orders are in actual practice. Since this follow-up of court orders into the domain of actual practice does not happen, it remains to be seen as to what effect judicial promotion of workers' rights does actually have on workers in their situated everyday experiences of work.

While these concerns make some scholars adopt a more cautious view of the labour rights as human rights strategy,[14] others see the strategy as useful for certain categories of workers, namely informal workers.[15] Guy Mundlak contends that the human rights strategy is particularly useful for workers who cannot undertake collective action and thereby participate in collective bargaining with employers in furtherance of their rights realisation.[16] Since informal workers are unorganised and are largely excluded from trade unionism, the judiciary-centric human rights strategy is more useful for them. In the absence of collective action, informal workers can formulate their claims against the state and have their claims vindicated through the judiciary. By examining human rights claims of informal migrant domestic workers in Europe, Virginia Mantouvalou concludes that judiciary-centred human rights claims are efficacious for workers who are excluded from the purview of statutory safeguard.[17] She argues, since informal (particularly undocumented migrant) workers are normally excluded from labour law safeguards, the human rights vocabulary offers some protection in cases of extreme violation of some of their justified claims.[18]

Jeemol Unni too advocates a human rights strategy for informal workers.[19] In the absence of the systematic and documented arrangements for informal work (and hence the uncertainty about the employer), Unni is concerned about who might be responsible for promoting informal workers' justified claims. Therefore, she argues that if the human rights of informal workers are vindicated through the judiciary, it would be easier to identify a responsible entity for the promotion of such rights.[20] According to her, there lies the significance of formulating informal

[14] KD Ewing, 'Foreword' in Colin Fenwick and Tonia Novitz (eds), *Human Rights at Work: Perspectives on Law and Regulation* (Oxford, Hart Publishing, 2010) vii, xiv–xv; Kolben, 'Labor Rights as Human Rights?' above n 7, 451–52.

[15] Guy Mundlak, 'Human Rights and Labor Rights: Why Don't the Two Tracks Meet?' (2012–2013) 34 *Comparative Labor Law & Policy Journal* 217–43; Guy Mundlak, 'Industrial Citizenship, Social Citizenship, Corporate Citizenship: I Just Want My Wages' (2007) 8 *Theoretical Inquiries in Law* 719–48; Mantouvalou, 'Servitude and Forced Labour in the 21st Century', above n 7; Virginia Mantouvalou, 'Human Rights for Precarious Workers: The Legislative Precariousness of Domestic Labor' (2012–2013) 34 *Comparative Labor Law & Policy Journal*, 133–66; Jeemol Unni, 'Globalization and Securing Rights for Women Informal Workers in Asia' (2004) 5: 3 *Journal of Human Development*, 335–54.

[16] Mundlak, 'Human Rights and Labor Rights', above n 15; Mundlak, 'Industrial Citizenship', above n 15.

[17] Mantouvalou, 'Human Rights for Precarious Workers', above n 15.

[18] Mantouvalou, ibid.

[19] Unni, 'Globalization and Securing Rights for Women Informal Workers in Asia', above n 15.

[20] ibid.

workers' claims as human rights. If her observation is correct, even if informal workers do not have an employer, their justified claims would be promoted by some entity (identified by the court) if their claims are recognised as human rights by the judiciary. While this is an attractive proposition, it lacks empirical corroboration or conceptual justification as to its viability. However, Unni adds that the International Labour Organization (ILO)-promoted core human rights guarantees are too restrictive to be of any help for the diverse categories of informal workers[21] whose claims are as varied as their activities.

Through her study of traditional trade unions' strategy involving their informal worker members in India, Rina Agarwala concludes that where industrial trade unions have been able to organise informal workers, they have formulated workers' claims against the state rather than employers.[22] This strategy of making demands against the state prevails even when informal workers are engaged in an employment relationship.[23] Agarwala notes that this strategy of identifying the state as the duty-bearing entity for informal workers' justified claims is reformulating the labour–capital relation as the citizen–state relation.[24] Informal workers' claims, then, are not based on their (agency-based) position as workers, but on their status as citizens.[25]

Agarwala's empirical analysis *prima facie* seems to support the position that the human rights strategy is more useful for informal workers because workers can hold the state directly responsible for the violation of their rights. However, a deeper examination will reveal that Agarwala's thesis only partly supports the proposition. While it might be true that trade unions are making claims against the state, that is, mainly the executive, their claims are not channelled through the judiciary. Instead, the state becomes their bargaining partner and their approach is political rather than juridical.

Even though informal workers' trade unions bargain their claims with the government in some limited instances,[26] making the state responsible secures no certain guarantee in promoting informal workers' human rights claims. More specifically, several scholars doubt the effectiveness of a court-based rights strategy to promote workers' claims.[27] Harry Arthurs, by citing the instances of jurisdictions wherein labour rights are constitutionally safeguarded, concludes that

[21] ibid, 340–41; also see the 1998 ILO *Declaration on Fundamental Principles and Rights at Work*.

[22] See generally Rina Agarwala, *Informal Labor, Formal Politics, and Dignified Discontent in India* (Cambridge, Cambridge University Press, 2013).

[23] ibid.

[24] ibid 4–6, 198–201.

[25] ibid.

[26] Limited because traditional trade unions, which Agarwala studies, are yet to integrate informal workers as a matter of normal practice.

[27] Harry Arthurs, 'The Constitutionalization of Employment Relations: Multiple Models, Pernicious Problems' (2010) 19: 4 *Social & Legal Studies* 403–22, 403–04, 416; Damian Brown and KD Ewing, 'Human Rights at Work: Possibilities and Problems' in KD Ewing (ed), *Human Rights at Work* (Liverpool, The Institute of Employment Rights, 2000) 203, 218–22; KD Ewing, 'Constitutional Reform and Human Rights: Unfinished Business?' (2001) 5 *Edinburgh Law Review*, 297–324.

treating labour rights as human rights and constitutionalising those rights does not always work for workers.[28] Amongst the several reasons that Arthurs extends as to why the court-based human rights strategy does not work, prominent are that the substantive rights standards may not address concrete concerns of workers; that workers' rights may have to be traded off against rights of other groups; that constitutional litigation is costly and remains out of reach of several workers; that the judiciary is unable to determine redistributive policies; and that the human rights strategy curbs democratic collective action.[29]

From a broader conceptual point of view, Keith Ewing reflects that although the human rights vocabulary appropriately places workers' claims in the public law domain, it cannot justify the basis of workers' rights.[30] Ewing goes on to emphasise that the human rights-based strategy, instead, suggests that scholars have given up on industrial democracy in improving conditions of workers.[31] Even scholars, who otherwise think that constitutionalisation of labour rights is a useful strategy, caution against the overdependence on that strategy.[32] Following this line of questioning of the human rights strategy, in the next part, I identify some of the problems with the human rights discourse insofar as it relates to improving conditions of informal workers.

III. Problems with the Labour Rights as Human Rights Strategy

As I mention, Arthurs notes several jurisdictions where labour rights are constitutionally safeguarded as human rights, in order to contend that such a strategy might not benefit workers. India and South Africa are prominent amongst these jurisdictions, while at the same time both of these jurisdictions are also known to have an enormous number of marginalised informal workers. The Indian constitution is possibly the most comprehensive one in safeguarding labour rights. Labour rights are constitutionally promoted as justiciable civil-political rights and non-justiciable socio-economic rights.[33] The safeguarded human rights standards

[28] Arthurs, 'The Constitutionalization of Employment Relations', above n 27.

[29] ibid, 404–06; also see Brown and Ewing, 'Human Rights at Work' above n 27. Kolben adds that the human rights movement is too legalistic, adopts a top-down approach to workers' rights, and is based on the idea of philanthropy rather than workers' agency. See Kolben, above n 7, 452, 475–81.

[30] Ewing, 'Foreword', above n 14, ix, xi.

[31] ibid, x–xi.

[32] Judy Fudge, 'Constitutionalizing Labour Rights in Europe' in Tom Campbell, KD Ewing and Adam Tomkins (eds), *The Legal Protection of Human Rights: Sceptical Essays* (Oxford, Oxford University Press, 2011) 244, 267.

[33] See Constitution of India, 1950, Part III and Part IV. Although the Indian judiciary, well known for its judicial activism, has devised the strategy of interpreting socio-economic rights as part and parcel of civil-political rights, the result of such a strategy has been mixed in promoting an integrated view of human rights. See generally Supriya Routh, *Enhancing Capabilities through Labour Law: Informal*

range from the very broad rights against forced labour and child labour to the narrowly detailed rights such as maternity benefit and workers' participation in management.[34]

Labour rights so enumerated in the Constitution of India are individualistic and tiered. Following the international human rights standards, civil-political rights have a higher status, followed by socio-economic rights. The recognition of group rights (for example, the right to development) is, then, tertiary to this human rights standards framework. This way of organising human rights standards adheres to the so-called First, Second, and Third Generation human rights hierarchy. This hierarchy is inherent to the way human rights are conceptualised. Even though there are religious underpinnings to it, the human rights regime in its present form is conceptualised against the backdrop of a specific political philosophy, that is, a liberal constitutional democracy. It is, then, no surprise that substantive civil and political rights are recognised as properly human rights. This individual-centric hierarchised ordering of human rights is oblivious to the specific needs of workers, particularly informal workers. From the several ILO missions and scholarly studies what emerges is that social, economic, and group rights are oftentimes more important for informal workers than civil and political rights.[35]

While civil and political rights are no less important, the hierarchy of human rights standards relegates informal workers' main concerns to secondary status, thereby prioritising formal industrial workers. Not only does the hierarchy of human rights standards ignore informal workers' specific circumstances, the top-down substantive rights formulation is disrespectful of their autonomy. Following the human rights' vocabulary, workers' rights are what are already determined and enumerated. Workers need to fit their concerns and demands within the given substantive human rights standards. The inflexibility of the politically

Workers in India (New York, Routledge, 2014) 48–59; also see generally O Chinnappa Reddy, *The Court and the Constitution of India: Summits and Shallows* (Oxford, Oxford University Press, 2010).

[34] Constitution of India, above n 33.

[35] See generally, eg, ILO, *Informality and the quality of employment in G20 countries*, Report prepared for the G20 Labour and Employment Ministerial Meeting Melbourne, Australia, 10–11 September 2014; Tanya Goldman, *Organizing in South Africa's Informal Economy: An Overview of Four Sectoral Case Studies*, Working Paper No 60, Series on Representation and Organization Building, ILO, 2003; Paul E Bangasser, 'The ILO and the Informal Sector: An Institutional History', Employment Paper 2000/9 (Geneva, ILO, 2000); also see generally Routh, *Enhancing Capabilities through Labour Law*, above n 33; the different chapters in Supriya Routh and Vando Borghi (eds), *Workers and the Global Informal Economy: Interdisciplinary Perspectives* (New York, Routledge, 2016); Martha Alter Chen et al, 'Supporting Workers in the Informal Economy: A Policy Framework', Paper Prepared for ILO Task Force on the Informal Economy, Women in Informal Employment – Globalizing & Organizing, November 2001; Martha Alter Chen et al, *Mainstreaming Informal Employment and Gender in Poverty Reduction: A Handbook for Policy-makers and Other Stakeholders* (London, Commonwealth Secretariat & International Development Research Centre, 2004); the different chapters in Martha Chen et al (eds), *Membership-Based Organizations of the Poor* (London, Routledge, 2007); WIEGO Country Reports on Law & Informality, http://wiego.org/informal_economy_law/country-reports, accessed 2 January 2017.

determined substantive rights makes it difficult for newer claims to attain the same rights status that were once decided. In a human rights-focused strategy, workers' aim then is to *fit the box* rather than articulate their own aspirations and entitlement proposals in their own language. This disjuncture between *is* (existing substantive human rights) and *ought* (what claims are worthy of attention) makes scholars emphasise the opposite pull of the legally protected human rights and collective organisation and self-determination of workers.[36]

Substantive human rights are also temporally determined. Consider these constitutional safeguards in India: employment of children below 14 years in factories and mines is prohibited; gender equality in payment for work; right to public assistance for unemployment; provision for a living wage; workers' participation in management.[37] These constitutional safeguards are primarily aimed at the formal industrial production processes. This is, however, not to deny that there are certain constitutional provisions that take account of the agricultural production processes, many of which might not be formally organised.[38] In any case, constitutionally protected labour rights are conceptualised against the backdrop of the employment relationship. This is far from being a uniquely Indian experience. Internationally, labour rights were originally formulated against the backdrop of "industrial mass production" in a specific historical time.[39] Thus, it is doubtful as to how far constitutional labour rights that were formulated in the context of industrial employment relations can afford adequate safeguard to the interests of a wide range of workers, such as self-employed, own-account, family-labour and other non-typical workers, outside the industrial employee category.[40]

Thus, the inventory of rights of labour is now a determinate set of claims formulated as claims against the employer and the state, primarily the executive. Constitutional litigation is set in motion in cases of violation of these rights. The problem of using the human rights strategy in realising claims of informal workers is that their claims need to be couched in the existing rights language. An already existing rights lens is employed to understand workers' problems and

[36] Jennifer Gordon, *Suburban Sweatshops: The Fight for Immigrant Rights* (Cambridge, MA, The Belknap Press of Harvard University Press, 2005) 148–49.

[37] Constitution, above n 33, Arts 24, 39(d), 41, 43, 43A.

[38] ibid, Part IV.

[39] Gordon, *Suburban Sweatshops*, above n 36, 23, 152; also see Judy Fudge, 'Fragmenting Work and Fragmenting Organizations: The Contract of Employment and the Scope of Labour Regulation' (2006) 44:4 *Osgoode Hall Law Journal*, 609–48; Judy Fudge, 'Feminist Reflections on the Scope of Labour Law: Domestic Work, Social Reproduction, and Jurisdiction' (2014) 22 *Feminist Legal Studies*, 1–23, 10–11, 17.

[40] See generally Arthurs, above n 27. Some scholars, however, do not agree with this assertion, noting instead that the human rights strategy to labour rights actually helps non-typical workers to diversify their emancipatory strategies. See, eg, Guy Davidov, 'The Principle of Proportionality in Labor Law and its Impact on Precarious Workers' (2012–2013) 34 *Comparative Labor Law & Policy Journal*, 63–80, 76–78.

contingencies. The starting point, then, is legally safeguarded rights, not workers experiences at work. There is a logical inconsistency in envisaging informal workers' entitlement strategy in this manner. If the point of reference for existing labour rights were factory-based industrial employment it is only logical that legally promoted claims of informal workers should emerge from workers' own perspectives shaped by their work-related experiences.

Several scholars observe that even though the human rights vocabulary is extremely important as a rhetorical political tool, the substantive human rights safeguards are not enough to integrate a range of possible measures necessary for improving conditions of workers.[41] What follows is that the human rights discourse should open up to other possibilities that might be able to promote workers' justified claims even if those do not qualify as substantive human rights. However, the inventory of rights, since these are rhetorically entrenched into the imagination of law and workers' movements, impedes stakeholders from conceiving other possible emancipatory visions outside the rights claims.[42] Under such circumstances, there is a special need to refocus our attention to the actual lived experiences of workers. In the case of informal workers, because of the diversity in their working experiences, legislative policy ought to concentrate on each specific location or activity in order to legally institutionalise justified specific claims of such workers. Following institutional ethnographers, I elaborate the significance of experience-based policy making in the following section in proposing a human rights-plus approach to informal workers' entitlement.

Before so doing, the litigation-centric approach to human rights promotion needs a brief comment. In the labour rights as human rights strategy vindication of workers' rights happens through judicial adjudication. Judicial adjudication is set in motion through an individual or a collective complaint, and poses to the court one or more specific human rights question(s). Litigation is not appropriate for systematic promotion of justified claims including human rights of workers. Even in its limited scope of functioning, a litigation-focused strategy for the vindication of specific justified claims (that is, not systematic promotion) of informal workers is problematic. A litigation-centric strategy for the realisation of rights is prolonged, costly and intimidating, especially for people from marginalised communities.[43] More importantly, people from these marginalised communities

[41] Christian Brunelle, 'The Growing Impact of Human Rights on Canadian Labour Law' in Colin Fenwick and Tonia Novitz (eds), *Human Rights at Work: Perspectives on Law and Regulation* (Oxford, Hart Publishing, 2010) 119, 146; also see generally Ivan Hare, 'Social rights as fundamental human rights' in Bob Hepple (ed), *Social and Labour Rights in a Global Context: International and Comparative Perspectives* (Cambridge, Cambridge University Press, 2002) 153–81; also Bob Hepple, 'Introduction' in Hepple (ed), *Social and Labour Rights in a Global Context*, above, 8–14.

[42] See David Kennedy, 'The International Human Rights Movement: Part of the Problem?' (2002) 15 *Harvard Human Rights Journal*, 101–26, 108–11, 113–14, 122; Gordon, above n 36, 7, 181.

[43] Clark D Cunningham, 'The Lawyer as Translator, Representation as Text: Towards an Ethnography of Legal Discourse' (1991–1992) 77 *Cornell Law Review* 1298–1387, 1383–87; also see Arthurs, above n 27.

often find that they are unable to translate their experiences and aspirations into the language of law, and thereby feel ignored and let down by the judicial system.[44] Even scholars who otherwise view judicial strategies favourably caution about the limits of law and legally induced social change.[45]

My critique of the human rights discourse in this part is by no means complete. A comprehensive review of the human rights strategy is outside the scope of this chapter. There are several problems with the human rights discourse,[46] among which I only focus on those aspects that deny any role for workers in formulating their own justified claims against employers or the state. It needs to be emphasised that the human rights discourse is not completely irrelevant in improving conditions for informal workers. However, human rights-based strategies should be supplemented by policies emanating from informal workers' experiences. In the following section, I discuss why informal workers' experiences are immensely important as an informational basis for policy-making.

IV. Informal Work and Workers' Experience

Some legal scholars relegate informality and informal workers to the lawless black or grey economy (of course *white* signifies the formal industrial legal order).[47] Defining informal work on the basis of enacted statutes and thereby relegating the idea of *work* to black, grey, or illegal market/economy is an easy endeavour and simplistic in its outlook. It is true that several of the activities performed by numerous workers remain outside the scope of laws (including labour and taxation statutes), but this fact does not make the activities illegal/back/grey *per se*. If only one adopts an extremely narrow understanding of law (as statutory enactment), this thesis might hold some value, even if incomplete.

Activities that do not adhere to the *form* of industrial employment and are in that sense informal, do have detailed rules and laws that organise these activities.[48] And the state, even in industrial western jurisdictions, oftentimes either tolerates

[44] See generally Cunningham, 'The Lawyer as Translator, Representation as Text', above n 43.

[45] See generally Orly Lobel, 'The Paradox of Extralegal Activism: Critical Legal Consciousness and Transformative Politics' (2007) 120 *Harvard Law Review*, 937–88.

[46] See generally Makau Mutua, *Human Rights: A Political and Cultural Critique* (Philadelphia, University of Pennsylvania Press, 2002); David Kennedy, *The Dark Sides of Virtue – Reassessing International Humanitarianism* (Princeton, Princeton University Press, 2004); Upendra Baxi, *The Future of Human Rights* (Oxford, Oxford University Press, 2008).

[47] Mark Freedland and Nicola Kountouris, *The Legal Construction of Personal Work Relations* (Oxford, Oxford University Press, 2012) 349–58; also see Guy Davidov, 'Enforcement Problems in Informal Labor Markets: A View from Israel' (2006) 27 *Comparative Labor Law and Policy Journal*, 3–26; also Claire LaHovary, 'A new international labour standard for formalising the informal economy? A discussion of its desirability' in Routh and Borghi (eds) (n 35) 91.

[48] See generally Ana Maria Vargas, *Outside the Law: An Ethnographic Study of Street Vendors in Bogota* (Lund, Sweden, Lund University Press, 2016); also see Zoran Slavnic, 'The informal economy and the state' in Routh and Borghi (eds), *Workers and the Global Informal Economy*, above n 35, 51.

or encourages such regulations.[49] However, even on this narrow understanding of law, there are activities that receive statutory recognition but are too impractical (that is, inefficient and costly) to be administered. Finally, there are activities that are far off the legal imagination, but not illegal in any sense. This complexity is lost in the simplistic ascending categories of correctness suggested by black, grey, and white economies. It is this correctness that is reflected in policies such as the ILO's effort in Transition from the Informal to the Formal Economy.[50]

If one considers the following instances of informal work, the fallacy of the black/grey/white categorisation becomes all too evident. It is argued that oftentimes informal activities are an '*invention of the job*' by workers themselves.[51] In light of this assertion, consider the following observation by Ella R Bhatt:[52]

> A small farmer works on her own farm. In tough times, she also works on other farms as a laborer. When the agriculture season is over, she goes to the forest to collect gum and other forest produce. Year round, she produces embroidered items either at a piece rate for a contractor or for sale to a trader who comes to her village to buy goods. Now, how should her trade be categorized? Does she belong to the agricultural sector, the factory sector, or the home-based work sector? Should she be categorized as a farmer or a farm worker? Is she self-employed or is she a piece-rate worker? Because her situation cannot be defined and contained neatly in a box, she has no work status and her right to representation in a union is unrealized. She is denied access to financial services or training to upgrade her skills. The tyranny of having to belong to a well-defined 'category' has condemned her to having no 'identity'.

[49] Slavnic, The informal economy and the state', above n 48.

[50] See ILO, Recommendation No 204 concerning the Transition from the Informal to the Formal Economy, adopted 12 June 2015, available at http://www.ilo.org/wcmsp5/groups/public/---ed_norm/---relconf/documents/meetingdocument/wcms_377774.pdf (visited 20 August 2017).

[51] See Claudia Danani and Javier Lindenboim, 'Informal employment and precariousness: Where social inequality begins, and where it leads to; society and policies in Argentina, 2003–2014' in Routh and Borghi (eds), above n 35, 155, 160, quoting A Monza (emphasis mine).

[52] Ela R Bhatt, *We are Poor but So Many: The Story of Self-Employed Women in India* (Oxford, Oxford University Press, 2006) 17.

Likewise, a news report from *The Hindu* is also instructive:

> The old man [Mr. Maraiah] rears some 20 goats besides taking 20 other goats belonging to various farmers for grazing. Mr. Maraiah is paid Rs. 100 per month by farmers towards *Kapu Kooli* (labour charges for guarding the goats). Besides, Mr. Maraiah skilfully weaves sleeping mats with silver date palm leaves, which fetches him some more money every month. He is generally seen grazing goats and weaving sleeping mats during the daytime near Moosi River, 5 km away from his village. Mr. Maraiah weaves at least 10 mats in a month. He sells each mat for Rs. 200. The total income from *Kapu Kooli* and from weaving mats comes to Rs. 4,000 per month and he also earns some more by selling a few of his mature goats … Besides, he also cultivates paddy in a one-acre field to save money for his granddaughters' marriage.

See '70-year-old does three jobs to support his family' *The Hindu* (10 August 2016), http://www.thehindu.com/news/national/andhra-pradesh/70yearold-from-lakshmipuram-village-of-ramannapet-mandal-does-three-jobs-to-support-his-family/article6324637.ece, accessed 28 July 2016.

Or for the more industrialised part of the globe, consider Jennifer Gordon's narration:[53]

> [I]mmigrant workers on Long Island [USA] have little industry identification, and change jobs frequently. A Latino immigrant man in Long Island may work as a landscaper during the summer and in a restaurant in the winter; if he loses his restaurant job he may spend some time doing day labor and end up working for a roofer. A woman may begin as a live-in domestic worker and move on to a patchwork of factory work, live-out housecleaning, and part-time janitorial jobs.

Dorothy Smith's articulation of Mrs T's work, wherein the work of Mrs T, a homemaker, is shaped by the contingencies of her husband's work and her children's school, is also instructive in this respect.[54] A homemaker's work, it is argued, leads to and supports other market-valued coveted careers, but is still seen as a work of last resort.[55] Likewise, paid care work is for workers who are unable to secure a productive job in the economy.[56] Since labour rights pertain to productive industrial work, such rights are incapable of acknowledging the significance of homework, even if such work is fuelling the productive economy and has direct links to the market. This proposition is also true for the several other categories of work. Feminist lawyers and political economists have long noted this incapacity of existing framework of labour rights to take account of socially reproductive work.[57]

The above-mentioned instances suggest that laws generally, and legally protected labour rights in particular, have a more complex relationship with informality than a legal/illegal dichotomy might suggest. For example, in Sweden, informality resulting from absence of laws continued with complete state

[53] Gordon, above n 36, 22. Noting the divergence in sweatshop activities in the USA from car washing to landscaping, Gordon emphasises that painting informal activities as black or underground is shortsighted and misses the significance of the increasing informalisation of a range of activities. She points at the interconnectedness of formal and informal activities suggesting a continuum of these activities as indicated by Guha-Khasnobis et al, rather than a divergence between the two (Gordon, above n 36, 14–15, 47–48); also see Basudeb Guha-Khasnobis, Ravi Kanbur and Elinor Ostrom, 'Beyond formality and informality' in Basudeb Guha-Khasnobis, Ravi Kanbur and Elinor Ostrom (eds), *Linking the Formal and Informal Economy Concepts and Policies* (Oxford, Oxford University Press, 2006) 1, 2–3, 7, 16. Also see Compa, 'Workers' Freedom', above n 4, 43–44.

[54] Dorothy E Smith, *The Everyday World as Problematic: A Feminist Sociology* (Toronto, University of Toronto Press, 1987) 138–39, 190–96.

[55] Arlie Russell Hochschild, *Commercialization of Intimate Life: Notes form Home and Work* (Berkeley, CA, University of California Press, 2003) 2–5, 242–44.

[56] ibid, 2.

[57] Judy Fudge, 'Feminist Reflections on the Scope of Labour Law: Domestic Work, Social Reproduction, and Jurisdiction' (2014) 22 *Feminist Legal Studies* 1–23; Kendra Strauss, 'Unfree Again: Social Reproduction, Flexible Labour Markets and the Resurgence of Gang Labour in the UK' (2013) 45:1 *Antipode*, 180–97. (Both the articles offer an overview of the recent debates pertaining to social reproduction.) Also see generally Antonella Picchio, *Social Reproduction: The Political Economy of the Labour Market* (Cambridge, Cambridge University Press, 1992); Smith, above n 54.

knowledge, perhaps with some approval.[58] The Swedish Government's reluctance to regulate informal taxi drivers was influenced by the hope of controlling the somewhat monopolistic nature of the formal Swedish taxi industry, which itself is a legitimate policy ambition.[59] Other states too, such as China, adopt a similar approach.[60] While in the Swedish taxi industry informality may indicate lawlessness, in Colombia informal transport workers (rickshaw drivers) are subject to elaborate rules and regulations organising their work.[61] These regulations are instituted by the different associations of the workers.[62] Likewise in Cameroon while, on the one hand, informal transport workers (bikers) are subject to enacted legislation, on the other, some street vendors organise their own activities and continuously negotiate with the state apparatus in undertaking their work.[63]

Such local and activity-specific regulation and organisation of informal activities, where they exist, manifest a complex and nuanced domain of regulation, attuned to the unique characteristics of specific activities, workers' location within these activities, and the socio-economic-political context in which these activities are undertaken. These forms of regulation do not attempt to generalise the particular experiences of specific categories of informal workers. These regulations, even if not explicitly, do acknowledge that specific experiences of workers need to be the basis of any effective regulation aiming at improving conditions of such workers.

Specific concerns of informal workers are as varied as their work is. For instance, the main concern of informal Swedish taxi drivers (work undertaken mainly by the unemployed) is the increasing cost of operating formally.[64] Informal workers in Brazil struggle to get their work legally recognised as employment in labour courts.[65] While unjust taxes and a corrupt bureaucracy compel Russian workers to work informally and accept deplorable conditions at work, some informal workers in Cameroon do pay tax to the government as a condition of their continued operation.[66] The main concerns for Cameroonian informal workers are

[58] Slavnic, above n 48, 60–61.

[59] ibid, 62.

[60] Just as the Swedish Government, the Chinese Government too promotes informality to some extent in furtherance of legitimate economic policies. See Sandra V Constantin, 'Reforms, individualisation and informal employment in urban China' in Routh and Borghi (eds), above n 35, 67, 83.

[61] Vargas, above n 48, 89, 133–35, 141–55.

[62] ibid.

[63] Alioum Idrissou, 'The urban informal sector in Africa: New players, solidarity economy and socio-aesthetic transformations in Cameroon' in Routh and Borghi (eds), above n 35, 190.

[64] Slavnic, above n 48, 59, 61.

[65] Roberto Fragale Filho, 'When informal work becomes litigious in a labour courtroom' in Routh and Borghi (eds), above n 35, 108, 109, 111–12, 114–15. This recognition as employees is central for workers because claim to labour rights hinges on the employment relationship. If workers base their just claims on labour rights they need to establish a written labour contract, subordinated relationship, and continuous employment, all of which may be problematic in the context of informal workers.

[66] Petr Bizyukov, 'Precarious employment in Russia: A form of degradation in labour relations' in Routh and Borghi (eds), above n 35, 174, 175–76; also see Idrissou, 'The urban informal sector in Africa', above n 63, 201.

verbal and physical abuse and confiscation of their work tools by the authorities.[67] Confiscation and eviction from public spaces are also serious concerns of informal workers in Colombia.[68]

These experiences and concerns of informal workers are local and specific; these experiences may not be generalisable even throughout a specific country or region.[69] Accordingly, all these experiences may not be susceptible to be expressed in terms of universal rights claims. My own earlier empirical work with informal workers in India indicates that informal workers' needs and aspirations cannot be easily framed as existing human rights claims.[70] Oftentimes, informal workers' claims went beyond the existing human rights standards.[71] For example, one of the fundamental aspirations of these workers is the recognition of their activity as legitimate work and themselves as contributing members of the society. This aspiration could not be captured through the substantive human rights standards and goes beyond the narrowly described specific workers' rights.

The above-mentioned instances, which are only indicative of the diversity of informal workers and not exhaustive of the unique nature of informal activities, show the complex relationship between law, human rights, and informality that cannot be captured by a straightforward white/black dichotomy created according to legal criteria. These instances also go on to show that the diverse and unique range of activities that are not industrial employment may not easily fit the abstract categories of legally safeguarded rights. The problem with the labour/human rights language in the specific context of work is that it takes concrete forms of work and transforms them into *abstract industrial labour* and devises rights claims with reference to that abstract industrial labour.[72] Valid labour rights claims could be made only when working arrangements could fit into the documented employment relationship model.[73] Accordingly, labour rights claims centre on the debate on employee/independent contractor status rather than workers' specific context and their subjective experiences at work.[74]

Therefore, the human rights vocabulary becomes incapable of positively addressing informal workers' marginalisation. Having said that, there are some informal workers' agendas that are closer to the needs of industrial employees such as the claim to minimum wages, maximum working hours, benefits packages, which could be framed as legitimate human rights claims, but others such as recognition as workers, bureaucratic documentation of domicile, hiring processes, insecurities at work, certain conditions at work, and taxation may not

[67] Idrissou, above n 63, 199.
[68] Vargas, above n 48, 103–07.
[69] Gordon, above n 36, 10–16.
[70] Routh, above n 33, 200–20, 224–34.
[71] Gordon, above n 36, 178.
[72] Smith, above n 54, 108, 158.
[73] Fragale Filho, above n 65, 118–19.
[74] See generally Fragale Filho, ibid.

be susceptible to such formulation.[75] Additionally, human rights claims often give rise to conflicting and opposing demands. Since human rights are general claims available to all, competing human rights claims need to be resolved before promoting informal workers' rights. For example, rights of street vendors are often in conflict with rights to public space of the people.[76] A rights-based approach to informal workers' interest promotion here would be contingent on how the right to public space is decided.

Thus, the problem with the way *work* and workers' *rights* are conceptualised is that workers and their experiences of work-lives are brought to conform to the existing executive, legislative, and market orders, but not the other way round.[77] Even for some of the most formally structured work situations with a clear employment relationship and defined work profile, legal conceptualisations miss the subtleties of work experiences including workers' vulnerabilities, their quest for exceeding the defined job expectations, and the resultant imbalance and insecurities in their work-lives.[78] Legally guaranteed rights oftentimes operate on the assumption of disembodied workers who are disconnected from the non-work requirements of their lives.[79]

Institutional ethnographer Marjorie L DeVault notes that by focusing on workers' experiences, IE is able to offer a generous concept of work that is concerned with the notion of embodied worker, that is, the somewhat obvious notion that work cannot be understood in isolation from workers' bodies in their overall social context.[80] Workers' experience, then, constitutes the lens through which to understand the meaning of work, but one that does not essentialise the experiences of even similar groups of workers such as migrant or women workers.[81]

Institutional ethnographers are concerned with the exclusion of women and other marginalised people including workers from the legally organised patriarchal ruling apparatus.[82] They are mindful that only some aspects of workers'

[75] Bizyukov, 'Precarious employment in Russia', above n 66, 181–86. We would also have to remember that these claims are likely to arise in the context of waged informal workers rather than self-employed or own account workers. This possibility also reinforces the industrial employment orientation of the labour rights language. Also see Routh, above n 33; Gordon, above n 36, 24.

[76] See Vargas, above n 48, 100–04; Idrissou, above n 63, 201.

[77] Brenda Solomon, 'Training for Low-Wage Work: TANF Recipients Preparing for Health-Care Work' in Marjorie L DeVault (ed), *People at Work: Life, Power, and Social Inclusion in the New Economy* (New York, New York University Press, 2008) 141, 151.

[78] Solomon, ibid, 142, 146, 150; also see Catherine Richards Solomon, 'Personal Responsibility in Professional Work: *The Academic "Star" as Ideological Code*' in DeVault (ed), above n 77, 180; Payal Banerjee, 'Flexible Hiring, Immigration, and Indian IT Workers' Experiences of Contract Work in the United States' in DeVault (ed), above n 77, 97; also Marjorie DeVault, 'Mapping Invisible Work: Conceptual Tools for Social Justice Projects' (2014) 29: 4 *Sociological Forum*, 775–90, 785.

[79] Richards Solomon, 'Personal Responsibility', above n 78, 184.

[80] Marjorie DeVault, 'Introduction' in DeVault (ed), above n 77, 1, 2, 5–6; also see DeVault, 'Mapping Invisible Work', above n 78.

[81] DeVault, 'Introduction', above n 80, 5; Smith, above n 54, 107.

[82] Smith, above n 54, 4, 17–18, 65, 107.

experience find expression in the several legal and policy texts, but not all.[83] When law and policy engages with workers, it objectifies their subjectivities and consciousness.[84] Workers' representations in these texts are standardised and miss the nuances of their experiences. By analysing these texts and contrasting them with experience-based policy-making institutional ethnographers seek to unearth what it really means to be a worker in their respective embodied specific circumstances.[85] By focusing on workers' experience, it is possible to bring erstwhile invisible work to the attention of law and policy documents, which contribute to shaping future conceptualisations of work and accordingly, are more attuned to understanding workers' aspirations.[86]

In a different substantive context, employing IE, Ellen Pence articulates the disjuncture between the lived experiences of battered women and the law and the legal system's engagement with the problem.[87] Pence notes that law understands domestic violence differently to the understandings of battered women. While for the women violence means continued powerlessness including possible future harm, law focuses on violent events and the resultant (principally) physical injury.[88] Women's experiences need to fit into the categories developed by law and administrative agencies, which means that unless their experiences of violence fit into the given categories, the legal process could not be triggered and hence, so far as law is concerned, domestic violence did not occur.[89] She concludes that by textually limiting (by means of substantive clauses and administrative forms) its understanding of injury, the legal system misses the larger concept of harm, thereby missing the opportunity to effectively engage with the problem of battered women in its larger socio-economic context.[90] An analogy could be drawn with informal workers, whose experiences of work are bypassed by the abstraction of legally protected rights, as I mention above.

Thus, IE offers 'a way of seeing, from where we actually live, into the powers, processes, and relations that organize and determine the everyday context of that seeing'.[91] Accordingly norms, institutions and social ordering are to be examined

[83] DeVault, 'Introduction', above n 80, 7.

[84] Dorothy E Smith and Susan Marie Turner, 'Introduction' in Dorothy E Smith and Susan Marie Turner (eds), *Incorporating Texts into Institutional Ethnographies* (Toronto, University of Toronto Press, 2014) 6–7, 10.

[85] DeVault, 'Introduction', above n 80, 7–9, 17–19; Smith, above n 54, 160–61. There is, however, no one way of doing institutional ethnography; research methods for undertaking institutional ethnography are ever evolving. Although in all its variations institutional ethnography engages objectified texts and subjective lived experiences. See Smith and Turner, above n 84, 3–4.

[86] DeVault, 'Mapping Invisible Work', above n 78, 787–88; Smith, above n 54, 160–61.

[87] Ellen Pence, 'Safety for Battered Women in a Textually Mediated Legal System' (2001) 7: 2 *Studies in Cultures, Organizations and Societies*, 199–229.

[88] ibid, 205, 215, 220–22, 225.

[89] ibid, 203.

[90] ibid, 200–02, 226.

[91] Smith, above n 54, 9. According to Smith, in this research method, institutions signify a complex network of relations (but not a specific organisation) that constitutes a 'ruling apparatus' performing

from the location of the marginalised people, 'embodied in the local historicity and particularities of our lived worlds'.[92] IE, therefore, constitutes an alternative sociology rather than a social research method.[93] Several research methods could be employed in understanding the social relations of ruling from specific standpoints.[94] IE is a way of knowing – an epistemology – about society and social relations.[95] By employing this epistemology legal policy makers could access to knowledge that was hereinbefore unavailable to them.[96]

The *epistemic orientation* of IE is particularly helpful in understanding the idea of work in the context of informal workers and analysing the significance of a human rights strategy for the promotion of their aspirations.[97] Analytical understandings of informal work and workers should be grounded on the experiences of such workers at their work. Since these experiences fall outside the ruling framework of the human rights vocabulary, the critique of human rights should then be an outsiders' critique (that is, from the standpoint of workers) on generalisability of workers' conditions and their needs in disregard to specific contexts.[98] The understanding of informal work cannot be based on conceptual categories developed out of industrial employment in Europe, else we end up trying to fit all work-related characteristics within that model and lament the *death of labour law*[99] once realities do not fit the existing models.

Recognition of the centrality of experiences of workers in formulating an idea of work for legal cognisance is not unprecedented.[100] Gordon too underlines the significance of focusing on specific contexts and experiences of particular communities in order to understand and thereby effectively address the precarious plight of informal workers.[101] This increasing realisation of the significance of experience

a specific function such as legal, educational, welfare and so on; and ethnography means an examination of how something *actually works* rather than a commitment to specific research methods such as interviewing or participant observation. Institutional ethnography unearths the dialectic between institutions and everyday practice of people governed by those institutions. See Smith, ibid, 53, 147–48, 160–61.

[92] ibid, 8, 108.

[93] Dorothy Smith, *Institutional Ethnography: A Sociology for People* (Walnut Creek, CA, AltaMira Press, 2006) 2, 57.

[94] Explaining a people's standpoint-based sociology, Smith notes that writing sociology from people's standpoint, in distinction to a standpoint based in theory, means to begin the study in people's everyday lives, but eventually exploring 'social relations and organizations' that are hidden from their everyday interaction. When institutional ethnography is undertaken, 'it becomes a means of expanding people's own knowledge rather than substituting the expert's knowledge for our own'. See Smith, ibid, 1.

[95] 'Series Editors' Foreword', in Smith, ibid, xi.

[96] ibid.

[97] Smith, above n 54, 122, 215; also DeVault, 'Mapping Invisible Work', above n 78, 778.

[98] Smith, above n 54, 36, 78–80, 85, 88.

[99] Cynthia Estlund, 'The Death of Labor Law?' (2006) 2 *Annual Review of Law and Social Science* 105–23. Although Estlund is not concerned with informal workers in this essay – at least explicitly – her title couldn't have been more appropriate to explain the misfit between informality and labour law.

[100] Alain Supiot et al, *Beyond Employment – Changes in Work and the Future of Labour Law in Europe* (Oxford, Oxford University Press, 2001). Supiot and his colleagues forcefully articulate the pertinence of workers' experiences for conceptualising labour law.

[101] Gordon, above n 36, 16, 184.

in facilitating informal workers' aspirations should lead to mainstreaming informal workers' experience-based policy making in addition to the human rights strategy.

IE, in pointing to the gap between embodied workers and abstract generalised legal safeguards, might seem to ignore the complex socio-political interaction that constitutes the backdrop of substantive legal safeguards and instead take substantive rights as emanating merely from statutory texts. It might also seem problematic, although incorrectly, that a social research *method* – that is, IE – could offer any serious critique of *substantive* human rights safeguards. Both of these apprehensions, although appearing *prima facie* reasonable, emerge misplaced on deeper scrutiny. While IE grasps rights and policies from legal and policy texts, its critique lies against only those generalised principles that ignore embodied experiences of workers. Indeed, one of the aims of IE is to indicate the richness that substantive rights and policies might characterise if they integrate workers' experiences into policy making. Thus, IE's thin understanding of law is not *per se* problematic in mounting a critique of abstract rights that are unsuitable for specific situated experiences of workers.

As I mention above, it is this situated experience of workers that is central for the epistemology underlying IE. If actual knowledge emerges from situated experiences of workers, it seems reasonable – indeed essential – that a critique of generalised substantive human rights be made on the basis of such epistemology. Further, research methods do not exist in vacuum; they follow from epistemology. IE is an epistemology, a way of knowing, not a research method (as I mention above).[102] Several qualitative research methods such as interviewing, group discussion, participant observation, triangulation, and quantitative methods could be employed to undertake IE.[103] It is this epistemology, not methods of doing research, that I draw on in critiquing the human rights strategy. Thus, in employing an IE-based critique of the human rights language, I contend that substantive human rights fail to access people's situated knowledge that IE unearths and instead depends on objectified expert knowledge in articulating people's entitlements. And this failure is particularly detrimental in facilitating aspirations of non-industrial informal workers.

V. Conclusion: A Rights Plus Approach

It is true that in extraordinarily desperate situations for workers the human rights vocabulary as a political instrument might be an important recourse for them, perhaps the only recourse.[104] Legally safeguarded human rights are oftentimes also

[102] See generally Smith, *Institutional Ethnography*, above n 93.
[103] ibid.
[104] See Compa, 'Workers' Freedom', above n 4, 36–44; Gordon, above n 36, 10–39, 148–50, 165–69, 179–80.

important in promoting collective action of and negotiation by workers.[105] In spite of these advantages, scholars acknowledge that human rights are unable to go too far in addressing deeply entrenched structural injustices.[106]

Informality leads to structural injustices. By reason of the nature of their activity, informal workers are systematically bypassed by legal and policy imagination. Law and legally safeguarded human rights standards have not been able to find an appropriate way to engage with informal workers that leads to the promotion of their aspirations. This is because the human rights discourse seeks to subsume disparate experiences of working into an industrial mass production framework. While the original formulation of workers' human rights standards took industrial factory-based workers' experiences as their point of reference, its reluctance to take informal workers' experiences at work into account in reformulating its standards is ironic.

If the human rights discourse is to preserve its legitimacy as an effective emancipatory tool for workers, it needs to place informal workers at the centre of the discourse. Structural changes could be facilitated by placing workers' situated experiences at the centre of the challenge posed to the existing order of organising labour rights.[107] Since informal workers are mostly situated *outside* the ruling apparatus of human rights, it is only by looking at their embodied experiences in their locally situated context that one can hope to understand their needs and aspirations.[108] Without a better understanding of their aspirations, one cannot *a priori* conclude that human rights claims are destined to improve their working conditions and living situations.

Moreover, a court-based strategy, apart from being prolonged and costly, is ill-equipped in engaging with the nuances of the diverse nature of informal work. The judiciary tries to fit violation of justified claims in the given box of substantive human rights. It is unable to open up spaces for different entitlement conceptualisations on the basis of workers' unique experiences and aspirations. A court-based strategy, even when successful, is no substitute for collective action and continued dialogue amongst stakeholders.[109] Thus, while it may be useful to employ the human rights language in promoting workers' aspirations for certain justified claims, for others, informal workers need to continuously engage with the several stakeholders in shaping policies that take their experiences as the informational basis of policy making.

In closing, human rights are theoretically available to all human beings – one is born to that status rather than attains it. However, work is an active notion that requires peoples' commitment and toil. If workers' demands are to be made

[105] Gordon, above n 36, 148–50.
[106] ibid, 151.
[107] ibid, 155.
[108] Smith, above n 54, 46–47, 65.
[109] See generally Lobel, above n 45.

as human rights claims, one substitutes an active notion of human being characterising agency with a passive notion of human being attained by reason of birth. This strategy not only converts a worker into a passive claimant of rights (notwithstanding the historical struggle inherent in the human rights discourse), it also sidelines the very significance of work from social organisation. There is, then, some reason why even advocates of a human rights strategy for workers conclude that workers' collective action is essential for the success of the human rights discourse and that human rights cannot flourish if workers' claims are not respected.[110]

[110] Compa, 'Workers' Freedom', above n 4, 52.

5

Labour Law as a Luxury in the Global South? A Case Study from Zimbabwe

PAMHIDZAI H BAMU*

I. Introduction

Modern labour law is premised on the standard employment relationship, which is characterised by full-time, permanent wage work in the context of a bilateral relationship where the employee works on premises controlled by the employer. It emerged and became the norm for labour regulation during the post-war period of prosperity in North America and Western Europe. This period was marked by the rise of welfare state capitalism, which entailed a strong state role in altering the balance of power between employers and workers and the growth of income security and public welfare programmes.[1]

Labour law (understood broadly to include the regulation of employment relations, working conditions and social security)[2] in many countries of the global South has historically been modelled on labour law in the global North.[3] This is the case in many African and Asian states that were colonised by European settlers. This began with the transplantation of labour law systems during colonisation, and the dominance of the former colonies' labour law systems as models for labour law development post-independence.[4] Consequently, labour law in many of these

* LLB, LLM, PhD (Cape Town). I am grateful to the Stellenbosch University Faculty of Law, which provided the funds and institutional space for me to conduct the Post-Doctoral research that enabled me to write this chapter.

[1] See G Standing, *Global Labour Flexibility: Seeking Distributive Justice* (London, Macmillan, 1999) 53, 55; IU Haque, 'Globalization, Neoliberalism and Labour', United Nations Conference on Trade and Development Discussion Paper No 173 (2004) 6.

[2] K Sankaran, 'Labour Law in South Asia' in S Marshall and C Fenwick (eds), *Labour Regulation and Development* (Cheltenham, Edward Elgar, 2016) 213.

[3] See Sankaran, 'Labour Law in South Asia', above n 2 at 212–13.

[4] See C Fenwick, ER Kalula and I Landau, *Labour Law: A Southern African Perspective* (Geneva, International Institute for Labor Studies, 2007) 1–2.

countries has been, and continues to be, premised on the notion of the standard employment relationship in the context of a Fordist workplace.[5]

Using Zimbabwe as a case study, this chapter seeks to demonstrate that labour law's focus on the standard employment relationship is problematic in many countries of the global South, where a sizeable proportion of workers, especially women, labour in the informal economy. The informal economy refers to all economic units, economic activities and workers that fall outside the scope of regulation.[6] It comprises two components. The first is the *informal sector*, which comprises the production and employment that take place in unregistered enterprises.[7] The second is *informal employment*, which refers to paid employment – whether inside or outside the informal sector – that does not provide employment-based social protection.[8] The informal economy spans a diverse range of sectors and occupational groups.[9]

Research on the informal economy is riddled with conceptual challenges, as the formal and informal sector on the one hand and the formal and informal economy on the other are often used interchangeably. In addition, methodological challenges of reconciling the overlapping concepts of 'enterprise' and 'worker'[10] make it difficult to measure the different components of the formal and informal economies. Compounding these challenges is the reality that formality and informality are not discrete categories, but more closely resemble ends of a spectrum of diverse enterprises and employment relationships.

In this chapter, I will refer to the formal and informal *sectors*, as opposed to the formal and informal *economies* more broadly. This choice assumes that the standard employment relationship is predominantly found in the formal enterprises in the formal sector; and that work in the informal sector typically falls outside the standard employment relationship.

Using a political economy approach, I consider Zimbabwe's labour market in a historical context. My analysis spans five periods in the country's history, namely i) the colonial era (1890–1980); ii) the post-independence decade (1980–1990); iii) the Economic Structural Adjustment Programme (ESAP) period (1991–1996); iv) the crisis period (1997–2008); and v) the post-crisis period, beginning with the formation of the Government of National Unity (GNU) in 2009 to the end of the Mugabe era in 2017. I cover these periods in sections II to VI of this chapter, showing that employment in the formal economy has historically accounted for a limited proportion of the country's labour force.

[5] ibid.

[6] Martha Alter Chen, 'The informal economy: Recent trends, future directions' (2016) 26(2) *New Solutions: A Journal of Environmental and Occupational Health Policy* 155, 158–59.

[7] Martha Alter Chen, 'Women Informal Workers', A Policy Brief for the UN Secretary General's High-Level Panel on Women's Economic Empowerment (2016) 1.

[8] ibid.

[9] Chen, 'The informal economy', above n 6 at 158–59.

[10] See Sankaran,' Labor Law in South Asia', above n 2 at 218–19.

The chapter chronicles the post-independence relationship between the formal and the informal sectors at two levels, namely the level of the worker and the level of the household. Two trends in worker-level linkages are apparent, with the first being the movement of workers from employment in the formal sector to work in the informal sector. The second worker-level trend relates to individuals employed in the formal sector and concurrently engaging in informal economic activities on a part-time basis to supplement their wages. At the household level, many families have become increasingly dependent on informal sector earnings as opposed to wages from the formal sector.

In section VII, I draw together the analysis and underscore the informal sector's role in providing a source of livelihood for workers who fail to obtain formal employment, those who lose their formal employment, and those who need to supplement their income from formal employment. It is also an increasingly important source of income to many households in Zimbabwe. Recalling that labour law's focus is on the standard employment relationship in the formal sector, I argue that it constitutes a luxury for a small proportion of privileged workers and excludes the majority. Drawing on lessons from the International Labour Organization (ILO), I make recommendations for the extension of labour law's protection to workers in the informal sector. I end this contribution with brief reflections on issues for further research in section VIII.

II. The Colonial Period: 1890–1980

The land that is now called Zimbabwe was colonised by British settlers from 1890 to 1980. Ndoro reports that prior to the arrival of the British settlers, the indigenous population engaged in primary and secondary economic activities.[11] These included agriculture, gold and copper mining, copper smelting, foundry work, iron work and beer brewing.[12] The indigenous population recognised these as legitimate activities that were central to their economy in the territory. One could therefore argue that these activities constituted the formal sector.

The colonial government promoted the commercial interests of British capitalists by, inter alia, addressing the need for the latter's access to cheap labour from the indigenous communities.[13] The colonial government used two strategies to achieve this. First, it forced the indigenous people to seek work for the new capital

[11] H Ndoro 'Zimbabwe: The informal sector in a decontrolling formerly "Socialist" economy' in GCZ Mhone (ed), *The Informal Sector in Southern Africa: An Analysis of Conceptual, Research and Policy Issues* (Harare, SAPES Books, 1991) 23.

[12] ibid.

[13] See AE Sibanda, 'The Political Economy of Zimbabwe: Focus on the Creation of a Proletariat: Implications for the Labour Movement' (Harare, Zimbabwe Institute of Development Studies Discussion Paper Series, 1992), 5.

class through measures such as expropriation of land and the imposition of taxes on the African population.[14] Second, it introduced measures to discourage and prohibit black people from engaging in independent entrepreneurial activities.

The colonial government's direct and indirect labour policies created a migrant labour system and the 'split household' as African men migrated to work for capitalist concerns for meagre wages.[15] The families of migrant workers remained in the communal 'reserves' and survived on subsistence agriculture and shouldered the burden of migrant workers' illness or death.[16] The state reserved higher-skilled and better-paying positions for white workers, and confined black workers to unskilled and casual jobs that did not provide for their advancement.[17] White workers in industrial and mining enterprises were protected by the Industrial Conciliation Act of 1934, which prohibited Africans from organising or participating in collective bargaining. Domestic and agricultural workers fell under the Master and Servant legislation, which largely left them to their employers' devices.[18]

Securing the hegemony of the new capitalist class was premised on the suppression of pre-existing indigenous economic activities.[19] The colonial authorities usurped the power to confer legitimacy on existing economic activities and informalised black people's independent activities such as manufacturing, repairs, personal services and retail trade[20] by 'a heavy dose of stigmatization

[14] LM Sachikonye, 'Labour Legislation in Zimbabwe: Historical and Contemporary Perspectives' (Harare, Zimbabwe Institute of Development Studies Discussion Paper Series, 1985), 3; M Ncube, 'Employment, unemployment and the evolution of labour policy in Zimbabwe' (2000) XXVII(ii) *Zambezia* 161, 162; Sibanda, 'Political Economy of Zimbabwe', above n 13 at 5.

[15] G Kanyenze, T Kondo, P Chitambara and J Martens (eds), *Beyond the Enclave, Towards a Pro-Poor and Inclusive Development Strategy for Zimbabwe* (Harare, Weaver Press, 2011) 257.

[16] J Dhemba, 'Informal sector development: A strategy for alleviating urban poverty in Zimbabwe' (1999) 14(2) *Journal of Social Development in Africa* 5 at 8–9; Kanyenze et al, *Beyond the Enclave*, above n 15 at 257.

[17] M Ncube, 'Employment, unemployment and the evolution of labour policy in Zimbabwe', above n 14 at 162; NP Moyo, 'The State, Planning and Labour: Towards transforming the colonial labour process in Zimbabwe' (1988) 24(4) *The Journal of Development Studies*, 203, 205; C Bailey, W van Ginneken, R van der Hoeven, V Jamal, E Lee, A Marinakis, F Stewart, D Tajgman, *Structural Change and Adjustment in Zimbabwe* (Geneva, ILO, 1993), 107–08; GCZ Mhone, 'The Social Dimensions of Adjustment (SDA) Programme in Zimbabwe: A critical review and assessment' (1995) 7(1) *European Journal of Development Research*, 101, 102.

[18] NP Moyo, 'The State, Planning and Labour', above n 17 at 206.

[19] GCZ Mhone, 'Conceptual and Analytical Issues' in GCZ Mhone (ed), *The Informal Sector in Southern Africa: An Analysis of Conceptual, Research and Policy Issues* (Harare, SAPES Books, 1991), at 11–12. The colonial policies pursued in Zimbabwe mirrored those adopted in other Southern African colonies. See T Mkandawire, 'The informal sector in the labour reserve economies of Southern Africa with special reference to Zimbabwe' (1986) 11(1) *Africa Development/ Afrique et Développement* 61.

[20] Ndoro, 'Zimbabwe: The informal sector in a decontrolling formerly "Socialist" economy', above n 11 at 23; NP Moyo, RJ Davies, GCZ Mhone and L Pakkiri, 'The informal sector in Zimbabwe: Its potential for employment creation', Study prepared for the Ministry of Labour, Manpower Development and Social Welfare by ILO Southern Africa Team for Employment Promotion (Harare, SATEP, 1984) 24.

and legal sanction'.[21] The government denigrated black people's economic activities as 'inadequate', 'backwards', 'wasteful' and 'inefficient'.[22] It constrained their activities through a barrage of laws and regulations, including the expropriation of their fertile land and other productive resources,[23] racist licensing laws, restrictions on freedom of movement in urban areas and the express prohibition of Africans' engagement in lucrative economic activities.[24] The inequality was reinforced by a policy bias towards the formal sector in the provision of credit, infrastructure, foreign currency, training and the application of protective regulations.[25]

The outcome of these policies was the emergence of a dual economy in the country. There was a well-developed and relatively sophisticated economy.[26] Unlike the first generation of developed Western economies, the formal part of the economy did not evolve from internal growth, but was grafted onto the pre-colonial forms of production by the British settlers.[27] It therefore formed an enclave economy that was dependent on and constrained by external capital, external markets and imports.[28] Consequently, in 1980, formal employment accounted for about 25 per cent of the labour force.[29] About 10 per cent of the labour force were working in informal enterprises and 55 per cent in the communal areas, and the remaining 10 per cent of the labour force was unemployed.[30]

Significantly, patriarchal norms and sexist colonial policies conspired to relegate women to a lower position in the economy and labour market.[31] Women of

[21] Ndoro, 'Zimbabwe: The informal sector in a decontrolling formerly "Socialist" economy', above n 11 at 23.

[22] ibid.

[23] Mhone, 'The Social Dimensions of Adjustment (SDA) Programme in Zimbabwe', above n 17 at 102; NP Moyo, 'The State, Planning and Labour', above n 17 at 206.

[24] Bailey et al, *Structural Change and Adjustment in Zimbabwe*, above n 17 at 21; Zimbabwe Institute, *Labour Market and Sustainable Growth and Transformation in Zimbabwe* (Cape Town, Zimbabwe Institute, 2007), 17; F Siddiqui and RS Maya, *The Development Potential of Small-scale and Informal Sector Enterprises in Zimbabwe* (Harare, International Labour Office Employment and Manpower Planning Project, 1992), 1, 4; Ndoro, 'Zimbabwe: The informal sector in a decontrolling formerly "Socialist" economy', 23; Mkandawire, 'The informal sector in the labour reserve economies of Southern Africa', above n 19 at 16, 18.

[25] Mhone, 'The Social Dimensions of Adjustment (SDA) Programme in Zimbabwe', above n 17 at 107.

[26] Kanyenze et al, *Beyond the Enclave*, n 15 above at 5; The Zimbabwe Institute, *Labour Market and Sustainable Growth and Transformation in Zimbabwe*, above n 24 at 26.

[27] G Kanyenze, T Kondo, and J Martens (eds), *The Search for Sustainable Human Development in Southern Africa* (Harare, Alternatives to Neoliberalism in Southern Africa, 2006), 28–29.

[28] Kanyenze et al, *Beyond the Enclave*, above n 15, 4–5; JH Conning and JA Robinson, 'Enclaves and Development: An empirical assessment' (2009) 44 *Studies in Comparative International Development* 359 at 361.

[29] Kanyenze et al, *Beyond the Enclave*, above n 15, 4–5. AO Chimhowu, J Manjengwa and S Feresu, *Moving Forward in Zimbabwe: Reducing poverty and promoting growth* (Harare, Institute of Environmental Studies, 2010), Table 2.2.

[30] Ncube, 'Employment, unemployment and the evolution of labour policy in Zimbabwe', above n 14 at 165.

[31] ON Moyo and SM Kawewe, 'The dynamics of a racialized, gendered and ethnicised and economically stratified society: Understanding the socio-economic status of women in Zimbabwe' (2002) 8(2)

all races constituted a mere 17 per cent of the formal workforce in 1980, and dominated in the health and agricultural sectors.[32] They played a minor role in key sectors such as manufacturing and mining and comprised only 3 per cent of workers in the highest-paying electricity and water sector.[33] Black women were situated at the intersection of gender, race, ethnicity and class dynamics and were the most marginalised in the labour market.[34]

III. The Post-independence Decade: 1980–1990

At independence, the new government promulgated a series of socio-economic policies, which promised to bring about inclusive economic growth and an egalitarian society. However, it maintained the existing ownership structure of the private sector[35] and preserved the colonial order's interventionist and conservative macro-economic policies.[36] The pro-capitalist policies were juxtaposed with a 'socialist' agenda to expand the public sector and to extend the public administration, health and education sectors to the previously marginalised black majority.[37] The government also subsidised and controlled prices of basic foodstuffs and utilities to raise the living standards of lower income groups.[38]

Significant labour reforms were enacted to redress the labour market inequalities of the colonial era. The Minimum Wages Act set minimum wages for workers in various sectors. The Employment Act and several statutory instruments in the early 1980s protected security of employment and provided for maternity protection, which had been neglected by colonial labour laws.[39] The 1985 Labour

Feminist Economics, 163, 166–70; Kanyenze et al *Beyond the Enclave, Towards a Pro-Poor and Inclusive Development Strategy for Zimbabwe*, above n 15 at 256.

[32] Ncube, 'Employment, unemployment and the evolution of labour policy in Zimbabwe', above n 14 at 166.

[33] Kanyenze et al, *Beyond the Enclave*, above n 15 at 259.

[34] ON Moyo and Kawewe, 'The dynamics of a racialised, gendered and ethnicised and economically stratified society', above n 31 at 166–67.

[35] Sachikonye, 'Labour Legislation in Zimbabwe: Historical and Contemporary Perspectives', above n 14 at 8; G Kanyenze, 'Economic Policy Making Processes, Implementation and Impact in Zimbabwe', Paper prepared for the Centre for Rural Development (2006) 13–14.

[36] These include import substitution, foreign exchange control, and agricultural subsidies. Mhone, 'The Social Dimensions of Adjustment (SDA) Programme in Zimbabwe', above n 17 at 103; BM Chiripanhura and P Makwavarara, 'The Labour Market and Economic Development 1980–2000', undated paper for the Zimbabwean Congress of Trade Unions (ZCTU) at 9.

[37] F Siddiqui and RS Maya, *The Development Potential of Small-scale and Informal Sector Enterprises in Zimbabwe* (Geneva, ILO/UNDP/Zimbabwe Ministry of Labour, Manpower Planning and Social Welfare, 1992), above n 24 at 1; Mhone, 'The Social Dimensions of Adjustment (SDA) Programme in Zimbabwe', above n 17 at 102; Bailey et al, *Structural Change and Adjustment in Zimbabwe*, above n 24 at 23; Kanyenze et al, *Beyond the Enclave*, above n 15 at 35, 366–68, 300–305.

[38] C Peters-Berries, *The Urban Informal Sector in Zimbabwe: From Insignificance to the Employer of the Last Resort* (Geneva, International Labour Office, World Employment Programme, 1993) 1.

[39] For example, the Employment (Conditions of Service) Regulations 1981 Statutory Instrument 894 of 1981; Emergency Powers (Termination of Employment) Regulations of 1982 Statutory Instrument

Relations Act introduced additional rights, including freedom of association and worker participation, non-discrimination, provision for paid maternity leave, and the protection of the right to strike.[40]

The new government succeeded in increasing access to social services, especially health and education, to the majority.[41] By contrast, the economy did not achieve the targets set out in the national development plans as economic growth declined and inflation increased in the latter part of the decade.[42] The economy failed to create sufficient new jobs, with school leavers swelling the ranks of the unemployed.[43] The small increase in employment recorded during the decade was attributable to the expansion of the public sector, as opposed to growth in the productive sectors such as agriculture, manufacturing and mining.[44]

Moreover, employers made greater use of casual labour to avoid the obligations that the new legislation imposed on employers.[45] Female workers were more likely to be employed on a casual basis than male workers, under more precarious employment conditions than those of their male counterparts.[46] Women continued to be marginalised in the formal sector, where they represented less than 5 per cent of all skilled workers.[47] They continued to dominate the domestic sector, where they worked under poor conditions.[48]

748 of 1982; and Commercial Undertaking of Zimbabwe Employment Regulations (1983) Statutory Instrument 571 of 1983. See generally LM Sachikonye, 'The Protection of Security of Employment: the Zimbabwean Experience' (Harare, Zimbabwe Institute of Development Studies Consultancy Report No 14, 1990), 5–7.

[40] Ncube, 'Employment, unemployment and the evolution of labour policy in Zimbabwe', above n 14 at 187–88; Sachikonye, 'Labour Legislation in Zimbabwe: Historical and Contemporary Perspectives', above n 14 at 13–14.

[41] Mhone, 'The Social Dimensions of Adjustment (SDA) Programme in Zimbabwe', above n 17 at 104; Chiripanhura and Makwavarara, 'The Labour Market and Economic Development 1980–2000', above n 36 at 57.

[42] Kanyenze et al, *Beyond the Enclave*, above n 15 at 35–36; R Gaidzanwa, *Voting with their Feet: Migrant Zimbabwean Nurses and Doctors in the Era of Structural Adjustment* (Uppsala, Nordiska Afrikainstitutet, 1999), at 24; The Zimbabwe Institute, *Labour Market and Sustainable Growth and Transformation in Zimbabwe*, above n 24 at 29.

[43] Chiripanhura and Makwavarara, 'The Labour Market and Economic Development 1980–2000', above n 36 at 57; Mhone, 'The Social Dimensions of Adjustment (SDA) Programme in Zimbabwe', above n 17 at 104; Bailey et al, *Structural Change and Adjustment in Zimbabwe*, above n 14 at 109.

[44] Author's calculations from Chiripanhura and Makwavarara, 'The Labour Market and Economic Development 1980–2000', above n 36 at 57, and Chimhowu et al, *Moving forward in Zimbabwe: Reducing Poverty and Promoting Growth*, above n 29 at 23.

[45] Chimhowu et al, *Moving forward in Zimbabwe: Reducing Poverty and Promoting Growth*, above n 29 at 23; TD Shopo and S Moyo, 'Vulnerable Working Households in Zimbabwe's Segmented Labour Markets' (Harare, Zimbabwe Institute of Development Studies, Working Paper No 5, 1986), 49–52; Ncube, 'Employment, unemployment and the evolution of labour policy in Zimbabwe', above n 14 at 165–66.

[46] Chimhowu et al, *Moving Forward in Zimbabwe: Reducing Poverty and Promoting Growth*, above n 29 at 23.

[47] RS Maya, *Structural Adjustment in Zimbabwe: Its Impact on Women* (Harare, Institute of Development Studies Consultancy report No 13), 27; Ncube, 'Employment, unemployment and the evolution of labour policy in Zimbabwe', above n 14 at 166.

[48] Shopo and Moyo, 'Vulnerable Working Households in Zimbabwe's Segmented Labour Markets', above n 45 at 58–59, 62.

The number of informal micro-enterprises increased significantly following independence. The post-independence growth in informal economic activity was facilitated by the repeal of laws restricting freedom of movement, and the relaxation of restrictions on access to licences and vending sites.[49] The growth was also driven by increased rural–urban migration, slow economic growth and the economy's failure to generate adequate jobs in the formal sector.[50] In 1991, there were an estimated 845,000 non-farming and non-mining micro and small enterprises (MSEs) employing about 1.6 million people, including the proprietors.[51]

IV. The ESAP Period: 1991–1996

In an about-turn from its macro-economic policies during the post-independence decade, the government formally adopted the Economic Structural Adjustment Programme (ESAP) in 1991.[52] The key tenets of ESAP included the liberalisation of foreign exchange and trade regimes; the liberalisation of foreign investment regulations; the elimination of subsidies, reduction of social expenditures and levying of cost recovery rates for social services; the rationalisation of some public enterprises and privatisation of others; and the deregulation of the labour market. Following the economy's dismal post-independence performance, government hoped that ESAP would generate greater economic growth.

Proponents and critics of ESAP agree that the programme failed to achieve the desired results and that it worsened the socio-economic conditions in the country. Business performance declined as a result of ESAP's tight monetary policies including high interest rates, credit restrictions and the phased removal of export incentives.[53] Local manufacturing firms found it difficult to compete with the

[49] M Leubker, *Employment, Unemployment and Informality in Zimbabwe: Concepts and Data for Coherent Policy-making* (Harare, ILO, 2008), 4–5; Shopo and Moyo, 'Vulnerable Working Households in Zimbabwe's Segmented Labour Markets', above n 45 at 78.

[50] Mhone, *The Impact of Structural Adjustment on the Urban Informal Sector* (Geneva, International Labour Office Development and Technical Cooperation Department, 1998), 2.

[51] MA McPherson, *Micro and Small-scale Enterprises in Zimbabwe: Results of a Country-Wide Survey* (Maryland, Growth and Equity through Microenterprise Investments and Institutions, 1991). This will be referred to as the GEMINI study (1991). Although this report focused on micro and small-scale enterprises as opposed to informal enterprises per se, most of the enterprises surveyed were unregistered and therefore informal (see vii–viii).

[52] Although the comprehensive framework was adopted in 1991, the government 'had already taken several measures which provided the basis of the adjustment package'. See Bailey et al, *Structural Change and Adjustment in Zimbabwe*, above n 14 at 31; Kanyenze, 'Economic Policy Making Processes, Implementation and Impact in Zimbabwe', above n 35 at 14–15.

[53] P Gibbon, *Structural Adjustment and the Working Poor in Zimbabwe: Studies on labour, women informal sector workers and health* (Uppsala, Nordiska Afrikainstitutet, 1995) 9–10; International Labour Office Employment and Manpower Planning Project and Ministry of Labour, Manpower Planning and Social Welfare, *Employment Prospects in Zimbabwe Under the Economic Structural Adjustment Programme* (Harare, International Labour Office, 1992), 17–18.

influx of cheap imports after the liberalisation of the trade regime.[54] The country's exports, GDP and rate of economic growth declined during the 1990s.[55] The period was marked by high inflation, the erosion of the real value of earnings and a decline in consumer spending.[56]

Under these conditions, the economy was unable to maintain pre-ESAP levels of employment. Some private sector firms downsized or ceased to operate, and retrenched workers in terms of the amended labour regulations.[57] In the public sector, job losses were the result of ESAP's imperatives to 'rationalise' the public service and government parastatals.[58] Between 100,000 and 160,000 workers were retrenched between 1991 and 1995.[59] Unemployment also increased as the economy failed to absorb retrenched workers and new labour market entrants.[60] Job shedding was accompanied by the employment of workers on temporary and casual contracts.[61] The casualisation of the workforce brought greater job and income insecurity, and had a greater impact on female workers.[62]

[54] M Grant, 'Lodging as a migrant economic strategy in urban Zimbabwe' (2007) 24(1) *Development Southern Africa* 78 at 82; B Chiripanhura, 'Sneaking up and stumbling back: Textile sector performance under crisis conditions in Zimbabwe' (2010) 22 *Journal of International Development* 153 at 155–56; Kanyenze et al, *Beyond the Enclave*, above n 15 at 134, 218.

[55] Kanyenze et al, *Beyond the Enclave*, above n 15 at 38, 135.

[56] Gibbon, *Structural Adjustment and the Working Poor in Zimbabwe*, above n 53 at 9–10; Ncube 'Employment, unemployment and the evolution of labour policy in Zimbabwe', above n 14 at 184–85.

[57] Chiripanhura and Makwavarara, 'The Labour Market and Economic Development 1980–2000', above n 36 at 23, 45.

[58] Gaidzanwa, *Voting with their Feet: Migrant Zimbabwean Nurses and Doctors in the Era of Structural Adjustment*, above n 42 at 25; Ncube, 'Employment, unemployment and the evolution of labour policy in Zimbabwe', above n 14 at 165–67.

[59] See eg S Kawewe and R Dibie, 'The Impact of Economic Structural Adjustment Programmes (ESAPs) on Women and Children: Implications for Social Welfare in Zimbabwe' (2000) 27(4) *Journal of Sociology and Social Welfare* 79 at 94; Mhone, 'The Social Dimensions of Adjustment (SDA) Programme in Zimbabwe', above n 17 at 114; Ncube, 'Employment, unemployment and the evolution of labour policy in Zimbabwe', above n 14 at 165–67. However, official employment statistics during this period indicate a slight increase in overall (formal) employment during the early 1990s. See, eg, Chiripanhura and Makwavarara, 'The Labour Market and Economic Development 1980–2000', above n 36 at 57.

[60] Chimhowu et al, *Moving Forward in Zimbabwe*, above n 29 at 28; The Zimbabwe Institute, *Labour Market and Sustainable Growth and Transformation in Zimbabwe*, above n 24 at 35; BM Chiripanhura, 'Zimbabwe's labour market dynamics: prospects for recovery' (undated PowerPoint presentation). Unemployment data covering the 1990s is somewhat patchy, as official statistics use different definitions of unemployment and measure it at different points in time. Although government statistics consistently used the strict definition of unemployment, its different departments and institutions published widely varying figures for unemployment, even for the same year. For example, the Ministry of Public Service, Labour and Social Welfare put unemployment in 1993 at 44 per cent, while Central Statistical Office figures for the same year pegged it at only 7.9 per cent. Statistics provided by non-state institutions generally used a wider definition of unemployment, and their figures are much higher than the official statistics. However, the overall picture from official and unofficial statistics throughout the 1990s is a trend in rising unemployment during the 1990s.

[61] Chiripanhura and Makwavarara, 'The Labour Market and Economic Development 1980–2000', above n 36 at 45, 48; Mhone, 'The Social Dimensions of Adjustment (SDA) Programme in Zimbabwe', above n 17 at 108; Ncube, 'Employment, unemployment and the evolution of labour policy in Zimbabwe', above n 14 at 164; Bailey et al, *Structural Change and Adjustment in Zimbabwe*, above n 14 at 41.

[62] Chiripanhura and Makwavarara, 'The Labour Market and Economic Development 1980–2000', above n 36 at 45, 48; Bailey et al, *Structural Change and Adjustment in Zimbabwe*, above n 14 at 41.

Against this backdrop, the prevalence, depth and severity of poverty increased and the well-being of people in Zimbabwe declined.[63] Ordinary Zimbabweans associated ESAP with fewer job opportunities, the higher incidence of retrenchments, low pay levels, a higher cost of living and higher levels of poverty.[64] They came to refer to ESAP as the 'Extreme Suffering of African People'. Women and children bore the brunt of the declining socio-economic environment, and the decline in living conditions was more severe in urban than in rural areas.[65] Workers, trade unions and civil society expressed their dissatisfaction with their working and living conditions under ESAP through strike action and demonstrations.[66] Others 'voted with their feet' by migrating to countries such as South Africa, Botswana, the United Kingdom and the United States.[67]

The ESAP period was marked by the growth in the number of micro and small enterprises (MSEs) and an increase in the number of people employed in these enterprises. The growth in the informal sector was accompanied by a shift in its sectoral distribution, as the number of manufacturing and construction activities declined and that of trade activities increased.[68] This reflected the high growth in informal activities with minimal entry barriers.[69]

There were changes in the significance of the informal sector linkages with the formal sector at the worker and household levels. At the worker level, more workers were shifting from formal employment to become owners or employees in informal enterprises[70] due to retrenchments in the formal sector.[71] There was also

[63] A Hamdok, 'A poverty assessment exercise in Zimbabwe' (1999) *African Development Review* 290 at 291; J Alwang et al, 'Changes in poverty in Zimbabwe between 1990 and 1996: Worsening outcomes under adverse conditions' (2001) 18(5) *Development Southern Africa*, 553 at 556, 561–65; Mhone, 'The Social Dimensions of Adjustment (SDA) Programme in Zimbabwe', above n 17 at 79.

[64] See, eg, the findings from the ZCTU's public participatory forums to discuss the impact of ESAP in Chiripanhura and Makwavarara, 'The Labour Market and Economic Development 1980–2000', above n 36 at 40.

[65] Hamdok, 'A poverty assessment exercise in Zimbabwe', above n 63 at 297; Kanyenze et al, *Beyond the Enclave*, above n 15 at 216–18; Gibbon, *Structural Adjustment and the Working Poor in Zimbabwe*, above n 53 at 22–24; Chiripanhura and Makwavarara, 'The Labour Market and Economic Development 1980–2000' n 36 above at 24, 30; Bailey et al, *Structural Change and Adjustment in Zimbabwe*, above n 14 at 3; Kawewe and Dibie, 'The impact of Economic Structural Adjustment Programmes (ESAPs) on Women and Children, above n 59 at 90; Alwang et al, 'Changes in poverty in Zimbabwe between 1990 and 1996', above n 63 at 558–59; J Dhemba, 'Informal sector development: A strategy for alleviating urban poverty in Zimbabwe', above n 16 at 10–11.

[66] Gaidzanwa, *Voting with their Feet: Migrant Zimbabwean Nurses and Doctors in the Era of Structural Adjustment*, above n 42 at 7; Kanyenze, 'Economic Policy Making Processes, Implementation and Impact in Zimbabwe', above n 35 at 17–18; N Kanji and N Jadowska, 'Gender, structural adjustment and employment in urban Zimbabwe' 17(2) (1995) *Third World Policy Review* 133 at 152.

[67] Gaidzanwa, *Voting with their Feet: Migrant Zimbabwean Nurses and Doctors in the Era of Structural Adjustment*, above n 42 at 35; Mhone, 'The Social Dimensions of Adjustment (SDA) Programme in Zimbabwe', above n 17 at 118.

[68] L Daniels, *Changes in the Small-Scale Enterprise Sector from 1991 to 1993: Results of a Second Nationwide Survey in Zimbabwe* (Bethesda, GEMINI, 1994) 14.

[69] Daniels, *Changes in the Small-Scale Enterprise Sector from 1991 to 1993*, above n 68 at 16, 21–22; Mhone, *The Impact of Structural Adjustment on the Urban Informal Sector in Zimbabwe*, above n 50 at 34.

[70] Mhone, *The Impact of Structural Adjustment on the Urban Informal Sector in Zimbabwe*, above n 50 at 133; Alwang et al, 'Changes in poverty in Zimbabwe between 1990 and 1996', above n 63 at 560.

[71] ibid.

a greater tendency for some workers to straddle both the formal sector employment and informal economic activities.[72] This was necessary to supplement low wages considering declining real wages of formal sector workers.[73] The most notable amongst the ESAP era 'straddlers' were civil servants, who had formerly been regarded as the labour aristocracy.[74] Many engaged in 'moonlighting', traded during working time and engaged in corrupt activities.[75]

At the household level, there was an increase in the number of income earners and a diversification of the sources of household income, with informal sector earnings becoming more important. Whereas urban households could formerly survive on one (usually formal wage) income during the 1980s, more households depended on two or more income earners under ESAP.[76] Most of the new income earners were engaged in informal economic activities, either as proprietors or as employees.[77] In addition, proprietors were more likely to employ spouses, children and extended family members to supplement their incomes.[78] Despite earning less from informal activities than their male counterparts, women played a greater role in extending household incomes, and committed most of their earnings and profits to meeting household needs.[79]

V. The Crisis Period: 1997–2008

The decline of the Zimbabwean economy must be understood against the historical backdrop of 'colonial resource inequalities, narrow forms of capital accumulation that failed to build a proper productive base, a labour reproduction system based on low wages and migrant labour, problematic developmental strategies in both the "welfarist" 1980s and in the neoliberal 1990s'.[80] In addition

[72] Gibbon, 'Structural Adjustment and the Working Poor in Zimbabwe', above n 53 at 23. See also: ILO, SATEP study (1984), above n 20, p 21.

[73] Mhone, *The Impact of Structural Adjustment on the Urban Informal Sector in Zimbabwe*, above n 50 at 133; Alwang et al, 'Changes in poverty in Zimbabwe between 1990 and 1996', above n 63 at 560.

[74] Gibbon, 'Structural Adjustment and the Working Poor in Zimbabwe', above n 63 at 23; Bailey et al, *Structural Change and Adjustment in Zimbabwe*, above n 14 at 126–27.

[75] Bailey et al, *Structural Change and Adjustment in Zimbabwe*, above n 14 at 126–27.

[76] Grant, 'Lodging as a migrant economic strategy in urban Zimbabwe', above n 54 at 82–83; Alwang et al, 'Changes in poverty in Zimbabwe between 1990 and 1996', above n 63 at 559; Bailey et al, *Structural Change and Adjustment in Zimbabwe*, above n 14 at 85–86.

[77] Mhone, *The Impact of Structural Adjustment on the Urban Informal Sector in Zimbabwe*, above n 50 at 134. See also: GEMINI Study (1991), above n 51 at 9.

[78] Mhone, *The Impact of Structural Adjustment on the Urban Informal Sector in Zimbabwe*, above n 50 at 137.

[79] Kanji and Jadowska, 'Gender, structural adjustment and employment in urban Zimbabwe', above n 66 at 140–42; R Mupedziswa and P Gumbo, *Structural Adjustment and Women Informal Traders in Harare, Zimbabwe* (Uppsala, Nordiska Afrikainstitutet, 1998), 19; L Daniels, *Changes in the Small-Scale Enterprise Sector from 1991 to 1993*, above n 68 at 30; Gibbon, 'Structural Adjustment and the Working Poor in Zimbabwe', above n 53 at 23–24; Bailey et al, *Structural Change and Adjustment in Zimbabwe*, above n 14 at 43–44.

[80] B Raftopoulos, 'The crisis in Zimbabwe' in B Raftopoulos and S Mlambo (eds), *Becoming Zimbabwe: A history from the Pre-colonial Period to 2008* (Harare, Weaver Press, 2009), 219.

to these long-term causes, the economic decline has been attributed to more immediate causes, with the genesis of the crisis period being 14 November 1997, which is known as 'Black Friday'.[81] On this day, the Zimbabwe dollar's value tumbled 75 per cent within the space of four hours.[82] This was triggered by the government's earlier announcement that it would compensate about 50,000 war veterans who fought in Zimbabwe's struggle for independence.[83] Subsequent events and government decisions, including the controversial Fast-Track Land Reform Programme,[84] sent the country's economy into a downward spiral.

These developments led to international condemnation and the country's economic woes raised the country's risk profile and undermined confidence in the economy.[85] After Black Friday, input prices soared and producers were forced to hike prices to ensure the viability of their operations.[86] Interest rates increased and raised the cost and limited the availability of capital for entrepreneurs.[87] Unbudgeted spending and short-term borrowing inflated the country's budget deficit and external debt.[88]

During the crisis, the government controlled the exchange rate and overvalued the Zimbabwe dollar.[89] The government also incurred imprudent and unbudgeted expenditures, adopted price controls, and controlled wage increases.[90] Inflation escalated from 20.1 per cent in December 1997 to 231 million per cent in July 2008.[91] The loss of investor and donor funding and the economic decline led

[81] See, eg, G Kanyenze, T Kondo, P Chitambara and J Martens, *Beyond the Enclave: Towards a Pro-Poor and Inclusive Development Strategy for Zimbabwe* (Harare, Weaver Press, 2011), above n 15 at 40; R Parsons, 'The political economy of Zimbabwe 1996–2002' (2002), 17 *South African Journal of Economic History* 105, 118.

[82] Kanyenze, 'Economic Policy Making Processes, Implementation and Impact in Zimbabwe', above n 35 at 20.

[83] Chiripanhura, 'Sneaking up and stumbling back: Textiles sector performance under crisis conditions in Zimbabwe', above n 54 at 153, 156; Kanyenze et al, *Beyond the Enclave*, above n 15 at 40; Parsons, 'The political economy of Zimbabwe 1996–2002', above n 81 at 118. The government sought to pacify angry war veterans who had challenged it. The expenditure was not budgeted for and had to be funded through borrowing and printing of money. See generally W Mhanda, 'The role of war veterans in Zimbabwe's political and economic processes', Solidarity Peace Trust (2011), accessible at www.solidaritypeacetrust.org/1063/the-role-of-war-veterans/.

[84] See generally Kanyenze et al, *Beyond the Enclave*, above n 15 at 90–102.

[85] African Development Bank and Organisation for Economic Cooperation and Development, 'Zimbabwe' in *African Economic Outlook 2002–3* (Paris, AfDB/OECD 2003), 356; Chiripanhura, 'Sneaking up and stumbling back' above n 54 at 156, 168–89.

[86] Kanyenze et al, *Beyond the Enclave*, above n 15 at 40.

[87] Parsons, 'The political economy of Zimbabwe: 1996–2002', above n 81 at 117.

[88] Kanyenze et al, *Beyond the Enclave*, above n 15 at 41–42.

[89] J Coomer and T Gstraunthaler, 'The hyperinflation in Zimbabwe' (2011) 14(4) *Quarterly Journal of Austrian Economics* 311, 320–25.

[90] Price controls were introduced by Statutory Instruments gazetted in terms of the Control of Goods Act [Chapter 15:04]. In 2007, the government enacted the National Incomes and Price Commission Act of 2007, which established the National Incomes and Price Commission to control wage and price increases.

[91] Kanyenze et al, *Beyond the Enclave*, above n 15 at 139, 485; J Robertson, 'The Zimbabwean economy: Current position and the way forward' in P Bond, B Kagoro, J Makumbe, J Robertson, E Lahiff and R Cornwell (eds), *Zimbabwe's Turmoil: Problems and Prospects* (Pretoria, Institute of Security Studies, 2003), 45.

to foreign currency shortages. Foreign currency shortages in turn contributed to fuel and electricity shortages[92] and inhibited the maintenance and replacement of capital equipment in the public and private sectors. The banking sector also suffered a liquidity crisis, which curtailed its lending activities and undermined confidence in the banking system.[93] These circumstances resulted in a decline in production in all sectors of the economy and the overall contraction of the economy.[94]

Formal employment declined with the loss of 300 000 formal jobs and as formal enterprises failed to create additional jobs.[95] Hyperinflation, wage freezes and the concomitant decline in real earnings stripped formal employment of the privilege that it had conferred in the past. At the height of hyperinflation in 2007 and 2008, the average worker's monthly wage could not cover their basic transport and accommodation needs.[96] The loss of skilled workers to HIV- and AIDS-related illness, absenteeism, worker fatigue and hunger negatively affected labour productivity.[97] Another challenge was the brain drain, as thousands of workers including teachers, engineers, artisans and medical personnel migrated to other countries to escape the political and economic crisis.[98]

The crisis period was marked by increasing poverty and declining well-being amongst the population. This was evidenced by increasing food insecurity and greater demand for food aid, and the general population's inability to afford decent housing, health care and education.[99] Savings and social security schemes

[92] Robertson, 'The Zimbabwean economy: Current position and the way forward', above n 91 at 46, 48–50.

[93] Kanyenze et al, *Beyond the Enclave*, above n 15 at 485–94; Nathan Associates, 'Zimbabwe Economic Performance Assessment: A Benchmark Study' (2007) Unpublished research report prepared for United States Agency for International Development 26–27; P Robinson, 'Zimbabwe's Hyperinflation: The House is on Fire – But Does the Government Know it is Dousing the Flames with Petrol?' Hintergrundinformationen aus der internationalen Entwicklungszusammenarbeit: Afrika (Bonn, Fredrich Ebert Stiftung, 2006) 4.

[94] See UNDP *Comprehensive Economic Recovery in Zimbabwe: A discussion document* (Harare, UNDP Zimbabwe, 2008); Robinson, *Zimbabwe's hyperinflation*, above n 93; USAID, Zimbabwe Economic Performance Assessment (Harare, USAID, 2007) vi, vii.

[95] UNDP, *Comprehensive Economic Recovery in Zimbabwe*, above n 94 at 105; Kanyenze, 'Economic Policy Making Processes, Implementation and Impact in Zimbabwe' above n 35 at 44.

[96] T Mariwo, *Working Conditions and Labour Relation in the Private Security Sector: A Research Paper* (2008) 3; Chiripanhura, 'Sneaking up and stumbling back', above n 54 at 167; Kanyenze et al, *Beyond the Enclave*, above n 15 at 273.

[97] UNDP, *Comprehensive Economic Recovery in Zimbabwe*, above n 94 at 107; Chiripanhura, 'Sneaking up and stumbling back', above n 54 at 167.

[98] D Makina, 'Survey of profile of migrant Zimbabweans in South Africa: A pilot study' (unpublished research report, 2007), 5–6; Solidarity Peace Trust, 'Gone to Egoli: Economic survival strategies in Matabeleland' (unpublished research report, 2009), 15–16; E Gwaradzimba and A Shumba, 'The nature, extent and impact of the brain drain in Zimbabwe and South Africa' (2010) 42(1) *Acta Academica* 219–22; S Eppel, D Ndlela, B Raftopoulos and M Rupiya, *Developing a Transformation Agenda for Zimbabwe* (Cape Town, The Institute for Democracy in South Africa, 2009), 7.

[99] Solidarity Peace Trust, 'Gone to Egoli', above n 98 at 33–37; A Goebel, '"We are working for nothing": Livelihoods and gender relations in rural Zimbabwe' (2007) 41(2) *Canadian Journal of African Studies* 226, 235–37; A Chikanda, 'Medical migration from Zimbabwe' (2007) 24(1) *Development*

were rendered worthless as inflation ravaged the value of pension and insurance pay-outs.[100] Girls and women were severely affected by the crisis. They bore the brunt of choices to keep male children in school, had limited access to maternal health care and assumed the burden of caring for the sick and orphaned children.[101]

Physical, economic, institutional, social and personal displacement were hallmarks of the crisis period.[102] Informalisation underpinned the displacements associated with the economic crisis as formal enterprises, institutions and systems gave way to informal ones.[103] Small and medium enterprises virtually disappeared, thus expanding the chasm between a few large-scale enterprises and a growing number of informal enterprises.[104] The legacy of the dualistic pre-independence economy was entrenched by the virtual collapse of the formal sector and the greater prominence of the informal sector during the crisis.[105]

There is no comprehensive statistical data detailing the nature of activities accounting for the growth of the informal sector during the crisis. Arguably, this to some degree involved the expansion in the scale of existing informal economic activities that people engaged in prior to the crisis, namely small manufacturing units, fruit and vegetable vending, cross-border trading, the sale of second-hand clothing, and the provision of services such as repairs and hair dressing.[106] Moreover, illicit activities such as gold panning, unauthorised fishing and the unauthorised sale of game meat became more prevalent during this period.[107]

The expansion of the informal sector was partly attributable to the emergence of new opportunities during the crisis.[108] Ordinary people stepped in to supply foreign currency and commodities such as fuel and food.[109] Virtually everyone

Southern Africa, 47, 56–58; Chimhowu et al, *Moving Forward in Zimbabwe*, above n 29 at 27; L Masuko, 'Current performance of the education sector in Zimbabwe: Key policy Challenges facing the sector' (2005) Paper presented at workshop on Sectoral Economic Development, Policy Challenges and the Way Forward held at Harare International Conference Centre, 26–27 June 2003, at 27.

[100] UNDP, *Comprehensive Economic Recovery in Zimbabwe*, above n 94 at 61.

[101] Kanyenze et al, *Beyond the Enclave*, above n 15 at 219–24, 319.

[102] A Hammar, J MacGregor and L Landau, 'Displacing Zimbabwe: Crisis and Construction in Southern Africa' (2010) 36(2) *Journal of Southern African Studies* 281–82.

[103] Hammar et al, 'Displacing Zimbabwe', above n 102 at 269.

[104] UNDP, *Comprehensive Economic Recovery in Zimbabwe*, above n 94 at 4.

[105] ibid.

[106] T Mukwedeya, 'Zimbabwe's saving grace: The role of remittances in household livelihood strategies in Glen Norah, Harare' (2011) 42(1) *South African Review of Sociology*, 116, 126; P Matondi, *'I am doing my own thing!: Livelihoods diversity study in Zimbabwe* (Harare, Oxfam, 2011) 10–11.

[107] See AY Kamete, 'When livelihoods take a battering … Mapping the new "Gold Rush" in Zimbabwe's Angwa-Pote Basin' (2008) 65 *Critical Perspectives on Southern Africa* 36; J MacGregor, 'Patrolling Kariba's waters: state authority, fishing and the border economy' (2008) 34(4) *Journal of Southern African Studies* 861; PA Lindsey, S Romanach, S Matema, C Matema, I Mupamhadzi and J Muvengwi, 'Dynamics and underlying causes of illegal bushmeat trade in Zimbabwe' (2011) 45(1) *Fauna and Flora International* 84.

[108] See Hammar et al, 'Displacing Zimbabwe', above n 102 at 268.

[109] T Mufudza, M Jengeta and P Hove, 'The usefulness of strategic planning in a turbulent economic environment: a case of Zimbabwe during the period 2007–2009' (2013) 14(1) *Business Strategy Series*

became a 'dealer' as trading in scarce goods proved more lucrative than formal employment and long-term investments in production.[110] Goods were typically sold through layers of intermediaries, with a profit being made at each level.[111] Shona-speaking people coined the phrase *kukiya kiya* to describe informal economic activities.[112]

People involved in the informal sector adopted new ways of thinking and operating during the crisis. First, one had to be flexible and able to shift to new economic activities as government regulations and market dynamics were constantly changing and affecting the availability or scarcity of goods.[113] It was risky to rely on one activity, and most people engaged in a diverse range of activities in order to stay afloat.[114] Second, most people involved in informal economic activities suspended all conventions about what constituted proper and acceptable behaviour.[115] Exploitative pricing became rampant and the notion of 'reasonable' or 'fair' pricing ceased to exist.[116] Third, people increasingly engaged in illicit activities, including the solicitation of bribes during the course of employment.[117] Such unorthodox practices were justified on the grounds of economic necessity in the absence of conventional alternatives.[118]

Previously 'marginal' informal economic activities that had been associated with the lower classes became more significant in Zimbabwe's economy.[119]

24, 25; M Kadenge and G Mavunga, 'Linguistic innovation during a national crisis' (2009) 29(2) *South African Journal of African Languages*, 169, 170; Mukwedeya, 'Zimbabwe's saving grace', above n 106 at 125–6.

[110] Raftopoulos, 'The crisis in Zimbabwe', above n 80 at 221; Kanyenze et al, *Beyond the Enclave*, above n 15 at 273.

[111] Mukwedeya, 'Zimbabwe's saving grace', above n 106 at 125–26.

[112] This expression literally means 'to lock something repeatedly', and has come to mean 'employing unorthodox means to raise money for survival' or 'doing this and that'. Kadenge and Mavunga, 'Linguistic innovation during a national crisis', above n 109 at 182; Mukwedeya, 'Zimbabwe's saving grace', above n 106 at 125; JL Jones, 'Nothing is straight in Zimbabwe: The rise of the *kukiya kiya* economy 2000–2008' (2010) 36 (2) *Journal of Southern African Studies* 186.

[113] Mukwedeya, 'Zimbabwe's saving grace', above n 106 at 125.

[114] I Chirisa, 'Informality, deceit and conscience: a survey of ethical dilemmas in Harare' (2009) 11(2) *Journal of Sustainable Development in Africa* 257, 274; Kadenge and Mavunga, 'Linguistic innovation during a national crisis', above n 109 at 182.

[115] Jones, 'Nothing is straight in Zimbabwe: The rise of the *kukiya kiya* economy 2000–2008', above n 112 at 285.

[116] JL Jones, 'Freeze! Movement, narrative and the disciplining of price in hyperinflationary Zimbabwe' (2010) 36(2) *Social Dynamics* 338, 339; D Masaka, 'Moral paralysis in Zimbabwe's economy: A challenge to the Government of National Unity (GNU)' (2012) 2(2:2) *International Journal of Politics and Good Governance*, 1, 2, 4–5, 10–11; Solidarity Peace Trust, 'Gone to Egoli' above n 98 at 33–35.

[117] Mawowa and Matongo, 'Inside Zimbabwe's roadside currency trade: The "World Bank" of Bulawayo' (2010) 36(2) *Journal of Southern African Studies* 319, 329; Kadenge and Mavunga, 'Linguistic innovation during a national crisis', above n 109 at 180. See also T Chagonda, 'Teachers' and bank workers' responses to Zimbabwe's crisis: Uneven effects, different strategies' (2012) 30(1) *Journal of Contemporary African Studies*, 83, 84; Masaka, 'Moral paralysis in Zimbabwe's economy: A Challenge to the Government of National Unity (GNU)' 4–5, 10–11.

[118] Jones, 'Nothing is straight in Zimbabwe', above n 112 at 285.

[119] Mukwedeya, 'Zimbabwe's saving grace', above n 106 at 126; Jones, 'Nothing is straight in Zimbabwe', above n 112 at 286.

The new entrants into the informal sector included the country's political and economic elite. Jones argues that as the economic activities formerly relegated to the urban social margins became an important source of livelihood, Zimbabwe's economy came to be characterised as a *kukiya kiya* economy.[120]

Formal-informal linkages were manifested at various levels: at the level of individual workers as they navigated between formal employment and informal economic activities; at the level of the household, as more families became dependent on earnings from informal economic activities; and at the level of the firm, as formal firms became informalised and as transactions between formal firms and the informal sector increased.

Straddling formal employment and informal economic activities became a survival tactic of formally employed workers during the ESAP period. The crisis saw the acceleration and intensification of this trend as inflation daily eroded the real value of salaries. Despite the inadequacy of their salaries to cater for their basic needs, many workers chose to remain in employment because it provided opportunities for them to engage in informal economic activities.[121] Chirisa has described both forms of straddling as 'going to work to find work' or 'survivalist snowballing'.[122]

Some workers directly aligned their informal economic activities to their formal employment. Thus, bank workers engaged in foreign currency trading, service sector workers poached their employers' clients and teachers taught 'extra lessons' for a fee.[123] Other straddlers used office facilities such as telephones, computers and internet to engage in informal economic activities that were unrelated to the employer's line of business.[124] This meant that formal employers subsidised their employees' informal activities.

Another linkage at the worker level was the decline in formal employment and the increase in employment in informal enterprises.[125] While some workers engaged in informal economic activities and retained their jobs, other workers left their formal employment to engage in informal economic activities on a full-time basis. Some of these workers were forced to leave their employment due to retrenchments.[126] Other workers – including those in the

[120] Jones, 'Nothing is straight in Zimbabwe', above n 112 at 286.

[121] Chirisa, 'Informality, deceit and conscience', above n 114 at 260.

[122] ibid.

[123] Chirisa, 'Informality, deceit and conscience', above n 114 at 275–78; Chagonda, 'Teachers' and bank workers' responses to Zimbabwe's crisis', above n 117 at 88–90, 92–93; Mawowa and Matongo, 'Inside Zimbabwe's roadside currency trade', above n 117 at 331; Matondi, '*I am doing my own thing!*', above n 106 at 20.

[124] Hungwe, 'A review of the challenges and survival strategies of university workers during the economic crisis', 252–55; Kanyenze et al, *Beyond the Enclave*, above n 15 at 273; Mukwedeya, 'Zimbabwe's saving grace', above n 106 at 124.

[125] Chimhowu et al, *Moving forward in Zimbabwe*, above n 29 at 24.

[126] Hammar et al, 'Displacing Zimbabwe', above n 102 at 275; Kamete, 'When livelihoods take a battering', above n 107 at 48–54.

civil service – resigned from formal employment to focus on more lucrative informal economic activities.[127]

At the household level, wage income became less significant due to the decline in formal employment and the erosion of wages by inflation. As the number of people involved in informal economic activities increased during the crisis, so too did the number of households that depended on informal economic activities for their incomes. There was greater diversification of household income streams as household members increasingly engaged in various informal economic activities.[128] Conversely, household income from other sources such as remittances was used to finance informal economic activities by household members.[129]

Other aspects of the economy were informalised during the crisis. Government regulations made it unprofitable or impossible to transact via formal channels, and thereby fuelled linkages between formal enterprises and informal economic activities: for example, formal firms bought and sold foreign currency on the black market,[130] and became increasingly reliant on informal cross-border traders for scarce inputs and stock.[131] In addition, some firms engaged in lucrative sideline activities such as informal foreign currency trading to stay afloat.[132]

VI. The Post-crisis Period: 2009 to the End of the Mugabe Era

Following a protracted election battle between the ruling Zimbabwe African National Union-Patriotic Front (ZANU-PF) and the two formations of the Movement for Democratic Change (MDC) in 2008, a Government of National Unity (GNU) was formed in February 2009 and lasted until ZANU-PF's return to power in August 2013. Over the years, the ruling party was torn by speculation about the succession and by factionalism. In November 2017, the military staged a military take-over, which resulted in the resignation of then-President Robert Mugabe. He was succeeded by the former Vice-President Emmerson Mnangagwa. The general election was held in July 2018, with a narrow win for President Mnangagwa.

[127] Kamete, 'When livelihoods take a battering', above n 107 at 48–54; Kanyenze et al, *Beyond the Enclave*, above n 15 at 273; S Mawowa and A Matongo, 'Inside Zimbabwe's roadside currency trade', above n 117 at 328.

[128] Goebel, 'We are working for nothing', above n 99 at 235–38; Matondi, *'I am doing my own thing!'*, above n 106 at 20–22, Mukwedeya, 'Zimbabwe's saving grace', above n 106 at 124.

[129] Mukwedeya, 'Zimbabwe's saving grace', above n 106 at 121–22; F Magunha, A Bailey and L Cliffe, *Remittance Strategies of Zimbabweans in Northern England* (Leeds, School of Geography University of Leeds, 2009), 6–7; F Maphosa, 'Remittances and development: The impact of migration to South Africa on rural livelihoods in southern Zimbabwe' (2007) 24(1) *Development Southern Africa* 123, 130, 132.

[130] A Makochekanwa, *Zimbabwe's Black Market for Foreign Exchange*, Working Papers from University of Pretoria, Department of Economics, No 2007–13, 2007.

[131] Chiripanhura, 'Sneaking up and stumbling back', above n 54 at 165–66.

[132] S Gumbe and N Kaseke, 'Manufacturing firms and hyperinflation-survival options' (2010) *Journal of Management and Marketing Research*, 14–17.

The GNU dollarised Zimbabwe's economy shortly after its inauguration in 2009.[133] This has allowed the official use of a basket of currencies, with the United States dollar being the principal currency. The Zimbabwe dollar was effectively demonetised in 2015.The following year ushered in an acute cash shortage, resulting from a combination of factors including growing public borrowing from the banking sector and illicit financial flows from the country.[134] In response to this crisis, the Reserve Bank introduced cash withdrawal limits and measures to promote cashless transactions.[135] It also introduced limits on the physical and electronic externalisation of currency, and developed a priority list for foreign payments.[136] Significantly, it introduced 'bond notes' as a surrogate currency equivalent to the US dollar.[137] These measures have been introduced alongside initiatives to restrict imports and promote exports in a bid to improve the balance of payments.

The adoption of a multi-currency regime brought some stability to the Zimbabwean economy, and producers and retailers are more willing to use formal distribution channels.[138] One of the improvements has been a decline in inflation since the crisis.[139] Overall, the country's economy is recovering from the crisis, but economic performance remains sub-optimal. Economic growth increased significantly after 2009 but has declined since 2012.[140] Economic performance has been hampered by challenges including the fiscal indiscipline, corruption and mismanagement of public finances.[141] Another challenge has been the undercapitalisation of the economy because of, inter alia, loss of savings after dollarisation and low investor and donor confidence in the country.[142]

Under its new leadership, the government has embarked on an aggressive drive to re-engage international financial institutions and development partners

[133] Ministry of Finance, '2009 National Budget Statement', presented to the Parliament of Zimbabwe by Minister Tendai Biti on 17 March 2009.

[134] See World Bank, *Zimbabwe Economic Update: The State in the Economy* Issue 2 (Washington, World Bank, 2017) at viii–ix; Reserve Bank of Zimbabwe 'January 2016 Monetary Policy Statement' by Governor Dr JP Mangudya (2016) at 4–6.

[135] See Reserve Bank of Zimbabwe, 'January 2016 Monetary Policy Statement, above n 134 at 66–71.

[136] Reserve Bank of Zimbabwe, 'September 2016 Monetary Policy Statement', by Governor Dr JP Mangudya (2016) at 52–57.

[137] See Reserve Bank of Zimbabwe, 'September 2016 Monetary Policy Statement', above n 136 at 56–62; RJ Southall, 'Bond notes, Borrowing and Heading for Bust: Zimbabwe's Persistent Crisis' (2018) 51(3) *Canadian Journal of African Studies* 389.

[138] See, eg, S Mawowa, 'The Political Economy of Artisanal and Small-scale Gold Mining in Central Zimbabwe' (2013) 39(4) *Journal of Southern African Studies* 926–27.

[139] Ministry of Finance and Economic Development, '2018 National Budget Statement' (2018) at 22–24.

[140] World Bank, *Zimbabwe Economic Update*, above n 134 at vii.

[141] Ministry of Finance and Economic Development, '2018 National Budget Statement' (2018), above n 139 at 1–3.

[142] See Ministry of Finance, '2012 National Budget Statement', presented by Minister Tendai Biti to Parliament on 15 November 2012, accessed at http://archive.kubatana.net/docs/econ/min_fin_budget_2012_111124.pdf at 20.

to access funding. It is also courting investors with the mantra that 'Zimbabwe is open for business'. International financial institutions and development partners have demonstrated a willingness to engage with the government, and potential investors have been making enquiries and submitting their proposals to do business in the country. It remains to be seen whether these positive responses will translate into tangible agreements and undertakings and will contribute towards improved economic performance and job creation. The modest economic gains have not translated into an informal sector employment.[143] After the crisis, there was a dramatic increase in retrenchments, from 31,102 in 2009 to 84,789 in 2013.[144] While there were about 204,731 retrenchments between 2011 and 2013, permanent employment remained constant at 15.5 per cent during the same period,[145] suggesting that the job losses were offset by new jobs. The informal sector continues to be an important source of livelihood for many Zimbabweans, who lack viable alternatives or who seek to supplement their salaries.[146] Many Zimbabwean households continue to derive part or all their income from the informal economic sector.

The changes in the political economy have had an impact on the nature of informal activities that people engage in. The dollarisation of the economy initially limited the opportunities for speculative trading based on price and market distortions, forcing people to engage in more conventional informal economic activities to earn a living. However, circumstances have changed with the liquidity crisis, which prompted the return of the black market for foreign currency. Moreover, restrictions on cash withdrawals and external payments have limited imports of inputs and stock and provided opportunities for the informal sector to meet these needs.

Workers in the informal sector are involved in different activities: buying and selling goods; producing goods including cooked food, poultry, clothing, crafts, and furniture; providing services including hair dressing, cellular phone repairs, and transport. They operate in various locations, including private homes, mines, landfill sites, public spaces, and offices. Some are mobile operators – hawkers who sell their wares in public spaces and from door to door; 'car boot' traders who sell goods from their cars wherever they can attract customers; and traders and service providers who operate across borders. During the post-crisis period, certain informal sector activities, such as informal trading, waste picking and small-scale manufacturing have become more visible, suggesting an increase in their scale.

[143] Mawowa, 'The Political Economy of Artisanal and Small-scale Gold Mining in Central Zimbabwe', above n 138 at 927.

[144] Zimbabwe Statistical Agency (ZIMSTAT), *2014 Labour Force Survey* (Harare, ZIMSTAT, 2014) 244.

[145] ibid, 1–2.

[146] Ministry of Finance, '2012 National Budget Statement', above n 142 at 126–27.

VII. Reflections on Zimbabwe's Labour Market and the Implications for Labour and Social Security Law

At its inception, labour law applied to a minority of workers located at the intersection of two inter-related features of the colonial economic system. The first was the establishment and legitimation of an economy owned and controlled by white settlers, which was predicated on the suppression and marginalisation of pre-existing indigenous economic activities. The latter activities were therefore informalised and formed the roots of what is now the country's informal sector. The second feature was that labour law was only applicable to the dominant or formal sector, and worse still, excluded black workers from the standard employment relationship by confining them to casual employment.

The post-independence regime represents both a break from, and continuity with, the colonial labour regime. A break, because the law has dismantled racial discrimination in the labour market. Continuity, because labour law is still tied to the standard employment relationship. This is at odds with the realities of a labour market in which paid permanent employees employment accounted for almost 19 per cent of employed workers in the labour force in 2004. This has declined to 15.5 per cent in 2011 and 2014.[147]

This chapter has focused on worker-level linkages between formal employment and the informal sector and considered the trends over time. Many workers have a long history of engaging in informal sector activities after failing to obtain formal or losing formal employment. Others have – voluntarily or involuntarily – moved between formal employment and the informal sector and have straddled both in response to changes in the labour market and the availability of opportunities in the informal sector. Transcending the vicissitudes of this sector, and the diversity and fluidity of workers' experiences within it, is the reality that the informal sector is an inevitable and enduring feature of labour markets in the global South. This is because expectations that the modernisation of developing economies would result in the absorption of more workers in the formal sector have not been realised.[148] Labour law's crisis in the global South is not that the standard employment relationship was the norm and is being weakened by non-standard employment relationships. Admittedly, employers in Zimbabwe have used non-standard employment to weaken the standard employment relationship,[149] and

[147] Zimbabwe Statistical Agency (ZIMSTAT), *2004 Labour Force Survey* (Harare, ZIMSTAT, 2004) 37; *2011 Labour Force Survey* (Harare, ZIMSTAT, 2011) 57, *2014 Labour Force and Child Labour Survey* (Harare, ZIMSTAT, 2014) 68.

[148] J Fudge, 'Blurring the Boundaries: Regulating for Decent Work' in J Fudge, S McCrystal and K Sankaran, *Challenging the Legal Boundaries of Work Regulation* (Oxford, Hart Publishing, 2012) 5–6.

[149] See F Ncube, 'Precarious employment as survival strategy: An emerging reality in Zimbabwean hotels' (2017) 5(2) *International Journal of Business Management* 67.

labour law reforms should address this challenge. However, the real crisis of labour law in this and other developing countries is that it revolves around the standard employment relationship, which is and continues to represent the exception, rather than the norm. Consequently, labour law is a luxury far beyond the reach of many of the country's workers.

This crisis is gendered because most female workers are largely under-represented amongst paid employees, let alone standard employees. The informal sector is an important source of livelihood for women, who represent less than 40 per cent of paid employees in Zimbabwe.[150] This shows women's continued situation at the intersection of race, class and gender, where they are marginalised in the labour market and excluded from labour law's scope.

The ILO's Decent Work Agenda calls for global, regional and national efforts to promote its four pillars, namely opportunities for work, rights at work, social protection and social dialogue.[151] The Decent Work Agenda reiterates the ILO Constitution's call for the improvement of 'conditions of labour', which applies to all workers.[152] The Decent Work Agenda embraces all work, 'whether organised or not, and wherever work might occur, whether in the formal or the informal economy, whether at home, in the community or in the voluntary sector'.[153]

In addition, the ILO adopted the Recommendation concerning the Transition from the Informal to the Formal Economy, 2015 (No 204) (R 204). The Recommendation recognises 'the diversity of characteristics, circumstances and needs of workers and economic units in the informal economy'.[154] It calls on Member States to address this diversity with tailored approaches by, inter alia, adopting an integrated policy framework to facilitate the transition to the formal economy.[155] This policy framework should address, inter alia, the adoption of an appropriate legal and regulatory framework to promote formalisation.[156]

Implementing the international principles will require labour ministries to radically re-orient their approach from an 'employment-centric' focus to recognising own-account workers in the informal sector as workers.[157] In contemplating the extension of labour law, they must consider which rights would be extended to own-account workers in the informal sector. Certain labour rights – such as those relating to working time, minimum wages and the provision of an employment contract – may not be relevant to these workers. However, they could benefit from the extension and adaptation of other protections, including occupational health and safety, work-related social security and social dialogue.

[150] ZIMSTAT, *2011 Labour Force Survey*, above n 147 at 58; *2014 Labour Force Survey*, above n 147 at 68.
[151] International Labour Conference (ILC), Report of the Director-General, *Decent Work*, at the 87th Session of the International Labour Conference (1999).
[152] ILC, Report of the Director-General, *Decent Work*, above n 151.
[153] ibid.
[154] Recommendation 204, para 7(a).
[155] ibid read with 10.
[156] ibid, para 10(b).
[157] See Sankaran, 'Labour Law in South Asia', above n 2.

Zimbabwe is beginning to recognise the need to extend labour legislation to those in the informal sector. In 2017, the government committed to including informal sector workers under the National Social Security Authority (NSSA) pension scheme, which covers the retirement, invalidity or death of a breadwinner. The NSSA pension scheme currently applies to employers and employees.[158] Although the NSSA has made progress towards the development of a voluntary pension scheme for the informal sector, it is unclear how this will be operationalised to provide appropriate collection measures and ensure that the contribution levels are realistic based on the workers' earnings. It remains to be seen whether the NSSA Act will be amended so that the legal framework underpins these operational changes and expressly recognises workers in the informal sector.

Informal workers labour under precarious conditions that expose them to health and safety risks, including dangerous chemicals, dust and fumes; ergonomic hazards; and fire, and do not have adequate knowledge or resources to prevent or address them.[159] Despite their vulnerability to these risks, informal sector workers are excluded from the scope of occupational health and safety legislation. In Zimbabwe, the relevant Statutory Instrument[160] should be amended to expressly cover own-account workers, including those who work in unconventional workplaces, including private homes and public spaces. This would give the NSSA a clear mandate to develop specific training programmes and compensation schemes for workers in the informal sector. Extending this protection would entail placing responsibility on stakeholders who control the workplace, even though they do not employ workers in the informal sector. Thus, local authorities would be called upon to provide infrastructure and equipment for informal workers operating in public spaces.[161]

The extension of labour law will require more than efforts to include historically excluded workers under the banner of existing protections: employment relations, working conditions and social security. It will also require a broadening of labour law's agenda to include issues that have not traditionally been included in its scope, including access to space, markets, skills development and credit. These have largely fallen under the auspices of ministries and agencies responsible for small business development. According to Sankaran, the provision of such facilities should 'be seen as necessary of a proactive labour policy addressing the needs of informal workers'.[162] This assertion resonates with R 204, which calls for an

[158] See National Social Security Authority Act No. 12 of 1989, section 3(1).

[159] See generally: S Jerie, 'An assessment of the application of occupational ergonomics principles in the informal sector of Harare and Mutare in Zimbabwe', 2017 2(7) *Review of Social Sciences* 1.

[160] See National Social Security Authority (Accident Prevention and Workers' Compensation Scheme) (Prescribed Matters) Notice, 1990, Statutory Instrument 68 of 1990, sections 4 and 6, which refers to workers and employers in an employment relationship.

[161] Jerie, 'An assessment of the application of occupational ergonomics', above n 159 at 5; PH Bamu, 'Extending Occupational Health and Safety Law to Informal Workers: The Case of Street Vendors in South Africa (forthcoming).

[162] Sankaran, 'Labour Law in South Asia', above n 2 at 220.

integrated policy framework that brings together traditional labour issues with business development measures.[163]

It is critical for these changes to be underpinned and facilitated by inclusive social dialogue. Inclusiveness will entail, on the one hand, the inclusion of workers' organisations representing those in the informal sector, who are largely excluded from tripartite negotiations.[164] On the other hand, it entails that government representation extend beyond the labour ministry, but include representatives of government responsible for other policy fields such as urban policy and public health; and where relevant different levels of government including local government.[165] Consequently, a multi-stakeholder approach will ensure that appropriate and effective measures are adopted to protect informal workers.

VIII. Conclusion: Opportunities for Further Research

In this chapter, I have considered the significance of the informal sector and explored the possibilities for extending labour law's protection to workers in this sector. Several challenges remain for further consideration in research and in policy debates. First, the paper analysed the linkages between the formal and informal sectors at the level of the worker and the household. It has shown that the informal sector has served as a primary or supplementary source of income in the absence of viable formal sector employment. It did not analyse the linkages between formal and informal sector operations, and the implications for extending labour law to workers in the latter. Further research should consider the possibilities for attributing employer responsibilities to informal sector firms which rely on the informal sector that form part of their supply chains and distribution channels.

The second relates to reconciling the dual identity of many informal sector workers as employers and as workers, and the implications thereof for regulation.[166] Moreover, the chapter has not considered workers in communal or subsistence farming, another category of workers that fall outside of the scope of employment, and which accounts for a sizable proportion of Zimbabwe's labour force. It will be necessary to consider their situation to determine their needs and how labour law can be extended to them.

[163] Recommendation 204, art 11.

[164] Sankaran, 'Labour Law in South Asia', above n 2 at 220.

[165] Bamu, 'Extending Occupational Health and Safety Law to Informal Workers', above n 161. See also Sankaran, 'Labour Law in South Asia', above n 2 at 224.

[166] Sankaran, 'Labour Law in South Asia', above n 2 at 218–19.

6

Insiders, Outsiders and Conflicts of Interest

RUTH DUKES*

'If labour law, as Arthurs puts it, "takes its purpose, form, and content from the larger political economy from which it originates and operates", what shape does or should labour law assume in response to the transformation of the political economy in countries of the global North, with the declining prevalence of the post-war model of full employment within a formal welfare state regime? Correspondingly, what is the proper role to be played by labour law and labour relations institutions in the development process within industrialising countries of the global South?'[1]

I. Introduction

This chapter considers the use made of the notions of conflicts of interest, and of insiders and outsiders, in academic and policy discourse regarding labour markets and labour law. It takes as its starting point the questions raised by Diamond Ashiagbor concerning the 'conceptual and normative narrative' of labour law.[2] It notes, especially, her forefronting of political economy as the source of labour law's 'purpose, form, and content' – but as something, too, which may, in turn, be shaped by the law. (The potentially transformative character of law is acknowledged by Ashiagbor, as I understand her, when she asks what shape labour law does or *should* assume today in the global North; what the proper role is to be played by labour law and labour relations institutions in the development process in the global South.) The argument that I seek to make, with Ashiagbor, is for the importance of the wider political economy to understanding labour law, and to assessing the capacity of particular laws and institutions to contribute to the

* School of Law, University of Glasgow.

[1] D Ashiagbor, *Conference Programme: Re-imagining labour law for development: informal work in the global North and South* (September 2016), citing H Arthurs, 'Labour Law After Labour' in B Langille and G Davidov (eds), *The Idea of Labour Law* (Oxford, Oxford University Press, 2011).

[2] ibid.

attainment of particular policy aims: job creation, decent wages and working conditions, economic security for workers and their dependants, the reduction of wealth and income inequalities.

In order to make this argument, the chapter begins by outlining briefly the significance of the notion of conflicts of interest to the foundational narratives of labour law, conceptual and normative. (The focus here, as throughout the chapter, is with labour law in the industrialised world and, especially, the UK.) It then illustrates the degree of emphasis given today by policy makers and commentators to the conflicting interests of different workers or groups of workers, observing that conflict between the social classes, in contrast, tends now to be underemphasised in both policy and scholarly discourse. It notes that the identification of conflicts of interest between workers or groups of workers is closely linked, often, to the claim or belief that flexible – 'free' – markets benefit all, raising employment levels and encouraging economic growth. Labour market segmentation should be addressed, so the argument goes, so as to maximise flexibility and ease market access for all.

In the course of this discussion, I seek to argue that approaches which begin from an identification of labour market insiders and outsiders can suffer from a number of weaknesses, chief among them a tendency to oversimplify complex constellations of interests, motivations, strategies, allegiances and collusions. As such, they can tend to overstate the incidence and the significance of conflicts of interest between the posited groups of workers, insiders and outsiders. Often such approaches adopt the kind of 'pure economic theory' forms of reasoning that are typical of law and economics scholarship, conceiving of markets in the abstract – as functioning according to the same set of rules regardless of place and time – and of market actors as purely economically motivated. In doing so, they can tend to obscure the role of the state, and of law, in giving specific form to labour markets and labour market institutions, and, of course, grossly to underemphasise the importance of any interest or value other than an economically rational one. A political economy framework, in contrast, allows for questions to be asked of labour markets as they are configured within particular localities, drawing scholars' attention directly to the state and to public policy as an expression of struggles between different actors over political influence.[3] Such a framework allows, importantly, for the impact of particular laws and policies to be considered over a period of real time, and not only in the 'snapshot' view captured by an economic model.[4] For these reasons, it allows the questions to be addressed in a much more nuanced way of who benefits and who is disadvantaged by particular labour laws and labour market institutions; in what respects they are advantaged or disadvantaged; and why that is so.

[3] G Menz, 'Employers and Migrant Legality: Liberalization of Service Provision, Transnational Posting, and the Bifurcation of the European Labour Market' in C Costello and M Freedland (eds), *Migrants at Work: Immigration and Vulnerability in Labour Law* (Oxford, Oxford University Press, 2015), at 49–50.

[4] J Robinson, 'Time in Economic Theory' (1980) 33 *Kyklos* 219.

In the final section of the chapter, I construct a case study of the agricultural sector in Scotland. In the context of a discussion of labour market insiders and outsiders, informed by the wider themes of this volume, the sector is of particular interest. Using the definitions of formality and informality developed by Ashiagbor in the volume's Introduction, we might say that the general trend in Scottish agriculture is to greater informality in employment relations. On the face of it, the sector could be characterised by the existence of a number of insider and outsider groups: employees whose terms and conditions are regulated by the Scottish Agricultural Wages Board, and casual workers, to whom the relevant rules do not apply; local workers, and temporary migrants from within the EU and elsewhere; workers employed directly by farmers, and those supplied to the farmers by labour market intermediaries or 'gangmasters'; the documented, and the undocumented. Resisting the easy characterisation of these groups as labour market insiders and outsiders, and the implication of 'inter-worker' conflicts of interest which such characterisation might bring with it, I seek instead to understand why it is that workers in the sector are generally low-paid and often ill-treated: what are the motivations and strategies of employing organisations; why are they under such pressure to employ low-wage labour; what is the role of the state in causing or failing to address the causes of such pressures? I also attempt to identify the possible consequences of amending the existing systems of regulation, and the potentially disastrous impact upon the sector of Brexit.

II. Conflicts of Interest and Labour Law

A. From Traditional Narratives to the Third Way

In early accounts of labour law – those which did the work of first presenting it as a distinct and coherent field of study and legal practice – employment relations were understood to be inherently conflictual.[5] Relying more or less directly on a Marxist analysis of capitalism, scholars understood the interests of the social classes – dependent labour, on the one hand, and the owners of capital, on the other – to be distinct and opposed.[6] Labour law was advocated as a means of empowering the weaker party in the relationship, the worker, so that his interests were not routinely subordinated to those of the more powerful employer. The goals of labour law were conceived accordingly to include the emancipation of the worker and democratisation of the economic sphere. Broadly speaking, the interests of the individual

[5] Section II of this chapter draws heavily on R Dukes, 'Conflict and the Crisis in Labour Law: From Weimar to Austerity' in PF Kjaer and N Olsen (eds), *Critical Theories of Crisis in Europe* (London, Rowman and Littlefield, 2016).

[6] See eg H Sinzheimer, *Grundzüge des Arbeitsrechts* 2nd edn (Jena, Gustav Fischer, 1927). On the influence of Marx upon Sinzheimer, see O Kahn-Freund, 'Hugo Sinzheimer' in R Lewis and J Clark (eds), *Labour Law and Politics in the Weimar Republic* (Oxford, Blackwell, 1981).

worker were understood to be identical with those of dependent labour as a class.[7] Conflicts of interest arising *between* workers were regarded, therefore, as largely illusory and, in any case, to be greatly ameliorated by systems of collective bargaining that ensured standardised wages across sectors and regions.[8]

For the duration of the *trente glorieuses*, these were the essential tenets of the dominant narrative of labour law. It was not until the 1980s that the narrative was challenged quite fundamentally on two fronts, each emphasising in different ways the existence of labour market insiders and outsiders, and conflicts of interest between groups of workers. In the first instance, scholars of neoclassical economics, Austrian libertarianism, and law and economics brought a particular form of economic reasoning to bear on the analysis of employment relations, characterising workers and employers alike as rational wealth-maximisers, and trade unions as rent-seeking monopolies.[9] Employment protection laws and collective bargaining were criticised for their propensity to raise the wages of some (ie 'insiders') above the 'natural' market level, causing lower wages or even unemployment elsewhere (ie to 'outsiders'). Ultimately, it was argued, protective labour laws and trade unions were damaging to the economy and so to the very workers that they were designed to protect. Feminist critiques of labour law, meanwhile, were directed at exposing the extent to which trade unions and established collective bargaining practices had failed, for many decades, to embrace certain categories of worker, including categories that were predominantly or wholly populated by women (and/or immigrant) workers. Focused, by their nature, on the furtherance of members' interests, unions routinely regarded the priorities and interests of 'non-standard' workers as marginal, or even contrary to members' interests. As a result, these workers ran the risk of being denied the protections afforded to others by way of the collective negotiation of employment terms and conditions.[10]

Notwithstanding the force of these challenges to the traditional labour law narrative, it remained the case that class conflict was still highly visible in the 1980s: picture a line of striking miners in the north of England eye to eye with an opposing line of police; a mounted policeman, truncheon raised; a roomful of young, male traders popping champagne corks as computer screens flash green around them. For the most part, scholars of labour law tended to frame

[7] In the work of Hugo Sinzheimer, for example, the condition of the individual worker was said to be determined by the conditions of the social class of which he was a member, so that any improvement in the former was dependent upon an improvement in the latter: H Sinzheimer, 'Demokratisierung des Arbeitsverhältnisses' (1928) in H Sinzheimer, *Arbeitsrecht und Rechtssoziologie: gesammelte Aufsätze und Reden* (Frankfurt, Europäische Verlagsanstalt, 1976) 121.

[8] See eg H Sinzheimer, 'Das Rätesystem' and 'Die Rätebewegung und Gesellschaftsverfassung', both in *Arbeitsrecht und Rechtssoziologie: gesammelte Aufsätze und Reden*, above n 7.

[9] The *locus classicus* is R Posner, 'Some Economics of Labor Law' (1984) 51 *University of Chicago Law Review* 988–1011. See also Lord Wedderburn, 'Freedom of Association and Philosophies of Labour Law' (1989) 18 *Industrial Law Journal* 1–38.

[10] J Conaghan, 'The Invisibility of Women in Labor-Law – Gender-Neutrality in Model-Building' 14 *International Journal of the Sociology of Law* 377–92; J Conaghan, 'Feminism and Labour Law: Contesting the Terrain' in A Morris and T O'Donnell (eds), *Feminist Perspectives on Employment Law* (London, Lawrence and Wishart, 1999).

their analysis accordingly.[11] It was not until the mid-1990s that the influential 'third way' discourse was developed by the centre left in an effort to transcend 'old' divides between left and right; to offer instead a vision of a win-win society in which rich and poor alike would be better off. In the UK, 'New' Labour devised a set of policies and legislative initiatives in the field of employment and employment relations which were introduced as offering 'fairness at work'.[12] The premise upon which the claim of fairness lay, quite explicitly, was that certain kinds of labour laws and legally enforceable standards could benefit employees and employers alike, improving the situation of the former while helping at the same time to make British businesses and the British economy more competitive. '[F]airness at work and competitiveness go hand in hand … one must reinforce the other. That is the cardinal principle'.[13] Describing the social policy of the European Union at the time, with reference to Karl Polanyi, Colin Crouch spoke of 'embedded neoliberalism'.[14] Neo-liberal strategies were pursued, but it was recognised that such strategies should be nested or embedded in certain forms of social protection, to gain legitimacy and to ease disruptive transitions. So-called 'flexicurity' programmes aimed, then, to increase the flexibility of action open to employers, especially their ability to dismiss workers, while offering those workers 'security' in the form of improved opportunities for alternative employment and adequate income support during periods of 'transition'.

During the early 2000s, many scholars of labour law, in the UK as elsewhere, were critical of third way policies and legislative initiatives, illustrating how measures which purported to benefit both sides of industry in truth served the interests of employers rather better than those of the workforce.[15] Others, however, glimpsed therein the possibility of a new narrative for the field; one which might constitute a convincing alternative to the 'deregulation' orthodoxy of the 1980s.[16] Without, of course, simply endorsing government policy and legislation uncritically, these scholars felt themselves able to identify within its terms a set of objectives that they could approve as setting an appropriate agenda for scholarly investigations. In their authoritative history of labour legislation and public policy in the years to 2007, for example, Paul Davies and Mark Freedland adopted a framework which assessed laws and policies primarily with reference to New Labour's stated objectives of maximising social inclusion and improving the competitiveness of the economy.[17] These were 'profoundly important social objectives', Davies and

[11] See eg Wedderburn, 'Freedom of Association', above n 9.

[12] UK Government (1998), White Paper, *Fairness at Work*, Cm 3968.

[13] ibid.

[14] C Crouch, 'Entrenching Neo-liberalism: The Current Agenda of European Social Policy' in N Countouris and M Freedland (eds), *Resocializing Europe in a Time of Crisis* (Cambridge, Cambridge University Press, 2013).

[15] eg T Novitz and P Skidmore, *Fairness at Work* (Oxford, Hart Publishing, 2001).

[16] R Dukes, *The Labour Constitution: the Enduring Idea of Labour Law* (Oxford, Oxford University Press, 2014) ch 5.

[17] P Davies and M Freedland, *Towards a Flexible Labour Market* (Oxford, Oxford University Press, 2007).

Freedland suggested, which scholars would do well to engage with.[18] In the UK and elsewhere, other authors developed a line of analysis which sought to make the case for labour law by demonstrating how it served to address 'labour market failures' or 'externalities', or to improve labour market efficiency.[19] On that logic, they were able to argue that certain labour rights and standards could be beneficial not only to workers and rights-holders, but to all.

B. Crisis, Austerity, and the Politics of Division

> Where is the fairness, we ask, for the shift-worker, leaving home in the dark hours of the early morning, who looks up at the closed blinds of their next-door neighbour sleeping off a life on benefits?
>
> George Osborne, UK Conservative Party Conference, October 2012

For a brief moment in 2008, the financial crisis appeared to reveal the deep-seated nature of the conflict of interests between those who (had) benefited from deregulated or 'lightly' regulated financial markets and those who had not. As a matter of more or less unanimous agreement, it seemed, the ostensibly 'win-win' strategies of the third way would be rethought: more stringent financial regulation would be introduced, bankers' salaries and bonuses reined in, no longer would we feel quite so 'intensely relaxed about people getting filthy rich'.[20] Before such steps could be taken, however, the crisis was quickly recast as one of swollen public sectors, over-generous welfare systems and rigid labour markets.[21] As billions of dollars and euros were spent by governments on propping up the banks, unemployment rates rose, welfare payments were reduced, and legal and institutional supports for better-than-minimum terms and conditions of employment were removed.[22]

In what has since become the mainstream analysis of 'failing' labour markets, labour market segmentation has routinely been attributed to the existence of market 'insiders' and 'outsiders'. Insiders are those who enjoy 'unnaturally' and, therefore, 'unfairly' high wages and good working conditions including, importantly, job security; outsiders are those without work or in precarious, low-paid work. Often 'insiders' are defined simply as those in a standard employment relationship (SER), enjoying all the legal protections that are accorded to (standard)

[18] ibid, 249.

[19] For discussion see RM Fischl, 'Labor Law, the Left and the Lure of the Market' (2011) 94 *Marquette Law Review* 947.

[20] As Peter Mandelson, a prominent member of Tony Blair's first government, stated in 1998 (https://www.theguardian.com/politics/2012/jan/26/mandelson-people-getting-filthy-rich).

[21] A Supiot, 'Towards a European Policy on Work' in N Countouris and M Freedland (eds), *Resocializing Europe in a Time of Crisis* (Cambridge, Cambridge University Press, 2013).

[22] For country-by-country analysis within the EU see C Clauwaert and I Schömann, 'The Crisis and National Labour Law Reforms: a Mapping Exercise', Annex to ETUI Working Paper 2014/4 (Brussels, 2014).

'employees', while 'outsiders' are correspondingly those in non-SER.[23] The characterisation of labour markets as dually segmented in this way encourages the conclusion that conflicts of interest arise – primarily and problematically – not between workers and their employers, but between different groups of workers. The logic implied by the diagnosis is that in order to improve the position of the outsiders, the insiders' rights should be weakened or forfeited: it is *because* the insiders' terms and conditions are unfairly high that those of the outsiders remain low.[24]

In the context of the financial crisis of 2008 and the ongoing crisis in the Eurozone, the EU Commission and its Troika associates have consistently identified dual segmentation as a primary cause of failing labour markets, high unemployment levels, and stunted economic growth.[25] Accordingly they have recommended or required national governments to reform employment protection legislation so as 'to reduce over-protection of workers with permanent contracts, and provide protection to those left outside or at the margins of the job market'.[26] With the stated aim of better 'balancing' the legal protection afforded to so-called insiders and outsiders, national governments have amended legislation so as to weaken the rights and lower the standards enjoyed by the former, without in fact strengthening the protections afforded to the latter.[27] Elsewhere, conflicts of interest have been deemed to arise between 'hard-working families' and 'welfare-scroungers', 'strivers' and 'shirkers', and used to legitimise cuts to welfare.[28] In an attempt to explain the imposition of draconian restrictions upon the right to strike, the interests of striking workers have been said to conflict with those of other worker-consumers, whose access to services is purportedly unfairly hindered by reason of the industrial action.[29]

The figment of conflicts of interests between workers also loomed large, of course, in policy debates and print media in the run-up to the 2016 Brexit referendum, and the Trump presidential campaign of the same year. Here, it took the form of the putative competition for jobs (and access to public services) arising

[23] V De Stefano, 'A Tale of Oversimplification and Deregulation: the Mainstream Approach to Labour Market Segmentation and Recent Responses to the Crisis in European Countries' (2014) 43(3) *Industrial Law Journal* 253.

[24] See eg the Kok Report, *Jobs, Jobs, Jobs. Creating more Employment in Europe* (Report of the Employment Taskforce, November 2003), cited in De Stefano, 'A Tale of Oversimplification and Deregulation', above n 23, 258.

[25] The term 'Troika' is widely used to refer to the EU Commission, European Central Bank, and International Monetary Fund acting together.

[26] EU Commission, 'Communication from the Commission to the European Parliament, the European Economic and Social Committee and the Committee of Regions, Annual Growth Survey' COM(2011) 11 final.

[27] De Stefano, 'A Tale of Oversimplification and Deregulation', above n 23, 264–74. For an assessment of such reforms see (2016) 32(4) *European Sociological Review*, special issue.

[28] See eg the Conservative Party of the UK, Manifesto 2015, and its bracketing together of welfare cuts and income tax cuts.

[29] UK Government, Department of Business Innovation and Skills, *Trade Union Bill: Consultation on Ballot Thresholds in Important Public Services* (July 2015).

between 'British', or 'American', and immigrant workers. In both cases, then, the 'villains' of the piece were the outsiders rather than the insiders; in both cases, the language and imagery used was routinely exaggerated and even inflammatory. Take, for example, *Leave.EU*'s notorious 'Breaking Point' poster, with its depiction of a snaking queue of hundreds of dark-skinned people, waiting – so we were clearly intended to understand – to gain entry to the country;[30] or the almost daily headlines in *The Sun*, the *Daily Express* and the *Daily Mail* referring to the 'hordes' of immigrants squeezing into 'full-up' Britain, at the insistence of the EU.[31] 'MILLIONS of EU migrants grab our jobs: Time for Brexit to FINALLY take control of borders' was fairly typical of the time, with its suggestion of a direct conflict of interest over work, and Brexit as the mechanism that would allow us to stem the immigrant flow.[32] After the event, analysis suggested that these narratives had been influential: immigration was one of the main issues to influence Leave voters' decision making; moreover, that readers of *The Sun*, the *Express* and the *Mail* were much more likely to vote Leave than Remain.[33]

C. Conflicts of Interest Depicted in Scholarship

In scholarly writing, the language of labour market insiders and outsiders is familiar, first and foremost, from the US and a line of analysis in the law and economics tradition which seeks to illustrate the allegedly damaging effects of trade union representation; particularly, the barriers put in the way of employers who would otherwise 'increase efficiency' by hiring cheaper, non-union labour.[34] In recent years, it has appeared, too, in the work of some left-wing, or centre-left, commentators. Perhaps the best-known example is Guy Standing and his identification of an emerging global class of low-paid workers with little or no job security: the 'precariat'.[35] As the dynamics of globalisation and government policies aimed at 'flexibilisation' have fragmented older class divisions, so Standing argues, several new social classes have emerged, which may be defined with reference, essentially, to the degree of vulnerability suffered by their members. Above the 'precariat' sit, then, among other classes, the 'salariat' (comprising those employed in large corporations and government administration on a full-time basis, enjoying job security, pensions and paid holidays) and the rump of the old working class (also employed under full-time, long-term contracts, enjoying both legal protections

[30] Leave.EU is an organisation that campaigned for Leave during the 2016 Referendum. The poster in question is reproduced here: https://www.theguardian.com/politics/2016/jun/16/nigel-farage-defends-ukip-breaking-point-poster-queue-of-migrants.

[31] J Martinson, *The Guardian*, 24 June 2016.

[32] The headline is taken from the *Daily Express*, 18 February, 2016.

[33] K Swales, *NatCen Report: Understanding the Leave Vote* (London, NatCen Social Research, 2016). At the time of writing, similar analysis of the 2016 US presidential election has yet to be published.

[34] De Stefano, 'A Tale of Oversimplification and Deregulation', above n 23, 262–64.

[35] G Standing, *The Precariat: the New Dangerous Class* (London, Bloomsbury, 2011). For criticism, see J Breman, 'A Bogus Concept?' (2013) 84 *New Left Review* 130.

and representation by trade unions). Below it sit the unemployed and the *Lumpen*. Implicit, and at times even explicit, in Standing's analysis is the suggestion that the interests of these different classes of worker conflict. From a social policy/basic income group perspective, for example, he describes current systems of welfare and labour law as 'labourist', effective only in supporting the shrinking and privileged population who are in stable and secure jobs. The centre-left must abandon the interests of 'labour', he argues, and turn its attentions instead to representation of the precariat.

In the field of labour law more specifically, several important works have focused in recent years on the question of inter-worker conflicts: by Valerio de Stefano, for example, already cited above, analysing the centrality of the notion of labour market segmentation to 'mainstream responses' to the financial crisis in the EU; by Guy Mundlak, and by ACL Davies.[36] Both Mundlak and Davies have sought in their writing to make the case for the importance of inter-worker conflicts; Mundlak arguing that they ought to be paid greater attention by policy makers and scholars alike, Davies building on that argument to consider how the law addresses such conflicts in the UK, and to begin the task of mapping out the law's various responses. In the course of his analysis, Mundlak has made the provocative claim that conflicts of interest between different workers or groups of workers are of the same 'order' as the conflict between labour and capital.[37]

> [T]he question labour scholars and practitioners often ask – who gains from any particular arrangement, employers or workers? – must be complemented by its counterpart – which workers gain and which lose? Sacrificing the interests of some workers for the benefit of 'labour' as a group is but one option, but clearly not the only one, nor necessarily the most redeeming, even if recognising the gains and losses of some groups risks the size of the aggregate gain, or labour's gain.[38]

III. An Outline Critique

The interests of individual workers and groups of workers can, of course, conflict. Competition between workers for jobs is as much a characteristic of market economies as conflict between workers and their employers over terms and conditions,[39]

[36] De Stefano, 'A Tale of Oversimplification and Deregulation', above n 23; G Mundlak, 'The Third Function of Labour Law: Distributing Labour Market Opportunities among Workers' in G Davidov and B Langille, *The Idea of Labour Law* (Oxford, Oxford University Press, 2011); ACL Davies, 'Identifying "Exploitative Compromises": the Role of Labour Law in Resolving Disputes Between Workers' (2012) 65 *Current Legal Problems* 269–94. See also J Rubery, 'Reregulating for Inclusive Labour Markets', Conditions of Work and Employment Series No. 65 (Geneva, ILO, 2015) and further references contained therein.

[37] Mundlak, 'The Third Function of Labour Law', above n 36, 323.

[38] ibid, 328.

[39] Characterised by Max Weber as 'Konkurrenzkampf' and 'Preiskampf': M Weber, *Economy and Society* (Berkeley, University of California Press, 1978) 72, 82, 93. *cf* Kahn-Freund's identification of 'universal' conflicts of interest between management and labour in P Davies and M Freedland (eds), *Kahn-Freund's Labour and the Law* 3rd edn (London, Stevens, 1983).

and the greater the inequality of rewards attached to particular jobs – within and between different countries – the more accentuated such competition is likely to be. Conflicts of interest can arise then, for example, between applicants for the same post, or between workers in a particular sector and others (eg young people, migrants) who would willingly do the same jobs for less. It is also manifestly the case that law can serve to intensify or to weaken such conflicts of interest, or to resolve them in favour of particular parties.[40] It can create mandatory minimum terms and conditions of employment, for example, applicable across whole localities or whole sectors. It can extend such minima to casual and migrant workers. It can guarantee a particular level of welfare to the unemployed. It can seek to prohibit discriminatory treatment of workers by employers on the grounds of race, gender or sexuality. In a situation of redundancies, it can stipulate the manner of redundancy selection. Which workers or groups of workers stand to benefit, and which to be disadvantaged, by particular labour laws is or should be a matter of concern to all scholars and policy makers working in the field.[41]

I want to suggest that it is nonetheless the case that approaches to the description or analysis of labour laws and labour markets which begin from an identification of conflicts of interests between workers – including, especially, those which employ the notion of insiders and outsiders as a heuristic device – can suffer from a number of weaknesses. Often, such approaches make use of the kind of microeconomic model which provides only an atemporal, spatially limited 'snapshot' of a single workplace or locality, from which the likely consequences of particular actions or events must be deduced. The use of such models can encourage analysts into making a number of assumptions: for example, that the amount of resources to be distributed between workers in any given situation – (good) jobs, wages, rights, risks – is fixed, so that if one worker secures a job, or a higher wage, or a right to take time off to care for dependants, another will necessarily miss out on those things. The disadvantage suffered by the outsider can accordingly be attributed directly to the advantage enjoyed by the insider.[42] Membership of posited 'insider' and 'outsider' groups of workers is similarly often assumed to be fixed rather than fluid – the unemployed will remain unemployed, while those in full-time, stable employment stay in full-time, stable employment. 'Labour' is assumed to be a homogeneous good, the labour of one person to be always easily replaceable with that of another.

[40] Davies, 'Identifying "Exploitative Compromises"', above n 36; Mundlak, 'Third Function', above n 36.

[41] Davies, 'Identifying "Exploitative Compromises"', above n 36; Mundlak, 'Third Function', above n 36; C Costello and M Freedland, 'Migrants at Work and the Division of Labour Law' in Costello and Freedland (eds), *Migrants at Work* (Oxford, Oxford University Press, 2014).

[42] See, eg, Mundlak, 'Third Function', above n 36, 323–24: 'those who pay the price to the benefit of others'; Davies, 'Exploitative Compromises', above n 36, 270: 'the introduction of the statutory right to request flexible working can be seen as a choice in favour of a particular group of workers – those with caring responsibilities – and against those who might want the benefit of flexible working for other reasons'.

Reintroducing a temporal and spatial dimension to the picture reveals that such assumptions may be unfounded. While it may be possible, in any given context, to establish that resources are fixed – so that a particular employer could not afford to hire extra staff without cutting the wages of existing employees; or so that the employment of an influx of migrant workers would necessarily entail the redundancy of others – this is not something that ought, without investigation, to be assumed. It might just as easily be the case that hiring extra staff would be economically viable for a particular firm because it would allow it to increase its customer base; that the employment of migrant workers would contribute to the growth of the economy and the creation of more jobs. Those who assume that resources are fixed overlook the fact that future resources are not; that action taken today may serve to increase, as well as to decrease, the quantity of resources available at a later date. Categorising workers as either insiders or outsiders, meanwhile, can tend to obscure not only the potentially temporary nature of membership of the posited groups, but also the possibility and the extent of *shared* interests between them. Workers in low-paid, insecure work may aspire to better jobs with better terms and conditions, and for that reason may not regard it as in their interests for systems of worker protection to be dismantled. Lowering the wages of one group of workers may impact negatively on the wages of others, and may additionally serve to legitimate cuts to welfare (on the basis that income tax revenue has fallen, or so as to ensure that 'work pays'). Many 'outsiders' share directly the interests of 'insiders' by reason of being partially financially dependent on an 'insider' family member. Regarding labour as homogeneous and workers as readily interchangeable overlooks the existence of many different segments or groupings in labour markets, arising not only by reason of the differing terms and conditions of workers, but also different skill-sets and levels of education, geographical locations, corporate structures, trade union membership and so on.[43]

A further significant weakness of the insider/outsider heuristic is its tendency to obscure the importance of employer interests and strategies in causing market segmentation. The very language of insiders and outsiders can appear to attribute the causes of inequalities among workers to the insiders (and not to capital or the state), and, as a consequence, to legitimise measures which aim to achieve greater equality by a process of levelling wages and conditions *down*. It is true that the lowering of insiders' terms and conditions is not the only possible policy response to a diagnosis of dual segmentation. As Deakin has identified, a number of alternative strategies exist, including 'mandating equal (or pro rata) protections for workers in atypical work relationships to those in the "core" ("levelling up")'; widening the scope of labour law protections so as to increase the proportion of workers who enjoy them; and using the law 'to stimulate alternative mechanisms of labour market regulation' such as 'collective bargaining, training policy and

[43] W Streeck, 'The Sociology of Labor Markets and Trade Unions' in NJ Smelser and R Swedberg (eds), *The Handbook of Economic Sociology* (Princeton, Princeton University Press, 2005).

fiscal incentives'.[44] In the current context of austerity, however, and in line with the economic orthodoxy regarding the benefits of ever-greater flexibility, it is levelling down which is almost invariably the preferred option of national governments and supranational institutions. The aim is decidedly to increase the number of jobs, and not to ensure their quality.

As was emphasised long ago by Engels, employers have much to gain by orchestrating and intensifying competition between workers.[45] It was, of course, precisely for that reason that workers sought to organise themselves into trade unions and to demand the standardisation of terms and conditions across whole sectors and countries, or regions, refusing to compete with one another on the basis of the price at which they were willing to sell their labour power. Those who advocate labour market 'flexibilisation' as a response to the existence of insiders and outsiders seem to overlook this point; to downplay the fact that some forms of flexibilisation – for example, the dismantling of established machinery for the collective representation of workers' interests – may serve to *increase* inequalities between workers, intensifying competition between them for (the better) jobs.[46] This is not true across the board, of course: certain types of labour market segmentation may serve the interests of employing organisations not only by keeping wages low, but also by weakening the capacity of labour for collective action.[47] The reorganisation of big firms in line with a core/periphery pattern, for example, may be undertaken with the specific aim of reducing labour costs, divesting the firm of non-core elements of the production process, and creating a two-tier workforce in the process. Inequalities between remaining 'core' employees and the rest – the employees of smaller contractors, 'zero hours' and other 'casual' workers, self-employed workers – are likely to be significant.

IV. Case Study

A. The Agricultural Sector in Scotland

In what follows, the aim is to give further consideration to the nature and implications of conflicts of interest in the field of work and labour market relations, focusing specifically on the agriculture sector in Scotland. In economic terms, the

[44] S Deakin, 'Addressing Labour Market Segmentation: the Role of Labour Law', *Working Paper No 52*, Governance and Tripartism Department (Geneva, ILO, 2013).

[45] '[C]ompetition of the workers among themselves is … the sharpest weapon against the proletariat in the hands of the bourgeoisie.' F Engels, *The Condition of the Working Class in England* (Leipzig, Otto Wigand, 1845).

[46] This is especially likely to be the case where the collective bargaining machinery previously in place was sectoral rather than company specific: De Stefano 271–74; Rubery cites evidence that deregulation can serve to increase the dispersion of employment conditions and rewards: Rubery, 'Reregulating for Inclusive Labour Markets', above n 36, 6.

[47] Breman, 'A Bogus Concept?', above n 35.

sector is small, accounting for only around 1 per cent of income and 1 per cent of jobs in Scotland.[48] In terms of its workforce, it is characterised by low pay across the board, and by a singularly high proportion of temporary migrant labour.[49] In 2010, it was estimated that as many as half of all employees in the sector were 'A8' migrants, from the eight Central and Eastern European countries that acceded to the EU on 1 May 2004.[50] This was a much larger proportion of the workforce than in any other sector in Scotland.[51] Between 1998 and 2008, the number of full-time employees in agriculture decreased by around 4,000, while the number of casual and temporary workers increased by around 2,000.[52] Full-time employees now constitute only around half of the workforce, the other half being part-time, casual and seasonal workers, with migrants providing much of the seasonal labour.[53]

In Scotland, as elsewhere, employment in the agricultural sector possesses certain features which can tend to make the situation of workers particularly precarious.[54] Much of the work is seasonal, leaving workers without a stable, guaranteed income throughout the year. Where they are only in post for short periods of time, workers are less likely to have been given proper health and safety information and training, or to have acquired the same level of expertise in using farm machinery as permanent employees, putting them at an even greater risk than usual of workplace accidents.[55] Often, agricultural work requires to be done in geographically isolated locations, meaning that farm workers are reliant on the accommodation and/or transport provided by their employer, with only very limited opportunities to seek advice, including legal advice, or to join a trade union. By reason of these various vulnerabilities, workers in agriculture may be more likely than others to accept any terms offered in a bid to get themselves hired, and less likely to be in a position to enforce their legal rights. Migrant workers may not be able to build up the periods of long-term continuous residence necessary to acquire more secure residence status. According to the Equality and Human Rights Commission, there is some evidence in the Scottish agricultural sector of

[48] The reference here to 'jobs' indicates that 'working occupiers' and 'working spouses' are excluded from the calculation, since they are generally treated as unpaid labour. Scottish Government, *Economic Report on Scottish Agriculture*, 2016 edn (Edinburgh, 2016); Scottish Government, *Regional Employment Patterns in Scotland: Statistics from the Annual Population Survey 2015* (Edinburgh, 2016).

[49] In April 2013, median full-time gross weekly earnings in agriculture in the UK were found to be £407.50, 21.3% lower than the median for all industries and services, £517.50: D Bovill, *Patterns of Pay: Estimates from the Annual Survey of Hours and Earnings, UK, 1997 to 2013* (London, Office for National Statistics, 2014).

[50] Czech Republic, Estonia, Latvia, Lithuania, Hungary, Poland, Slovakia, Slovenia. A Findlay, A Geddes, D McCollum, 'International Migration and Recession' (2010) 126(4) *Scottish Geographical Journal* 299–320, 314. No government statistics are available as to numbers of migrant workers employed across the sector.

[51] ibid.

[52] ibid, 316.

[53] Scottish Government Report, 2016, above n 48.

[54] ACL Davies, 'Migrant Workers in Agriculture' in C Costello and M Freedland (eds), *Migrants at Work: Immigration and Vulnerability in Labour Law* (Oxford, Oxford University Press, 2014), 80–81.

[55] Health and Safety Executive, *Fatal injuries in farming, horticulture and fish farming in Scotland from 2003/04 to 2013/14* (HSE, 2014).

human trafficking and forced labour.[56] The wages of migrant workers employed to plant and harvest soft fruit in Scotland, it has found, may be below the minimum wage.[57]

> [T]hey can lose significant parts of what they earn in commission to the gangmaster, as well as repaying exorbitant charges for being conscripted and brought in. They may also be charged for living accommodation in insanitary, dangerous portable buildings in the countryside, crammed to the seams with other workers.[58]

From 1943 until the end of 2013, the hiring of temporary migrant labour in agriculture across the UK was regulated by a series of temporary migrant worker programmes.[59] Most recently, the so-called Seasonal Agricultural Workers Programme accommodated as many as 25,000 workers per annum in the country, employed primarily in horticulture at harvest time.[60] From 2008, the programme was limited to so-called A2 nationals from Romania and Bulgaria.[61] It was brought to an end on 1 January 2014 to coincide with the lifting of restrictions on the rights of A2 nationals to work in the UK. Since then, the demand for seasonal workers in agriculture has been filled predominantly by A8 and A2 nationals who, as EU citizens, do not require a visa to work in the UK. This is consistent with government policy that demand for unskilled and low-skilled labour should be satisfied, for the moment, from within the EU.[62]

Since the beginning of 2014, then, no distinction has been drawn in law between temporary migrant and other kinds of agricultural labour when it comes to the regulation of workers' terms and conditions of employment. In Scotland, two separate and very different regulatory regimes are in force, in addition to the generally applicable norms of employment law: the Scottish Agricultural Wages Board (SAWB) and the Gangmasters Labour Abuse Authority (GLAA, formerly the Gangmasters Licensing Authority).[63] The SAWB is empowered by statute to set wages and other terms and conditions for the sector by way of statutory order.[64] Together with the Agricultural Advisory Panel for Wales, it is the sole survivor of a system of wages councils first set up under the Trade Boards Act 1909, the remainder of which were abolished during the 1980s, and, in the case of the Agricultural Wages Board for England and Wales, in 2013.[65] The original aim of the trade boards

[56] Equality and Human Rights Commission Scotland, *Inquiry into Human Trafficking in Scotland Report* (Equality and Human Rights Commission 2011), 8.

[57] ibid.

[58] ibid.

[59] S Scott, 'Making the case for Temporary Migrant Worker Programmes: Evidence from the UK's rural guestworker ('SAWS') scheme' (2015) 40 *Journal of Rural Studies* 1–11.

[60] At its 2004 peak: ibid. For an outline of the relevant rules, see ACL Davies, 'Migrant Workers in Agriculture', above n 54.

[61] The A2 countries are Romania and Bulgaria, which joined the EU on 1 January 2007. The access of A2 nationals to the UK labour market was restricted until January 2014.

[62] Scott, 'Making the case for Temporary Migrant Worker Programmes', above n 59.

[63] The Agricultural Wages Board for England and Wales was abolished in 2013.

[64] Agricultural Wages (Scotland) Act 1949.

[65] The Trade Boards Act 1909 was amended by the Trade Boards Act 1918. The Wages Councils Act 1945 repealed the two earlier Acts in their entirety and replaced them with a new set of provisions. In

legislation was to create a legislative substitute for collective machinery, involving representatives of labour and the employers directly in the setting of wages.[66] In line with that aim, the SAWB comprises 17 members: six nominated by Unite the Union, six nominated by the National Farmers Union Scotland and the Scottish Land and Estates, and five independent members appointed by Scottish Ministers. Its annual Wages Orders apply to all employees in the sector, guaranteeing them an hourly wage that is at least as high as the National Living or Minimum Wage (NLW/NMW) and in many cases higher, depending on the length of service and qualifications of the employee in question.[67] It also sets additional overtime rates, minimum paid holiday entitlements that are more generous than the generally applicable minima established under the Working Time Regulations, and other rules, including a requirement that employees be supplied by their employer with weather protective clothing and boots.[68] Enforcement of the rules contained in the Order is a matter for the Scottish Government Wages Enforcement Team, and the Agricultural Wages Inspector.[69]

The GLAA was first established in 2006 with the aim of protecting vulnerable and exploited workers in the agriculture, horticulture, shellfish gathering and associated processing and packaging sectors throughout the UK.[70] Because its method of seeking to achieve this aim involves operating a 'gangmaster' – or labour provider – licensing regime, it has no application to individuals who are employed directly by farm businesses. Under the terms of the relevant legislation, any labour provider must apply for and continue to hold a licence in order to operate lawfully in the relevant sectors. Before granting a licence, the Authority must inspect the applicant; where the business is new and not yet trading, it may return after granting the licence for a second inspection. The matter of whether to award or revoke a licence is judged by the GLAA with reference to eight labour standards, the majority of which seek to protect workers from exploitation and abuse, to ensure that they enjoy safe and decent working conditions, and to ensure a floor of basic rights.[71] Responsibility for monitoring and enforcement lies primarily with

agriculture, a Wages Board was first established under the Corn Production Act 1917. The Agricultural Advisory Panel for Wales was established under the Agricultural Sector (Wales) Act 2014.

[66] As discussed by Otto Kahn-Freund in O Kahn-Freund, 'Legal Framework' in A Flanders and HA Clegg (eds), *The System of Industrial Relations in Great Britain* (Oxford, Blackwell, 1954), 69.

[67] The Order uses the term 'worker' throughout but confines its application to workers 'employed' in agriculture: Agricultural Wages (Scotland) Order (No 63) 2015 [AWSO], Art 3. An employee with at least 26 weeks' continuous service is entitled to a higher hourly minimum, as is an employee with certain agricultural qualifications: AWSO, Arts 5, 6, 8.

[68] AWSO, Arts 9, 10, 27.

[69] Scottish Agricultural Wages Board, *Annual Report for 1 October 2015 – 30 September 2016*: http://www.gov.scot/Topics/farmingrural/Rural/business/18107/SAWBAnnualReport2016.

[70] Gangmasters (Licensing) Act 2004 (GLA 2004), since amended by the Immigration Act 2016. The types of agriculture and associated industry covered by the Act are stipulated in s 3. In the 2016 Act, provision has been made for the future extension of the GLAA's remit to cover all sectors of the labour market: GLA 2004, s 3(5) as amended.

[71] Gangmasters (Licensing Conditions) Rules 2009, SI 2009/307, Schedule 1. For explanation, see GLA, *Licensing Standards* (May 2012, reprinted July 2015), available at http://www.gla.gov.uk/media/2745/licensing-standards-aug-2016.pdf.

the GLAA. Where a gangmaster breaches a term of its licence, the GLAA may revoke the licence, or modify it.[72] It is a criminal offence to operate as a gangmaster without a licence, or to use labour from an unlicensed provider.[73]

In contrast to the Scottish Agricultural Wages legislation, the Gangmasters (Licensing) Act makes no provision for the setting of wages or other terms and conditions higher than those already stipulated as the NLW/NMW or by the Agricultural Wages Order. Instead, its 'added value' lies principally with the additional degree of scrutiny it ensures of labour provision practices in the sector, and of the terms and conditions of employment, and working and living conditions of the relevant workers. A second strength of the regime is its broad scope of application. Both gangmaster and 'worker' are defined very widely in the Act so as to include all workers provided by a gangmaster (whether an individual or agency, situated in the UK or elsewhere) or other intermediary, including those workers who have no contract of employment or 'workers' contract, and/or 'no right to be, or to work' in the UK.[74] The licensing system thus extends a number of employment rights, albeit indirectly, to workers who might not otherwise have had them – including the right to be paid a national minimum.[75] In operation for over a decade now, the Authority has been widely and highly praised for clamping down on rogue employers and preventing abusive practices.[76] Since 2010, significant budget cuts have raised a question mark over its continued capacity to function as effectively as it did in its first years.[77]

B. Agricultural Insiders and Outsiders?

On the face of it, then, the agricultural sector in Scotland comprises a variety of different groups of workers which could be thought of as comprising 'insiders' or 'outsiders': employees whose terms and conditions are regulated by the SAWB, and casual workers, to whom the relevant rules do not apply; local workers, and migrants from within the EU and elsewhere; workers employed directly

[72] GLA 2004, s 9.

[73] GLA 2004, ss 12 and 13.

[74] GLA 2004, ss 3 and 4.

[75] See 'Licensing Standard 2': 'A worker must be paid at least the National Minimum Wage (NMW) or, if applicable, in accordance with appropriate Agricultural Wages Order (AWO)… Failure against this standard will lead to the licence being revoked without immediate effect.' I say "indirectly", because the Act does not actually confer any rights on workers, but instead deems the paying of stipulated wages etc to be a "licensing condition".

[76] See eg Frances O'Grady, quoted in TUC press release, *TUC raises concerns over changes to the Gangmasters Licensing Authority*, 12 January 2016; A Balch, P Brindley, A Geddes, S Scott, *Gangmasters Licensing Authority: Annual Review 2008* (Nottingham, Gangmasters Licensing Authority, 2009); M Wilkinson, G Craig, A Gaus, *Forced Labour in the UK and the GLA* (Hull, Hull University Press, 2010). For a discussion of current threats to the continued effectiveness of the GLAA, see ACL Davies, 'The Immigration Act 2016' (2016) 45(3) *Industrial Law Journal* 431–42.

[77] Davies, 'Migrant Workers', above n 54; Davies 'The Immigration Act 2016', above n 76.

by farmers, and those supplied to the farmers by labour market intermediaries or gangmasters; the documented, and the undocumented. Categorising the workers in this way might prompt us to consider such questions as the following. In commanding higher wages than the national minimum by reason of the Scottish Agricultural Wages Order, are employees eating up an unnecessarily large portion of employers' budgets? Are they thereby preventing the hire of potentially greater numbers of (cheaper) casual and gangmaster-supplied workers? With their readiness to accept lower wages and harsher terms and conditions, are temporary migrant workers undercutting Scottish workers, and filling vacancies that would otherwise be filled by the locals? If, as a consequence of Brexit, EU workers were no longer able to work here without visas, causing labour shortages in the sector, would Scottish workers step forward to take up the jobs as they became available? Would employers offer higher wages in an effort to persuade them to do so?

The sketch of the sector drawn above principally comprises information regarding working relationships and the relevant regulatory regimes. If we supplement it with consideration of *employer* motivations and practices, it changes dramatically so that quite different questions appear to require answers. A useful example of such an employer- or demand-side-focused analysis is provided by Ben Rogaly in his study of horticulture in the UK.[78] Rogaly takes as his starting point the observation that it is harder, *as a general rule*, to make a profit in agriculture than in many other sectors. As Marx long ago observed, production time and labour time are not identical in agriculture, so that there are necessarily periods of idleness of labour and machinery, with consequent stalling of the turnover of capital.[79] In recent years, Rogaly goes on to explain, these basic difficulties have been compounded by the ever-growing power of supermarkets as the main buyers of horticultural produce, and their ability to appropriate ever-greater value from the producers.[80] In an effort to turn a profit nonetheless, producers have sought to intensify production in a variety of ways. Here, Rogaly adopts the broad definition of 'intensification' proposed by Guthman to include not only 'efforts to speed up, enhance or reduce the risks of biological processes', but also 'some nontechnical innovations in labour control … for example, the use of vulnerability to ensure a timely and compliant labour force come harvesttime'.[81] In British horticulture, he observes three examples of trends in employment practices which may be

[78] B Rogaly, 'Intensification of Workplace Regimes in British Agriculture: The Role of Migrant Workers' (2008) 14 *Population, Place Space* 497–510. Rogaly approves Krissman's arguments regarding the need for more demand-side-focused analyses of migration: Rogaly, 499 citing F Krissman, 'Sin coyote ni patron: why the "migrant network" fails to explain international migration' (2005) 39 *International Migration Review* 4–44.

[79] Rogaly, 'Intensification of Workplace Regimes in British Agriculture', above n 78, 498, citing S Mann, *Agrarian Capitalism in Theory and Practice* (Chapel Hill, NC, University of North Carolina Press 1990).

[80] Rogaly, 'Intensification', above n 79, 499, citing Competition Commission, *Supermarkets: a Report on the Supply of Groceries from Multiple Stores in the United Kingdom* (London, 2000).

[81] Rogaly, 'Intensification', above n 79, 498, citing J Guthman, *Agrarian Dreams: The Paradox of Organic Farming in California* (Berkeley, University of California Press, 2004).

understood to indicate such intensification: the increased employment of international migrant workers, the increased use of gangmaster labour, and the increased use of piece rates. On the basis of three case studies, he concludes that the drive towards intensification 'has been caused largely by corporate retailers' regulation of workplace regimes in the sector, through their requirements for volume, "quality" and low margins for the growers'.[82]

Of course, the oligopsony power of supermarkets is not only an issue for horticultural producers.[83] In her 2004 exposé of the supermarket sector, the food writer and journalist Joanna Blythman likened the relationship between retailers and producers to that of masters and servants.[84] Producers are beholden to supermarkets for the simple reason that they have no one else, often, to sell to.[85] In their relations with individual producers, supermarkets capitalise on their position of power by wielding the threat of 'delisting', that is ceasing to buy from, that producer.[86] At the same time as they present the producer with a list of incredibly detailed product specifications (stipulating precisely the size, shape, colour and general appearance of the items to be supplied), they refuse, as a rule, to make any binding commitment to purchase from that producer, then, or for any period of time to come.[87] Nor will they undertake to provide a minimum period of notice before cancelling an order.[88] In tailoring its produce, as it must, to comply with the supermarket's wishes, meanwhile, the producer becomes even more reliant on that specific buyer, since others will likely have different product specifications. As documented by the Competition Commission in 2000, the variety of ways in which supermarkets routinely abuse their resultant positions of power is quite startling: not only squeezing the price that they will pay for goods, for example, but actually requiring producers to *pay them*, in various ways, in return for stocking or promoting the producers' food and drink.[89]

In the Scottish agricultural sector, as elsewhere, the oligopsony power of the supermarkets is reflected above all in the very low profit margins of the majority of commercial farms, and in the high proportion of such farms reliant on subsidies.[90] As a result of efforts to intensify production, wages have been driven down and working practices amended so that it has become increasingly difficult for

[82] Rogaly, 'Intensification', above n 79, 506.

[83] J Blythman, *Shopped: The Shocking Power of British Supermarkets* (London, Harper Perennial, 2005); Rogaly, 'Intensification', above n 79.

[84] Blythman, *Shopped*, above n 83, 177.

[85] In 2011, supermarkets in the UK were estimated to command 76% of the supply of food products to consumers: P Shears, 'Grocery Suppliers Code of Practice: Fairness for Farmers?' (2013) 3 *International Journal of Agricultural Management* 59.

[86] Blythman, *Shopped*, above n 83, ch 18.

[87] ibid, ch 27.

[88] ibid, ch 22.

[89] Competition Commission, *Supermarkets: a Report on the Supply of Groceries from Multiple Stores in the United Kingdom*, above n 80.

[90] According to Government figures, in 2014/15 average farm business income, including from subsidies, was only £23,000. Excluding support from grants and subsidies, the average farm made a loss of £17,000 in 2014: Scottish Government, *Economic Report*, above n 48.

employers to recruit local workers.[91] Migrant workers fulfil a 'complementary' rather than 'substitutional' workforce function, performing work that would not otherwise be done by locals.[92] In the light of these findings, the question that begs to be answered is not so much one of conflicts of interest between different worker groups, but rather that of the potentially disastrous consequences of Brexit for the sector. As was noted above, more than half of all workers in the sector are currently thought to be EU citizens exercising their freedom of movement. Evidence suggests that they could not be replaced with Scottish or British workers, at least, not without a rise in wages of a magnitude that could threaten the viability of many producers, for example, if supermarkets chose to buy imports instead.[93] If the demand for cheap, exploitable labour cannot otherwise be filled, however, the threat arises of increased incidences of undocumented work, trafficking and forced labour.[94]

As to the role of government in all of this, Rogaly has highlighted the interest which the state has in reducing food prices, and retail price inflation more generally.[95] In furtherance of that interest, successive governments have offered all kinds of support to supermarkets since the end of the Second World War: from the funding of trips for the directors of Tesco and Sainsbury to study emerging multiple grocery stores in the United States, to the abolition of the retail price mechanism in 1964.[96] In 2001, the Labour Government responded to the 2000 Report of the Competition Commission, which had recognised the frequent abuses by supermarkets of their positions of power, by issuing a Supermarkets Code of Practice.[97] Voluntary rather than binding in nature, and reliant upon individual producers brave enough to bring complaints against the retail giants, however, the Code was widely criticised for its ineffectualness.[98]

In 2010, the Coalition Government introduced a new Grocery Suppliers Code of Practice which, since 2013, has its own Groceries Code Adjudicator.[99] Under the terms of the relevant legislation, the Adjudicator is authorised to arbitrate disputes between retailers and suppliers, investigate complaints from suppliers, and where there has been a breach of the Code, to publish that information and/or to impose a fine.[100] Importantly, the Adjudicator may rely on evidence from third parties in deciding whether to launch an investigation, and need not therefore wait

[91] Findlay et al, 'International Migration and Recession', above n 50, 316–17.

[92] ibid, 313.

[93] Migration Advisory Committee, *Report on Migrant Seasonal Workers* (London, Home Office, 2013).

[94] With respect to forced labour, the Equality and Human Rights Commission Scotland has identified demand for cheap, exploitable labour as a pull factor to 'destination' countries: Equality and Human Rights Commission Scotland, *Inquiry into Human Trafficking in Scotland*, above n 56.

[95] Rogaly, 'Intensification', above n 79, 507.

[96] ibid, 506–07.

[97] For discussion, see Blythman, *Shopped*, above n 83, ch 24.

[98] ibid; Shears, 'Fairness for Farmers', citing Office of Fair Trading, *The Supermarkets Code of Practice: Report on the Review of the Operation of the Code of Practice* (2004).

[99] https://www.gov.uk/government/organisations/groceries-code-adjudicator.

[100] Groceries Code Adjudicator Act 2013.

for a plucky producer willing to raise her head above the parapet. These are positive developments indeed, which have already resulted in the public admonishing of Tesco for breaches of the Code relating to delayed payments.[101] Whether the Adjudicator is sufficiently resourced to make a significant and lasting difference to supermarket behaviour remains, however, to be seen.[102] In this respect, it ought also to be borne in mind that the Code aims at ensuring 'fair and lawful' treatment of producers by retailers, and not at transforming the essential nature of their relationship across the sector.

On the matter of Brexit, and the labour shortages that it will almost certainly bring with it, the government has not undertaken, at the time of writing, to guarantee the right of EU citizens to continue working in this country; nor to introduce any kind of alternative temporary work visa scheme. In her speech to the annual conference of the National Farmers' Union in February 2017, the Environment Secretary acknowledged the 'vital role' that seasonal migrants from the EU played, especially in horticulture, but was also quick to remind the audience that controlling immigration was a 'key factor' behind the vote to Leave.[103] Labour shortages would best be avoided, then, she seemed to suggest, through encouraging British workers and apprentices into the sector, and through technological innovation.

V. Conclusion

In policy discourse, the rhetoric of labour market insiders and outsiders is often deployed in support of measures aimed at weakening labour rights and protections, sometimes as part of a wider-ranging politics of division. As scholars of labour law, we ought always to be attentive to conflicts of interest between workers, and the ways in which law can accentuate, alleviate, or resolve these. We must be equally attentive, however, to the possibility that such conflicts have been overemphasised by government or other commentators, purported or assumed to exist where they may not. Where conflicts of interest between workers are overstated – as can be the case, in particular, where the notion of insiders and outsiders is used as a heuristic – the danger arises that the motivations and strategies of employing organisations, and the role of the state, might each be obscured. Workers might feel encouraged into the belief that legislative protections and collective institutions are not for them; as a consequence, support for the protective legislation and collective institutions in question might be weakened, and their efficacy undermined.[104]

[101] Groceries Code Adjudicator Annual Report 2015/16.

[102] In 2015/16, the single investigation into Tesco's breach of the Code lasted almost a year from launch through to publication of the report, taking over 50% of the Adjudicator's time and 25% of the total office resource: ibid.

[103] https://www.gov.uk/government/speeches/environment-secretary-speaks-at-nfu-conference, accessed 23 February 2017.

[104] S Marshall and C Fenwick, *Labour Regulation and Development: Socio-Legal Perspectives* (Cheltenham, Elgar, 2016).

7

The Different Meanings of Formalisation. Experiments from the South: The Case of Argentina

LORENA POBLETE*

I. Introduction

Informality is a structural feature of the labour market in developing countries, particularly in Latin America. Historically, in Argentina, at least one-third of the people perform so-called informal activities. During the 1990s, the informality rate rose to 35 per cent, climbing to 45 per cent in 2002, after the profound economic crisis which took place in 2001. More recently, as the result of various formalisation policies, the informality rate has decreased, though 34 per cent of the working population can still be considered informal workers.

Since 1991, Argentinian legislators have prioritised formalisation, introducing a slew of laws seeking to formalise the situation of these workers. However, the rationale underpinning this process of formalisation changed during this period. Between 1991 and 2001, in accordance with the neoliberal policies that characterised the decade, formalisation and flexibility were considered part of the same equation. All the legislation enacted under the auspices of the Labour Reform initiated in Argentina in the 1990s promotes labour flexibility in classical ways: short-term contracts, part-time jobs, internships, and different kinds of subcontracting arrangements like temporary employment agencies or the promotion of self-employment. Since 2004, with the so-called counter Labour Reform,[1]

* Centro de Investigaciones Sociales del Instituto de Desarrollo Económico y Social, CONICET (CIS-CONICET/IDES) Argentina. This research received special funding from Argentina's National Research Council (CONICET-PUE 22920160100005CO). I am very grateful for Diamond Ashiagbor's very detailed reading of my work and her suggestions, also for the interesting comments received during the workshop 'Re-imagining labour law for development: Informal work in the global North and global South' at SOAS University of London.

[1] See especially A Goldín, 'Reforma y contrareforma laboral en Argentina, crónica simple de un proceso pendular' (2012) 68 *Derecho PUCP* 63, 91. According to this author, in 2004 the process of reconfiguring Argentina's institutional labour protection system began, re-establishing essential labour rights like minimum wage and collective bargaining. The aim was to undo a great part of the sweeping labour reform in the 1990s that had minimised labour rights and limited the power of labour institutions.

formalisation has been used as a way to expand social protection. In line with the approach of the International Labour Organization (ILO), the main goal is to provide decent work to all workers.

While the reasons for formalisation are clearly different in the two periods, the way in which formalisation was conceived and implemented is quite similar. This chapter seeks to analyse – from a socio-historical perspective – the different regulatory responses to informality adopted in Argentina since the 1990s. Analysing changes in labour law, social security norms, tax regulations and congressional debates, this research assesses different experiments in formalising the situation of precarious workers such as wage-earners working in small businesses, own-account workers and domestic workers. These experiments introduced some regulatory innovations and novel enforcement mechanisms.

The first experiment addressed own-account workers in the informal labour market and small business employers and wage earners. Thus, the legal category of 'self-employed' was reshaped to include not only liberal professions but also unqualified own-account workers with low incomes. The second experiment aimed to formalise paid domestic work. Using different strategies, the state strove to implement new regulations that would give domestic workers the same rights as all workers.

The chapter shows that, in Argentina, formalisation policies principally entailed reforms to the tax regime and the social security system, although labour law was also adjusted to allow informal workers to become formal. Social security benefits – like health insurance and pensions – were the main goal of formalisation policies and also served as an incentive for informal workers. For these workers, formalising a labour relationship becomes desirable when it grants access to social protection. The acknowledgement of labour rights is important but not determinant in the decision of domestic workers and wage earners working for small businesses to ask employers to formalise their labour relation or for low-income own-account workers to enrol themselves.

The chapter will be organised in five sections. Following this Introduction, section II will discuss the concept of informality – particularly from the Latin American sociological perspective – seeking to understand the purpose of the formalisation policies in Argentina. Section III will focus on the revised definition of the self-employed worker category based on its transformation during the period; and section IV, the new law on domestic work and its implementation. The conclusion, section V, will present the results of these experiments.

II. Informality: A Polysemous Concept

A little over a decade ago, informality became a core topic in the academic debates within industrialised countries. The international crisis of 2008 revealed the complexity of the labour market transformation that had begun at the end of the twentieth century.[2] This transformation demonstrated the limits of the explanatory power of the two concepts most commonly used to explain labour market changes: precarious work and non-standard work. The first concept – conceived as a deterioration of the salaried worker's status; and the second – understood as an alternative to the employment relationship – proved ineffective when attempting to explain innovative and unconventional ways to participate in the labour market.[3] In this context, the concept of informality – which had previously been used to explain the structure and dynamic of labour markets in countries of the South – was introduced (or imported) to analyse the changes in industrialised countries. Mediated by the definitions proposed by the ILO, this concept has been widely adopted and employed to understand substantially different phenomena.

A. A Sector, an Economy or a Type of Job?

The adjective 'informal' has been used to characterise a sector within the economy, a labour market sector, a method of production, a kind of job or even an 'employment' type.[4] Over the past decade, however, a plethora of studies on these different phenomena have indiscriminately used and even vulgarised the term 'informality', as if this word alone could capture all of them.

The ILO is undoubtedly the entity responsible for producing and disseminating this concept. For over 40 years, at different moments and with different intentions, 'informal' gradually adopted new meanings. Studies on the topic note that the definition of 'informal sector' proposed in 1972 by the employment mission to Kenya gave origin to the concept. In the context of a wide-ranging debate on the evolution of labour markets in developing countries that followed Arthur Lewis's 1954 article, Hans Singer and Richard Jolly's mission into Kenya showed that there is a traditional sector of the economy capable of creating employment and thus reducing poverty.[5] This is when the concept of the 'informal sector' became a focus in the discussions in developing countries.

Since then, different actors within and related to the ILO have proposed new definitions in order to refine the meaning of the concept.[6] In some cases, these

[2] See generally R Castel, *Les métamorphoses de la question sociale. Une chronique du salariat* (Paris, Fayard, 1995); M Lallement, *Les gouvernances de l'emploi* (Paris, Desclée de Brouwer, 1999).

[3] See generally A Supiot (ed), *Au-delà de l'emploi. Transformations du travail et devenir du droit du travail en Europe* (Paris, Flammarion, 1999); M-L Morin, 'Sous-traitance et relations salariales. Aspects de droit du travail' (1994) 60 *Travail et Emploi* 23, 44; M-L Morin (ed), *Prestation de travail et activité de service* (Paris, La Documentation Française, 1999).

[4] See, eg, A Trebilcock, 'Using Development Approaches to Address the Challenge of the Informal Economy for Labour Law' in G Davidov and B Langille (eds), *Boundaries and Frontiers of Labour Law* (Portland, International Institute for Labour Studies-Hart Publishing, 2006).

[5] See, eg, M Chen, 'The Informal Economy: Definitions, Theories and Policies' (2012) *WIEGO* (Women of Informal Employment: Globalizing and Organizing), Working Paper 1.

[6] See generally C La Hovary, 'The Informal Economy and the ILO: A Legal Perspective' (2015) 30 *International Journal of Comparative Labour Law and Industrial Relations* 391, 441.

clarifications were aimed at developing statistical measures of informality; in others, the aim was to draft recommendations for formalisation policies.

In 1991, taking into account the Latin American debate – and particularly, the studies by the PREALC ILO[7] – the informal sector, according to the report 'The Dilemma of the Informal Sector',[8] comprised small-scale production units and independent unskilled workers with little capital, a low technological level, and low and erratic income.[9] Although the sector is acknowledged as heterogeneous, the activities developed within the sector are considered a survival strategy among the urban poor in developing countries.[10] Following this definition, in 1993 the ILO International Conference of Labour Statisticians (ICLS) emphasised that the 'informal sector' refers to the firms in which informal jobs are done but does not make reference to the personal characteristics of those working there or the jobs they do. The focus is on a sector of the economy, not on methods for regulating work arrangements in the labour market.[11]

In 2002, the ILO 'Resolution Concerning Decent Work and the Informal Economy' introduced a wide notion of informality through the concept of informal economy, which 'refers to all economic activities by workers and economic units that are – in law or in practice – not covered or insufficiently covered by formal arrangements'.[12] A year later, with the goal of measuring and characterising the informal economy, the ICLS introduced the concept of 'informal jobs'. Following its definition: 'Employees are considered to have informal jobs if their employment relationship is, in law or in practice, not subject to national labour legislation, income taxation, social protection or entitlement to certain employment benefits (advance notice of dismissal, severance pay, paid annual or sick leave, etc.).'[13] Thus, according to the ILO approach, informal economy and informal jobs are considered as complementary concepts.[14]

In 2015, the 'Transition from the Informal to the Formal Economy Recommendation' (R204) renewed the 2003 definition of informal economy, providing a more precise characterisation of the economic units as involving 'units that employ hired labour; that are owned by individuals working on their own account – either alone or with the help of contributing family workers; cooperatives and social and

[7] Regional Employment Programme for Latin America – ILO.

[8] ILO, "The Dilemma of the Informal Sector", Report of the Director-General, International Labour Conference, 78th Session, 1991, Geneva.

[9] See especially J Neffa (ed), *La informalidad, la precariedad laboral y el empleo no registrado en la provincia de Buenos Aires* (Buenos Aires, CEIL-PIETTE/CONICET-OIT, 2008).

[10] See C La Hovary, 'The Informal Economy and the ILO', above n 6.

[11] See, eg, R Hussmanns, 'Statistical definition of informal employment: Guidelines endorsed by the Seventeenth International Conference of Labour Statisticians (2003)' (2004), 7th Meeting of the Expert Group on Informal Sector Statistics (Delhi Group).

[12] ILO, "The Resolution concerning decent work and informal economy", International Labour Conference, 90th Session, 2002, Geneva.

[13] ILO, *Guidelines concerning a statistical definition of informal employment, endorsed by the Seventeenth International Conference of Labour Statisticians (November–December 2003)* (2003).

[14] See, eg, R Hussmanns, 'Measuring the Informal Economy: From employment in the informal sector to informal employment' (2004) ILO, Policy Integration Department, Working Paper 53.

solidarity economy units'. However, the recommendation applies to all workers, that is those working in both informal and formal economic units.

As Davidov has noted,[15] the opacity of the myriad definitions of the concept of informality proposed by the ILO can be attributed to the overlapping of two different issues. On the one hand, informality refers to the exclusion of certain categories of workers from the law; this brings up gaps in the existing legislation, which does not cover all of the positions in the labour market. On the other hand, informality is presented as a question of noncompliance with the law – or even fraud. Therefore, state intervention can take two very different paths: it must expand the legal framework on the one hand and implement effective enforcement mechanisms on the other.

B. Informal Sector vs Informal Jobs in Latin America's Debate

During the 1980s, an intense debate around the concept of informality took place across Latin America, mainly due to the industrial sector's effeteness for labour absorption in the countries of the region.[16] This is why different theories have been put forward in an attempt to explain why certain productive units and certain workers remain excluded from the modern sector of the economy.[17] According to dependence theory, Latin America faces a particular obstacle to a dynamic process of industrialisation: the region is technologically dependent on developed countries. Instead, the modern sector has grown at a sluggish pace and unemployment has risen.[18] Another explanation provided by the theory of marginality is that the low absorption of the workforce into industry could be attributed to the lack of qualified labour.[19] According to the structuralist vision of the researchers associated with the PREALC-ILO, the informal sector's growth resulted from an imbalance between the supply and demand for work in the modernised parts of the economy, given that the number of rural workers moving to urban areas could not be absorbed by the modern sector.[20] The 'underground' economy literature

[15] G Davidov, 'Enforcement Problems in "Informal" Labor Markets: A View from Israel' (2005) 27 *Comparative Labor Law and Policy Journal* 3, 26.

[16] See, eg, C Rakowki, 'Convergence and Divergence in the Informal Sector Debate: A Focus on Latin America, 1984–92' (1994) 22 *World Development* 501, 516.

[17] See especially Deakin, Marshall and Pinto, this volume.

[18] See, eg, FH Cardoso, *Cuestiones de Sociología del Desarrollo en América Latina* (Santiago de Chile, Editorial Universitaria, 1969).

[19] See, eg, J Nun, JC Marín and M Murmis, 'La marginalidad en América Latina' (1967) *Programa conjunto ILPES-DESAL*, Documento de trabajo, no. 2, Santiago de Chile.

[20] See, eg, E Klein and V Tockman, 'Sector informal: una forma de utilizar el trabajo como consecuencia de la manera de producer y no viceversa. A propósito del artículo de Portes y Benton' (1982) 6 *Estudios Sociológicos* 205, 212; A Portes, 'The Informal Sector: Definition, Controversy, and Relation to National Development' (1983) 7 *Review Fernand Braudel Center* 151, 174.

argues that it is necessary to understand the ties between the informal and formal sectors in order to fully grasp the problem of informality.[21]

This debate yields two different and conceptually opposing notions of informality: the informal sector on the one hand and informal work on the other. Those who consider informality as a feature of the structure of production argue that the informal sector refers to a mode of production originating in the structural heterogeneity characteristic of the economies of Latin America: companies with little capital, rudimentary technology and no access to formal credit.[22] On the other side of the debate, the notion of informal work is used to emphasise the informality inherent in certain institutional practices, particularly noncompliant employer–worker contractual arrangements (that is, the absence of a labour contract).

To measure informality (understood as the informal sector), statisticians suggest focusing on four worker categories: own-account workers (not including professionals), employers and workers in micro-enterprises (fewer than five workers), unpaid family workers and domestic workers. Those who consider that informality is associated with hiring terms propose using exclusion from the social security system as an indicator of informality, which means that any worker not enrolled in that system would be considered informal.[23]

Since then, these two coexisting notions of informality have been the basis for diverse policies that seek to formalise both the positions of those who work within the informal sector as well as those of informal workers. This alignment of conceptually opposing perspectives seems possible because empirically these notions partially overlap.

C. How Can Informality be Tackled? Argentina's Responses

In Argentina, although the standardised measurement of informality corresponds to informal labour (referred to as 'unregistered labour' in public statistics), both notions of informality are present in the formalisation policies that have been developed since the 1990s. The main goal of these policies is to integrate into the social security system own-account workers from the least productive sectors of the economy; employers and workers within micro-enterprises in these same sectors; unpaid workers, especially rural labourers; and domestic workers.

The legislation on formalisation addresses the two issues that overlap in the way informality is conceived by the ILO – the scope of the law and noncompliance with

[21] See, eg, A Portes, M Castells and L Benton, *The Informal Economy: Studies in Advanced and Less Developed Countries*, (Baltimore, Johns Hopkins University Press, 1989); L Benton and A Portes, 'Desarrollo industrial y absorción laboral: una reinterpretación' (1981) 5 *Estudios Sociológicos* 111, 137.

[22] See Klein and Tockman, ' Sector informal', above note 20.

[23] See, eg, V Tokman, 'The Informal Economy, Insecurity and Social Cohesion in Latin America' (2007) 146 *International Labour Review* 81, 107.

the law.[24] In all cases, the content of the law appears to be the same:[25] to guarantee social protection to all workers, or at least its two main benefits (that is, health insurance and retirement pension).

In the first case analysed here, that of employers and workers in micro-enterprises in sectors with low productivity, and the set of non-salaried workers with low incomes, informality is the result of noncompliance with existing regulations. Nevertheless, it is interpreted as a problem with the scope of the law. According to the legislator, noncompliance cannot be considered as legal disobedience because of the inapplicability of the law. Although these workers are covered by the law, the conditions it imposes for compliance are impossible for them to meet given their low income. Therefore, the legislator proposed a new law that amended existing regulations, in order to integrate these workers in practice. It thus became necessary to modify the law before designing more effective enforcement mechanisms capable of ensuring compliance with the legislation.

In the second case analysed, that of domestic workers, informality is connected to both the scope of the law and noncompliance. Until 2000, the prevailing regime – the Domestic Workers' Regime approved in 1956 – covered only 47 per cent of domestic workers, which is why that same year a special social security regime was created to include the majority of domestic workers within its scope. The 2013 law then incorporated additional measures to extend the scope of the law to all domestic workers.

Enforcement did not become an issue until 2000, when the majority of domestic workers were covered by the law. At that moment, considering on the one hand the impossibility for the state to verify compliance with the law inside homes and, on the other, the form this labour relationship traditionally takes (generally based on personal ties), indirect mechanisms were established to ensure compliance with the law. These mechanisms were broad, covering everything from fiscal incentives to new forms of ex officio implementation.

III. Reshaping the Self-Employment Category

Argentina's informal workers have historically represented around 35 per cent of the working population. In 1997, the year before a new regime was created for non-salaried workers, the informality rate reached a high of 48 per cent.[26] The two categories of workers most affected by informality were the employees of

[24] See Davidov, 'Enforcement problems in "informal" labor markets', above n 15.

[25] La Hovary underlines the need to take into account the content of the law to understand the differences that exist in terms of effective rights, even when the workers are within the scope of the law and the law is applied to them. La Hovary, 'The Informal Economy and the ILO', above n 6.

[26] See, eg, L Beccaria, J Carpio and A Orsatti, 'Argentina: informalidad laboral en el nuevo modelo económico', in J Carpio et al, *Informalidad y exclusión social* (Buenos Aires, Fondo de Cultura Económica-SIEMPRO-OIT, 1999).

small businesses (fewer than five employees) and own-account workers. The first category represented around 30 per cent of all informal workers and the latter 50 per cent.[27] Moreover, it is estimated that in that year, 72 per cent of self-employed workers already enrolled in social security did not pay their contributions.[28] Such high levels of informality can mainly be attributed to noncompliance with the law. Hefty social security contributions excluded low-income own-account workers de facto but also hindered the integration of wage earners in small businesses.[29] However, for the legislator the main problem was the restrictive scope of the law.

Thus, in order to facilitate the formalisation of their activities and guarantee their participation in the social security system, in 1998, as part of the tax reform, the Simplified Regimen for Small Taxpayers, known as Single Tax Regimen, was created. This regime specifically sought to formalise the activities of workers such as own-account workers; employers and wage earners in small firms in sectors with low productivity; and workers with non-standard statuses such as domestic and rural labourers by lowering the social security contributions.

The Single Tax Regimen arose in the context of a significant labour market reform whose main objective was to increase the market's flexibility. The justification for the reform was the need to adapt the labour market to the neoliberal economy. Proponents of orthodox economics asserted that market liberalisation necessitated a deregulated labour market in order to achieve acceptable levels of international competitiveness. Therefore, a rigid legal framework would only strengthen the unregulated segment of the labour market, thus exacerbating the dualism of the labour market in developing countries.[30]

This was the argument put forth to justify the set of laws included in the labour reform, though legislators significantly mischaracterised the existing legislation during this process. First, the existing legal framework was already sufficiently flexible, for example, in terms of layoffs. For some authors, the Argentinian regime is one of 'relative instability' or 'free layoffs',[31] in that dismissals were common and cost-free for the employer. Moreover, arrangements between employers and employees which evade or ignore legal requirements continue to be very common.[32]

[27] See, eg, E Lepore and D Schleser, 'La heterogeneidad del cuentapropismo en la Argentina actual. Una propuesta de análisis y clasificación' (2006) Ministerio de Trabajo, Empleo y Seguridad Social, *serie Trabajo, Ocupación y Empleo, No 4.*

[28] See, eg, Beccaria et al, 'Argentina', above n 26.

[29] See, eg, M Jimenez, 'Caracterización del trabajo independiente en Argentina. Un análisis descriptivo de largo plazo, 1974–2009' in F Bertranou and R Maurizio, *Trabajadores independientes, mercado laboral e informalidad en Argentina* (Buenos Aires, OIT, 2011) 39, 94.

[30] See generally A Marshall, '¿Contrataciones 'flexibles' o trabajo precario? El empleo temporario y a tiempo parcial' in P Galin and M Novick, *La precarización del empleo en la Argentina* (Buenos Aires, CEAL/CIAT/CLACSO, 1990); L Beccaria and P Galín, *Regulaciones laborales en Argentina. Evaluación y propuestas* (Buenos Aires, Fundación OSDE/CIEPP, 2002).

[31] See, eg, M Meik and O Zas, 'Desregulación y flexibilización normativa de la protección en el ordenamiento laboral argentino' in P Galin and M Novick, *La precarización del empleo en la Argentina* (Buenos Aires, CEAL/CIAT/CLACSO, 1990).

[32] See, eg, A Marshall, 'Empleo temporario y trabajo a tiempo parcial en la Argentina' (1989) Instituto Internacional de Estudios Laborales, OIT, *Discussion Papers* 17.

Thus, the local labour market is characterised by a sort of de facto flexibility due to noncompliance with the regulations. In this context, the Single Tax Regimen appeared as a regulatory framework that allowed workers who already had flexible labour relations to be integrated into the formal labour market. In this sense, it permitted the formalisation of existing flexible models of labour relations.[33]

For informal workers, the biggest advantage of this regime was the social benefits, especially health insurance. During the debate over the reform of the social security system in 1993, health insurance was presented as a fundamental incentive for self-employed workers to make regular contributions to the social security system. The main argument was that social benefits offered in the present (such as medical insurance) were more effective motivators than future benefits (like retirement pensions) to encourage ongoing payment to the social security system.[34] In the case of the Single Tax Regimen, medical insurance also served as an incentive for timely tax paying.[35]

Thus, the Single Tax Regimen established low levels of social contributions (and in some cases, no contributions at all) on the one hand; on the other, it created new mechanisms to ensure the formalisation of those with limited ability to pay, that is, workers in the economy's least productive sectors.

A. The Formalisation of Non-Salaried Workers

When the Single Tax Regimen was presented to the Chamber of Deputies in May 1998, the Deputy with responsibility for introducing the measure outlined the principal reasons why this law was necessary:

> Three years ago, a group of street vendors visited the Budget and Finance Commission, arguing that they wanted to be included under the law, that is, in the same system as all the other workers. I remember them saying, 'We are not second-class citizens, we want to be treated like everyone else. The only difference between us and them is that we earn less – but we want to pay what we can.'
>
> At a certain point, the tax system had to change. People could no longer make their retirement contributions. When self-employed workers abandoned social security, this led to a mass desertion from the tax system. Thousands of Argentines are moving towards an unregistered economy: they work hard and they produce, but they have no clear identity, that is, they can't be citizens like everyone else …
>
> Moreover, since they are outside the law, they are subject to extortion and blackmail: 'I can pay you this much and if you don't like it, get out.' Obviously, this cannot

[33] See, eg, C Olmedo and M-J Murray, 'The Formalization of Informal/Precarious Labor in Contemporary Argentina' (2002) 17 *International Sociology* 421, 443.

[34] Law 24,241, 18 October 1993, on the Integrated Retirement and Pension System (in force until 2008) does not include health insurance within the social security benefits for self-employed workers.

[35] The idea of a single contribution that would integrate the income tax with social security contributions first appeared in 1993, during the debate over Law 24,241. Senate Sessional Diary 22 and 23 September 1993, and Chamber of Deputies Sessional Diary 2 and 3 May 1993.

> occur in a democratic system where citizens, whatever their condition, should have the same rights.[36]

Two outstanding aspects of the legislature's depiction of the scenario include the reference to informal workers' explicit demand for legal protection and the need to keep self-employed workers from 'deserting' the social security system and tax regime. For the legislature, which interpreted this demand as a desire for fiscal equity, it was essential to recognise that not all workers had the same abilities to contribute to state finances, given that they participated in the labour market in different ways. Many of them remained outside the scope of applicable regulations due to their low income. Informality was thus considered an 'involuntary' condition.[37] Consequently, evasion was not a choice but the result of inappropriate legislation; evaders, then, were not to blame for tax and social security fraud. Social contributions and tax evasion are thus considered problems that need to be addressed within the law, which is why the new regime seeks to integrate *de jure* those who were excluded *de facto* from the legislation.

Within a democratic regime, the state, as the legislature noted, should guarantee that all citizens have the same rights. In this sense, Law 24,977,[38] which established the Single Tax Regimen, sought to establish equal access to social benefits. However, given that access to social benefits in Argentina depended principally (though not exclusively) on contributions, the state needed to design a system that would integrate workers with less ability to contribute. These were the workers excluded in practice by the existing social security regimes; that is, the general regime for salaried workers and the regime for self-employed workers. Income level thus appeared as the main condition of eligibility for participating in this integrated system which unified tax payments (VAT and income tax) and social security contributions.

The Single Tax Regimen established eight categories of contributors according to four criteria: gross income, surface area of the business establishment, energy consumption and unit price. However, gross income would be the decisive criterion for the classification of taxpayers.[39] The maximum income level established for the highest category was 12 times higher than that stipulated for the lowest. The regime thus provided for the inclusion of workers with a wide range of incomes. During the first year, workers in the lowest income category represented 40 per cent of all single taxpayers; those in the intermediate categories represented 32 per cent; and those enrolled in the highest income categories 28 per cent. Nevertheless, in the following years, most workers joined the lowest categories. The vast majority of

[36] President of the Budget and Finance Committee. Chamber of Deputies Sessional Diary 6 May 1998.

[37] See especially J Salim and W D'Angela, *Evolución de los Regímenes Simplificados para Pequeños Contribuyentes en la República Argentina* (Buenos Aires, AFIP, 2006).

[38] Law 24,977, 6 July 1998.

[39] Art 17, Chapter VIII of Law 24,977 establishes certain exclusions, defined by the type of labour activity. These exclusions cover contributors who are expected to join the social security system as self-employed workers.

those who were incorporated by this regime were own-account workers from the service sector, trade or retail.[40] In practice, then, the main result of the Single Tax Regimen was the formalisation of own-account workers with low incomes.

In the context of wide-ranging labour reform, the creation of this special regimen – which seeks to formalise non-salaried workers – fosters non-standard types of participation in the labour market. In particular, it favours complex outsourcing networks of independent service providers. The 'self-employed worker' category, particularly in the 'single tax-payer' version, was used as a new legal tool to make labour relations more flexible. This particular use can be observed both within highly regulated labour markets (for example, the civil service) and in less regulated markets such as the agricultural sector.[41] Moreover, the formalisation of low-income own-account workers allowed them to be hired as independent contractors in all economic sectors.

B. Temporary Self-employed Workers

During its first three years, the Single Tax Regimen successfully integrated many self-employed workers into the social security system who had hitherto remained outside the scope of labour regulations. Between 1998 and 2001, 1,225,000 workers enrolled as single taxpayers.[42] However, beyond these achievements, it became apparent that a large number of workers continued to be excluded due to the manner in which their activities were structured. For this reason, a special regime of single taxpayers was created with the goal of integrating the self-employed working on a casual basis.

In 2001, the Single Tax Regimen included temporary workers for the first time. Until then, this type of activity had not been of particular interest to the state, given that it was considered to merely supplement someone's main activity. However, the situation changed in the late 1990s because of the spike in unemployment and the rising precarity of contractual arrangements. At that time, temporary work became a common way of joining the labour market, generally informally. In response, a presidential decree[43] created a new category of single tax payers, allowing workers whose activities were temporary in nature or sporadic to join the Single Tax Regimen. This means that, in principle, this regime excluded those who worked on a regular basis, regardless of whether they were paid sporadically. However,

[40] See especially Salim and D'Angela, *Evolución de los Regímenes Simplificados para Pequeños Contribuyentes en la República Argentina*, above n 37.

[41] See especially L Poblete, 'Flexibilidad en la normativa y flexibilización en los usos. El régimen de contratación de trabajadores independientes en la administración pública argentina (1995–2008)' (2016) 33 *Revista Latinoamericana de Estudios del Trabajo* 59, 88; L Poblete, 'De trabajadores inamovibles a trabajadores móviles. El caso de una región vitivinícola de Mendoza (1995–2010)' (2012) 30 *Cuadernos de Relaciones Laborales* 519, 539.

[42] See Salim and D'Angela, above n 37.

[43] Presidential Decree 1401/01, 4 November 2001. This order was repealed by Art 3 of Law 25,865, 10 January 2004, which modified the regimen for temporary workers.

in exceptional cases, the regime authorised the incorporation of single taxpayers earning very low incomes – those registered in the lowest category of the Single Tax Regimen. In this case, a low income was considered equivalent to casual work.

The Executive provided two reasons for creating this category, the first being the 2001 economic crisis:

> Due to the severe social vulnerability that has resulted from the current economic scenario, it has become necessary and urgent to create measures extending social protection to a great number of low-income citizens working in informal conditions. These citizens require priority attention within a framework of rational, efficient and effective public expenditure.

The second objective in creating the new category was to formalise certain activities and facilitate the payment of contributions. In conjunction with the arguments presented when the Single Tax Regimen was created, the Executive argued that 'To achieve equity and social justice, it is necessary to create a tax regimen for taxpayers whose business activity does not allow them to meet the tax obligations outlined in current tax law.'[44]

The state was striving to ensure that the most vulnerable workers – and thus, the most likely to require state support – would have access to all areas of social protection. Own-account workers whose activities are often temporary and whose incomes vary are also vulnerable. This means that a great number of small taxpayers are not able to regularly make social security contributions or pay their taxes. Although these workers are less able than others to contribute, the goal of this sub-regimen is to incorporate them into both the tax regime and the social security system. As a result, a variable combined tax was established (VAT plus income tax) that represented 5 per cent of gross annual earnings. This regime thus keeps social contributions and taxes to a minimum but the amount a worker pays varies based on how much he/she earns in any given month.

Through the single taxpayer statute, the government thus sought to adapt the structure of the social security system to different ways of participating in the labour market. In addition to self-employed workers, it included workers who did not fit within the traditional categories (and thus could not comply with existing regulations) due to the nature of their work activity. This new legal framework allowed workers in atypical situations in the economy's least-productive sectors to access social benefits. In this sense, the Single Tax Regimen represented an initial attempt to formalise the extensive informal part of labour market that has been one of the persistent characteristics of the Argentinian labour market.

C. Social Protections for Low-income Non-salaried Workers

Following the so-called 'counter' labour reform, the Single Tax Regimen became one of the key social policy tools. In 2004, another special regime – the Social

[44] Presidential Decree 1401/01, 4 November 2001.

Single Taxpayer – sought to incorporate workers barely able (or unable) to pay their contributions. The addition of the word 'social' to this category indicates its proximity to non-contributory social protection. The workers enrolled under this special regime were exempt from making their contributions for two years following their enrolment, and received a 50 per cent discount on their health insurance contributions.[45] Own-account workers in highly precarious positions were eligible for this category, either because they fell within the two lowest categories of single taxpayers,[46] because they had long-term unemployment and were working under state-led employment programmes[47] or because they were members of work cooperatives.[48] This category juxtaposed different types of labour relationships. In the first case, it applied to own-account workers with low, frequently irregular incomes not because they were engaged in a fixed-term contract or temporary work but because they were employed in the least-productive sectors of the economy. In the other two cases, the labour relationships were similar to that of wage earners. In state-led employment programmes, the institution that administered the programme functioned as a worker's employer, even if a true labour relationship did not exist. Those who worked in cooperatives were in a similar situation, given that in many cases the cooperative could be considered the principal employer.

Members of work cooperatives represent a particular case among the social single taxpayers. The law allows small cooperatives with a maximum of three employees and an annual income lower than the first category of the general single taxpayer regime to enrol as a cooperative once their 'productive service project' has been certified by the Ministry of Development. These workers, who are mainly employed in the social economy – particularly domestic production units – are exempt from their social security contributions.

In practice, this subcategory of single taxpayers incorporated more low-income earners than workers employed under the state-led employment programmes. In fact, in order to enrol temporary and fixed-term contract workers with the lowest incomes, in 2004 the law allowed the categories to be combined, creating the temporary/social single taxpayer.[49]

The single taxpayer regime remained unchanged until 2009,[50] when two new sub-regimes were created. The first, the 'Single Taxpayer Regimen for the Social Integration and Promotion of Independent Labour', aimed to help young professionals join the labour market in the first two years after finishing their degree. In order to help these young professionals establish their business, the state offers them discounted social contributions for the first two years after enrolling in the

[45] Law 25,865, 19 January 2004 (Arts 34 and 49 of the annex).

[46] Law 25,865 (Art 12 of the annex).

[47] The Social Single Taxpayers Regimen category was aimed at workers registered in the National Registry of Local Development and Social Economy Participants of the Ministry of Social Development, Presidential Decree 186/04 (Art 1).

[48] Law 25,865 (Art 48 of the annex).

[49] Law 25,865 (Art 34 of the annex).

[50] Law 26,565, 26 December 2009.

Single Tax Regimen. The idea is that after this period, these professionals will be able to enter the higher single taxpayer categories or join the general independent labour regime.

The second single taxpayer sub-regime created in 2009 sought to integrate rural workers, extending the category to include small agricultural producers. The goal was to formalise the position of small family producers and give them access to social security benefits. In this case, the workers are exempted from contributions. The Ministry of Agriculture and the Ministry of Social Development make these workers' contributions and for this reason, the regimen is presented as the 'cost-free single taxpayer regimen'. Based on the model of the small work cooperatives implemented by the 'social volunteering' law,[51] this sub-regime sought to integrate rural workers in low-productivity sectors into the formal labour market.

Since 2004, the single taxpayer regime has been a tool to formalise the activities of workers unable to make contributions. Some are not able to pay because they were left without an income (or with a drastically reduced one) after Argentina's 2001 economic crisis, which has a massive impact in the labour market; others are unable to pay because they are just getting started as self-employed workers. The inability to make contributions among workers affected by the economic crisis is associated with their labour activity and these particular workers are expected to remain in this regime, which represents in practice a sort of social policy. In contrast, for young professionals, the integration into the sub-regime of the single taxpayer regimen is only temporary since they are expected to later switch into the general single taxpayer or the general independent worker regime.

D. Simplifying Paperwork as a Compliance Strategy

Although the diverse regimes included in the Single Tax Regimen extend legal coverage to different worker categories in the informal labour market, their incorporation to the tax regime and social security system represented a major challenge in practice. The historic exclusion of many of these workers from the formal market was an obstacle to the implementation of this new regime for small taxpayers. The state came up with two strategies to make this formalisation successful: simplifying paperwork and continuously adapting social security and tax obligations based on each taxpayer's ability to pay. As part of the first strategy, each worker received a unique identification number; this was followed by a new programme in 2005, 'Program for the Simplification and Unification of Labour and Social Security Enrolment'.[52] By using an IT platform, workers could easily enrol as single taxpayers, change taxpayer categories and select different payment options. To achieve the second strategy, a system was established for periodically

[51] Law 25,865, 19 January 2004.

[52] Public Treasury Resolution 440/2005, 2 July 2005.

assessing one's tax category (on a quarterly or annual basis). This means that based on their income level in a given period, single taxpayers can move up or down a category, increasing or reducing (respectively) the amounts contributed to social security system and their taxes. In addition, contributions are made monthly to ensure greater compliance.

IV. Formalising Paid Domestic Work

Domestic work in Argentina constitutes a significant portion of female work, namely, 17 per cent of all working women and 23 per cent of all female wage earners. Most domestic workers are Argentinian; 31 per cent have migrated from other provinces to the metropolitan area of Buenos Aires, but 14 per cent are migrants from neighbouring countries. Though 35 per cent are secondary workers, 39 per cent are heads of households, so their household's income depends on their labour market activity.[53]

Domestic work is characterised by precarity. It is rare for a female worker to work a full eight-hour day. Only 19.6 per cent work over 40 hours per week; 39.6 per cent work between 16 and 39 hours per week; 32.4 per cent work between six and 15 hours; and 9.3 per cent work less than six hours. It is also a sector characterised by high rotation. In 2010, 28.7 per cent had been working for their current employer for less than a year; 47.9 per cent, between one and five years; and only 23.3 per cent had remained in the same position for over five years.[54] Regarding hiring terms, traditionally most workers have had just one employer and very few reside in the employer's household (less than 2 per cent). However, the number of workers with a single employer decreased between 2004 and 2014, while the quantity of those working for two or more employers has increased accordingly. In 2004, workers with a single employer accounted for 79.2 per cent of total domestic work,[55] and in 2014, this rate had fallen to 70.5 per cent. Workers with two employers increased from 12 to 17 per cent, and those with three or more employers increased from 8.5 to 13.3 per cent in the same term. Those who work more than 16 hours per week for the same employer represent only 41.4 per cent.[56]

Enrolment in the social security and tax system in this sector is very low. Although it has increased during the last years (from 5 per cent in 2003 to

[53] See, eg, M Álvarez and A Beccaria, 'Las trabajadoras domesticas en la Argentina actual. Límites y avances en torno a su sindicalización' (2013) *X Jornadas de sociología de la UBA*, Buenos Aires.

[54] See, eg, F Pereyra, 'La regulación laboral de las trabajadoras domésticas en Argentina. Situación actual y perspectivas' in V Esquivel, E Faur and E Jelin, *Las lógicas del cuidado infantil. Entre las familias, el Estado y el mercado* (Buenos Aires, IDES/UNICEF/UNFPA, 2012) 165, 199.

[55] See, eg, Ministerio de Trabajo, Empleo y Seguridad Social, *Situación laboral del servicio doméstico en Argentina* (Buenos Aires, Argentina, 2006).

[56] See especially F Pereyra and L Poblete, '¿Qué derechos? ¿Qué obligaciones? La construcción discursiva de la noción de empleadas y empleadores en el debate de la ley del Personal de Casas Particulares (2010–2013)' (2015) 30 *Cuadernos del IDES* 73, 102.

16 per cent in 2013), 84 per cent of domestic workers were still unregistered when the new law was passed in 2013.[57] As unregistered workers, they do not have access to the social security system and are earning less than the amounts established by the state for the sector. In fact, the average monthly wage of unregistered workers is 48 per cent less than the average monthly wage of registered workers.[58]

A. Defining 'Domestic Worker'

Initially, informality was a problem associated with the scope of existing legislation since more than half of domestic workers were excluded. The 'Special Statute on Domestic Work' (Presidential Decree 326/56), the only regulation in force between 1956 and 2000 which sought to govern domestic work, only allowed the enrolment of workers who resided in the employer's household or performed activities in the same household at least four hours a day, four days per week. According to data from the Ministry of Labour, 52.8 per cent of all domestic workers were excluded from this regulation because, first, half of the workers with just one employer worked less than 16 hours a week, and second, most workers employed by more than one employer did not work 16 hours for any one of them.[59]

In order to prevent this legal exclusion, in 2000, Law 25,239 established the 'Special Social Security Regime for Domestic Workers' that extended social security benefits to all domestic workers performing activities for a single employer for at least six hours per week. This expansion of legal coverage was achieved not by broadening the scope of the 1956 statute but by creating a special social security regime for all domestic workers excluded from that regime. Because of the characteristics of the contributory system, these two different regimes established certain inequalities among workers in the same occupation. Domestic workers covered by the 1956 regime enjoy almost the same rights as employees, while domestic workers covered by the 2000 Social Security Regime only have the right to social security benefits. Also for some of the domestic workers included the latter, the access to social security benefits depend on their capacity to make contributions.

This new social security regime is structured as a contributory system, financed by mandatory contributions by the employer and 'voluntary' contributions by the worker. When a domestic worker works at least 16 hours a week for a single employer, that employer is responsible for the total amount of compulsory contributions that entitle the worker to social benefits. Those working less than 16 hours per week can supplement the amount the employer pays to have access to social benefits, but Law 25,239 stipulates that the nature of these contributions is voluntary.

[57] See, eg, Álvarez and Beccaria, above n 53.
[58] See, eg, F Pereyra, 'La regulación laboral de las trabajadoras domésticas en Argentina', above n 52.
[59] See MTEySS, *Situación laboral del servicio doméstico en Argentina*, above n 55.

The 'voluntary' contributions are calculated taking into account the difference between the minimum established by law and the sum the employer is required to pay based on the number of hours worked. When a domestic worker works for different employers for less than 16 hours each, the partial contributions made by each of the employers are combined. Thus, the amount of supplementary contributions that domestic workers need to make depends on the number of employers they have. This regime thus provides a clear distinction between domestic workers whose employers pay their social security in full and those who must contribute to social security in order to access its benefits.[60]

In 2000, due to these two coexisting regimes, 90.6 per cent of domestic workers qualify for formal employment under one of these two.[61] In order to integrate the remaining 9.4 per cent excluded from previous regulations, in 2004, it was established that all domestic workers working less than six hours per week for one or more employers could enrol as self-employed workers in the Single Tax Regimen.[62] In this case, the domestic workers must pay their own social contributions and taxes since they are considered independent service providers. The enrolment of domestic workers in this system appeared unlikely because those who work just a few hours for several employers rarely end up working full days; therefore, they earn considerably less than those who work at least six hours for a single employer. In addition, hourly domestic work generates an unsteady income since it depends greatly on the changing needs of the households where the domestic workers are employed. From that year on, enrolment options were available to all domestic workers under one of these existing regimes. However, only seven per cent of domestic workers were in fact legally registered as formal domestic workers in 2005.[63]

Though informality decreased significantly during the first decade of the 21 century, it still remained very high. The challenge for legislators was to draft a regulation that would successfully formalise domestic work. For that reason, after a three-year debate on several different draft bills, Law 26,844 was passed in 2013. This law represented a major step forward in the legislation on domestic work, as it granted labour and social rights to all domestic workers providing at least one hour of service a week. This assured them a limit on the number of working hours, weekly rest, worker compensation, a trial period, severance pay, extra hours, annual mandatory bonuses, and paid holidays, sick leave and maternity leave. After the new law on 'Personal Household Staff' (Law 26,844) was passed, domestic work began to be governed by a new Special Regime, but the rights of

[60] See, eg, L Poblete, 'New Rights, Old Protections: the New Regulation for Domestic Workers in Argentina' (2015) Labour Law and Development Research Laboratory, McGill University, Working Papers Series No 5.

[61] See MTEySS, above n 55.

[62] Presidential Decree 804/04, 23 June 2004.

[63] See, eg, F Groisman and ME Sconfienza, 'El servicio doméstico en Argentina. Particularidades y desafíos de un sector relegado (2004–2012)' (2013) 25 *Carta Económica Regional* 151, 172.

domestic workers are comparable to those conferred by the 'Labour Contract Law' that regulates the activity of employees in the private sector.

Even if the legislature had wanted to design a Special Regime instead of merely including domestic workers in the 'Labour Contract Law', the new regulation recognises almost the same rights for domestic workers as those granted by that law to employees. By taking this approach, the legislature distinguishes domestic work and emphasises that it is 'work like no other'.[64] However, domestic workers must be treated just like every other labourer. In contrast to what can be found in the literature, according to the legislature, what renders this work special in some way are not the characteristics of the workplace or the features of the relationship between the employer and the employee,[65] but the attributes of the employer.[66] The latter is defined by legislators as an employer-worker, meaning an employer who is also a worker him/herself. In terms of the difference between the 'typical' employer under the labour law and a family who hires a domestic worker, the employer-worker 'does not obtain a direct profit or benefit' from the activity performed by the domestic worker. For that reason, the employer-worker can only partially comply with the obligations arising from the employment relationship. That is why the new law on 'Personal Household Staff' does not appear to consider the practical consequences of keeping the 'Special Social Security Regime for Domestic Workers' (created by Law 25,639) in force and unchanged. During legislative sessions, this matter was not discussed. The legislature seemed more concerned to ensure that domestic workers enjoy the same rights as private sector wage-earners than to ensure that all workers within the same domestic worker category have the same rights. That is why the inequalities introduced by this special social security regime remained invisible during the congressional debate.

With the goal of formalising a type of work that is overwhelmingly done informally, the different regulations on domestic work gradually modified the definition of domestic worker. The definition in 1956 was tailored to the usual employment arrangement at that time – that is full-time or live-in domestic work – but by the end of the century, it applied to very few domestic workers. In 2000, the law considered any person cleaning in a household at least six hours a week for a single employer to be a domestic worker. As with ILO Convention 189, this regulation seeks to include exclusively those domestic workers who do this type of work on an 'occupational basis'. In 2013, acknowledging the diverse types of employment arrangements and the increase in hourly work in the sector, the law did not establish a minimum number of work hours, which meant that

[64] See, especially, A Blackett, 'Making domestic work visible: the case for specific regulation' (1998) *Labour Law and Labour Relations Programme*, Working Paper No 2, International Labour Office, Geneva.

[65] See, especially A Blackett, 'Introduction: Regulating Decent Work for Domestic Workers' (2011) 23 *Canadian Journal of Women and the Law* 1, 45; M Chen, 'Recognizing Domestic Workers, Regulating Domestic Work: Conceptual, Measurement, and Regulatory Challenges' (2011) 23 *Canadian Journal of Women and the Law* 167, 184.

[66] See Pereyra and Poblete, above n 56.

any person cleaning or providing personal care in households was considered a domestic worker, regardless of how many hours she worked. Since then, in terms of the scope of application, the law covers all domestic workers.

B. Enforcement without Labour Inspection

Domestic work is also relegated to the informal sector due to the limited enforcement of the legislation. Given that the workplace is someone's home, it is difficult to ensure compliance with the law. The state does not have the legal or institutional capacity to carry out household inspections. First of all, the inviolability of the home prohibits the state from showing up at people's houses;[67] second, the state also lacks institutional capacity, that is, a special team of labour inspectors. For this reason, in order to ensure higher levels of compliance with domestic labour law, the government developed four different strategies. The first was similar to one of its strategies to promote the single taxpayer regime: the paperwork (a common obstacle to formalisation) was simplified. Second, tax incentives were offered. The third strategy involved setting up a compulsory enrolment system for domestic workers who were presumably working informally. Finally, public campaigns were launched to inform the public on the rights of domestic workers and the duties of employers.

The incorporation of new information technologies has contributed significantly to simplifying the regime. In 2002, the public treasury established an online system to simplify both enrolment and the payment of social security contributions. Following the passage of Law 26,844 in 2013, three easy enrolment options were offered: domestic workers could be enrolled on the public treasury website, by calling a free hotline, or on home banking websites. The goal was to make enrolment of domestic workers as easy as clicking a mouse.

Second, for the purpose of promoting the enrolment of domestic workers, Law 26,063 establishes a tax exemption for employment providers. Subject to the limit prescribed by the Federal Tax Agency (sec. 16), employers of a domestic worker may be able to deduct the total amount of social contributions and even the worker's wages from their income tax returns. From the beginning, this measure proved very effective and for this reason, the tax incentives have remained in force. During the first year, formal employment in the sector almost tripled, soaring from 52,150 domestic workers enrolled in 2004 to 142,200 in 2006.[68]

[67] See generally MG Loyo and MD Velásquez, 'Aspectos jurídicos y económicos del trabajo doméstico remunerado en América Latina' in ME Valenzuela and C Mora, *Trabajo doméstico: un largo camino hacia el trabajo decente* (Santiago de Chile, Oficina Internacional del Trabajo, 2009) 21, 70; J Rodgers, 'Cambios en el servicio doméstico en América Latina' in ME Valenzuela and C Mora, *Trabajo doméstico: un largo camino hacia el trabajo decente* (Santiago de Chile, Oficina Internacional del Trabajo, 2009) 71, 113; M Vega Ruiz, 'L'administration et l'inspection du travail dans le domaine du travail domestique: les expériences de l'Amérique latine' (2011) 23 *Canadian Journal of Women and the Law* 341, 358.

[68] See Salim and D'Angela, above n 37.

Third, the law established what was referred to as an 'ex officio formalisation' in order to estimate which households might be employing domestic workers informally and thus encourage employer compliance. In keeping with the legislation on social security fraud in 1970 (and its amendment in 2004) and based on a formula for estimating social security debts of employers in the textile industry and construction sector,[69] in 2013, the Minimum Domestic Work Indicator was established.[70] This indicator was based on gross annual income and personal assets (especially real estate) as declared by the taxpayer. In cases in which the gross annual income and the value of the home exceeded the minimum established by the indicator, the state would assume that there was a domestic worker in the home who had not been enrolled. In such cases, the public treasury would send a warning to the taxpayers, giving them a certain period of time to formalise the presumed employee. If the taxpayer did not enrol a domestic worker within said period, the public treasury would proceed to collect the corresponding social security contributions and taxes. This measure, which became known as 'presumption of a domestic worker', was controversial but effective – at least for the first year. In 2016, considering that the indicators were insufficient to presume the existence of an informal domestic worker, the measure was repealed.[71]

Finally, the last strategy for reducing informality in the sector involved public campaigns on the rights of domestic workers and the obligations of employers. In collaboration with the ILO, the Ministry of Labour developed campaigns that targeted domestic workers on the one hand and employers on the other; in some cases, the campaigns targeted domestic workers in other countries who were planning to migrate to Argentina and those who had migrated recently.

The efficacy of the strategies has varied over time but enrolment levels continue to be very low. In 2006, formal domestic workers represent 5.5 per cent of all domestic workers,[72] 16.2 per cent in 2012,[73] and today they represent only 21 per cent.[74]

V. Conclusion

In Argentina, the formalisation of labour relations has gradually acquired various meanings over the last two decades. In the 1990s, different meanings coexisted.

[69] Public Treasury Resolution 2927/10, 21 October 2010.

[70] Public Treasury Resolution 3492/13, 30 April 2013.

[71] Public Treasury Resolution 3828/16, 19 February 2016.

[72] See, eg, MTEySS, above n 55.

[73] See, eg, L Casanova, E Lepore and D Schleser, 'Profundización y redefición De Políticas Para La Formalización Laboral: Ley De Promoción Del Empleo Registrado Y Prevención Del Fraude Laboral' in F Bertranou and L Casanova (eds), *Caminos hacia la formalización laboral en Argentina* (Buenos Aires, OIT-Ministerio de Trabajo, Empleo y Seguridad Social, 2015).

[74] Pereyra, F, 'Trabajadoras domésticas y protección social en Argentina: avances y desafíos pendientes', *Serie de Trabajo* No 15 (Buenos Aires, OIT, 2017).

Formalisation can be conceived of as a legal protection measure; as a mechanism for increasing tax revenues; as a matter of merely improving the accuracy of the administrative record; or as a means to access social protection. At certain points, the different meanings contended with one another, yielding contradictory policies; at other times, some of the meanings prevailed, resulting in specific measures. Starting in 2000, this last meaning – formalisation as access to social protection – became the most widely accepted and, as a result, formalisation policies focused on guaranteeing social benefits for enrolled workers.

During the debate preceding Law 24,977 that led to the single taxpayer regime in 1998, some legislators argued that the goal of formalisation was to ensure legal protection. One legislator said, 'We've designed this regimen with the fisherman on the Paraná River in mind. When this fisherman gets back to port, what he hears is, "I'll buy your fish under the table for x amount. And if you don't like it, throw it back in the water".' Also, in the case of Law 26,844, which established the new Special Regime for domestic workers in 2013, the goal was to provide these workers with a certain number of legal guarantees against employer abuse. The rights deemed fundamental included vacation time, sick leave and maternity leave, overtime and severance pay, among others.

For other legislators, formalisation had additional goals like increasing tax revenues and upping social security contributions. Although the meagre contributions that workers are able to make would not raise tax revenues significantly, increasing the quantity of contributors to the system was viewed as important. As predicted, during the first two years in force, the single taxpayer regime represented just 1.5 per cent of total tax revenues.

Other legislators believed that in the case of low-income labourers with precarious work, formalisation served only to provide a record of how many people worked in different sectors and some information about these workers. This record was perceived as a bureaucratic formality. One senator even argued that 'the single taxpayer regimen has become a system for tax fraud'. In other words, enrolment in this regime had no consequences whatsoever: it did not increase workers' access to social security or help the state buttress its tax revenues.

Finally, for other legislators – probably the majority – the main objective of formalisation was to provide social benefits to workers who had been fully excluded from the social security system. This reasoning behind formalisation was present from the time when the labour reform began in the 1990s, and as the years passed, it became the predominant meaning of the term. In Argentina, social security is based on employment-related contributions,[75] so access to the system's benefits depends on having formal labour relationships. This is why legislators became so focused on expanding the scope of the law and ensuring compliance.

In summary, the process of formalisation that has occurred in Argentina since the end of the 1990s can be described as successive experiments in social

[75] Although the Social Security System is based on both employer and worker contributions, only 40 per cent of the system is funded by these contributions. The rest comes from indirect taxes.

security regimes. The innovative approach consisted in expanding social security benefits without redefining either the employee or the independent worker categories, though informal workers of different kinds were treated as a new type of employee, self-employed worker or a combination of both. Thus, new social security contribution schemes combined the two main systems adopted in the 1950s: the wage-earner regime – based on employer and worker contributions – and the self-employed worker regime – where the workers alone are responsible for their contributions. In addition, the state began participating in these schemes as a third contributor in the case of more vulnerable workers.

In order to expand social protection to low-income non-salaried workers, three subtypes were established in the single taxpayer regime. The first is a replica of the general self-employed worker regime but contributions are simplified and reduced to fit with these workers' limited ability to contribute. Within this system, it is expected that as the own-account workers gain a stronger foothold on the labour market, they can move up and eventually enrol in the general social security regime for self-employed workers. In the second, which can be defined as temporary, the state exempts workers just entering the system from paying a portion (or all) of their contributions for a two-year period. After that, they are expected to join the general Single Tax Regimen or the self-employed regime – in the case of young professionals. In the third regime, workers are not expected to make any contributions; instead, the Ministry of Labour and Ministry of Social Development make their contributions for them. This final subtype could be viewed as social assistance but in order to emphasise the connection between formality and social protection, the state has opted to retain the structure of contributions to the system.

In the legislation on domestic work, the same logic of expanding social security benefits applies. However, a different regime was established in the case of domestic workers because they have an employer. Under the 2013 law, the Special Social Security Regime for domestic workers reinforced the duality of the system. For domestic workers who are employed at least 16 hours a week for a single employer, the employer is responsible for the entirety of the worker's social contributions. For these workers, the social security system applies as it would to employees. However, in the case of those who work fewer than 16 hours for several employers, a more complex and innovative regime applies and both employers and workers must make contributions. The coexistence of two different structures of contributions is a source of inequality among domestic workers, as some are guaranteed social security benefits through employer contributions while others rely on their capacity to make their own contributions.

These varied social security regimes provide registered workers with two types of social benefits: retirement pensions and health insurance. Given the structure of the retirement system, regardless of how many years they contribute, these workers will receive the minimum when they retire. These amounts will probably be the same (or slightly higher) than the social security benefits provided under Argentina's non-contributory retirement regime. Therefore, health insurance is the only additional social benefit received by single taxpayers and domestic workers once they are enrolled as formal workers. Although the Argentine healthcare system[76] does provide the option of universal free healthcare, for these low-income workers, health insurance is a critical social benefit since it ensures much easier access and better care than the public hospital system.[77]

Formalisation thus became synonymous with health insurance for these informal workers. However, the regimes are structured so that access depends on making regular contributions. This means that extending the scope of the law to integrate the majority of workers does not suffice: it is critical to effectively guarantee their compliance with the law to ensure their access to social benefits.

[76] The healthcare system has three components: universal free healthcare provided by state-run hospitals and medical centres, a health insurance system for those engaged in formal labour relationships, and private (optional) healthcare services.

[77] See, eg, L Poblete, 'Vers la protection du travail informel. Le régime du monotribut en Argentine (1998–2013)' (2014) 2 *Revue Française d'Affaires Sociales* 120, 136.

8

Supply Chains and Temporary Migrant Labour: The Relevance of Trade and Sustainability Frameworks

TONIA NOVITZ*

I. Introduction

This chapter considers how labour law can be re-imagined to address the increasing role played by migrant labour in supply chains in the twenty-first century both within the European Union (EU) and in the context of global trade. The chapter begins by identifying some key issues regarding the intersection of supply chains, trade in services and exploitation of migrant workers who move between countries on a temporary basis. It is suggested that various factors enable the divide between the informal (or irregular) and formal (regular) worker to become, in this context, a sliding scale of precarity which can be exploited by the corporate entity at the top of a supply chain.

The chapter then goes on to consider the extent to which the contemporary regulation of EU and global trade seeks to address such issues, suggesting that these rules are insufficient for the protection of those temporarily moving as 'natural persons' as part of trade in services. This is because the worker posted from one jurisdiction to another is deemed not to enter the labour market of the host state and therefore is not treated as a suitable subject for regulation.

It is suggested that a preferable approach may be one emerging within the larger UN framework, whereby it is possible to mobilise under the 2015 Sustainable Development Goals to establish global norms regarding the obligations of states. Both substantive and procedural norms can arise from recognition of the relevance of SDGs, so that there should be scope for participation by workers and their organisations in regulatory strategies concerning supply chains, the terms of trade and treatment of migrant workers.

* Professor of Labour Law, University of Bristol. Tonia Novitz is a member of Sustainable Market Actors for Responsible Trade (SMART) (smart.uio.no). SMART has received funding from the European Union's Horizon 2020 research and innovation programme under grant agreement No 693642, and its support is gratefully acknowledged here.

II. Connections between Supply Chains, Trade in Services and Migrant Labour

This section of the chapter seeks to introduce the scope of a contemporary problem arising from the intersection of supply chains, trade in services and migrant labour. It is important to consider what may be identified as a 'supply chain', how trade in services remains relevant to such a mode of corporate or business organisation, and where migrant labour fits within this framework.

It is suggested here that contemporary modes of manufacture and service provision, combined with forms of technological change, have led to significant transnational cross-border sites of production and delivery. Multinational corporate enterprises (MNEs) subcontract across national boundaries and, in this way, utilise different legal regimes and lower costs in specific countries. In so doing, there is scope to distance the commercial enterprise which ultimately profits from the labour on which it draws. An increasing feature of global markets is trade in services which, as I shall argue, involves the commodification of work and its usage whether they ultimately can be linked to manufacture of tradeable goods or not. What is evident within this frame is that longer-term migration is no longer a feature of attempts to enhance service delivery or manufacturing. Rather, the evidence suggests that transport of labour to sites of provision (or production) has become increasingly temporary in nature.[1] In so doing, workers experience 'informality' through the insecurity of their immigration status (which does not give them longer-term rights or even any rights to remain in the country in which they are working, thereby affecting their bargaining power in the workplace whether individually or collectively) and their employment status (which may not give them full or indeed any rights under the labour laws of the host state in which their work is situated).

A. Identifying Supply Chains

Supply chains may be understood as 'the cross-border organization of the activities required to produce goods or services and bring them to consumers through inputs and various phases of development, production and delivery'.[2] For the sake of consistency and clarity, I shall use this definition as a basis for analysis in this chapter, including, as an International Labour Organization (ILO) report of 2016 did, the use of foreign direct investment (FDI) by multinational enterprises (MNEs)

[1] For a review of the evidence, see Joanna Howe and Rosemary Owens, 'Temporary Labour Migration in the Global Era: The Regulatory Challenges' in Joanna Howe and Rosemary Owens (eds), *Temporary Labour Migration in the Global Era: The Regulatory Challenges* (Oxford, Hart Publishing, 2016), at 12.

[2] ILO, Report IV: Decent Work in Global Supply Chains, ILC, 105th Session (Geneva, ILO, 2016), at 2.

and engagement of the same through diverse corporate forms and subcontracting in the hiring of labour.[3]

In the literature on 'supply chains' one finds a variety of more specific definitions and analyses. For example, there is frequent reference to 'commodity chains' in the sphere of political economy, namely 'networks of [labor] and production processes whose end is a finished commodity'.[4] In this body of research, the consumption of particular services at various 'nodes' is given considerable attention. In this setting, cheap labour can be drafted to make the production of goods profitable and skilled labour imported to satisfy supply side problems.[5] In a more positive fashion, supply chains (operating around the cross-border production of commodities) can be understood as 'global value chains', to the extent that value is added at each stage (and in each country) of the process. Policy makers in the World Bank have proposed that value should not only be created in the global North where the product is designed, but should extend to (even multiple) countries in the South so as to fuel development.[6] Beyond this, work on 'global care chains' tends to consider the services delivered by women across national borders relating to provision of reproductive labour, including care for the elderly, childcare and the traditional business of women's work such as cooking and cleaning.[7] There has been a move by Nicola Yeates and others to link 'global care chains' to commodity chain analysis around the commodification of care.[8]

The 2016 ILO Report recognised at length the vulnerability of workers in all stages of supply chains, but did not pay specific attention to the situation of migrant workers. In some senses, this may be because the ILO, like the World Bank, sees the benefits for workers in developing and emerging countries of global 'value' chains that provide 'new opportunities for employment … including for workers who had difficulty accessing wage employment or formal jobs, such as women, young people and migrant workers'.[9] However, there was mention in the report of dangers for migrant workers in supply chains by virtue of the ways in

[3] ibid.

[4] Terence K Hopkins and Immanuel Wallerstein, 'Commodity Chains in the World Economy prior to 1800' (1986) 10(1) *Review* 157 at 159, cited in Gary Gereffi and Miguel Korzeniewicz (eds), *Commodity Chains and Global Capitalism* (Westport, CT, Prager, 1994) at 2.

[5] Stephanie Ware Barrientos, '"Labour Chains": Analysing the role of labour contractors in global production networks' (2013) 49(8) *The Journal of Development Studies* 1058.

[6] For a very positive view of their operation and its development potential, see Daria Taglioni and Deborah Winkler, 'Making Global Value Chains Work for Development' (2014) *The World Bank – Economic Premise*, No 143, especially at 1–2 and 8.

[7] See Arlie Hochschild, 'Global Care Chains and Emotional Surplus Value in Will Hutton and Anthony Giddens, (eds), *On the Edge: Living with Global Capitalism* (London, Jonathan Cape, 2000) at 131: 'a series of personal links between people across the globe based on the paid or unpaid work of caring'.

[8] Nicola Yeates, 'Global Care Chains' (2004) 6(3) *International Feminist Journal of Politics* 369; and Nicola Yeates, 'Global Care Chains: A state-of-the-art review and future directions in care transnationalization research' (2012) 12(2) *Global Networks* 135. See also for an extension of this approach, Ann Stewart, *Gender, Law and Justice in Global Markets* (Cambridge, Cambridge University Press, 2011).

[9] ILO, Report IV: Decent Work in Global Supply Chains, ILC, 105th Session (Geneva, ILO, 2016), at 17.

which they enter another country for work, acknowledging that 'the cross-border flows of workers have also resulted in a greater risk of forced labour and trafficking in persons' and that while MNEs may take action to prevent such practices 'there is a risk they may become associated with forced labour through business links to contractors and suppliers who may conceal unlawful practices'.[10] There was also a short discussion of migrant workers' particular vulnerability, in that they 'are often found in non-standard forms of employment',[11] which of course preclude access to standard labour law protections. In this respect, the 2016 Report mentioned 'enforcement gaps', 'fragmentation of norms', alongside particular difficulties for those 'in an irregular situation and in the informal economy'.[12] The scale of this problem was not discussed in any detail, perhaps because it is not possible now to quantify its dimensions when so many workers lie outside the scope of formal legal protections. Moreover, while the ILO report demonstrated an appreciation of supply chains (and migrant labour within them) as an emergent problem, the link to extant trade regimes seemed to be absent.

B. The Role of Services in Trade

The emergence of supply chains and the role of workers within them has not emerged in a vacuum, but arguably reflects the growth in cross-border trade in 'services'.[13] Adam Smith termed this 'unproductive labour',[14] but as we shall see it has become the lifeblood of a transnational supply chain economy. The variety of forms that 'services' may take has been ably identified by writers such as Michael Hardt and Antonio Negri,[15] but also Jane Kelsey.[16] This section draws on their analysis and seeks to explain their connection to trade in services, drawing from some earlier work of my own.[17]

Hardt and Negri have described free-standing supply of services as 'immaterial labour', that is, labour not linked to an identifiable 'product'. In this sense, their identification of 'affective labour', traditionally associated with women's work, and

[10] ibid, 26.

[11] ibid, 25, paras 75–76.

[12] ibid, 25 and 32.

[13] The services sector now accounts for approximately 70% of world GDP, as explained in Prakash Loungani, Saurabh Mishra, Chris Papageorgiou, and Ke Wang, *World Trade in Services: Evidence from A New Dataset* (2016) available at http://pubdocs.worldbank.org/en/180141480958603384/World-Trade-in-Service-February-2017.pdf.

[14] Adam Smith, *The Wealth of Nations* (first published 1776; London, Penguin, 1977), 429–30.

[15] Michael Hardt and Antonio Negri, *Empire* (Cambridge, MA, Harvard University Press, 2000), 290–93.

[16] Jane Kelsey, *Serving Whose Interests? The Political Economy of Trade in Services Agreements* (Abingdon, Routledge, 2008), at 119 et seq.

[17] See also Tonia Novitz, 'Evolutionary Trajectories for Transnational Labour Law: Trade in Goods to Trade in Services?' (2014) 67 *Current Legal Problems* 239 at 242–46, from which this analysis is taken and adapted.

the supply of labour by the state providing healthcare and other care work for children, the elderly and the disabled, can be linked to contemporary value care chains, namely the sale of women's reproductive labour across borders.[18] Their categorisation could also be further extended to what has been described as women's 'abject labour', which is also reproductive in character, such as sex work, bar-dancing and commercial surrogacy. These activities can, again, have significant cross-border 'trade' elements, as is evident from recorded forms of trafficking but also market-led choices made by the women concerned.[19] An interesting question, in these instances of reproductive labour, however, is whether they are truly 'immaterial' as it could be said that women's own bodies are commodified within these processes.

Another category identified by Hardt and Negri is 'analytical labour', which poses the difficulty that 'the growth of … knowledge-based jobs … implies a corresponding growth of low-value and low-skill jobs of routine symbol manipulation, such as data entry and word processing. Here begins to emerge a fundamental division of labour within the realm of immaterial production'.[20] This offers an insight into the differential market value of labour which poses problems in global value chains, where the design-based labour in the North is more highly valued and rewarded than that in the global South. Despite World Bank advisers' best intentions, it seems that such stark divisions pose barriers to development.

Also useful for our purposes is Hardt and Negri's idea of the decentralisation of production through 'networks',[21] or what Kelsey describes as 'labour for institutionalised production'.[22] Kelsey views these as 'services related to manufacturing, mining, forestry, fisheries and agriculture, the placement and supply of persons in activities such as construction, and supply chain operations such as transport and distribution'.[23] This category of services seems more concerned with subcontracting than with the absence of a product. As I have observed elsewhere, a contractor may be on site to provide a 'service', for example to cook, to design, to draft and there may be a product at the end of the day, such as an item of food, an architectural plan, or a legal contract. Yet we talk about catering services, design services and legal services as if there were no end product in sight. In the same way, agencies can also be regarded as providing 'services', even though their 'service' is to supply people to do a job which may also involve production of a manufactured item.[24] Subcontracting of labour through global supply chains in this way allows additional profit to be made by the supplier of the labour (usually the recruitment and placement agency) before the workers begin to make the products in question.

[18] Kelsey, *Serving Whose Interests?*, above n 16 at 119 et seq.

[19] Prabha Kotiswaran, 'The Laws of Social Reproduction: A Lesson in Appropriation' (2013) 64(3) *Northern Ireland Legal Quarterly* 317; and Prabha Kotiswaran, 'Abject Labors, Informal Markets: Revisiting the Law's Re(Production) Boundary' (2014) 18 *Employee Rights and Employment Policy Journal* 111.

[20] Hardt and Negri, *Empire*, above n 15 at 291–92.

[21] ibid, 293–94.

[22] Kelsey, above n 16 at 12.

[23] ibid.

[24] Novitz, above n 17 at 244.

Arguably, what all these manifestations of the term 'services' have in common is that we use the term to signify that instead of services *being a component part of* making a product, the service (or even the worker) *is* the product. Commodification (even of care work) is thereby inherent in this creation of a market in services, especially in the context of multinational companies and franchises operating through commodity chains.

C. The Function of Migrant Labour

Services are now being bought and sold temporarily across borders, as workers are recruited to provide work within the various countries engaged within supply chains at sites of construction (architectural or building services), project management (managerial consultancy, legal, accountancy, IT and human resources services), service consumption (care, catering, cleaning) and even production of goods (delivered through subcontracting or agencies to the factory floors). The focus is now on short-term migration to fill gaps wherever the production or service delivery is based. Indeed, temporary migration is now more common than longer-term migration.[25]

Work will be performed under the ultimate control of a multinational company (usually originating in the global North) in the place (usually although not invariably in the South) that offers the greatest profit margins for the outlay of investment. For example, workers from the South may be supplied through an agency to a subcontractor on a site in the North, such that the larger corporate (or state) interests which benefit from the hiring are not held accountable for the experience of those whose labour is hired cheaply. To offer a second example, migrant labour may be deployed from one country in the South to another country also in the South, where a franchisee or subsidiary of a larger North-based corporation operates to satisfy a temporary skills gap or provide cheap labour for a limited period. In this way, labour migration is changing and the intersection of trade in services within supply chains is linked to these changes.

In the UK, care-worker recruitment is carried out by agencies attached to the National Health Service (NHS). One such agency is the 'Helping Hands Homecare' recruitment service now attached to the NHS, which seeks to place EU nationals, for example from Portugal and Romania, to provide live-in or visiting care for the elderly or otherwise dependent. The overall ratings on review sites do not look problematic (4 stars for the clients and the carers) but the actual comments raise serious concerns.[26] Clients raise concerns over language and

[25] Eric Tucker, 'Intra-Company Transfers and Fissured Workplaces: *CS Wind* and the Challenge of Union Organizing in Canada', Paper prepared for ReMarkLab Final Conference: New Foundations of Labour Law in the Globalised Market Economy? Stockholm, May 2016. See also Howe and Owens, 'Temporary Labour Migration in the Global Era: The Regulatory Challenges', above n 1.

[26] See http://www.nhs.uk/Services/careproviders/ReviewsAndRatings/DefaultView.aspx?id=47580; and https://www.indeed.co.uk/cmp/Helping-Hands/reviews.

qualifications, but also the treatment of carers, with one comment being that 'they were not valued as care workers or adequately supported in their stressful work'. Carers have complained of low pay, long hours, lack of communication and even a 'culture of fear'. Both websites indicate that the commercialisation of care meant that clients and carers viewed the agency as profit-orientated rather than providing adequate assistance or organisation centred on clients' or workers' needs.

This is interesting, given what we already know about the treatment of individual migrant domestic (or homecare) workers in the UK, surfacing in cases before courts regarding their claims arising under contracts of employment of doubtful legality and even torts relating to racial discrimination involving physical abuse.[27] In this respect, the UK Government's immigration provisions under the 'domestic workers visa' has been identified as a contributing factor to the entrapment and subsequent ill-treatment of these workers.[28] It may be that uncertain long-term immigration status for even EEA nationals since the Brexit referendum is playing into insecurity and vulnerability at work. There is now a substantial academic literature emerging on UK care workers, examining their treatment within cross-border supply chains, which are rendered problematic by migrant status compounded by gender,[29] and the difficulty of establishing a standard employment relationship which could lead to coverage by national labour laws.[30]

Another reprehensible example of ill-treatment can be found in Qatar, where an estimated 1.8 million temporary migrant construction workers are engaged in various subcontracted building works. There are allegations of deaths on site and widespread experience of extreme exhaustion and dehydration, including various other forms of what Amnesty International identifies as 'exploitation and abuse'.[31] It should be added that UK businesses, including corporations based in the UK, are actively engaged in investment in Qatar supported by the current UK Government.[32] The ILO gave the Emir of Qatar until November 2016 to make significant changes to the *kafala* sponsorship system, following the publication of the ITUC reports in 2015 and 2016.[33] These experiences of migrant workers are

[27] See Joined cases *Onu v Akwiwu* and *Taiwo v Olaigbe* [2016] IRLR 719 (SC); also *Hounga v Allen* [2014] ICR 847, SC.

[28] For recent comment, see Virginia Mantouvalou, '"Am I Free Now?" Overseas Domestic Workers in Slavery' (2015) 42 *Journal of Law and Society* 329.

[29] Stewart, *Gender, Law and Justice in Global Markets*, above n 8; also Bridget Anderson, *Doing the Dirty Work? The Global Politics of Domestic Labour* (London, Zed Books, 2000).

[30] Leah F Vosko, *Managing the Margins: Gender, Citizenship and the International Regulation of Precarious Employment* (Oxford, Oxford University Press, 2010); LJB Hayes, *Stories of Care: A Labour of Law – Gender and Class at Work* (London, Palgrave Macmillan, 2017).

[31] Amnesty International Report 2015/16: The state of the world's human rights, published February 2016, available at: https://www.amnesty.org/en/documents/pol10/2552/2016/en/. At pp 209–300, there are also reports of inadequate housing, low pay and late wages.

[32] See https://www.gov.uk/government/world/qatar. See, for critical media comment, eg, https://www.theguardian.com/world/2016/nov/09/qatar-world-cup-2022-amnesty-hits-out-at-uk-silence-on-human-rights-during-visit-greg-hands.

[33] *The Case Against Qatar*, ITUC Special Report, March 2014 available at http://www.ituc-csi.org/IMG/pdf/the_case_against_qatar_en_web170314.pdf; and *Qatar: Profit and Loss* (2016) available

illustrative of the role that not only companies but state regulatory frameworks (including those relating to immigration and access to justice) can play in perpetuating forms of exploitation in supply chains. Here, both the responses of the Qatari and UK Governments can attract criticism. Finally, in November 2017, after considerable criticism from the international community, Qatar agreed with the ILO to make substantial reforms from 2018 onwards, which have been endorsed by the ITUC.[34] It will be interesting to see whether other Middle Eastern states now follow suit.

In part, the problems for temporary migrant workers may be the modes of recruitment by subcontractors and agencies, as has been recognised by the 2016 ILO General Principles and Operational Guidelines for Fair Recruitment.[35] These Guidelines specifically recognise the significance of recruitment into supply chains,[36] and are now also the subject of a programme undertaken in partnership between the ILO and European Commission called 'Global Action to Improve the Recruitment Framework of Labour Migration (RE-FRAME)'. Yet, it is not only the process of recruitment that is problematic in the context of commodity chains, but the employment to which the worker is eventually put. Two factors can immediately be highlighted: first, the vulnerable immigration status of the temporary worker and, second, the intentional distancing of that worker from labour law regimes which might offer protection in the state within which they work. In the next section of this chapter, we see that this scenario has been maintained under EU internal trade law and the global World Trade Organization (WTO) General Agreement on Trade in Services (GATS).

III. The Role of Trade Law in Maintaining Vulnerability of Temporary Migrants in Contemporary Supply Chains

Supply chains obviously envisage *geographical* distance. The aim is to pursue the cheapest means of finding, collecting and assembling materials for the purpose of profitable trade. As a result, the processes of manufacture and service supply may be fragmented across national boundaries. This splintering is designed to maximise profitability for the parent company. The cost price of the good or service (to which profit can then be added) is reduced by production or labour involving countries in the South which add value and increase profit margins. For example,

at: https://www.ituc-csi.org/new-ituc-report-qatar-profit-and?lang=en. See a very helpful discussion in https://www.pressreader.com/lebanon/the-daily-star-lebanon/20170414/281702614581573.

[34] See http://www.ilo.org/global/about-the-ilo/newsroom/news/WCMS_592473/lang--en/index.htm; https://www.independent.co.uk/sport/football/international/qatar-2022-world-cup-workers-rights-kafala-system-migraints-middle-east-a8182191.html; and https://www.ituc-csi.org/ilo-decision-heralds-new-era-for.

[35] See http://www.ilo.org/wcmsp5/groups/public/---ed_protect/---protrav/---migrant/documents/genericdocument/wcms_536263.pdf.

[36] See Guidelines, para 3.1, para 14 and para 15.5.

a corporate entity may depend on its subsidiary in another country to commission the making of goods by a manufacturer, which relies on the supply of primary materials by a distributor from a third country that are then processed by workers hired from an agency from a fourth country.

An interesting question is the extent to which the original corporate entity can be obliged to compensate workers further down the supply chain, overcoming not only the geographical but the *legal* distance that might seem to exist between the parties. There have been interesting innovative strategies suggested, regarding for example claims in tort (involving potential claims of vicarious liability and joint as well as several liability),[37] the development of norms regarding contracts governing each step of the chain,[38] as well as a multiplicity of transparency measures designed to embarrass the parent company.[39] However, the straightforward option of access by a temporary migrant worker to domestic labour law protections is not acknowledged either under EU internal trade or global trade norms. This section of the chapter examines the legal instruments and rules which prevail in both contexts and the exploitation (including human rights violations) to which each can lead. Notably, neither was examined in the context of the 2016 ILO Report.[40]

A. Temporary Work in EU Supply Chains

Workers in the European Union (EU) and European Economic Area (EEA) can migrate by virtue of the right to 'free movement of workers' and, in so doing, can plug the gaps in demand across the common market.[41] In addition, the EU provides a pathway for temporary migrant labour. Exercising their rights to free movement of services, employers may temporarily 'post' workers from one EU state to another.[42]

[37] Vibe Ulfbeck and Andreas Ehlers, 'Tort Law, Corporate Groups and Supply Chain Liability for Workers' Injuries: The Concept of Vicarious Liability' (2016) 13(5) *European Company Law* 167.

[38] eg the International Finance Corporation (IFC) *Policy and Performance Standards on Social and Environmental Sustainability* (2012) PS2, paras 27–29 regarding use of child labour and forced labour in supply chains. See also Anna Louise Vytopil, 'Contractual Control in the Supply Chain. On Corporate Social Responsibility, Codes of Conduct, Contracts and (Avoiding) Liability' (2015) available at: https://business-humanrights.org/en/multinationals-unlikely-to-be-held-liable-for-csr-violations-due-to-lack-of-transparency-research-finds.

[39] Directive 2014/95/EU of the European Parliament and of the Council of 22 October 2014, amending Directive 2013/34/EU as regards disclosure of non-financial and diversity information by certain large undertakings and groups, Official Journal of the European Union L330/1-330/9; California Transparency in Supply Chains Act 2012 (SB 657); and Modern Slavery Act 2015, s 54. See, for analysis, Susan Ariel Aaronson with Ethan Wham, 'Can Transparency in Supply Chains Advance Labor Rights? A Mapping of Existing Efforts' IIEP-WP-2016-6 available at: https://www2.gwu.edu/~iiep/assets/docs/papers/2016WP/AaronsonIIEPWP2016-6.pdf.

[40] See above n 1.

[41] See Art 45 of the Treaty on the Functioning of the European Union (TFEU).

[42] See Art 56 of the TFEU and Directive 96/71/EC of the European Parliament and of the Council of 16.12.96 concerning the posting of workers in the framework of the provision of services [1997] OJ L18/1 (Posted Workers Directive).

According to a judgment of the Court of Justice of the European Union (CJEU) in *Rush Portuguesa*,[43] when a service provider sends a worker temporarily to another EU Member State for the delivery of services, ordinary work permit requirements are inappropriate, because such a worker returns after the completion of the service and, notably, does not at any time gain access to the labour market of the host state. However, the judgment in *Rush* did contemplate a discretion for the state in which the work was carried out to impose their labour standards on the employer and worker engaged in such temporary posting.[44]

Article 1(3) of the Posted Workers Directive now clarifies when posting takes place: through a contract between the undertaking employing the posted worker in one State and the party for whom the services are intended in another; via an inter-corporate transfer within a company or group of companies across EU national boundaries; or where an agency hires out a worker from one Member State to a user undertaking in another Member State.[45] These are classic forms of subcontracting across national borders within supply chains.

However, the Posted Workers Directive also limits the discretion of the state (acknowledged in *Rush*) to regulate labour standards with respect to such workers. States must, in the construction industry, lay down minimal standards for posted workers regarding matters set out in Article 3(1) of the Posted Workers Directive, and can do in respect of other industries under Article 3(10). The legitimate scope of regulation in Article 3(1) encompasses provisions relating to pay, hours and holidays, health and safety, provision for pregnant workers and maternity leave, and equality of treatment between men and women, as well as 'other provisions on non-discrimination'. It is clear, since the controversial case of *Laval*, that a Member State may not be able to impose its collective bargaining procedures or terms arising from collective agreements on a service provider posting workers, for to do so is to prevent a service provider being able to ascertain potential liabilities before applying for a contract.[46] There may be a right to strike (under, inter alia, Article 28 of the EU Charter of Fundamental Rights), but it is not wholly operative in this context.[47] Terms from a collective agreement must be given legislative effect to be

[43] Case C-113/89 *Rush Portuguesa Lda v Office national d'immigration* [1990] ECR I-1417.

[44] ibid, para 18.

[45] Much of this analysis is taken from Tonia Novitz, 'Collective Bargaining, Equality and Migration: The Journey to and from Brexit' (2017) 46(1) *Industrial Law Journal* 109 at 124 et seq.

[46] Case C-341/05 *Laval un Partneri v Svenska Byggnadsarbetareförbundet* [2007] ECR I-11767 (*Laval*), para 110: 'collective action such as that at issue in the main proceedings cannot be justified in the light of the public interest objective … where the negotiations on pay, which that action seeks to require an undertaking established in another Member State to enter into, form part of a national context characterised by a lack of provisions, of any kind, which are sufficiently precise and accessible that they do not render it impossible or excessively difficult in practice for such an undertaking to determine the obligations with which it is required to comply as regards minimum pay.' See also for exploration of the Nordic context for this decision, the work of the FORMULA project led by Professor Stein Evju in Stein Evju (ed), *Cross-border Services, Posting of Workers, and Multilevel Governance* (Oslo, University of Oslo, 2013); and Stein Evju (ed), *Regulating Transnational Labour in Europe: The Quandaries of Multilevel Governance* (Oslo, University of Oslo, 2014).

[47] See *Observations on Freedom of Association and Protection of the Right to Organise Convention No 87 1948* United Kingdom (2010) at 208–09; and Report (2013) at 196.

effective as the means of regulation under Article 3(1), setting, for example, terms regarding pay, hours and holidays.

The limited ability of posted workers to enforce what domestic labour law rights they can claim in the host state has been evident in some high-profile incidents, including those occurring in the Flamanville nuclear power plant in France where there were deaths on site alongside non-payment of wages.[48] A result was the adoption of a Posted Workers Enforcement Directive in 2014, which makes specific reference to health and safety inspectorates as well as trade unions in the enforcement of posted workers' rights.[49] The Court of Justice has also now indicated that local trade unions may at least assist posted workers in individual claims regarding non-payment of wages to which they were clearly entitled,[50] although it might also be observed that the UK Regulations implementing this Directive (effective as at June 2016) do not mention the role of trade unions as agents for enforcement and are limited to the enforcement of posted workers' rights solely in the construction sector.[51] In reality, posting of workers across Europe has been found to be significant not only in construction, but also in manufacturing, road transport, processing and in various service sectors, including care, medical and business services. It also arises in terms of seasonal agricultural work.[52] Posting through agencies is also becoming a more common phenomenon.[53]

An example of the latter was the troubling case of Bogdan Chain, a Polish worker, seemingly brought by him against an Irish recruitment company, Atlanco Rimec, over unpaid social insurance.[54] Atlanco were headquartered in Dublin but registered in Cyprus, so *Bogdan Chain v Atlanco* began in the District Court in Nicosia, Cyprus – and was then referred to the European Court of Justice (CJEU). However, Chain claimed that he did not know about the case, which was initiated by a Belgian legal firm that formerly represented the Atlanco Rimec Group

[48] *Working conditions of posted workers in the EPR construction site in Flamanville (France)*, 27 June 2011, Parliamentary Question for oral answer to the Commission, Rule 115, Stephen Hughes, Alejandro Cercas, Rovana Plumb, Pervenche Beres, Estelle Grelier, on behalf of the S&D group. O-000168/2011. See text at http://www.europarl.europa.eu/sides/getDoc.do?pubRef=-//EP//TEXT+OQ+O-2011-000168+0+DOC+XML+V0//EN; and Sarah Clarkson, GMB Brussels, 'Why free movement of labour must guarantee equal treatment for workers: the case of posted and seasonal workers', Presentation delivered at IER Seminar, Developments in European Employment Law, 21.3.12.

[49] Directive 2014/67/EU of the European Parliament and of the Council of 15 May 2014 on the enforcement of Directive 96/71/EC concerning the posting of workers in the framework of the provision of services and amending Regulation (EU) No 1024/2012 on administrative cooperation through the Internal Market Information System ('the IMI Regulation') Text with EEA relevance (the Enforcement Directive), especially Art 11(3).

[50] See also Case 396/13 *Sähköalojen ammattiliitto ry v Elektrobudowa Spółka Akcyjna*, judgment of 12 February 2015.

[51] The Posted Workers (Enforcement of Employment Rights) Regulations 2016 SI 2016/539.

[52] European Commission, *Commission Staff Working Document, Impact Assessment*, Strasbourg, 8.3.2016 SWD(2016) 52 final, at 8.

[53] Rutvica Andrijasevic and Devi Sacchetto, '"Disappearing Workers": Foxconn in Europe and the Changing Role of Temporary Work Agencies' (2016) *Work, Employment and Society* 1.

[54] C-189/14 *Bogdan Chain v Atlanco Ltd*, 11 June 2015, Request for a preliminary ruling.

(the company named as defendant). This state of affairs was exposed by Frank Shouldice at RTÉ in Ireland, whose investigations led him to find Chain in Poland apparently suffering from a work-related injury for which he had not been compensated and seemingly unaware of the case he had supposedly brought for social security compensation. The CJEU heard detailed legal arguments on 12 March 2015, but eventually abandoned the case, which seems to have been an attempt to set up a test case that could legitimate some of Atlanco's practices as an agency around social insurance (under a market rationale, given recent judgments regarding the claims of posted workers and workers exercising free movement rights).[55] The material on the EU website has vanished.[56] This is perhaps the ultimate in commodification of the litigant – achieved again by forms of *geographical* and *legal distance*. The injured migrant worker did not complain himself. He lacked access (both geographical and financial) to the services of a Belgian law firm or the Cypriot courts and the Polish courts could not help him.

In 2016, the European Commission announced proposals for further reform of the Posted Workers Directive on the basis that the scale of so-called temporary posting by service providers is growing (since 2012 by almost 49 per cent) and that the effects have been deleterious.[57] Further, the Commission has found that posted workers usually earn substantially less (often up to 50 per cent less) than local workers for the same job, affecting the ability of local workers to find employment when the cost of their labour is so undercut.[58] The Commission directly referred to supply or, as they termed it, 'subcontracting' chains. There was to be a 'new rule' which gave the faculty to Member States to oblige undertakings to subcontract only to undertakings that grant workers certain conditions on remuneration applicable to the contractor, including those resulting from non-universally applicable collective agreements. This was to be possible on a proportionate and non-discriminatory basis and would thus in particular require that the same obligations be imposed on all national subcontractors.[59] However, the 2018 amended Directive[60] makes no such provision.

[55] Starting with Case C-341/05 *Laval un Partneri v Svenska Byggnadsarbetareförbundet* [2007] ECR I-11767; see also for recent trends Rebecca Zahn, '"Common Sense" or a Threat to EU Integration: The Court, Economically Inactive EU Citizens and Social Benefits' (2015) 44(4) *Industrial Law Journal* 573.

[56] http://curia.europa.eu/juris/liste.jsf?language=en&num=C-189/14#.

[57] Commission Proposal to amend the Posted Workers Directive COM(2016) 128 final. These estimates would seem to be based on the use of portable social security (known as 'A1') documents, which record posting. A 2016 study produced for the European Parliament Committee on Employment and Social Affairs stressed that there is likely to be more posting that is not documented in this fashion, but does not have access to reliable sources of statistical evidence. Instead, the study highlights a very rapid increase in the use of posting in particular sectors after the financial crisis, which include the construction sector, but also manufacturing, education, health, care and social work. See European Parliament, Study for the Committee on Employment and Social Affairs, *Posting of Workers Directive – Current Situation and Challenges* (2016) IP/A/EMPL/2016-07 available at: http://www.europarl.europa.eu/RegData/etudes/STUD/2016/579001/IPOL_STU(2016)579001_EN.pdf.

[58] ibid.

[59] ibid, 7–8.

[60] Dir 2018/957/EU of the European Parliament and of the Council of 28 June 2018 amending Dir 96/71 concerning the posting of workers in the framework of the provision of services.

B. GATS Mode 4 and FTA Provision for Temporary Movement of Natural Persons in Supply Chains

There is implicit endorsement in the General Agreement on Trade in Services (GATS) of the legitimacy of a human element to trade in services, whereby temporary migrant labour is treated in a manner akin to 'posted work' under the trade rules of the EU under what is known as GATS Mode 4. An Annex on Movement of Natural Persons Supplying Services under the Agreement seems to reiterate the view taken in an EU context that such persons do not seek access to the labour market of the state to which they are posted.[61] As such, these workers would seem to lie outside the remit of the host state's labour laws.

There is also an explicit statement in paragraph 4 of the Annex to the effect that, if these do not affect their trade commitments, a WTO Member State may take 'measures to regulate the entry of natural persons into, or their temporary stay in, its territory, including those measures necessary to protect the integrity of, and to ensure the orderly movement of natural persons across, its borders'. In other words, unlike posted work within the EU, WTO states retain discretion in relation to their immigration laws in relation to trade in services even when these contribute to forms of exploitation.[62] Arguably, this combines the worst of the EU posted workers' regime with an international agreement that allows temporary workers to be rendered additionally vulnerable due to their insecure immigration status.

Similar concerns may arise under a free trade agreement (FTA). Free trade agreements dealing with services can be regarded as authorised under WTO rules under Article V bis and Article V of the GATS. Article V bis GATS allows for integration of labour markets but only if the relevant agreement (a) exempts citizens of parties to the agreement from requirements concerning residency and work permits; and (b) is notified to the Council for Trade in Services. The EU–EEA is one such labour integration agreement. More common are FTAs permissible under Article V of the GATS, which contemplates 'substantial sectoral coverage' and non-discrimination measures. An Article V GATS agreement can include movement of natural persons and indeed a chapter regarding temporary movement of natural persons, as is common in EU new generation trade agreements, such as EU–Korea,[63] EU–Singapore[64] and the Comprehensive Economic Trade Agreement (CETA) between the EU and Canada.[65]

An example of the potential effect of an FTA on regulation of workers temporarily resident in another country comes from New Zealand (NZ), which has

[61] Case C-113/89 *Rush Portuguesa Lda v Office national d'immigration*, 27 March 1990, [1990] ECR I-1417.

[62] See above nn 31–34.

[63] See Art 7.17, available at: http://eur-lex.europa.eu/legal-content/EN/TXT/PDF/?uri=OJ:L:2011:127:FULL&from=EN.

[64] See Ch 8, available at http://trade.ec.europa.eu/doclib/docs/2013/september/tradoc_151747.pdf.

[65] See Ch 10, available at: http://ec.europa.eu/trade/policy/in-focus/ceta/ceta-chapter-by-chapter/.

signed such an agreement with China.[66] In NZ, KiwiRail Ltd, an entirely state-owned enterprise, had purchased locomotives from a state-owned company in China, CNR Corporation Ltd. On arrival in NZ, the locomotives were found to contain asbestos. CNR then sent 40 workers, not hired directly but through two different subsidiary companies, to NZ to remove the asbestos and rebuild the locomotives, which was dangerous work. The companies refused to disclose the workers' remuneration, although one company said that the salary paid was what was paid in China, plus a daily allowance for working abroad. Insufficient disclosure was made by the subsidiaries or the workers to determine whether there was compliance with either the minimum NZ employment standards set out in relevant legislation or the terms of the multi-employer collective agreement (MECA) to which KiwiRail is a party. A NZ Ministry of Business, Innovation and Employment (MBIE) investigation revealed no answers, but found no evidence that the Chinese workers lived in cramped conditions or had inadequate food, despite the allegations made by local NZ workers in this regard.[67] Curiously, the MBIE inspectorate noted:

> it is also unclear that [New Zealand minimum employment standards law] would apply to or be enforceable against CNR in the circumstances in which the workers are working in New Zealand. Having taken advice, it is concluded that in all the circumstances of the case, it is more than likely that minimum standards law would not apply.[68]

In other words, there is an assumption that (like posted workers in the EU) the posted Chinese workers would be hired predominantly on terms set under the laws of their home state and not the host state. Further, unlike Article 3 of the Posted Workers Directive, no exceptions are envisaged in relation to this general rule.

The Rail and Maritime Transport Union (RMTU), representing the local NZ workers, however, expressed alarm at such findings. First, the RMTU was concerned that the outsourcing of labour was in breach of the MECA where it undercut the cost of NZ labour, a concern which the European Commission has identified in the EU context. Also, the RMTU argued that the work carried out by the temporarily resident Chinese workers through the supply chain should be declared to be 'subject to New Zealand minimum code legislation' and that KiwiRail was in breach of statutory duties of good faith. KiwiRail responded that, as they were not the employers of the Chinese workers, they had no legal obligations to prevent exploitation and no knowledge or control. As CNR (the Chinese parent company from which they bought the asbestos-contaminated locomotives) was not party to the MECA and had no direct relationship with the

[66] Available at: https://www.mfat.govt.nz/en/trade/free-trade-agreements/free-trade-agreements-in-force/china-fta/.

[67] Ministry of Business, Innovation and Employment, *Summary of Labour Inspectorate Investigation of Alleged Breaches in Employment Standards of the Chinese Workers at KiwiRail's Workshops* 17 April 2015.

[68] ibid, at 10.

RMTU, the union was precluded from seeking enforcement of the collective agreement against that commercial entity. The Employment Relations Authority in NZ subsequently refused to refer the matter for a Court to determine.[69] The RMTU General Secretary put a question which in NZ (as elsewhere) remains unanswered: 'If New Zealand employment law doesn't cover workers who are working in New Zealand … Where does it begin and when does it end? What would have happened if China loco had sent out some 15-year-old kids or younger? Would we say that was acceptable?'[70]

So, this raises an important question: in protecting migrant workers within supply chains in the context of trade in services, *who* are we aiming to protect and from *what*? Do we need the migrant workers themselves to make complaints and in doing so exercise their own personal agency? If so, do we need to establish the conditions that make it safe for them to complain (that goes beyond concerns merely over recruitment identified by the ILO Fair Recruitment Guidelines)? Chinese workers potentially subject to black jails and brainwashing centres (the successors to 're-education through labour' camps)[71] on return from a temporary assignment may be particularly reluctant to be seen to make trouble, as have been the workers on construction sites in Qatar.

If we do not require an actual complaint, is it only the most vulnerable, the trafficked and the children whom we seek to protect? Or should all workers, even when temporarily posted, be granted equal rights to home workers? And who should enforce these rights on their behalf?

There is always the risk that a union will be acting in a protectionist fashion to protect host state jobs for workers already resident in the host state, thereby obstructing aspects of enhanced income (the potential for real value in a global value chain) for those in the global South. Would we rely on *jus cogens* to assert national protection from the worst abuses, perhaps focusing on ILO core labour standards as human rights (as identified in the ILO Declaration on Fundamental Principles and Rights at Work 1998) and perhaps adding in health and safety for good measure (as an asbestos case like this one suggests we should)? Or do we assert the sovereignty of states to assert a set of measures which also reflect home state workers' interests in only a limited range of matters, as the PWD does?

[69] [2015] NZERA Wellington 105, 5560304, determination of 30 October 2015.

[70] 'RMTU case against KiwiRail's use of Chinese workers heads to ERA', available at http://stuff.co.nz/business/71462127/RMTU-case-against-Kiwirails-use-of-Chinese-workers-heads-to-ERA.

[71] See Amnesty press release December 2013, available at: https://www.amnesty.org.uk/press-releases/china-abolition-re-education-through-labour-camps-just-cosmetic-change; and the more recent report regarding the experience of a Swedish human rights activist at: https://www.theguardian.com/world/2017/jan/03/human-rights-activist-peter-dahlin-secret-black-prison-xi-jinpings-new-china. The term 'black jail' denotes an unofficial and undocumented place of detention where it is known that detainees are held, but for which the state refuses to accept responsibility. 'Brainwashing centres' as described by Amnesty International use a variety of techniques to persuade detainees to renounce their religious or other beliefs.

An alternative could be to utilise Article XIV of GATS, which would enable action to be taken by the host state on grounds of, for example, (a) 'public morality', (b) human life and health, or such matters as 'privacy', 'confidentiality' or 'health'. Or could we amend the Annex on Movement of Natural Persons to craft a solution particular to supply chains mirroring the European Commission proposal in respect of posted workers? My suggestion is that such questions might be answered with reference to the evolving United Nations (UN) role in the promotion of sustainable development which chimes with human rights protections, recognising the role of the state in this context.

IV. Sustainable Development Goals as a Basis for State Action to Protect Migrants in Supply Chains

In the ILO 2016 report on *Decent Work in Global Supply Chains*, different methods of governance are identified which might address the problems associated with supply chains: public, private, social partners' and multilateral initiatives.[72] While softer private and social partner initiatives may be of limited assistance for temporary migrant workers,[73] the ILO is correct to identify as highly problematic the failure of states to 'promote compliance and enforce national labour laws and regulations, and to ratify and implement international labour standards'.[74] One difficulty, however, is that the ILO report does not acknowledge, in the context of 'multilateral initiatives', the extent to which the EU and global legal regimes regarding trade in services may affect outcomes for workers in supply chains. Perhaps for this reason, the multilateral initiatives identified in the ILO report seem unduly narrow. They also fail to consider how the emergence of a normative order orientated around sustainable development might assist in reshaping state conduct alongside the rules of trade. This final section of the chapter flags the potential role for state action in the prevention of exploitation of temporary migrant workers within supply chains, with reference to the Sustainable Development Goals (SDGs) set out in the Resolution adopted by the UN General Assembly on 25 September 2015: *Transforming our world: the 2030 Agenda for Sustainable Development*.[75]

A. The Idea of Social Sustainability and its History

There are arguably two strands of international legal history that led to the current SDGs. One is the powerful idea of environmental (inter-generational)

[72] See above n 2, at 40.
[73] *cf* text accompanying nn 37–39.
[74] See above n 2, at 40.
[75] A/Res/70/1, available at https://sustainabledevelopment.un.org/post2015/transformingourworld/publication.

sustainability. This has its origins in the Stockholm Conference on the Human Environment of 1972 and the resultant 'Stockholm Declaration of Principles', with the Brundtland Report coining the phrase 'sustainable development' 15 years later.[76] The other is the increasing significance of an economic and social 'development' agenda. This intra-generational aspect received UN recognition in the 1972 Declaration under Principles 1 and 8,[77] but was more powerfully acknowledged in the UN Declaration on Right to Development.[78] In particular, Article 1 of the 1986 Declaration stresses that idea of 'economic, social, cultural and political development' as 'an inalienable' human right, which arguably maps on to the conception of Amartya Sen of 'development as freedom'.[79]

Sen resists the idea that humans can be regarded as commodities but wishes to see them exercise individual and collective agency at the level of the state, so as to determine what capacities are to be valued and able to be pursued. In this he is not prescriptive:

> It is not being suggested that there is some unique and precise "criterion" of development in terms of which the different development experiences can always be compared and ranked. Given the heterogeneity of distinct components of freedom as well as the need to take note of different persons' diverse freedoms, there will often be arguments that go in contrary directions. The motivation underlying the approach of 'development as freedom' is not so much to order all states – or all alternative scenarios – into one "complete ordering", but to draw attention to important aspects of the process of development, each of which deserves attention.[80]

Nussbaum is more determined to identify plausible bases for capabilities. She takes each person as 'an end', 'holding that the crucial good societies should be promoting for their people is a set of opportunities, or substantial freedoms'. Her concern is with addressing '*entrenched social injustice and inequality*, especially capability failures that are the result of discrimination or marginalization. It ascribes an urgent *task to government and public policy* – namely, to improve the quality of life for all people, as defined by their capabilities'.[81] For this reason,

[76] See Report of the World Commission on Environment and Development: Our Common Future (1987), esp chs 2 and 3, available at https://sustainabledevelopment.un.org/post2015/transformingourworld/publication.

[77] Principle 1 stated that: 'Man has the fundamental right to freedom, equality and adequate conditions of life, in an environment of a quality that permits a life of dignity and well-being, and he bears a solemn responsibility to protect and improve the environment for present and future generations. In this respect, policies promoting or perpetuating apartheid, racial segregation, discrimination, colonial and other forms of oppression and foreign domination stand condemned and must be eliminated.' Principle 8 recognised that: 'Economic and social development is essential for ensuring a favorable living and working environment for man and for creating conditions on earth that are necessary for the improvement of the quality of life.'

[78] GA Resolution 41/128 4 December 1986, available at: http://www.unhchr.ch/html/menu3/b/74.htm.

[79] Amartya Sen, *Development as Freedom* (Oxford, Oxford University Press, 1999).

[80] ibid at 33.

[81] Martha Nussbaum, *Creating Capabilities: The Human Development Approach* (Cambridge, MA, Harvard University Press, 2011), at 18–19.

she offers a list of 'Central Capabilities', of which two affiliation and practical reason, play an 'architectronic' role – 'they organize and pervade the others'.[82] These are also skills that are universally valued, arguably because they promote intergenerational and intragenerational policy solutions, which can operate in durable, that is, sustainable ways. This vision is one which is arguably manifested in the 1992 Rio Conference on Environment and Development (and its famous Declaration of Principles).[83] Principle 10 outlined the importance of 'participation of all concerned citizens at the relevant level' including women, young persons and indigenous peoples (Principles 20–22).

While the Millennium Development Goals have been criticised as target-ridden and donor-centric rather than qualitative and participatory,[84] this talisman of participation was again picked up in the Johannesburg Declaration of 2002. That instrument recognised the particular effects of globalisation on sustainability,[85] but also the importance of participation in policy formation,[86] and made an explicit link between sustainability and the ILO Declaration of Fundamental Principles and Rights at Work 1998.[87] In this way, development becomes less a matter for technical experts and more a matter for engagement, requiring protection of human rights and (at least) core labour standards by the state alongside multilevel deliberation (and arguably international cooperation) as to their realisation.

B. The SDGs on Migration, Supply Chains, Human Rights and Participation

It is evident historically that sustainability discourse gives us an avenue to link human rights to an analysis of the treatment of labour. Certainly, the 2015 SDGs stress the importance of protecting those rendered vulnerable by migration. For example, the UNGA SDG Resolution states:

> We recognize the positive contribution of migrants for inclusive growth and sustainable development. We also recognize that international migration is a multidimensional reality of major relevance for the development of countries of origin, transit and destination, which requires coherent and comprehensive responses. We will cooperate internationally to ensure safe, orderly and regular migration involving full respect for human rights and the humane treatment of migrants regardless of migration status.[88]

[82] ibid, 33–39.

[83] See http://www.un.org/documents/ga/conf151/aconf15126-1annex1.htm/.

[84] See http://www.unmillenniumproject.org/goals/gti.htm; criticised, e.g., by Jan Vandemoortele, 'The MDG Conundrum: Meeting the Targets without Missing the Point' (2009) 27(4) *Development Policy Review* 355; Maya Fehling, Brett D Nelson and Sridhar Venkatapuram, 'Limitations of the Millennium Development Goals: A Literature Review' (2013) 8(10) *Global Public Health* 1109; and Jason Hickel, 'The True Extent of Global Poverty and Hunger: Questioning the Good News Narrative of the Millennium Development Goals' (2016) 37(5) *Third World Quarterly* 749.

[85] See para 14. Available at http://www.un-documents.net/jburgdec.htm.

[86] ibid, para 26.

[87] ibid, para 28.

[88] See above n 75 at para 29.

This statement, which chimes with SDG 8.8, may not constitute explicit recognition of the precarity of temporary migrant labour, but arguably comes closer to this than any prior UN action. For example, recognising the drivers for such migration, SDG10.c makes specific provision for migrant workers to send 'remittances', that is, a portion of their salary, home. However, it is arguably disappointing that the only express reference to 'supply chains' is in an environmental capacity regarding food waste (under SDG 12.3).

In terms of the 'labour rights' specifically mentioned in the UN Resolution and SDG8, these do not obviously indicate recognition of 'freedom of association'. The statement in paragraph 27 of the Resolution is limited to eradicating 'forced labour and human trafficking and … child labour in all its forms', which are really only two of the four core labour standards recognised in the ILO Declaration on Fundamental Principles and Rights at Work, but it has to be also acknowledged that effective protections by states of even these two would make a concrete difference to construction workers in Qatar.[89]

There is further a nod to capabilities theory with the subsequent statement that: 'All countries stand to benefit from having a healthy and well-educated workforce with the knowledge and skills needed for productive and fulfilling work and full participation in society.' So, the answer to my question regarding the list of human rights or labour standards to be protected under FTAs (or indeed GATS Mode 4) may not be so very limited after all. They may include health and safety, as well as training, and even adequate remuneration. Potentially linking also to Nussbaum's ideas regarding affiliation and practical reason, is the statement in SDG 16.7 that the aim is to: 'Ensure responsive, inclusive, participatory and representative decision-making at all levels.' One would hope that this principle is to be applied to the workplace – for acknowledgement of this participatory aspect of sustainability would seem to connect to the entitlements of civil society (including trade unions) in the Johannesburg Declaration.[90] For these reasons, the ILO when considering 'strengthening development cooperation to improve rights and conditions in global supply chains'[91] may find the language, values and mobilisation behind SDGs to be helpful.

Indeed, a link can be made here between achievement of sustainability and the activities of international organisations relating to trade. One key target in SDG17 is to achieve 'a universal, rules-based, open, non-discriminatory and equitable multilateral trading system under the World Trade Organization',[92] presumably relating not only to trade in goods, but trade in services too. There may be a route

[89] See discussion at nn 31–34 above.

[90] See para 26 of the Johannesburg Declaration on Sustainable Development 2002, discussed in Tonia Novitz, 'The Paradigm of Sustainability in a European Social Context: Collective Participation in Protection of Future Interests?' (2015) 31(3) *The International Journal of Comparative Labour Law and Industrial Relations* 243 at 245–46.

[91] See above n 2 at para 202 and p 66.

[92] SDG 17.10. See above n 73.

here towards reform of the most problematic trade rules, whether through the Doha Development Agenda or otherwise.

V. Conclusion

This chapter has reviewed the potential and proven connections between supply chains, trade in services and temporary migrant labour. It has argued that current rules for trade in services both within the EU and internationally are unsustainable in that they can lead to problematic forms of exploitation. The chapter has explored the potential for connections between a sustainability and a human rights agenda, suggesting that states must be encouraged to address the ways in which immigration rules promote exploitation in breach of the 'social pillar'.

Further, following on from sustainable development principles, states should retain responsibility for protection of those who work within their territory and must make provision not only for access to justice, but the means to exercise agency. It is conceded that this is a bold set of claims, which have only received nascent protection on the international stage. But, at a time of trends towards nationalism and protectionism, it is arguable that it has never been more urgent for our rules of trade to be seen to benefit all – to be genuinely global value chains – and to be legitimate according to accepted sustainability and human rights standards.

There is therefore a case for reforming the current rules of global trade, so that sustainable development objectives (and their associated human rights protections, including substantive and procedural rights for workers) can be more closely integrated within GATS. The EU Enforcement Directive in respect of posted workers demonstrates the scope to amend and improve temporary work regimes within supply chains; it may be time for the WTO to enable (if not encourage) comparable protections for workers and even be as ambitious as the European Commission's 2016 proposals. If we are to take human rights provisions, guarantees of labour standards and sustainable development chapters in FTAs seriously,[93] we might expect more attention to their enforcement regarding temporary migrant workers within host states.

Further, it might be possible to supplement the amendment of trade provisions with more rigorous participatory measures. These might be legislative provisions to promote organisation and representation of migrant workers in supply chains, which could perhaps entail representation on a works council at

[93] See ILO, Assessment of labour provisions in trade and investment arrangements (Geneva, ILO, 2016) available at: http://www.ilo.ch/global/publications/books/WCMS_498944/lang--en/index.htm. For discussion of the relative merits of human rights and sustainable development chapters, see also Lore Van den Putte and Jan Orbie, 'EU bilateral trade agreements and the surprising rise of labour provisions' (2015) 31(3) IJCLLIR 263 and also Lorand Bartels, 'Human rights and sustainable development obligations in EU Free Trade Agreements' in Legal Studies Research Paper Series, University of Cambridge Faculty of Law, Paper No 24/2012, http://www.academia.edu/1902855/Human_rights_and_sustainable_development_obligations_in_EU_free_trade_agreements.

local levels, but also more stringent protections from dismissal and deportation in the event of acting as a representative or voicing opinions directly to an employer. Such an initiative would, as noted above, be consistent with the emergent ILO Fair Recruitment Guidelines.[94] In this context, we might draw on norms beginning to be set in international framework agreements regarding core labour standards and their implementation.[95] In other words, we need human rights, but also, as Sen and Nussbaum acknowledge, agency through voice for all persons whether migrant labour or not (and temporary or otherwise). This entails practical as well as legal means of ensuring access and protection within a supply chain. There will have to be greater attention to the details, practicalities and legal status of procedures which mediate between economic and social objectives, as well as the agency of the actors within them.

These suggestions may seem counterintuitive to some. We are, after all, discussing global trade within supply chains that by their very nature traverse national boundaries, thereby limiting the jurisdiction of the state over their operations. However, my point is that, in relation to labour within their territory, states can play a key regulatory role which the international community need not discourage or indeed abandon, but can rather reinforce. That objective can be achieved by utilising what is being learnt about the dimensions of sustainable governance and using acceptance of these principles to guide reform of trading rules. International law can, in this way, bolster the role of government in the protection of temporary migrant workers, thereby setting fairer standards for competition in trade in services when delivered by natural persons.

[94] See above n 35.

[95] Hans Wolfgang Platzer and Stefan Rüb, 'International Framework Agreements: An Instrument for Enforcing Social Human Rights?' (2014) Friedrich Ebert Stiftung Working Paper, available at https://www.hs-fulda.de/fileadmin/user_upload/Zentren_und_Verbuende/Cinteus/Europaeische_und_globale_Arbeitsbeziehungen/Veroeffentlichungen/PlatzerRueb_2014_IFAs_and_Social_Human_Rights.pdf; Cesar F Rosado Martin, 'Organizing with International Framework Agreements: An Exploratory Study' (2014) 4 *UC Irvine Law Review* 727; also Aalt Colenbrander, 'International Framework Agreements' (2016) 12 *Utrecht Law Review* 109.

PART III

Empirical Approaches: Regulating Informality

9

What is Actually Regulating Work? A Study of Restaurants in Indonesia and Australia

PETRA MAHY, RICHARD MITCHELL, JOHN HOWE AND MARIA AZZURRA TRANFAGLIA

I. Introduction

Much of the discussion of informal work in recent years has been couched in terms of the 'failure' of formal labour law to regulate and protect many millions of workers around the world.[1] This is usually seen as a failure of the state, either as a deliberate policy or through institutional weakness, to apply and enforce labour laws and standards in both developed and developing economies. As a result, the imagined picture created is of a circle drawn around the centre of state power within which labour laws are applicable, enforced and effective, and beyond which there is a void of regulation where workers are exploited and denied basic labour and human rights. Those who fall within the circle are labelled as formal employees and those outside as informal workers. While there has certainly been some recognition of the continuum between formal and informal work,[2] this understanding still seems submerged beneath the apparently more enduring image of a duality. Statistical data collection, such as that conducted using the International Labour Organization's (ILO's) definitions of the *informal sector* and *informal employment*,[3]

[1] See, eg, G Davidov and B Langille (eds), *Boundaries and Frontiers of Labour Law* (Oxford, Hart Publishing, 2006); J Fudge, K Sankaran and S McCrystal (eds), *Challenging the Legal Boundaries of Work Regulation* (Oxford, Hart Publishing, 2012); T Teklè (ed), *Labour Law and Worker Protection in Developing Countries* (Oxford, Hart and International Labour Office, 2010).

[2] See, eg, B Guha-Khasnobis, R Kanbur and E Ostrom, 'Beyond Formality and Informality' in B Guha-Khasnobis, R Kanbur and E Ostrom (eds), *Linking the Formal and Informal Economy: Concepts and Policies* (Oxford, Oxford University Press, 2006); MA Chen, 'Rethinking the Informal Economy: Linkages with the Formal Economy and the Formal Regulatory Environment' in B Guha-Khasnobis, R Kanbur and E Ostrom (eds), *Linking the Formal and Informal Economy: Concepts and Policies* (Oxford, Oxford University Press, 2006).

[3] ILO, *Measuring Informality: A Statistical Manual on the Informal Sector and Informal Employment* (Geneva, ILO, 2013); ILO, *Women and Men in the Informal Economy: A Statistical Picture* 2nd edn (Geneva, ILO, 2013).

is predicated on this duality where the business or the worker is counted as being either formal or informal.

However, when we move away from this traditional vision of labour law and instead take a regulatory approach to the study of work arrangements,[4] the picture that emerges is rather different. Regulatory approaches recognise that our view of social and economic ordering can be de-centred from the state by acknowledging the involvement of various interacting institutions, actors and sources of regulation. In such an approach, any particular work arrangement can be conceptualised as a regulatory space where a plural and often complex array of formal and informal regulation can have influence.[5] Individual work arrangements also exist within, and contribute to constituting, larger regulatory spaces from that of the enterprise and the local area up to state and transnational systems. In this approach it is the *regulation* that can be labelled as being either formal or informal rather than the business or the worker. Formal labour regulation is defined here as that which originates from, or is officially sanctioned by, the state, including legislation and case law, bureaucratic decision making and collective bargaining agreements.[6] Informal labour regulation, on the other hand, can take many forms[7] including corporate self-regulation, private (often transnational) regulation through civil society organisations and consumer power,[8] regulation by clusters of similar and/or

[4] See J Howe, 'Labour Regulation Now and in the Future: Current Trends and Emerging Themes' (2016) 59 *Journal of Industrial Relations* 209; J Howe, 'A Different World: The Regulatory Project in Labour Law' in J Howe, A Chapman and I Landau (eds), *The Evolving Project of Labour Law: Foundations, Development and Future Research Directions* (Sydney, The Federation Press, 2017); P Mahy, 'The Functional Approach in Comparative Socio-Legal Research: Reflections Based on a Study of Plural Work Regulation in Australia and Indonesia' (2016) 12 *International Journal of Law in Context* 420; A Frazer, 'Labour Law, Institutionalist Regulation and the Employing Organisation' (2014) 20 *International Employment Relations Review* 4; P Gahan and P Brosnan, 'The Repertoires of Labour Market Regulation' in C Arup et al (eds), *Labour Law and Labour Market Regulation: Essays on the Construction, Constitution and Regulation of Labour Markets and Work Relationships* (Sydney, The Federation Press, 2006). In many ways, regulatory studies overlap conceptually with that of 'new legal pluralism' which accepts that plural normative orders are found in all societies (SE Merry, 'Legal Pluralism' (1988) 22 *Law & Society Review* 869, 872–73). See, eg, L Benton, 'Beyond Legal Pluralism: Towards a New Approach to Law in the Informal Sector' (1994) 3 *Social & Legal Studies* 223.

[5] L Hancher and M Moran, 'Organizing Regulatory Space' in R Baldwin, C Scott and C Hood (eds), *A Reader on Regulation* (Oxford, Oxford University Press, 1998); C Scott, 'Analysing Regulatory Space: Fragmented Resources and Institutional Design' [2001] *Public Law* 329; G Morgan and K Soin, 'Regulatory Compliance' in G Morgan and L Engwell (eds), *Regulation and Organizations: International Perspectives* (Oxford, Routledge, 1999); Frazer, 'Labour Law, Institutionalist Regulation and the Employing Organisation', above n 4, 15.

[6] Collective bargaining and similar self-regulatory activities can be difficult to classify in this formal/informal dichotomy – bargaining can occur under the auspices of state meta-regulation and thus could be classified as 'formal', but in some circumstances it occurs entirely outside state control and would be more properly designated as 'informal'.

[7] For an extensive literature review on these sources of informal regulation, see P Mahy et al, *The Plural Regulation of Work: A Pilot Study of Workers in Yogyakarta, Indonesia* (Centre for Employment and Labour Relations Law, University of Melbourne, 2017).

[8] See, eg, P Martin Dumas, 'Regulating Informal Work through Consumocratic Law: Empirical and Theoretical Insights from the RugMark/GoodWeave Experience' in S Routh and V Borghi (eds),

spatially linked businesses,[9] regulatory agency by worker groups and individuals,[10] regulation through 'institutions of social identity' such as gender, class, ethnicity and religion,[11] social norms and other moralities,[12] customary law,[13] and also via an array of patron–client and real and fictive kinship type relationships.[14]

Descriptions of the nature and content of informal labour regulation tend to be found scattered across research from various disciplines including anthropology, labour geography, gender studies, migrant labour studies, employment relations, human resource management and political science. While such research often documents the realities of informal regulation of the workplace around the world, it usually does not include reference to the content or effects of formal labour law. Because doctrinal studies of labour law also tend largely to ignore the existence of informal regulation, the intersection and overlap between formal and informal forms of labour regulation is inadequately examined. There are seemingly just a few exceptions to this inter-disciplinary blind spot.

Some of these exceptions demonstrate how law can have influence in otherwise informal contexts. For example, Benton described how the working conditions of informally regulated workers in Spain often referred very closely to the standards set by formal labour law.[15] Similarly, Sugiarti et al found that labour conditions in informally regulated tea plantations in West Java, Indonesia, often partially imitated the formal sector.[16] Others have noted situations where the imposition of law has changed informal norms. Kondo documented how the introduction

Workers in the Global Informal Economy: Interdisciplinary Perspectives (Oxford, Routledge, 2016); K MacDonald and S Marshall, 'Transnational Business and the Politics of Social Risk: Re-embedding Transnational Supply Chains through Private Governance' in B Lange, F Haines and D Thomas (eds), *Regulatory Transformations: Rethinking Economy–Society Interactions* (Oxford, Hart Publishing, 2015).

[9] See, eg, E Yoruk, 'Labour Discipline in the Informal Economy: The Semi-Formal Professional Code of Istanbul's Apparel Urban Factory' (2009) 53 *Berkeley Journal of Sociology* 27; A Bloch and S McKay, 'Hidden Dishes – How Food Gets to Our Plates: Undocumented Migrants and the Restaurant and Takeaway Sector' (2013) 17 *Journal of Workplace Rights* 69.

[10] AM Vargas, 'Organization and Self-Regulation among Informal Workers: An Ethnographic Study of Rickshaw Drivers in Bogotá, Colombia', paper presented at Regulating for Decent Work Conference, ILO, 8–10 July 2015; T Sportel, 'Agency within a Socially Regulated Labour Market: A Study of Unorganised Agricultural Labour in Kerala' (2013) 47 *Geoforum* 42.

[11] B Harriss-White, 'Work and Wellbeing in Informal Economies: The Regulative Roles of Institutions of Identity and the State' (2010) 38 *World Development* 170.

[12] CC Williams and J Windebank, *Informal Employment in the Advanced Economies: Implications for Work and Welfare* (Oxford, Routledge, 1998) 40–42; D Isik, 'On Sabir and Agency: The Politics of Pious Practice in Konya's Carpet Weaving Industry' (2008) 10 *International Feminist Journal of Politics* 518.

[13] See, eg, EE Koodoh, A Alim and Bacharuddin, *Hukum Adat Orang Tolaki [The Customary Law of the Tolaki People]* (Yogyakarta, Teras, 2011) ch 8.

[14] See, eg, G De Neve, *The Everyday Politics of Labour: Working Lives in India's Informal Economy* (New Delhi, Social Science Press, 2005).

[15] L Benton, *Invisible Factories: The Informal Economy and Industrial Development in Spain* (New York, State University of New York Press, 1990); L Benton, 'Beyond Legal Pluralism: Towards a New Approach to Law in the Informal Sector' (1994) 3 *Social & Legal Studies* 223.

[16] KL Sugiarti and S Novi HP, 'Buruh dalam Industri Teh Rakyat Ciwidey, Jawa Barat' [Labourers in the People's Tea Industry, Ciwidey, West Java] in AF Safaria, D Suhanda and S Riawanti (eds), *Hubungan Perburuhan di Sektor Informal: Permasalahan dan Prospek [Labour Relations in the Informal Sector: Problems and Prospects]* (Bandung, Akatiga, 2003).

of the Meiji Civil Code in Japan in 1898 interacted with and changed the prevailing modes of labour relations based on fictive kinship.[17] Showing influence in the opposite direction, Petersen speculated that a norm of consideration of family life, particularly of women's family responsibilities, was moderating the effects of formal labour law in Denmark.[18] Ram et al also demonstrated that any effects of the National Minimum Wage in the United Kingdom depended on deeper processes of informality.[19] Finally, it is also possible to discern more complexity of interactions among different forms of labour regulation. For example, Charlesworth documents the 'regulatory space' of care work in Australia and the three-way interactions and conflicts between (i) Federal and State labour laws, (ii) the funding market created by governments setting the price of contracted-out care work, and (iii) the social norms of gender and care.[20]

These studies are few, fairly limited in geographic scope, and have yet to demonstrate fully the benefits of approaching the study of work arrangements through a regulatory lens. There is arguably a need for greater efforts to expose the workings and interactions of plural forms of labour regulation in different contexts in order to counter the view that employment outside the purview of the state is necessarily *unregulated* and to counter the view that there is a distinct binary division between formal and informal employment. Recognition of plural work regulation is, for example, conspicuously absent in ILO policy documents on 'formalising the informal' which largely emphasise the state-centric need for greater enforcement of formal labour laws.[21]

With these considerations in mind, we designed a research methodology aimed at investigating the plural regulation of work and then conducted a pilot project in one economic sector in two locations. We collected interview data on the regulation of work arrangements in restaurants in two very different cities: Melbourne, Australia, and Yogyakarta, Indonesia.[22] By interviewing workers across a range of restaurants based on size, business model, and geographical location within each city, the project was specifically designed to capture a spectrum of work arrangements ranging from those that are more formally regulated through

[17] DK Kondo, *Crafting Selves: Power, Gender and Discourses of Identity in a Japanese Workplace* (Chicago, The University of Chicago Press, 1990) ch 5.

[18] H Petersen, *Home Knitted Law. Norms and Values in Gendered Rule-Making* (Aldershot, Dartmouth Publishing, 1996) 52–55.

[19] M Ram, P Edwards, M Gilman and J Arrowsmith, 'The Dynamics of Informality: Employment Relations in Small Firms and the Effects of Regulatory Change' (2001) 15 *Work, Employment, Society* 845; M Ram, P Edwards and T Jones, 'Staying Underground: Informal Work, Small Firms, and Employment Regulation in the United Kingdom' (2007) 34 *Work and Occupations* 318.

[20] S Charlesworth, 'Decent Working Conditions for Care Workers? The Intersections of Employment Regulation, the Funding Market and Gender Norms' (2010) 25 *Australian Journal of Labour Law* 107.

[21] See ILO, *The Informal Economy and Decent Work: A Policy Resource Guide Supporting Transitions to Formality* (Geneva, ILO, 2013).

[22] This research was funded by a collaborative University of Melbourne Interdisciplinary Seed Grant for the project titled 'How are Low Protection Workers Regulated? A Pilot Study in Australia and Indonesia' (S Cooney, M Boese, J Howe, P Mahy, R Mitchell and J-C Tham) (2013). For the full results of the Yogyakarta research see Mahy et al, *The Plural Regulation of Work*, above n 7.

to those that are more informally regulated. This innovative methodology has allowed us to collect rich datasets in two very different contexts, which should permit us to bridge, at least to some extent, the lack of connection between the literature on informality in developed and developing nations.[23] The twin studies indicate some important differences as well as unexpected similarities in both the content of informal forms of regulation and the ways that formal and informal regulation interact to determine work arrangements.

There are at least two major implications arising from our research. First, in demonstrating the ubiquity and importance of informal regulation, this research suggests a need to expand the empirical research question asked in relation to informality in labour markets from the usual and somewhat myopic 'Is labour law performing its expected functions?' to a much broader question of '*What is actually regulating work?*'[24] Investigating this question and taking account of both formal and informal regulation should provide a much more holistic measure of the extent to which workers enjoy benefits and security in their employment compared to merely focusing on labour law and its effects. Second, and following from this, our research indicates some possibilities for turning to empirical knowledge of plural labour regulation to design and reform labour regulation systems. That is, if we pay greater attention to the existence of, and interactions among, different regulatory orders and actors, then this could potentially provide an evidence base for moving towards more nuanced interventions aimed at increasing worker security and well-being, or for understanding when interventions may be counterproductive.[25]

The next section of the chapter sets out our research methodology and analytical approach, while the two subsequent sections discuss the results of our interviews in Yogyakarta and Melbourne respectively. Section V presents our reflections on the two studies viewed together, while section VI elaborates on the implications of our research. The final section concludes.

II. Research Methods and Analytical Approach

This research project set out to develop and test a methodology for examining the plural regulation of work arrangements. This explains the selection of the two research sites, as we deliberately chose two very different locations – one in

[23] CC Williams and J Windebank, *Informal Employment in the Advanced Economies: Implications for Work and Welfare* (Oxford, Routledge, 1998) 112; S Routh and V Borghi, 'The Idea of Form, Informality and Aspirations of Workers' in S Routh and V Borghi (eds), *Workers and the Global Informal Economy: Interdisciplinary Perspectives* (Oxford, Routledge, 2016) 6.

[24] R Mitchell, P Mahy and P Gahan, 'The Evolution of Labour Law in India: An Overview and Commentary on Regulatory Objectives and Development' (2014) 1 *Asian Journal of Law and Society* 413, 447.

[25] C Sage and M Woolcock, 'Legal Pluralism and Development Policy: Scholars and Practitioners in Dialogue' in BZ Tamanaha, C Sage and M Woolcock (eds), *Legal Pluralism and Development: Scholars and Practitioners in Dialogue* (Cambridge, Cambridge University Press, 2012).

a developing economy (Indonesia) and one in a developed economy (Australia). The specific cities of Yogyakarta and Melbourne were selected for practical reasons of access and familiarity to the research team. The restaurant (food services) sector was chosen as it is known to have a significant degree of informality in both places.[26]

In each city, around 30 interviews were conducted with restaurant workers. In Yogyakarta, participants were recruited mostly by simply approaching workplaces to ask for permission to speak to one of their workers. In Melbourne, advertisements with a small financial incentive were placed and interviewees were entirely self-selected. The difference in participant recruitment strategies was due to the greater likelihood that informal workplace practices could be construed by authorities as illegal in Melbourne than in Yogyakarta. The interviews covered the full scope of issues relating to the interviewees' work arrangements including their personal employment history, recruitment, existence of a contract or agreement, wages, hours, leave, discipline, workplace relationships, knowledge of formal labour laws and informal norms and their personal attitudes towards their work. These interviews were transcribed and analysed for recurring patterns using a qualitative data analysis programme.

We were interested in finding out what was regulating work arrangements in practice. The interview material contains factual descriptions of particular work arrangements, but does not directly infer what type of regulation was ordering or shaping those arrangements. In cases where the work arrangements specifically replicated the detail of a particular law, such as where wages precisely followed the minimum wage, then it was easier to infer that law was the cause. This process is much more difficult in terms of informal norms, particularly because norms have two parts to them: what is subjectively considered 'ought' to be done, and what 'is' done in reality.[27] Mere recurrent patterns of behaviour may not necessarily signify the existence of a norm.[28] Hence, for this project we also needed to rely in part on what workers subjectively considered to be the source of the regulation of their particular work arrangement. In Yogyakarta, for instance, some workers said that although they knew about Indonesian labour laws, their work arrangements were based only on informal norms. Similarly, in Melbourne, many workers explained that it was a 'secret rule' that Asian restaurants paid a particular standard hourly (below minimum) wage to their workers. Thus the source of the regulation affecting the work arrangement, at least subjectively, was established.

[26] Fair Work Ombudsman, 'Annual Report 2013–2014' (Fair Work Ombudsman, Australian Government, 2014); Asian Development Bank and BPS-Statistics Indonesia, *The Informal Sector and Informal Employment in Indonesia* (Asian Development Bank and BPS-Statistics Indonesia, 2011).

[27] HLA Hart, *The Concept of Law* (Oxford, Clarendon Press, 1961) 81; R Banakar, *Normativity in Legal Sociology: Methodological Reflections on Law and Regulation in Late Modernity* (Dordrecht, Springer, 2015) 216.

[28] M Baier, 'Relations between Social and Legal Norms' in M Baier (ed), *Social and Legal Norms: Towards a Socio-Legal Understanding of Normativity* (Aldershot, Ashgate, 2013) 63.

III. Findings in Yogyakarta, Indonesia

The interview data from the restaurants in Yogyakarta[29] indicated that the important regulatory actors were business owners and individual workers, with very little, if any, direct influence from the local department of labour or other bodies such as trade unions or NGOs.[30] The data indicated the existence of a spectrum of work arrangements ranging from the more formally regulated end, where work arrangements followed Indonesian labour law to a greater degree, through to those affected more by informal norms and institutions. These informal norms were often explicitly termed by interviewees as *kekeluargaan* or 'family-ness' and this was distinguished very clearly from formal labour law. According to the interviewees, *kekeluargaan* encompasses a range of ideas and practices including reciprocity, patron–client or parent–child type relationships, understanding and leniency towards a worker's social and family responsibilities, a relaxed attitude towards rules, a lack of explicit discussion of wages and terms and even laughing and joking in the workplace. It also included such practices as *kasbon*, where workers may expect their business owners or managers to provide them with interest-free loans to cover sudden personal needs such as a child's medical costs. In other words, the interviews indicated two well-defined sources of regulation – formal labour law and *kekeluargaan* norms.

The existence of a written contract of employment was just one element in terms of the degree to which a work arrangement was formally or informally regulated. For instance, we found a number of work arrangements in the spectrum which used written fixed-term contracts but were in contravention of the formal restrictions around their use. Fixed-term contracts are only permitted for work that is not of a permanent character, and may only be for a maximum of two years' duration with one year's extension.[31] The use of fixed-term contracts outside these limitations is apparently very common as employers seek to avoid high severance payments and other compulsory benefits that must be paid to permanent workers.[32] The acceptance of the use of fixed-term contracts outside these legal stipulations appears to be quite a well-established informal norm.

[29] For the full results of this study in Yogyakarta, see Mahy et al, *The Plural Regulation of Work*, above n 7.

[30] On the weak enforcement of labour law in Indonesia see T Warnecke and A De Ruyter, 'The Enforcement of Decent Work in India and Indonesia: Developing Sustainable Institutions' (2012) 46 *Journal of Economic Issues* 392, 397; ILO, *Labour and Social Trends in Indonesia 2012* (Geneva, ILO, 2013); O Dupper, C Fenwick and T Hardy (2016), 'The Interaction of Labour Inspection and Private Compliance Initiatives: A Case Study of Better Work Indonesia,' Better Work Discussion Paper Series No 21 (June 2016).

[31] Law No 13/2003, art 59; Minister for Labour Decision No 100/2004 on the Implementation of Fixed-term Employment Contracts.

[32] I Tjandraningsih, R Herawati and Suhadmadi, 'Praktek Kerja Kontrak dan Outsourcing Buruh di Sektor Industri Metal di Indonesia' [The Practice of Work Contracts and Labour Outsourcing in the Metal Industry Sector in Indonesia] (AKATIGA–FSPMI–FE, 2010); R Herawati, R Dewayanti and W Sriyuliani (2011) 'Penelitian Praktek Kerja Outsourcing Pada Sub-Sektor Perbankan: Studi Kasus Jakarta, Surabaya dan Medan' [Study of Outsourcing Work Practices in the Banking

In the middle areas of the spectrum there were also businesses which used some elements of formal labour law even where there was little expectation of actual enforcement; that is, it was evident that formal labour laws were having at least some normative force beyond the scope of enforcement by the state. The eight-hour working day with one-hour rest and minimum wages in particular were often found across this section. At the same time, many of the interviewees with such work arrangements also described themselves as being in *kekeluargaan*-influenced relationships with both the business owner and with co-workers even if they had once been complete strangers. These fictive kin relationships seemed to be strengthened in the common situation where business owners provided accommodation to their workers, because bringing someone under one's roof tended to increase parental-like obligations towards them. In other words, there was clear mixing of formal and informal forms of regulation within particular work arrangements in the middle of the spectrum.

At the very informally regulated end of the spectrum, work arrangements were described by interviewees as being based entirely in *kekeluargaan* norms, although there still seemed to be some weak influence from the distant shadow of the law in terms of setting general standards and expectations. The most informally regulated work arrangements often had little to no explicit discussion about wages and conditions, just acceptance of what was given. Here, business owners were more likely to employ family members or friends, or friends of current employees as a way of ensuring that the worker could be trusted. However, this was not always the case; businesses using informally regulated work arrangements would still advertise and take on a stranger if they could not get anyone else. Towards the informal end of the spectrum there was also a greater sense of workers being taken on permanently, and that dismissing them was very difficult because of moral feelings of responsibility on the part of the business owner. Hence, sometimes there was actually greater security for them compared to those workers who were on short fixed-term contracts towards the more formal end of the spectrum. That is, formality was not always a guarantee of better employment security.

Institutions of social identity,[33] such as gender and ethnicity, also had real but less explicitly acknowledged effects across the spectrum. Such factors undoubtedly influenced the preferences of particular employers when recruiting workers, but they did not function as hard and fast rules across the sector. So, for example, while one employer had a preference for male kitchen staff, not far away another restaurant employed all women. There was also a relationship between hours of work and gender, with some employers preferring not to employ women late at night due to perceptions of moral and physical danger for women travelling to

Sub-Sector: A Case Study in Jakarta, Surabaya and Medan] (AKATIGA – OPSI – FES 2011); I Landau, P Mahy and R Mitchell, 'The Regulation of Non-Standard Forms of Employment in India, Indonesia and Vietnam' (ILO-INWORK Working Paper no. 63, 2015).

[33] Harriss-White, 'Work and Wellbeing in Informal Economies', above n 11.

and from work. Religion was also a commonly cited source of regulation of workplace arrangements, either as a discriminatory factor in recruitment or as a source of moral values used by employers to decide on their management strategies. In terms of ethnicity, there was the odd exceptional source of regulation, where ethnicity-based restaurants such as Padang restaurants, which originate in West Sumatra, sometimes kept to their own traditional profit sharing models of remuneration of workers.

IV. Findings in Melbourne, Australia

In our study of restaurant work in Melbourne, similar to Yogyakarta, the main regulatory actors mentioned in the interviews were individual business owners and workers, with very little evidence of direct regulatory activity by state institutions or other actors.[34] We also found a spectrum of regulation in the Melbourne interviews with some work arrangements in the middle of the spectrum that clearly used some combination of formal and informal regulation. We interviewed workers who had entirely, or mostly, formally regulated work arrangements, through to those completely 'off-the-books', as well as some in between. However, unlike in Yogyakarta with its strong dual pattern of regulation, the sources of regulation in Melbourne seemed more diverse in terms of type of business and particularly their ethnic associations.

The interviews indicated that clusters of businesses often have their own shared informal labour standards, such as restaurants in Chinatown, restaurants in the Italian-dominated Lygon Street, eateries on a university campus, or cafés with no ethnic connections in a particular neighbourhood. This was especially noticeable in terms of hourly wages, with many workers reporting being paid cash-in-hand (that is, without being declared formally for taxation and superannuation purposes), and being paid quite standard rates across similar businesses. As noted above, many of our interviewees reported that 'Asian' restaurants across the city had a common flat rate of about $8 per hour, well below the legal minimum of $16.37 per hour.[35] The interviewees were also not being paid the required additional 'casual loading' wage premium or weekend penalty rates.

[34] This is not to say that other actors were entirely absent, but merely that they were not identified by our interviewees. On actors in the work regulation space in Australia generally, see T Hardy, 'Watch This Space: Mapping the Actors Involved in the Implementation of Labour Standards Regulation in Australia' in J Howe, A Chapman and I Landau (eds), *The Evolving Project of Labour Law: Foundations, Development and Future Research Directions* (Sydney, The Federation Press, 2017).

[35] This was the hourly minimum wage for introductory level permanent employees covered by the Restaurant Industry Award (2010) and the Hospitality Industry (General) Award (2010). The minimum wage for Level 1 employees covered by the Fast Food Industry Award (2010) was higher at $17.98 per hour. These figures are the bare minimum and do not take account of role classifications, casual loading which requires a wage premium to be paid to casual workers, or penalty rates for work at weekends, on public holidays and on night shifts.

Most of the respondents referred to themselves as being 'casual' workers. Casual work is a very common, formally recognised form of employment in Australia, where workers have no ongoing right to shifts and are not paid for times that they cannot work providing that certain higher minimum wage rates are applied (casual loading).[36] While many of the interviewees described themselves as 'casual', they were actually employed informally (without a written contract) and were generally being paid cash-in-hand. Often such work arrangements otherwise approximated casual employment with similar approaches to scheduling of shifts and so on and it may be that this demonstrates a spill-over or shadow effect of legal categories of employment on what is otherwise informally regulated work.

Despite the diversity of informal labour norms in Melbourne that were based on geographical location and ethnic ties, some common practices were reported. Frequently described across the interviews was the incidence of unpaid trials for job seekers – sometimes just a few hours, in other cases a few days. The use of informal regulation also appeared heightened in situations where employers and employees accepted that the work would be temporary, such as work that was performed by students or temporary migrants. Few of the interviewees in the pilot study reported any encounter with formal workplace inspection, and few were given any specific training or awareness of health and safety issues. Disciplining of workers by giving them, or threatening to give them, fewer shifts appeared very common. It was also very common for free food and drink to be provided to workers, and these were often highly valued as a 'perk' of working in hospitality. Practices around the distribution of tips seemed very variable and idiosyncratic to particular workplaces, but were a common site of unwritten and/or unspoken rules in the workplace, where workers were usually expected to figure out workplace customs for themselves through observation.[37]

The interviews indicated a strong entanglement between personal relationships in the workplace and justifications for informality. Many expressed a reluctance to complain to authorities about their work conditions or to otherwise cause problems due to social ties and personal feelings of responsibility to their employer and to their co-workers. The amount of notice that a worker said that they would give their employer, in particular, seemed to be shaped by a worker's individual standards of decency balanced with their assessment of the quality of workplace relationships ('I would let them know in time so they can find a replacement for me' versus 'I don't feel I owe them anything'). Justifications for informality ranged from those who were naïve and said that they did not know that they should have been entitled to legal protections through to those workers who had made a conscious preference to avoid the law.

[36] A Stewart et al, *Creighton & Stewart's Labour Law* 6th edn (Sydney, The Federation Press, 2016) ch 10.1; I Campbell, 'Casual Work and Casualisation: How does Australia Compare?' (2004) 15 *Labour & Industry* 85; A O'Donnell, '"Non-Standard" Workers in Australia: Counts and Controversies' (2004) 17 *Australian Journal of Labour Law* 89.

[37] See also A Gow and A Frazer, 'Who Owns Tips? Hospitality Workers and the Distribution of Customer Gratuities' (2015) 28 *Australian Journal of Labour Law* 89.

A few of the work arrangements in Melbourne were described as 'family-like'. While we heard about a couple of restaurants holding daily 'family meals' with employees, for example, or encouraging after-work activities, lots of the workplaces that paid cash-in-hand seemed to make no effort at all to foster personal ties with their staff. This creates a puzzle as to how employers created enough trust in workers with no personal ties to them to minimise any possibility that the workers would later report the employer for underpayment or other breaches of minimum labour standards. It seems likely that employers were relying on workers' vulnerability and need for paid employment. It was very rare for workplace fictive kinship to form a source of social security in Melbourne – quite different from the Yogyakarta case.

In terms of institutions of social identity, these were key factors in recruitment and a basis for discrimination. Many of the interviews reported that ethnicity, gender, age and physical appearance were obvious factors in the selection of front of house staff particularly where the restaurant served a particular type of ethnic food. Meanwhile, for kitchen staff this mattered far less, although kitchen hands were far more likely to be male and were often selected based on the language(s) spoken by the head chef. None of the interviewees mentioned any religious aspects in the regulation of work arrangements in Melbourne.

V. Reflections on the Results of the Two Studies

This brief coverage of the results of our empirical research project clearly demonstrates a spectrum of regulation affecting work arrangements in both locations, with some arrangements more strongly regulated by formal labour law and others by informal norms. There was no clear dividing line between the two; work arrangements in the middle of the spectrum showed the influence of both formal law and informal norms.

The study shows that the character of this regulatory pluralism can, however, be quite different. In Yogyakarta we found two strongly defined sources of regulation – state labour law and *kekeluargaan* norms – which were mixed to varying degrees in regulating particular work arrangements. These two sources of regulation, state law and *kekeluargaan*, were both affected by institutions of social identity. Meanwhile, in Melbourne we found evidence of recognisable informal labour norms but these seemed more disparate and less readily identified by interviewees than in Yogyakarta. In Melbourne, we did find evidence of regulatory effects of business clusters where norms had developed in particular spatially- or ethnicity-linked businesses. Again, institutions of social identity were also influencing both the effectiveness of formal law and the content of informal norms.

The differences in the character of regulatory pluralism found in the two studies may be explained by the different historical pathways through which contemporary conditions of plural labour regulation was reached.[38] While both countries have long had formal labour laws and standards, in Indonesia, with its comparatively weak rule of law compared to Australia,[39] state capacity for enforcement has been lower.[40] We argue, however, that it would be a mistake to see *kekeluargaan* in Indonesia as a pure remnant of pre-capitalist times. It would seem more likely that this bundle of norms has developed over time and has been affected by the evolution of the law itself and by larger societal and economic changes.

Our research results indicated that models of employment established by the labour law of each place also correlated with the informally regulated work arrangements among restaurants. In Indonesia, informally regulated workers were more likely to be permanent full-time workers which mirrors the dominant formal employment model. Although non-standard forms of employment, including fixed-term contracts and outsourcing, were permitted in certain circumstances and had been increasing in recent years,[41] this was not the norm in the restaurant sector. Almost all of the informally regulated workers interviewed in Yogyakarta reported that they were employed on a permanent and full-time basis. Meanwhile, in Australia, 'casual' work has become the norm in the hospitality sector, and this is true of workers who are both more formally or informally regulated with very similar patterns of shift scheduling. While this might lead to the observation that law is creating a shadow that reaches further than its actual enforcement, saying for sure which came first in both of these cases – formal labour law or informal norms – may be a 'chicken or egg' proposition. But what is clear is that there are links between formal and informal regulation and most likely the employment forms have developed in tandem in each place.

In both places, the interviews indicated, for those with informally regulated work arrangements, the entanglement of personal motivations and relationships with justifications for informality. However, the types of narratives and explanations of how interviewees saw their relationship with formal law were quite different. In Melbourne, many of the interviewees were students or on working holiday visas and thus often saw their work in restaurants as temporary. While some were blasé about the possibility of being caught breaking the law, others were clearly uneasy. Only a very small minority had clear motivations of avoiding tax or other state regulations, and most expressed rather more complicated

[38] BZ Tamanaha, 'The Rule of Law and Legal Pluralism in Development' in BZ Tamanaha, C Sage and M Woolcock (eds), *Legal Pluralism and Development: Scholars and Practitioners in Dialogue* (Cambridge, Cambridge University Press, 2012) 46.

[39] See, eg, the World Justice Project Rule of Law Index (https://worldjusticeproject.org) where in 2016, Australia was given an aggregate score of 0.81 while Indonesia scored 0.52.

[40] On labour standards enforcement in Indonesia see references above at n 30. On labour standards enforcement in Australia see T Hardy and J Howe, 'Partners in Enforcement? The New Balance Between Government and Trade Union Enforcement of Employment Standards in Australia' (2009) 23 *Australian Journal of Labour Law* 306.

[41] Landau et al, 'The Regulation of Non-Standard Forms of Employment in India, Indonesia and Vietnam', above n 32.

attitudes towards their employment status and towards informal regulation. In Yogyakarta, meanwhile, *kekeluargaan* norms were often described in terms of being a legitimate alternative to the formal law, which was often seen as only being relevant to large companies. In both places, many interviewees explained that they felt morally responsible towards their employer, and hence that they would base decisions on requests for overtime and giving notice to end employment on their own sense of personal integrity.

Researching the plural regulation of work in such different contexts, and particularly presenting evidence from a 'developing' and a 'developed' economy, supports the argument that regulatory pluralism is not an 'unfinished stage in development',[42] but rather 'pervades the globe'[43] and must be viewed as a reality. While the character of pluralism in labour regulation in different contexts may well be different, we can identify the importance of understanding both the nature of informal labour regulation and the interactions that occur between different regulatory sources. Further, and very importantly, it is clear that taking a regulatory approach to researching work leads to a much fuller picture of the conditions and protections of workers within any particular context compared to approaches which merely focus on the content and effectiveness of formal labour law.

VI. Plural Work Regulation and Promoting Worker Security and Well-being

This project has, as discussed above, demonstrated the importance of widening our view beyond traditional labour law analyses in order to gain a more accurate picture of how work arrangements are regulated and the outcomes of this for workers. Additionally, by empirically researching the question '*what is actually regulating work?*', this project may also have implications for the design and reform of regulatory systems aimed at promoting worker security and well-being. First, however, there are some clear difficulties with gaining the requisite empirical knowledge of informal work regulation, given all the social and context-specific complexities of informal regulations and the need to take account of the fluidity and multi-level nature of the regulatory spaces where they have influence.[44] Different forms of informal regulation can be compatible or contradictory with each other; some are imperative and others facilitative,[45] and as noted above in Section 2, have both 'ought' and 'is' constitutive elements. Informal norms are also not frozen in time and hybridisation or co-evolution can occur through the

[42] Tamanaha, 'The Rule of Law and Legal Pluralism in Development', above n 38, 46.

[43] GR Woodman, 'The Development "Problem" of Legal Pluralism' in BZ Tamanaha, C Sage and M Woolcock (eds), *Legal Pluralism and Development: Scholars and Practitioners in Dialogue* (Cambridge, Cambridge University Press, 2012).

[44] ibid, 135.

[45] ibid.

accumulation of choices that a range of regulatory actors make.[46] Definitively disentangling the effects of different forms of regulation is necessarily a very difficult task, and fully understanding the interactions between multiple forms of work regulation is even more daunting.

Given this reality, there is no doubt that this particular research project has only just begun to capture some of these complexities within the boundaries set for the research (geographical locations and the restaurant sector). It has not yet ventured into action research and obviously cannot alone form the basis of any technical interventions. Without aiming to produce any concrete policy recommendations for Indonesia or Australia here, given the limited nature of our empirical data, we nonetheless want to point to some possibilities for how this kind of empirical material, if comprehensively gathered, has the potential to be used. Inspiration for these possibilities are drawn from both the regulatory design, and the legal pluralism and development, sets of literature.

This research indicates that a starting point for any reform of work regulation should be an objective measure of the regulation and its relationship to worker well-being without automatically assuming that a greater or more limited reach of the state necessarily has particular consequences for workers.[47] For example, the *kekeluargaan* norms in Indonesia do appear to provide, at least in some cases, greater security of employment than some formal arrangements (especially fixed-term contracts and other forms of legal, but non-standard, employment). At the same time, we also need to avoid being overly romantic about informal regulation and its effects and to recognise where it has deleterious effects for workers, such as the norm of underpayment in Asian restaurants in Melbourne. In other words, the outcomes of different existing forms of regulation need to be empirically established and normatively evaluated.

Recent thinking has challenged the positivist assumptions inherent in 'command and control' styles of regulation and in traditional 'law and development' type interventions, such as the transplantation of off-the-shelf laws, by pointing out that ignoring legal or regulatory pluralism can lead to policy disasters.[48] Informal norms and institutions are often strongly embedded in social practice and are resilient to imposed change. While development practitioners might see informal regulation as backward, irrational and as perpetuating legal uncertainty, its users may have different attitudes. Conversely, informal regulation can also be seen as an opportunity – something to be engaged with constructively through well-targeted interventions.[49] Any solutions devised, it is clear, must

[46] K Meagher, 'Unlocking the Informal Economy: A Literature Review on Linkages between Formal and Informal Economies in Developing Countries' (WIEGO working paper No 27 2013) 19; F and K von Benda-Beckmann, 'The Dynamics of Change and Continuity in Plural Legal Orders' (2006) 53–54 *Journal of Legal Pluralism & Unofficial Law* 1.

[47] For the general argument that neither greater nor lesser reach of the state is necessarily better, see Guha-Khasnobis et al, *Linking the Formal and Informal Economy*, above n 2.

[48] ibid, 4–5; Sage and Woolcock, 'Legal Pluralism and Development Policy', above n 25, 2.

[49] Sage and Woolcock, 'Legal Pluralism and Development Policy', above n 25, 2.

respond on a case-by-case basis to the specific context and particular moment in time,[50] and will need to encompass 'the whole configuration of resources and relations within the regulatory space'.[51] We also need to understand which interest groups might be affected by any reform and are likely to support or oppose it,[52] and where an intervention may be counterproductive and it would be better to maintain the status quo.

After these foundational issues have been acknowledged, two sets of possibilities may arise. The first set of possibilities can aim to use knowledge of informal regulation, and its interactions with formal state regulation, to bolster the strength and effectiveness of the formal labour regulation system. The second set of possibilities is much more radical and would involve purposively de-centring labour regulation from the state – an approach which is unlikely to gain favour with labour rights activists or international bodies like the ILO which insist on 'formalising the informal',[53] but is nonetheless worth raising. We will discuss these sets of possibilities in turn.

In the first set of possibilities, the efficacy of state labour law could be strengthened through knowledge and use of informal regulation.[54] Such approaches would involve questioning to some extent positivist assumptions made about the instrumental effects on behaviour of formal law, but nonetheless the centrality of the state is maintained. To begin with, the state can produce law that replicates existing informal regulation. It could identify informal labour regulation that is beneficial to workers and formalise it as state labour law and hence make it enforceable via existing state legal institutions. For example, if it were to be decided as a matter of policy that the distribution of tips in restaurants in part of, or all of, Australia needed to be formalised, a new law could be based on selected pre-existing informal norms. Such a new law would have a higher likelihood of being effective as it would reflect pre-existing regulation, and by implication would make more aspects of work formally regulated and hence formally protected. However, a potential drawback of legislating in this way would be to risk making the informal regulation more rigid and uniform and hence reducing any positive aspects of flexibility and context specific responsiveness that the informal regulation may have, as occurred during many colonial regimes when they codified 'customary law' to make it more legible to the state.[55]

[50] I Ayres and J Braithwaite, *Responsive Regulation: Transcending the Deregulation Debate* (Oxford, Oxford University Press, 1992) 5.

[51] Scott, 'Analysing Regulatory Space' above n 5, 331.

[52] Woodman, 'The Development "Problem" of Legal Pluralism', above n 43.

[53] ILO, *The Informal Economy and Decent Work*, above n 21.

[54] See S Marshall, 'Revitalising Labour Market Regulation for the Economic South: New Forms and Tools' in S Marshall and C Fenwick (eds), *Labour Regulation and Development: Socio-Legal Perspectives* (ILO and Edward Elgar, 2016) 308.

[55] Woodman, above n 43, 138; P Burns, *The Leiden Legacy: Concepts of Law in Indonesia* (Leiden, KITLV, 2004); M Chanock, *Law, Custom and Social Order: The Colonial Experience in Malawi and Zambia* (Cambridge, Cambridge University Press, 1985).

It is also possible for the state to acknowledge the existence of informal regulation without necessarily giving it formal legal status.[56] Acknowledgement can take the form of a specific prohibition on detrimental forms of informal regulation and targeted enforcement strategies designed to eradicate it. Similarly, the state can identify actors who have negative regulatory influence and seek to curb their power. Or, the state could positively encourage any informal regulation which supports or complements formal labour law, without formalising it. In Yogyakarta, for instance, the common practice of business owners or managers providing interest free loans to workers (*kasbon*) operates as a form of social security alongside formal requirements, and it could be encouraged via government discourse.

Empirical knowledge of, and acknowledgement of, informal labour regulation, and particularly its interactions with formal labour law, could also allow the design of more effective enforcement strategies. For example, strongly entrenched informal labour regulation could be made a primary target for eradication through focusing on particular labour law enforcement activities, or perhaps even the opposite could occur where weaker informal regulation is targeted first in the hope that this will make it easier to gain purchase against the stronger informal regulation. In other scenarios, understanding which formal labour laws have the most power in otherwise informally regulated work arrangements, might allow enforcement efforts to initially focus on strengthening the effectiveness of those norms, as a form of spearheading strategy, while planning to follow with the enforcement of other formal legal norms at a later date. For example, our evidence showed that the eight-hour working day and minimum wages had far greater purchase than other formal labour requirements in Yogyakarta, and hence enforcement efforts could concentrate on pushing these regulations even further into otherwise informally regulated work arrangements.

The state can also temporarily acknowledge informal regulation through the creation of what Adler et al have called 'interim institutions'.[57] They define these as hybrid, process-based institutions that are based in local knowledge and political realities while simultaneously aimed at promoting rule-based principles and equitable relationships of power.[58] The labour relations example that they provided was that of the Arbitration Council in Cambodia which was a hybrid rule-of-law and social dialogue institution – its existence was mandated by law but rather than producing enforceable outcomes, it was more geared to negotiated solutions to labour disputes.[59] Adler et al saw this as a pragmatic interim step that

[56] W Twining, 'Legal Pluralism 101' in BZ Tamanaha, C Sage and M Woolcock (eds), *Legal Pluralism and Development: Scholars and Practitioners in Dialogue* (Cambridge, Cambridge University Press, 2012) 119.

[57] D Adler, C Sage and M Woolcock, 'Interim Institutions and the Development Process: Opening Spaces for Reform in Cambodia and Indonesia' (Brooks World Poverty Institute Working Paper 86, 2009).

[58] ibid, 2, 4.

[59] ibid, 4–9. Other proposals for alternative social dialogue and arbitration institutions that make use of non-traditional industrial relations actors have also been made: see Marshall, 'Revitalising Labour Market Regulation for the Economic South', above n 54, 310–11.

acknowledged the present power of informal actors and regulation but with the aim of eventually evolving into a more formalised and enforceable system.

The second set of possibilities involves deliberately de-centring labour regulation from the authority of the state to some extent. The idea of deliberately de-centring state power, is of course, quite radical in general, but particularly so in labour regulation. The state has long been seen as providing the only possible corrective to the inequalities of the market and as the sole legitimate provider of minimum standards of protection for workers. While the state may be willing to allow bargaining, as a form of self- or meta- regulation, this usually may only occur above these minimum standards. To stray too far from this ideal would perhaps risk 'creating a neo-liberal normative agenda which is sceptical of the capacity of the state to steer market actors',[60] weakening hard-won labour rights and institutions[61] or producing fragmentation and deference to what could be seen as illegitimate norms.[62] However, research shows that state 'command and control' systems have important limitations, and more creative regulatory solutions are possible and have been shown to have promising outcomes in some circumstances.[63] This is not to advocate for 'deregulation' as such, as this term implies that it is possible to create a regulatory vacuum, which this research indicates is impossible. It is only possible to shift the balance between different forms of regulation – to decrease state regulatory power is to give greater space to informal regulation, and vice versa.

In certain circumstances it might be desirable to permit informal regulation to inhabit certain regulatory spaces – where the informal regulation is beneficial and perhaps has qualities that cannot be replicated through state law. In such situations, a state could recognise informal regulation and allow it to have force in certain defined spaces. This could mean, for example, permitting informal regulation to apply in businesses of a certain size or in a certain sector or location, or to a certain aspect of a work arrangement, without providing any recourse to state dispute resolution mechanisms. In countries such as India, this occurs by default, where formal labour law is deliberately limited to coverage of certain sectors of the

[60] Scott, above n 5, 352.

[61] J Murray, 'The Sound of One Hand Clapping? The "Ratcheting Labour Standards" Proposal and International Labour Law' (2001) 14 *Australian Journal of Labour Law* 1, 19. See also discussion in Howe, 'A Different World: The Regulatory Project in Labour Law', above n 4, 76–79.

[62] PS Berman, 'Non-State Lawmaking Through the Lens of Global Legal Pluralism' in MA Helfand (ed), *Negotiating State and Non-State Law: The Challenge of Global and Local Legal Pluralism* (Cambridge, Cambridge University Press, 2015) 16; H Arthurs, 'Corporate Self-Regulation: Political Economy, State Regulation and Reflexive Labour Law' in B Bercusson and C Estlund (eds), *Regulating Labour in the Wake of Globalisation: New Challenges, New Institutions* (Oxford, Hart Publishing, 2007) 33.

[63] See, eg, N Gunningham, P Grabovsky and D Sinclair, *Smart Regulation: Designing Environmental Policy* (Oxford, Clarendon Press, 1998); N Gunningham, 'Enforcement and Compliance Strategies' in R Baldwin, M Cave and M Lodge (eds), *The Oxford Handbook of Regulation* (Oxford, Oxford University Press, 2010); C Coglianese and E Mendelson, 'Meta-Regulation and Self-Regulation' in R Baldwin, M Cave and M Lodge (eds), *The Oxford Handbook of Regulation* (Oxford, Oxford University Press, 2010); K Kolben, 'Integrative Linkage: Combining Public and Private Regulatory Approaches in the Design of Trade and Labor Regimes' (2007) 48 *Harvard International Law Journal* 203.

economy or size of enterprise, but there the state does not determine what should operate instead.[64] Rather, what is being canvassed here is taking such a step only if the relevant informal regulation has desired beneficial outcomes for workers. Such an approach might be characterised as a form of meta-regulation,[65] where the state actively encourages self-regulatory solutions in particular spaces or creates state–private regulatory partnerships.[66]

Beyond this, there are more creative possibilities for working within the spaces of interaction between regulatory orders. Berman advocated that 'we might deliberately seek to create or preserve spaces for productive interaction among multiple, overlapping legal systems by developing procedural mechanisms, institutions, and practices that aim to manage, without eliminating, the legal pluralism we see around us'.[67] Such an approach, he argued, is more likely to draw people together in a common space than will asserting universalist laws. Although writing about global legal pluralism, Berman's ideas may also apply at the local regulatory level. This could involve identifying and empowering private regulatory actors who are able to 'navigate the interaction of normative systems and [use] those systems strategically'.[68] It could also imply the creation of novel 'procedures, institutions and discursive practices' that seek to manage rather than to eliminate regulatory pluralism.[69] Thus Berman's ideas for creating permanent mechanisms and institutions are different to the approach advocated by Adler et al (see discussion above), who saw moderating institutions as being only a temporary, interim step towards promoting the rule of law.

This survey of possibilities is, of course, merely that – possibilities. We are not necessarily advocating for all or indeed any of them in our research context of Yogyakarta and Melbourne or elsewhere. They are also posed here in unavoidably vague terms given that any regulatory design must be based in a specific context and be underpinned by robust empirical evidence of plural labour regulation. Action research would also be needed to test the efficacy of any proposed regulatory solutions.

VII. Conclusions

In terms of this book's theme of 're-imagining labour law for development', our research evidence suggests the need to re-imagine labour law in terms of a

[64] Mitchell et al, 'The Evolution of Labour Law in India', above n 24.
[65] Coglianese and Mendelson, 'Meta-Regulation and Self-Regulation', above n 63.
[66] Marshall, 'Revitalising Labour Market Regulation for the Economic South, above n 54, 309.
[67] PS Berman, *Global Legal Pluralism: A Jurisprudence of Law Beyond Borders* (Cambridge, Cambridge University Press, 2012) 10.
[68] Berman, 'Non-State Lawmaking Through the Lens of Global Legal Pluralism', above n 62, 18.
[69] Berman, *Global Legal Pluralism*, above n 67.

regulatory approach. We need to be far less fixated on formal labour law and its definitional scope and effectiveness, and rather shift our attention to the webs of plural and intersecting regulation that can simultaneously affect any one individual work arrangement and larger regulatory spaces. Using a regulatory approach in order to research work arrangements empirically allows us to produce a picture of worker protection and conditions that is much closer to reality than can be obtained through a vision of labour law orthodoxy. We have demonstrated here that work arrangements in restaurants in both developed and developing states are deeply affected by informal regulation of varying types, even if the exact character of the informal regulation is different. In our study sites of Yogyakarta and Melbourne, we found clear evidence of a spectrum of work arrangements in each place. In Yogyakarta, the spectrum was constructed by a strong dual pattern of regulatory sources, while in Melbourne, the informal regulatory sources were comparatively more disparate. In each place, informal regulation and the degree to which it interacted with formal labour law was key to explaining workers' real conditions and degree of security.

The kind of empirical evidence collected in this research project, we argue, gives rise to a number of possibilities for regulatory reform which do not exist if our vision is restricted to formal labour law. These possibilities fall into two general categories: first, using informal regulation to bolster the effectiveness of state labour law and, second and more radically, de-centring labour regulation from the authority of the state in order to permit and even encourage informal regulation in certain circumstances. Neither of these two sets of regulatory possibilities provide easy solutions to promoting worker well-being and development, and they certainly would require a much stronger empirical basis than that gained through these two initial studies in Yogyakarta and Melbourne. The consequences of attempting such creative regulatory interventions are still yet to be researched. Nonetheless, asking and comprehensively researching the question '*what is actually regulating work?*' brings these possibilities firmly into view.

10

Labour Laws, Informality, and Development: Comparing India and China

SIMON DEAKIN, SHELLEY MARSHALL AND SANJAY PINTO*

I. Introduction

With 1.37 billion and 1.25 billion people, respectively, China and India together account for 36 per cent of the world's population. Because their populations are younger than the global average, they comprise an even larger share of global employment, nearly 40 per cent.[1] No discussion of the nature of work across the world should take place without addressing the development trajectories of these two countries, including important differences in how their labour markets have evolved. One marked difference concerns their experience of informal labour. Informal work is widespread in India, and while formal employment has increased recently, this is only to a very small extent. In China, however, a variant of the standard employment contract, in which a number of social protections are attached to the status of wage labour, appears to be emerging. We discuss reasons for the divergence between the Indian and Chinese cases, and consider the relationship between formality and developmental outcomes in the two countries.

To assess the prevalence of labour informality and its significance for the global economy it is first necessary to disentangle some of its possible meanings from the multiple usages of the term in labour statistics. As we see in section II, the definitions used by international agencies are not uniform, and different countries have distinct approaches. Definitions have also evolved according to underlying

* Respectively University of Cambridge (s.deakin@cbr.cam.ac.uk), RMIT University (shelley.marshall@rmit.edu.au) and Cornell and Rutgers Universities (sanjaypinto@gmail.com). We are grateful for funding from the DFID-ESRC Joint Fund for Poverty Alleviation (Project ES/J01942/1, 'Labour Law and Poverty Alleviation in Low- and Middle-Income Countries').

[1] ILO, *Statistical Update on Employment in the Informal Economy* (Geneva, ILO, 2012).

theories of the law–development nexus. The idea that informal labour represents a residue of the subsistence economy which will be displaced by industrialisation has given way to a view of informality as a feature of contemporary trends towards casualised and precarious work. In the process, the definition of informal labour has been expanded, but may also have lost some of its coherence.

It is also important to understand the formalisation and informalisation of work as historical processes. There is a trend towards employment and away from own-account work and self-employment in many regions of the world, particularly in East Asia where the proportion of the labour force in waged employment has doubled over the past three decades. However, the transition to wage labour does not necessarily bring with it access to labour law protection. Employment is on a spectrum of formality and security. This is the context within which a debate has developed over the multi-dimensional nature of informality. Thus the question of informality needs to be seen in the context of long-run capitalist dynamics. In section III we set out a 'systemic' conception of labour law that sees labour market regulation as co-evolving with the emergence and stabilisation of labour markets and, more generally, of capitalist work relations. Here we build on previous work in which we have interrogated the relationship between socioeconomic development and the development of labour markets in other countries. In this work we found that the long-term trend towards more formal labour markets in the global North was the consequence not just of industrialisation, but of the emergence of state capacity underpinning labour market institutions, including those shaping social insurance and collective bargaining. Can the same be said today of the two largest workforces in the world? Section IV looks more closely at the co-evolution of labour market regulation and labour markets in India and China, after which we go on to examine the extent and nature of formalisation and informalisation in each country in section V. In section VI we conclude by examining some of the implications of the steady growth of formal work in China, in contrast to the much slower formalisation of Indian labour markets.

II. Defining Informality

There is no single, generally accepted definition of informal work. Various definitions inform the collection of data, which in turn informs what we know and do not know about the extent of informal work and its various dimensions. These definitions are informed by theories of economic development, if only implicitly.

The term 'informal' or 'informality' gained intellectual purchase thanks to Keith Hart's work in Ghana in the early 1970s and to the International Labour Organization's (ILO's) subsequent interest in the issue. Hart argued that the masses who were surplus to requirements for wage labour in African cities were not 'unemployed', but rather were working in ways not captured by standard categories, even if often for erratic and low returns.[2] Later, Hart expressed discomfort at the term's widespread uptake in the absence of greater precision in its use and clarity around its intellectual origins.[3] For Hart, the 'informal economy does not exist in any empirical sense: it is a way of contrasting some phenomena with what we imagine constitutes the orthodox core of our economy'.[4] The dualism of the definition, for Hart, begs reflection on the orthodoxy of our assumptions about what makes up the core.

Perhaps due to the legacy of modernist conceptions of the 'economy' which privilege oppositions between developed and undeveloped, market and non-market, such reflection has not been at the heart of scholarly or policy work in the field of informality. This modernist legacy is one of the reasons it has been possible to think about informal work as an anomaly destined for extinction via the transformative and universalising effects of socioeconomic development. There is a growing recognition that the economy, markets and, indeed, capitalism, can take multiple forms both between countries and within countries and that these differences are not anomalies but instead are grounded in cultural and institutional histories.[5] Yet because these insights are difficult to translate into policy strategies, they have not consistently found their way into development programmes and regulatory discourses. As we shall see, the different institutional histories of India and China have resulted in vastly contrasting patterns of employment and informality both between the countries and between sectors and geographical spaces within each country. The complexity of these patterns challenges conventional ideas about the nature of informality.

In 1993, participants in the 15th International Conference of Labour Statisticians (ICLS) marked an historic turning point by agreeing that informal workers should be counted in labour force surveys to improve analyses on the modern global economy.[6] An internationally consistent, operational definition of the informal economy was viewed as a first step toward collecting and analysing data on the subject. ICLS participants drafted a definition that was

[2] K Hart, 'Informal Income Opportunities and Informal Employment in Ghana' (1973) 11 *Journal of Modern African Studies* 61.

[3] K Hart, 'Informal Economy' in J Eatwell, M Milgate and P Newman (eds), *The New Palgrave: A Dictionary of Economics* 1st edn (London, Palgrave-Macmillan, 1987), http://www.dictionaryofeconomics.com/article?id=pde1987_X001135.

[4] ibid.

[5] P Hall and D Soskice (eds), *Varieties of Capitalism: The Institutional Foundations of Comparative Advantage* (Oxford, Oxford University Press, 2001); C Crouch, *Capitalist Diversity and Change: Recombinant Governance and Institutional Entrepreneurs* (Oxford, Oxford University Press, 2005).

[6] ICLS, *Report III: Statistics of Employment in the Informal Sector – Fifteenth International Conference of Labour Statisticians* (Geneva, ILO, 1993).

subsequently incorporated into the 1993 System of National Accounts. According to Ralf Hussmanns of the Bureau of Statistics at the ILO, in order to obtain an internationally agreed definition of the informal sector which was acceptable to labour statisticians as well as national accountants, the informal sector had to be defined in terms of characteristics of the production units (enterprises) in which the activities take place (the 'enterprise approach'), rather than in terms of the characteristics of the persons involved or of their jobs (the 'labour' approach).[7]

As a result, the ICLS defined the informal economy in terms of the structure of firms rather than by reference to the characteristics of workers. The definition focused on enterprises that had a low level of organisation, little or no division between capital and labour as factors of production, and labour relations underwritten by informal social relationships rather than formal contracts. Under this definition, the informal economy comprised only unregistered or unincorporated enterprises owned by households that produce goods and services to generate employment. The first statistical definition, then, was enterprise-based.

By the end of the 1990s, the 1993 ICLS definition was being criticised for the failure to include the growing group of informal workers operating in formal enterprises, as well as workers who move back and forth between, or work simultaneously in, informal and formal employment. Furthermore, the ICLS definition excluded the vast numbers of (often women) workers who are especially dependent on informal social networks, because they worked alone at home or in multiple locations (as in the case of street vendors); these workers were excluded from the definition because their workplaces were not counted as 'enterprises'.[8]

Thanks to the work of Ralf Hussmanns[9] along with many others, in 2003 the 17th ICLS adopted guidelines for measuring informal employment that attempted to address these criticisms (see Table 1). The ICLS concluded that 'employment in the informal sector' (based on the enterprise as unit of observation) and 'informal employment' (based on jobs as units of observation) were distinct concepts referring to different aspects of the 'informalisation' of employment and to different targets for policy making.[10] Both concepts needed to be defined and measured in a coherent and consistent manner, so that one could be clearly distinguished from the other.

[7] R Hussmanns, 'Measuring the Informal Economy: From Employment in the Informal Sector to Informal Employment', Working Paper No. 53, Policy Integration Department, Bureau of Statistics (Geneva, ILO, 2004).

[8] R Agarwala, 'The Economic Sociology of Informal Work: The Case of India' in N Bandelj (ed), *Economic Sociology of Work* (Bingley, Emerald, 2009).

[9] Hussmanns, 'Measuring the Informal Economy', above n 7.

[10] ICLS, *Seventeenth International Conference of Labour Statisticians* (Geneva, ILO, 2003).

Table 10.1 17th ICLS Guidelines for Measuring Informal Employment (2003)

(a)	own-account workers and employers employed in their own informal enterprises;
(b)	members of informal producers' co-operatives (not established as legal entities), if any;
(c)	own-account workers producing goods exclusively for own final use by their household (if considered employed given that the production comprises an important contribution to the total household consumption and is included in the national definition of employment);
(d)	contributing family workers in formal or informal enterprises; and
(e)	employees holding informal jobs in formal enterprises, informal enterprises, or as paid domestic workers employed by households. In line with the international definition, countries for which data are shown, define employees holding informal jobs as employees not covered by social security as employed persons, or as employees not entitled to other employment benefits.

The 2003 ICLS definition of informal work focuses on the 'nature of employment' in addition to the characteristics of enterprises and includes informal employment both within and outside agriculture.[11] It has played a crucial role in increasing the visibility of informal work in the statistical and policy platforms of the ILO and other multilateral organisations, and has been implemented in statistical analysis in many countries around the world.

Although the 2003 ICLS definition deals with a number of earlier criticisms of the 1993 definition, it continues to suffer from a number of flaws. First, it has not fully overcome the previous, dichotomous approach to informal work. It still represents informal work as an irregular phenomenon, rather than one which is shaped by institutions and social relations and which is the norm in many countries. Second, the definition does not recognise the structural interdependencies that link informal and formal economies. Third, the definition's utility is largely limited to aggregate-level statistical analysis. Deeper study is required to discover more about the nature of the work being conducted and other important work-related characteristics of economic relationships. Finally, the ICLS definition of informality and the broader conceptual framework in which it is embedded tell us nothing about the capacity of workers to demand access to legal entitlements or to organise collectively. For this reason, Dae-Oup Chang has argued for a system of classification that recognises the importance of workers' capacity to enjoy their legal entitlements as a determinant of formality. His point is that the capacity to be engaged in and enjoy the rights that are attached to the standard form of employment is based on power.[12] Thus, enacting new labour regulations or making work

[11] M Chen, *Rethinking the Informal Economy: Linkages with the Formal Economy and the Formal Regulatory Environment* (New York, United Nations Department of Economic and Social Affairs, 2007) 2.

[12] D-O Chang, 'Informalising Labour in China's Global Factory' (2009) 39 *Journal of Contemporary Asia* 161.

relations more 'formal' by expanding legal definitions will not improve the lot of workers if they have no powers of enforcement. Chang's definition is set out in Table 2.

Table 10.2 Chang's Pathways to Informality

A. Labour in the Informal Sector
Informal self-employed (street vendors, home workers, teleworkers, garbage pickers, shoe shiners, non-self-subsistence small-scale farmers, artisans), informal employees (family business workers, domestic workers, landless agricultural workers), migrant workers[13]
B. Increasing Informal Labour of the Formal Sector: Atypical Labour Not Protected by the Regulatory Framework
Contracted workers (including daily workers), agency or dispatched workers, task-based casual workers, formal self-employed, disguised formal self-employed, migrant workers
C. De Facto Informal Labour: Formal Workers in Informalising (or Informalised) Formal Economy, Workers Who Have No Power to Enjoy the Legal and Institutional Regulation and Standards to which They Are Entitled
Contracted workers, agency workers, part-timers, migrant workers, workers in export processing zones (EPZ), workers in developing countries with no or few democratic trade unions

Source: D-O Chang, 'Informalising Labour in China's Global Factory' (2009) 39 *Journal of Contemporary Asia* 161.

This definition has the merit of recognising that some types of informal work are less visible or less easy to identify than others. Labour in the informal sector (Category A) is most visible. This is why workers in this sector were the focus of early literature on informality and of statistical definitions. However, informal labour in the informalising formal sector (Category C) is less readily visible as it exists *within* the existing regulatory framework. The informal sector is larger and more obvious in less developed countries, but non-standard or precarious work within the formal sector is relatively more common in developed countries, and would be classified as informal under Chang's definition (Category B). De facto informal labour, as described by Chang (Category C), is prevalent both in developing and developed countries.

Contract workers, agency workers and part-timers come under what Chang classifies as de facto informal workers (Category C). Many of these workers are, in principle, covered by the relevant regulatory framework in their country, but

[13] The appearance of migrant workers three times in Chang's framework may either demonstrate the lack of precision of the categories or the strong correlation of migrant worker status and precariousness of different types.

the exploitative nature of their employment and, in some sectors, high levels of mobility, effectively exclude them from protection. Even where they are protected by laws on labour standards, those workers face numerous de facto barriers to organising. The largest population in this informalising formal economy is found in developing countries where even workers with formal employee status often lack solidarity-based forms of protection for job security. Migrant workers in the formal sector are frequently in a similar situation when they fail to attract the protection of unions and therefore cannot in practice assert the labour rights that are, in principle, recognised by law. This points to the crucial impact of the interaction of employment law and immigration law.

Many workers with non-standard or atypical employment relations and workers who have little power to demand the protections to which they are entitled (Chang's Category B and C) continue to be overlooked by existing studies of the extent of informal labour. This has implications for their policy visibility. Such workers instead tend to be called 'precarious'. Whether it is useful for precarious work to be classified as 'informal' is a particularly pressing issue in the Chinese and Indian cases and one we return to below (see section V).

Definitions of informality are essential if the extent of informal work is to be properly mapped and policy debates effectively informed, but there is a risk of definitions presenting an overly static picture of the nature of informal work. Ideas about the nature of work have developed in a dynamic fashion, as a response to industrialisation, while also shaping it, as we shall now explore.

III. Formalisation and Informalisation in Historical Perspective

Rather than simply defining the nature of work in abstract terms, it may be productive to study how forms of work have been shaped by laws, institutions and social relations. Work may be characterised as informal in the sense that the worker performing it does not enjoy the rights and protections of labour laws, while still being shaped indirectly by those laws and by other formal and informal institutions. Informal work does not sit outside of laws, institutions and social relations, but is embedded within social relations as well as being a response to the way in which formal work is defined and constituted. Both formal and informal work have developed over time, responding to a range of economic and non-economic factors.

The way in which work relations are constituted is, in the final analysis, a consequence of long run capitalist dynamics. The process of industrialisation which began in the global North in the early modern period and is having a transformative impact on parts of the global South today, in particular China, takes many varied forms, but also has common features which include the commodification of labour power and the related institutionalisation of wage labour as the 'normal' form of employment.[14] A 'systemic' conception of the relationship between labour market regulation and labour markets and capitalist work relations can be helpful for understanding the relationship between informal work and labour market regulation.

A 'systemic' conception of labour law sees labour market regulation as co-evolving with the emergence and stabilisation of labour markets and, more generally, of capitalist work relations. According to the systemic approach, labour law rules are seen as evolved or emergent solutions to co-ordination problems in particular market contexts.[15] These solutions are based on distributional compromises which are often contingent in nature; the arrangements they embody are not necessarily optimal and may not be particularly stable.[16] However, they are capable of contributing to economic growth and to development more generally in a number of ways.

In the European context, legal and economic systems have co-evolved, developing in parallel with each other in particular national or regional contexts. Thus, the core institutions of labour law – the individual employment relationship, collective bargaining and social insurance – have evolved in parallel with the emergence of labour markets in market economies.[17] Labour law institutions serve certain ends which are specific to societies in which labour markets are established – that is to say, societies in which a significant proportion of the adult population is engaged in waged or salaried labour of some kind.

Historical research has shown that the process of constituting the labour market in Western Europe required the active deployment of the legal and fiscal arms of the state.[18] The state's involvement in shaping market relations during this period was, in many contexts, coercive and even punitive, but legislation played a role in mitigating risks associated with the transition to the market from an early stage, and thereby contributed to industrialisation rather than simply responding to it.

For example, late sixteenth-century England already had in place a nationwide system of poor relief, administered locally but governed by a unified legislative framework, through which taxes were levied on households according to the value of their property in land and related assets. In the eighteenth century the term 'poor' was already being applied to the wage dependent ('those who labour to live,

[14] S Deakin and F Wilkinson, *The Law of the Labour Market: Industrialization, Employment, and Legal Evolution* (Oxford, Oxford University Press, 2005).

[15] A Hyde, 'What is Labour Law?' in G Davidov and B Langille (eds), *Boundaries and Frontiers of Labour Law: Goals and Means in the Regulation of Work* (Oxford, Hart Publishing, 2006); S Deakin and P Sarkar, 'Assessing the Long-Run Economic Impact of Labour Law Systems: A Theoretical Reappraisal and Analysis of New Time Series Data' (2008) 39 *Industrial Relations Journal* 453.

[16] M Khan, 'State Failure in Weak States: A Critique of New Institutionalist Explanations' in J Harriss, J Hunter, and C Lewis (eds), *The New Institutionalist Economics and Third World Development* (London, Routledge, 1995).

[17] Deakin and Wilkinson, *The Law of the Labour Market*, above n 14.

[18] ibid.

and such as are old and decrepit, unable to work, poor widows, and fatherless children, and tenants driven to poverty').[19] Anticipating the logic of the twentieth-century welfare state, the lawyers and jurists who administered the pre-industrial poor law regarded poverty as a condition engendered 'not by riot, expense and carelessness, but by mischance'.[20] Expenditure on poor relief in England during the period of industrial transition was seven times the amount spent in other Western European countries such as France, and doubled as a percentage of GDP in the course of the century to 1800.[21] Although the overall amount of national income spent on poor relief was low compared to modern-day levels of expenditure on the welfare state, replacement rates for unemployment benefits in some regions were comparable to those operating in Britain in the 1980s.[22] Thus the historical evidence points to the conclusion that the

> creation and elaboration of the poor law system from the reign of Elizabeth onwards was an important reason for the development of a capitalist system in England, affording the kind of protection for those in need which gave individuals a degree of protection against the hazards of life that in typical peasant cultures was provided by kin.[23]

Contrary to the neoclassical economic argument that social protection will only serve as a disincentive to employment,[24] economic historians recognised that the poor law helped to support the move to a market economy by offsetting the effects on workers and households of loss of access to the land. It paved the way for capitalism and the industrialisation of work with the associated separation of labour and capital.

The development of a welfare or 'social' state was of course far from continuous in most of the early industrialising nations. The demise in England of the 'old poor law' under the pressures of industrialisation in the final decades of the eighteenth century eventually ushered in the disciplinary regime of the workhouse, which was designed to make the receipt of poor relief as demeaning as possible and to avoid the subsidisation of wages. The expectation of the Poor Law Amendment Act 1834[25] was that once this strict regime was in place, wages would 'naturally' rise to a subsistence level. When this failed to happen, and when real wages instead began to fall during the 'great depression' between 1873 and 1896,

[19] M Dalton, *The Country Justice: Containing the Practice, Duty and Power of the Justices of the Peace, as Well in as Out of their Sessions* (London, Lintot, 1747).

[20] ibid. See generally Deakin and Wilkinson, above n 14, ch 3.

[21] P Solar, 'Poor Relief and English Economic Development before the Industrial Revolution' (1995) 42 *Economic History Review (NS)* 1.

[22] K Snell and J Millar, 'Lone Parent Families and the Welfare State: Past and Present' (1987) 2 *Continuity and Change* 387.

[23] EA Wrigley, *Continuity, Chance and Change: The Character of the Industrial Revolution in England* (Cambridge, Cambridge University Press, 1988) 120.

[24] P Fallon and R Lucas, 'The Impact of Changes in Job Security Legislation in India and Zimbabwe' (1993) 5 *World Bank Economic Review* 395.

[25] 4 & 5 Will 4, c 76.

the initial response of policy makers was to make the workhouse regime even more punitive. The expensive failure of 'test workhouses' convinced reformers at the turn of the century that an alternative was needed. Sidney and Beatrice Webb and William Beveridge were among those who made the argument for a combination of social insurance and collective bargaining to put in place a floor to terms and conditions of employment.[26] It was these reforms which reversed the trend towards casual (or 'informal') work at extremely low rates of pay which had become the norm in major cities and industrial centres in Britain at the end of the nineteenth century, a pattern which was repeated across the industrialised countries of Europe and North America at this time.

The emergence of the 'standard employment relationship' (SER) as the focal point of labour law regulation in the early decades of the twentieth century was the result, in part, of employer strategies which at that point favoured the vertical integration of production; but it was also the consequence of the rise of collective bargaining and of the passage of social legislation in the areas of workmen's compensation and insurance against unemployment.[27] The SER was a compromise in which 'subordination' within the workplace was the condition of access to protection against labour market risks.[28]

In the global North, as new forms of work proliferate, the association of the SER with full-time, 'permanent' or indeterminate work, and a predominantly male-orientated breadwinner wage, has put a question mark over its future. Factory production has declined and precarious employment has increased across the economies of the global North since the 1970s.[29] Still, the prevalence of labour law across market economies may suggest that it has a functional relationship of some kind to emergence of capitalism and also to the embedding of democratic political institutions, although the fit is not exact. We argue, therefore, that the relationship between the emergence of industrialised capitalism and labour market regulation is one that demands investigation.

For instance, there is a long tradition of labour law regulation in Latin America, which saw the emergence of mature forms of collective bargaining and social insurance in the middle decades of the twentieth century. These arrangements were put into question in the period of neoliberal policy ascendancy which began in the 1970s, but from the 1990s there was a switch in policy back to support for

[26] S Webb and B Webb, *The Public Organisation of the Labour Market: Being Part Two of the Minority Report of the Poor Law Commission* (London, Longmans, Green & Co, 1909); W Beveridge, *Unemployment: A Problem of Industry* (London, Longmans, Green & Co, 1909).

[27] Deakin and Wilkinson, above n 14.

[28] A Supiot, 'Introduction' in A Supiot (ed), *Au delà de l'emploi. Transformations du travail et devenir du droit du travail en Europe* (Paris, Flammarion, 1999) 10.

[29] G Standing, *The Precariat: The New Dangerous Class* (London, Bloomsbury, 2011); K Stone and H Arthurs, 'The Transformation of Employment Régimes: A Worldwide Challenge' in K Stone and H Arthurs (eds), *Rethinking Workplace Regulation: Beyond the Standard Contract of Employment* (New York, Russell Sage Foundation, 2013).

collective bargaining and solidaristic forms of social security, which reversed the previous trend towards informality.[30]

Although there is wide variation across different countries and regions, reforms aimed at building institutions to mitigate labour market risks are a feature of many fast-growing economies across the global South. As a result of factors including institutional reform and labour-intensive economic growth, East Asia has seen the largest rise in waged employment and corresponding decline in own-account work and similar types of informal work relationships over the past 20 years.[31]

The prevalence of labour law as a type of regulation found in virtually all market economies strongly suggests that it has a relationship of some kind to the emergence of capitalism and also to the embedding of democratic political institutions. In many cases, the fit is not exact and labour law has not co-evolved with industrial forms, but rather has been transplanted with colonisation. In the next section, we look at the evolution of labour law in China and India to attempt to better understand the way it has developed in India after independence and in China since 1979 with the fostering of managed markets.

IV. The Evolution of Labour Market Regulation in India and China

A. The Evolution of Labour Market Regulation in India

In India, the low percentage of workers covered by labour laws today has roots in colonial law making. The restricted coverage of labour laws flowed in part from the colonial deployment of labour laws to secure a limited supply of labour, and partly due to the post-colonial association of labour with *industry*. In the early years of colonisation the British authorities adopted versions of the English Masters and Servants Acts aimed toward securing labour supply and discipline and very much not toward the protection of workers' interests.[32] From about the 1880s onwards, the colonial government began to introduce legislation similar to the protective Factories Acts then operating in the United Kingdom. This legislation, which included the Factories Acts of 1881, 1891, and 1911, was designed

[30] L Fraile, 'Lessons from Latin America's Neoliberal Experiment: An Overview of Labour and Social Policies since the 1980s' (2009) 148 *International Labour Review* 215.

[31] ILO, *World Employment and Social Outlook: The Changing Nature of Jobs* (Geneva, ILO, 2015) ch 1.

[32] E Noronha, 'Bombay Dock Labour Board, 1948–1994: From Insecurity to Security to Insecurity?' (2001) 36 *Economic and Political Weekly* 4851; P Mohapatra, 'Regulated Informality: Legal Constructions of Labour Relations in Colonial India, 1814–1926' in J Lucassen and S Bhattacharya (eds), *Workers in the Informal Sector: Studies in Labour History 1800–2000* (New Delhi, Macmillan India, 2005).

to regulate working hours and conditions, holidays, safety, and so on, and had a particular focus on the welfare of women and children.[33]

In the 1920s, the emergence of a strong nationalist movement, the development of a powerful trade union movement with the formation of the All India Trade Union Congress in 1920, and the spread of Communist influence in the labour movement following the Bolshevik Revolution in Russia in 1917 placed pressure on the government to further elaborate the labour law regime. The formation of the ILO also had some influence. A volume of new protective legislation, including laws pertaining to hours of work, rest periods, female and child labour protections, and health and safety provisions was enacted. This period of international influence in the 1920s also gave rise to the first industrial relations legislation in India. The Trade Unions Act of 1926 provided for the registration of trade unions, although registration was not made compulsory. Registration provided unions with legal status and some protections against civil and criminal liability in the course of an industrial dispute. This Act was followed by the introduction of the Trade Disputes Act of 1929, which provided for the compulsory reference of industrial disputes to a Conciliation Board or Court of Inquiry, and tightly regulated the right to strike.

Later revisions to labour law purposefully restricted the scope of protection. The Royal Commission on Labour (known as the Whitley Commission), for example, appointed in 1928, determined that protection should only be extended to a small proportion of workers, so as not to impose undue costs on employers at this early stage of India's industrial development. The policy of depriving workers of social and employment security was meant to encourage workers to migrate to urban centres for periods of employment but return to villages between bouts of work. The Whitley Commission was boycotted by the All India Trade Union Congress, but most of its recommendations made their way into a string of new labour laws enacted in the 1930s. Virtually all of this legislation was aimed at protecting individual workers in factories and mines and, prior to the Second World War, there were few attempts to experiment further with laws concerning collective labour relations.

India secured independence from the United Kingdom in 1947. The Constitution of India (1949) contained several guarantees specific to labour's interests, including 'the right to work', the right to 'just and humane conditions of work', the right to a 'living wage' and the right to form trade unions, among others. One of the first acts of the new government was to introduce the Industrial Disputes Act, which continues, along with the Trade Unions Act of 1926, to provide the basic national legal framework within which the Indian industrial relations and labour market systems are structured. The government was outwardly labour-focused, treating the worker as an enfranchised citizen. However, for the architects of

[33] S Cooney et al, 'The Evolution of Labor Law in Three Asian Nations: An Introductory Comparative Study (India, Indonesia, China)' (2014) 36 *Comparative Labor Law and Policy Journal* 23.

post-colonial India, the 'worker' worked in the modern economy. Policy making was captured by the idea that the rural–agrarian order would soon be replaced by an urban–industrial one. The National Planning Committee, established in 1940 and chaired by Jawaharlal Nehru, focused primarily on *industrial* relations. The regulations it proposed were modelled on those already implemented in the industrialised world.[34]

The barriers to thinking more broadly about the regulation of work were not just conceptual, but also political. The industrial sector had an established and influential trade union movement that was intricately intertwined with the Indian independence movement.[35] This labour movement grew exponentially following independence. In 1929, the number of registered trade unions in India was 29; in 1951 it was 3,987.[36] Although the unions cared for the interests of only a small fraction of the labouring classes, that minority was vocal. The fear of the radicalisation of the factory proletariat was high, and labour laws were designed to stifle unrest.

At the start of India's independence era industrial labourers formed less than 6 per cent of the total workforce.[37] Despite its relatively small size, this group of workers was seen as key to India's future prosperity. The implicit assumption was that a social system would eventually emerge which would mirror that of the West, with industrialisation powering the way towards prosperity. Jan Breman has suggested that little thought was given to the way in which local and historical conditions in India had shaped the working class and the ways that India's historical conditions differed from advanced economies.[38] The labour law regime that emerged was more reflective of future ambition than it was attentive to the characteristics of the majority of workers in India.[39] The restricted scope of labour laws combined with the limited ambition of land reforms at this time created a mass of workers who circulated from the countryside to urban centres and back again in search of work. The work they found was largely precarious and insecure.

Today, it is estimated that well over 90 per cent of the workforce falls outside of the law's putative protection and organisation.[40] Only a very small proportion of India's workers are members of trade unions,[41] and a similarly small proportion

[34] J Breman, *Outcast Labor in Asia: Circulation and Informalization of the Workforce at the Bottom of the Economy* (New Delhi, Oxford University Press, 2010) 131.

[35] Agarwala, 'The Economic Sociology of Informal Work', above n 8.

[36] OA Ornati, *Jobs and Workers in India* (Ithaca, NY, Cornell University Press, 1955), xi.

[37] ibid, 9.

[38] Breman, *Outcast Labor in Asia*, above n 34, 133.

[39] R Jhabvala, 'Excluding the Majority: Workers, Producers and Categories of Employment' (2001) 44 *Indian Journal of Labour Economics* 243.

[40] VN Prasad, *Labour Regulation in Small Enterprises: Coverage and Impact* (New Delhi, Institute for Studies in Industrial Development, 2008).

[41] K Shyam Sundar, 'State in Industrial Relations System in India: From Corporatist to Neo-Liberal?' (2005) 48 *Indian Journal of Labour Economics*, 917; R Gopalakrishnan and L Tortell, 'Access to Justice, Trade Union Rights, and the Indian Industrial Disputes Act 1947' (2006) 22 *International Journal of Comparative Labour Law and Industrial Relations* 529, suggesting 2%.

are covered by collective agreements. In the late 1990s, it was estimated that 2 per cent of the total workforce or 30 per cent of formal sector workers were involved in collective bargaining.[42] Coverage since then has continued to be very low. As Sean Cooney and his coauthors put it:

> The application of much Indian labour law – including key provisions such as the *Industrial Disputes Act 1947* and a good deal of the protective legislation regulating hours of work, health and safety, and other conditions – is limited in varying ways by reference to size of an establishment, type of economic activity, type of employment relationship, type of employment position, and so on. The reach of formal labour law is limited accordingly. Moreover, even where labor laws do apply in principle, the law is often easy enough to evade in practice, and enforcement is generally very poor.[43]

For workers covered by labour laws, however, the law is formally highly protective when compared with labour laws in other countries.[44] The most controversial law is s 25N of the Industrial Disputes Act, which was introduced in 1976 (amending legislation going back to 1947) and extended in 1984. Under the 1976 law, the permission of the state, via the state labour bureau, was required for all 'retrenchments' in establishments of 300 employees or more. This threshold was reduced to 100 employees in 1984. The constitutionality of s 25N was not clearly established until 1992 but it was effectively in force prior to that point in several states. The 1976 changes also saw an extension of the legally mandated minimum notice period for dismissals from one month to three, and a widening of the powers of the courts to grant reinstatement for an unjust dismissal.

The 1976 changes were passed during the period of the Emergency, when democratic institutions were suspended, and their immediate aims were not worker-protective; instead they were part of a 'Bonapartist' strategy of placing the state in a position to mediate between labour and capital, with the interests of labour subordinate to the development of the economy.[45] A number of studies have argued that s 25N is discouraging the growth of formal-sector employment. The most convincing are those which have shown a tendency for the establishment size to cluster just below the 100-employee threshold.[46]

The most recent period of labour law reform in India arose as a result of the economic crisis that confronted the country in the late 1980s. Under the influence of the World Bank and the International Monetary Fund, the Indian state adopted a neoliberal orientation to macroeconomic policy. Public enforcement of labour standards was scaled back, leaving unions, which had become dependent

[42] P-S Ahn, *The Growth and Decline of Political Unionism in India: The Need for a Paradigm Shift* (Geneva, ILO, 2010).

[43] S Cooney et al, 'The Evolution of Labor Law in Three Asian Nations', above n 33, 35.

[44] S Deakin, P Lele and M Siems, 'The Evolution of Labour Law: Calibrating and Comparing Regulatory Regimes' (2007) 146 *International Labour Review* 133.

[45] Cooney et al, above n 33, 37.

[46] A Ahsan and C Pagés, 'Are All Labor Regulations Equal? Evidence from Indian Manufacturing' (2009) 37 *Journal of Comparative Economics* 62.

on the state, in an increasingly vulnerable position. Most change in labour laws occurred with respect to the employment of women at night, greater ease in shift working, and relaxed regulation on the use of contract labour. Perhaps of more impact was the deregulation of a number of sectors previously controlled by the state through licensing requirements of various kinds, coupled with the opening of the economy to overseas trade and capital flows. This helped trigger vertical disintegration of supply chains and, eventually, de-industrialisation in a number of industries including textiles.

Jan Breman has recently described how this process unfolded in the state of Gujarat. Ahmedabad's integrated textile mills were closed in the 1990s and around 125,000 workers 'thrown into the informal economy'.[47] The employers were 'basically merchants rather than industrialists [who] didn't invest in the mills, they just took the profits and started using them for land speculation, while the machinery had become obsolete; some of it went back to the nineteenth century'. The end of regular employment in the textiles sector was accompanied by changes to housing policy which saw the demolition of communal living areas near the former industrial sites and the displacement of their inhabitants to poorly constructed neighbourhoods in the suburbs. In this newly informalised economy, households 'barely' survive.[48]

In the same period Gujarat also became one of the most lightly regulated states from the viewpoint of labour laws, as its government took advantage of India's federal structure to opt out of the Industrial Disputes Act in favour of a regime of no-fault dismissal. Gujarat's model of minimal labour market regulation coupled with incentives for inward investment became the template for much anticipated national reforms under the Bharatiya Janata Party administration which took office in 2015.[49]

Labour law enforcement is recognised to be a major problem in India, but it is only partially related to long-standing issues of the underfunding of courts and labour inspectors. In the course of the fieldwork we conducted between 2013 and 2016, collusion between employers and inspectors was repeatedly raised as a problem. Where officials did not simply authorise retrenchments under s 25N (something which occurred in '98 per cent of cases' in the Delhi region according to one of our interviewees), firms would often find other ways to evade the law:

> Employers get round section 25N … by employing just fewer than 100 employees. Or they just relocate. There was a case of a pharma company in Gurgaon. It had been there for 30 years. There was a union. It was not affiliated to any political party. Every three to four years the collective agreement would be renegotiated. Then the employer said

[47] J Breman, 'Jan Breman Interview: A Footloose Scholar' (2015) 94 *New Left Review* 45.
[48] ibid, 60.
[49] S Deakin and A Haldar, 'How Should India Reform Its Labour Laws?' (2015) 50 *Economic and Political Weekly* 48.

> he had to cut salaries, the bank was putting him under pressure. The Gurgaon plant was shut down. The same company, making the same product, reopened at an export zone in Haryana. The new workers were now getting a quarter of the former salary. At the old site the company was closed and the banks repossessed the site. Now the employer makes 10 times as much profit. The same thing goes on in Uttar Pradesh. (Labour lawyer, interviewed in Delhi, 2013)

From a neoclassical economic perspective, India's large informal sector is a consequence of restrictive labour laws which do not reflect the diversity of forms of work that exist in practice. A systemic view suggests that other forces were at work, including government strategies of segmenting the labour force and employer strategies of pursuing informalisation as a way of cutting costs and offloading social responsibilities. The inability of successive governments to modernise the labour laws is also an issue: the concept of the 'ossification' of labour law, applied to the US context by Cynthia Estlund,[50] could equally well be applied to India.

Today the labour market in India is highly fragmented, with workers in formal enterprises, often protected by labour laws but lacking effective means of enforcing their rights, having a vastly different experience of work from the large majority of workers who have never worked in formal enterprises or received a contract of employment. For those who are not covered by labour laws, other informal regulations apply: those of caste, class, gender, patronage relations, tribal and village affiliations and so on. Thus the Indian labour market is very far from being ungoverned or unregulated, but is, at the same time, largely beyond the reach of formal laws. Claims that labour legislation is holding back the development of a formal labour market in India need to be understood in this context.

B. The Evolution of Labour Market Regulation in China

Because China has undergone such far-reaching changes in the state's management of the economy over the last century, it is not possible to trace a single trajectory in the co-evolution of labour markets and labour market regulation. Instead, we can track three periods: the Nationalist period from 1928, the Communist period from 1949, and the period of gradual re-regulation along market principles from 1979.

China's labour law has been effectively developed from scratch since 1979, with some of the most significant developments occurring from 2007 onwards. However, there are certain important features of today's labour markets that owe their structures to the Communist period, including the distinction between rural and urban workforces.

Unlike India, China was never fully colonised by European powers, although significant parts of the country, such as Hong Kong and a major section of

[50] C Estlund, 'The Ossification of American Labor Law' (2002) 102 *Columbia Law Review* 1527.

Shanghai, were subjected to extraterritorial rule by Western nations during the nineteenth century, and certain regions of the country were occupied by the Japanese during the parts of the twentieth. Passage of national labour laws was not possible until 1928 when the Nationalists defeated the Beiyang government and succeeded in unifying the country. The underlying contractual principles for labour contracts were set out in the Civil Code that was promulgated in 1929. The Civil Code was strongly influenced by continental European and Japanese labour law systems. The key law regulating labour standards was the Factory Law of 1929, directed at poor working conditions in many of the burgeoning industrial enterprises. The Factory Law applied only to industry and only to factories using mechanical power, restricting its coverage to a small proportion of the workforce. Trade unions were regulated by the Trade Union Law, which was highly repressive of freedom of association rights, and by the Labour Disputes Settlement Law.

Following the Communist Revolution, the Chinese Communist Party (CCP), which assumed control of the country in 1949, abolished the Nationalist legal system and began constructing a new economic and legal order. During the Communist era in China, any contractual basis for employment – in larger urban firms at least – was displaced by the administrative assignment of work. The freedom to strike was formally recognised for much of the Communist period.[51]

Particularly important from the perspective of understanding the contemporary situation of rural migrants was the consolidation of a sharp distinction between urban and rural workers, constructed around the *hukou*, or household registration system, which severely limited migration within the country. Many urban workers enjoyed relatively privileged conditions, being engaged on a permanent basis in large state-owned enterprises. In contrast, rural workers in collectivised farms experienced widespread poverty.

After the death of Mao, liberalisation began. Reforms in the 1980s and 1990s saw state enterprises privatised or shut down, in the process shedding millions of jobs. A large pool of labour for new firms was created, but also significant informality of work and related social problems.

The elimination of labour law under Mao meant that at the start of the period of market-led reforms in the late 1970s, there was virtually no regulatory framework in place to govern labour relations. A new system had to be created. From 1979, national and local Chinese governments began to dismantle the administrative ordering of the labour market in favour of one based on labour contracting. By the late 1980s, labour contracts had been introduced systematically across the urban economy, becoming a central institution for governing work. At the same time as this marketisation of working relations was being promoted, the freedom to strike was removed in the 1982 Constitution in a move by the CCP to tighten its grip and quash the emerging democratic movement.[52]

[51] K Chang and FL Cooke, 'Legislating the Right to Strike in China: Historical Development and Prospects' (2015) 57 *Journal of Industrial Relations* 440.

[52] ibid.

After over a decade of debate, in 1994, a more comprehensive national Labour Law was developed which remains in force today. One of the issues driving the debate was concern over how to regulate labour contracts without commodifying labour. The solution arrived at required a radical separation between labour contracts and all other forms of contracting. The Labour Law dealt only briefly with labour contracting, with the result that there was an absence of detailed rules regulating various aspects of the individual labour relationship. There were some working time protections and a right to notice and redundancy pay, but minimal controls over the dismissal decision. Not all employers during this period were under a duty to provide social insurance which largely operated through regional or city-wide programmes. This allowed many abuses and unfair terms to develop within labour contracts.

Thus the transition from the 'iron rice bowl' model was one from a protected, if highly state-directed, version of the labour relationship, to one mediated by contract. In contrast to India at this time, the underlying legal regime was weak, not just in its enforcement but in terms of its content too.

In 2007, however, China enacted a nationwide Labour Contract Law, which came into force the following year. Enactment of the 2007 law marked a highly significant change of direction in China's approach to labour market regulation coming after an extended internal debate over the merits of a more worker-protective approach, and in the face of concerted opposition from groups representing overseas employers including the American Chamber of Commerce.[53] The law was a response to growing levels of worker militancy and unrest in the rapidly industrialising coastal regions dating back to the 1980s, including actions such as go-slows, strikes and petitions. The Labour Contract Law was at the same time part of a larger institutional redesign aimed at increasing what official sources referred to as 'social harmony'. It was also part of an industrial strategy of encouraging firms to reduce their reliance on low-cost labour in favour of a strategy of organisational and technological 'upgrading'.[54] The move echoes the English poor law, which we described earlier in the chapter, which helped to support the move to a market economy by offsetting the effects on workers and households of loss of access to the land. In England, the poor law paved the way for capitalism and the industrialisation of work with the associated separation of labour and capital. It may be the case that the Labour Contract Law is performing a similar role in China in its transition to capitalism.

The 2007 law established the right of a worker in a relationship based on wage dependence or employer control to receive a written labour contract. Evidence of wage dependence can be presented in the form of pay slips, engagement letters, or

[53] M Gallagher and B Dong, 'Legislating Harmony: Labour Law Reform in Contemporary China' in S Kuruvilla, C Lee and M Gallagher (eds), *From Iron Rice Bowl to Informalization: Managers, Workers and the State in a Changing China* (Ithaca, NY, Cornell University Press, 2011).

[54] R Brown, *Understanding Labor and Employment Law in China* (Cambridge, Cambridge University Press, 2009).

even evidence from a security camera of a worker coming and going from work. As in most labour law systems around the world, the effect of an employer failing to provide a written contract is not the exclusion of the worker from legal protections; the worker remains within the coverage of labour law either way. Employer non-compliance, conversely, is a breach of the law which may be compensated by damages representing a doubling of the worker's salary for the period when no contract was provided. The written terms must normally be supplied within a month of the employment beginning.

The Labour Contract Law also strengthened the statutory floor of rights within the employment contract, in particular by providing for a right to claim reinstatement for unjust dismissal and by tightening the rules on dismissal procedures, notification of dismissals, redundancy selection, and priority re-employment following redundancy. In a related reform in 2008, a low-cost labour arbitration system was introduced for the resolution of disputes. Since that time the number of disputes resolved through the arbitration system has risen rapidly year on year.[55]

The situation of rural workers also changed. The *hukou* system was partially dismantled, allowing many rural workers to enter cities, where they became available to work in new forms of industrial and service enterprises. Yet sharp distinctions between rural and urban existences continue to shape labour markets. Between 1980 and 2010, some 150–160 million persons without official household permits for urban residence migrated to work in cities.[56] The Labour Contract Law appears to be making some headway in reducing disparities between urban dwellers and migrants from the countryside, and with it, informality. A survey of migrant workers conducted before and after the 2007 law was passed suggests that it substantially increased the likelihood that migrant workers would obtain a written contract, and that workers who were given a contract were more likely to have social insurance and a union presence at their workplace, as well as being less likely to experience wage arrears.[57]

There appears to be a trend towards increasing formalisation of work in the major industrial areas. During the 1990s and 2000s, the southern coastal province of Guangdong became 'one of the key nodes of the global economy, thanks to the combined interests of retailers like Wal-Mart and brand-defined companies like Nike, Mattel and Eileen Fisher', with parts of the province benefiting from a light-touch regulatory regime equivalent to 'a virtual free trade zone, attracting

[55] E Zheng and S Deakin, 'Pricing Labour Capacity: The Unexpected Effects of Formalising Labour Contracts in China' (2016) Centre for Business Research, University of Cambridge Working Paper No 479, https://www.cbr.cam.ac.uk/fileadmin/user_upload/centre-for-business-research/downloads/working-papers/wp479.pdf.

[56] S Li, 'Rural Migrant Workers in China: Scenario, Challenges and Public Policy', Working Paper No 89, Policy Integration and Statistics Department (Geneva, ILO, 2008).

[57] F Cui, Y Ge and F Jing, 'The Effects of the Labour Contract Law on the Chinese Labour Market' (2013) 10 *Journal of Empirical Legal Studies* 462; X Li and R Freeman, 'How Does China's New Labor Contract Law Affect Floating Workers?' (2015) 53 *British Journal of Industrial Relations* 711.

a wide range of manufacturers in search of low corporate taxes and lax environmental and planning regulations, and a workforce thought to be both compliant and cheap'.[58] While the implementation of the 2007 law in Guangdong was not straightforward, the evidence that many employers were going to considerable lengths to avoid it, while others moving their operations to low-cost provinces elsewhere in China or outside the country altogether,[59] suggests that it was seen from an early stage as having an impact on employers' costs.

On some estimates, the proportion of workers receiving written contracts in Guangdong province increased from 12 per cent before the passage of the Act to over 60 per cent afterwards.[60] There is survey evidence to suggest that the law of 2007 has had a similar tangible impact on the level of benefits provided to employees in other of the more industrialised regions including the Yangtze River delta area.[61] At the same time, there are indications, however, that the implementation of the 2007 law varies widely across different regions of China.[62] Concerns over its effectiveness have been voiced,[63] particularly in relation to the use of agency or 'despatch' labour and fixed-term employment, both of which are widespread across various manufacturing sectors including textiles and automobile production.[64]

It is not clear, however, how far the use of fixed-term or agency work should be equated with informality. Agency workers and fixed-term employees are not formally outside the scope of Chinese labour law and, like other workers, are entitled to a written contract; they also benefit, in principle, from a number of legal protections. Thus their work may be characterised as 'precarious' to varying degrees, without being 'informal'. Under the 2007 law, agency workers became entitled to equal terms and conditions with those employed in a regular employment relationship, and their position was further strengthened from 2013. Fixed-term employees are entitled to permanent employment but only after two successive employment contracts with a cumulative duration of ten years or more. Thus the weak protection of fixed-term employees is at least in part a function of the underlying law rather than its implementation or enforcement. Agency and fixed-term workers are not necessarily employed in 'informal work' according

[58] H Wang et al, 'China's new Labour Contract Law: Is China Moving towards Increased Power for Workers?' (2010) 30 *Third World Quarterly* 485, 486.

[59] ibid, 488.

[60] Z Cheng, R Smyth and F Guo, 'The Impact of China's New Labour Contract Law on Socioeconomic Outcomes for Migrant and Urban Workers' (2015) 68 *Human Relations* 329.

[61] S Cooney et al, *Law and Fair Work in China* (London, Routledge, 2013); Li and Freeman, 'How Does China's New Labor Contract Law Affect Floating Workers?', above n 57.

[62] Wang et al, 'China's new Labour Contract Law', above n 58.

[63] M Gallagher, C Lee and S Kuruvilla, 'Introduction and Argument' in S Kuruvilla, C Lee and M Gallagher (eds), *From Iron Rice Bowl to Informalization: Managers, Workers and the State in a Changing China* (Ithaca, NY, Cornell University Press, 2011).

[64] L Zhang, 'The Paradox of Labour Force Dualism and State–Labour–Capital Relations in the Chinese Automobile Industry' in S Kuruvilla, C Lee and M Gallagher (eds), *From Iron Rice Bowl to Informalization: Managers, Workers and the State in a Changing China* (Ithaca, NY, Cornell University Press, 2011).

to the 17th ICLS Guidelines for Measuring Informal Employment, and whether they are classified as informal according to Chang's schema depends on contextual information such as the extent of job security and access to benefits they enjoy in practice.

China's adoption of the Labour Contract Law has the potential to change not only its own developmental path but to alter the global dynamics associated with its rapid industrialisation and entry into world markets. For China to adopt a labour-protective measure at such a critical stage in its development implies that globalisation is not inevitably associated with a race to the bottom in labour standards, nor with irreversible declines, either globally or in particular regions, in the quality of employment. There is evidence from econometric research to suggest that the passage of the Labour Contract Law has led to improvements in total factor productivity in listed firms in regions with stronger state capacity. Although the impact of the law is mediated by the level of economic development across regions and by differences in the quality of the institutional environment, the reported effect is compatible with the theory that labour law can help stimulate industrial upgrading.[65] Whether this trend will persist and whether it will serve as an example to other developing countries (or even to developed ones contemplating deregulation of labour standards) remains to be seen, but it implies that policies articulated at national level can continue to shape labour market outcomes even in a period of global economic integration.

V. A Closer Look at Informality in India and China: Statistical Data and Interview Evidence

As we have seen in the previous sections, labour market regulation has evolved very differently in China and India. The limited coverage of labour law in India is traceable to its colonial roots and to post-colonial aspirations that have not yet been realised. Although the newly independent country of the early 1950s had only a small industrial workforce, forming less than 6 per cent of the total workforce,[66] it was this group for which labour laws were designed. The future of India's prosperity and growth was seen to hinge on this group of workers and its growth and displacement of the non-industrialised workforce. This historical legacy continues to resonate today in the structure of the Indian economy, where a vast majority of the population are informally employed.

[65] S Deakin and B Wang, 'The Effects of Employment Protection on Productivity: Cross-Provincial Evidence from China' (forthcoming) Centre for Business Research, University of Cambridge Working Paper.

[66] Ornati, *Jobs and Workers in India*, above n 36, 9.

China's path paralleled India's in certain respects during its Nationalist period starting in the late 1920s, but diverged dramatically with the onset of the Communist period in the mid-twentieth century. As in India, labour laws enacted during the Nationalist period focused on regulating the relatively small urban industrial sector. Under Mao, workers in different sectors of the economy came to be formally registered, even though there were large differences in standards of living and social benefits across the urban–rural divide. The advent of marketisation and shifting role of the Chinese state since late 1970s led initially to an increase in the share of people working informally, but today this group still comprises less than a third of the non-agricultural workforce, and there are signs of growing formalisation driven by legal and institutional reforms.

In this section we take a closer look at patterns of informality in India and China. We start by looking at comparative data on informality in the context of long-run economic forces shaping the development of the two countries, before examining the contours of informal employment in each country in more detail.

A. Comparing the Evolution of Informality in China and India: Aggregate Data

Cross-national data collected by the ILO using a person-based definition of informality provide one of the few bases for making a direct statistical comparison between the Indian and Chinese experiences. According to the ILO,[67] 32.6 per cent of China's non-agricultural working population was in informal employment in 2010, as opposed to 83.6 per cent of India's non-agricultural working population in 2009 (see Table 3). The difference in the overall rate of 'persons in informal employment' in the two countries stems primarily from the level of 'employment in the informal sector', which is 67.5 per cent in India and 21.9 per cent in China. The share of persons in 'informal employment outside the informal sector' – that is to say, within the formal sector – is more similar: 16.8 per cent in India, and 12.5 per cent in China.

Table 10.3 Rates of Persons in Informal Employment, China and India

	Persons in informal employment, as a percentage of non-agricultural employment	**Persons employed in the informal sector,** as a percentage of non-agricultural employment	**Persons in informal employment outside the informal sector,** as a percentage of non-agricultural employment
China (2010)	32.6%	21.9%	12.5%
India (2009)	83.6%	67.5%	16.8%

Source: ILO, *Statistical Update on Employment in the Informal Economy* (Geneva, ILO, 2012).

[67] ILO, *Statistical Update on Employment in the Informal Economy*, above n 1.

In order to make sense of these contrasting data, it is important to see recent developments in the context of the longer-term economic trajectories of the two countries. In 1980, according to the best data we have, China and India were nearly identical in their level of development as measured by GDP per capita.[68] In the ensuing three decades, however, China's GDP per capita grew at *three times* the rate of India's, placing the two countries in far different positions by 2010, when the comparative ILO data on informal employment was reported, showing China's significantly lower informality rate.[69]

Related to the varying growth rates of China and India over recent decades is the difference in their evolving sectoral profiles. Simply put, China moved away from being an agricultural economy – with people moving into industry and services – at a far higher rate than India.[70] Between 1990 and 2012, the share of the working population employed in agriculture went from 59.6 per cent to 32.6 per cent in China and from 62.4 per cent to 47.0 per cent in India. China also urbanised at a much faster clip, going from 20 per cent urban in 1980 to 50 per cent in 2010 as India inched upward from 25 per cent to 30 per cent.[71]

China's lower levels of informal employment relative to India's stem in large measure from its history under Communism, which, meant that, as of the late 1970s, a very high share of its workforce was formally registered in the state-run economy. After 1979, with the roll-out of market reforms, there was a substantial increase in the number of Chinese people working informally. But it still bears asking why the share of people working informally in China did not rise far more dramatically, to levels approaching those seen in India. To help account for the fact that informal employment still comprises less than a third of the Chinese workforce, we need to unpack the relationship between informality and economic development.

In the cross-national literature on informality, perhaps the strongest relationship that has been identified is the significant negative correlation between rates of informal employment and levels of economic development as measured by GDP per capita.[72] In part, this stems from the sectoral transformation that tends to be part and parcel of processes of economic development. Economic development generally entails a shift away from agriculture and towards industry and services, and, since informal employment is generally more prevalent in agriculture, the process of economic development tends to press in the direction of greater formalisation. A related process that often attends economic development and

[68] A Acocha, S Chattaraj and S Wachter, 'Urban Governance and Development of Informality in India and China' in E Ladner Birch, S Wachter and S Chattaraj (eds), *Slums: How Informal Real Estate Markets Work* (Philadelphia, University of Pennsylvania Press, 2016).

[69] ibid.

[70] ILO, above n 1.

[71] Acocha et al, 'Urban Governance and Development of Informality in India and China', above n 68.

[72] R La Porta and A Shleifer, 'Informality and Development' (2014) 28 *Journal of Economic Perspectives* 109.

contributes to increases in formal employment is urbanisation, as city dwellers are more likely to become incorporated into the formal economy than their rural counterparts.

Given what we know about this established set of relationships, China's extraordinarily high rates of economic growth in recent decades and its rapid industrialisation and urbanisation have helped to keep its rate of informal employment at lower levels than they otherwise would have been, even with the substantial informal workforce that can be found in construction and other segments of China's industrial sector.[73] But these broader transformations also warrant deeper explanation. Fully accounting for China's explosive growth and socioeconomic development goes beyond the scope of this chapter. However, highlighting some key aspects of the *political* economy of China's developmental trajectory can take us closer to understanding why it has modernised so rapidly and steered clear of even more widespread informalisation.

In China, industrialisation and urbanisation have been propelled at least in part by the organisation of the Chinese state. On the one hand, even amid recent waves of labour protest, Chinese government officials have *not* had to respond to demands from the labour force in the same way they would in a more democratic society. In particular, labour laws in China cannot be understood as responding to the emergence of collective bargaining from below, that is, at plant or company level, as was the case in Western Europe and North America in the early decades of the twentieth century.[74] On the other, decentralisation of authority and control over resources, coupled with a mandate from the central government to promote economic growth, *have* created a situation whereby local officials seek to develop the infrastructure necessary to pave the way for industrial development and support and attract an industrial workforce. Owing in part to these dynamics, the development of public housing and other forms of infrastructure is far more extensive in China than in India, where informal urban settlements are more pervasive. There is a relationship between living and working formally, and the Chinese government has promoted a set of conditions under which both are more likely than in India for its ever growing number of urban residents.[75]

B. A Closer Look at Informality in India

The *India Labour and Employment Report 2014*, prepared by the independent, Delhi-based Institute of Human Development, cites a figure of 92 per cent for the

[73] S Swider, *Building China: Informal Work and the New Precariat* (Ithaca, NY, Cornell University Press, 2015).

[74] E Zheng and S Deakin, 'State and Knowledge Production: Industrial Relations Scholarship under Chinese Capitalism' (2016) Centre for Business Research, University of Cambridge Working Paper No 480, https://www.cbr.cam.ac.uk/fileadmin/user_upload/centre-for-business-research/downloads/working-papers/wp480.pdf.

[75] Acocha et al, above n 68.

proportion of the labour force engaged in informal work, which on the face of it is little changed from previous years.[76] To understand what this figure means, however, it is necessary to distinguish between the size of the informal *sector* and those in informal *employment*. As we have seen, these two categories differ because there can be 'informal' employment within the formal sector.

According to the IHD, the formal sector has been growing in India, from 11.8 per cent of all employment in 2004/05 to 17 per cent in 2011/12, and the proportion of formal employment within the formal sector has also been increasing. The IHD analysis, based on survey data, suggests that 7.5 per cent of the working population was engaged in 'regular, formal employment', meaning 'regular, full-time employment with social protection', in 2011/12, up from 6.6 per cent in 2004/05. On this basis, the Institute concluded that 'the process of informalisation of the workforce seems to have halted since 2004–5'. One of the factors responsible for the decline has been the Mahatma Gandhi National Rural Employment Guarantee Scheme (NREGA), a programme introduced from 2005 under which the state provides a minimum of 100 days of paid manual work per year to rural households. A number of studies suggest that NREGA has contributed to an increase in the level of wage and in the stability of employment in rural areas,[77] although funding cuts may now be threatening the success of the programme.[78]

A complementary picture is provided by data published by the Government of India Labour Bureau's Report on Employment in Informal Sector and Conditions of Employment in 2015. The Bureau's survey excludes the part of the agricultural labour force which is engaged in subsistence farming. Of the segment of the working population that is left when subsistence farming is excluded, 72 per cent were ineligible for social security benefits, 68 per cent had no written work contract, and 80 per cent had no trade union affiliation in 2011/12. Looking at the same data differently, from the standpoint of enterprise types, 38.9 per cent of workers were employed in 'proprietary' enterprises (a category related to the concept of own-account work), and 12.9 per cent in 'partnerships' (unincorporated enterprises with a focus on a household or group of households). 24 per cent of the non-subsistence workforce were employed in registered companies or in the public sector.[79]

If these data suggest that the size of the informal sector in India is somewhat less than the nine-tenths figure which is often cited and that formal employment is

[76] IHD, *India Labour and Employment Report 2014: Workers in the Era of Globalisation* (Delhi, Institute for Human Development, 2013).

[77] ibid, ch 7.

[78] J Ghosh, 'India's Rural Employment Programme Is Dying a Death of Funding Cuts', *The Guardian* (London, 5 February 2015), https://www.theguardian.com/global-development/2015/feb/05/india-rural-employment-funding-cuts-mgnrega.

[79] Labour Bureau, *Report on Employment in Informal Sector and Conditions of Employment (2013–14)* (Chandigarh, Government of India, Ministry of Labour and Employment, 2015).

slowly growing, other data reported by IHD suggest that informalisation in parts of the economy, and in particular in the manufacturing sector, has been intensifying. Contract workers (a category defined by legislation to refer to those employed on a subcontract or quasi-independent basis) accounted for 13 per cent of total manufacturing employment in 1995, but 34 per cent by 2011. The share of value added in manufacturing allocated to wages (as opposed to profits), which was 45 per cent in the 1980s, was only 25 per cent by 2009/10. The Institute's assessment in 2013 was that the increasing '"informalisation" of employment has gradually eroded the strength of the trade unions' leading to an increase in plant closures, a fall in the coverage of collective bargaining, and 'a significant rise in industrial unrest outside the normal channels of social dialogue'.[80]

Informality in the Indian context is associated with structural inequalities. Access to formal employment in India correlates strongly with caste and religious affiliation. The IHD reports that casual work is concentrated among disadvantaged social classes including the so-called scheduled castes and Muslim workers, while regular work is concentrated among high-caste Hindus, Christians and Jains.[81] Wage gaps between casual workers and those in organised employment are huge: in 2011/12, 'a rural casual worker earned less than 7 per cent of a public-sector employee'. The employment rate for women is falling and is estimated to be between and one half and two thirds that for men. Women are more likely than men to be employed in 'low-productivity, low-income, insecure jobs in farms and in the unorganised and informal sectors'.[82]

Dualism within firms and establishments, and not just at a macro level, is a common phenomenon not confined to smaller enterprises. Two accounts given to us in the course of fieldwork conducted in India in 2013 provide a sense of how informal employment is structured within the formal sector. A labour economist interviewed in Delhi described the consequences of lack of enforcement of labour laws and the constant circulation of labour from the countryside to the city in Punjab:

> In dirty and dangerous factories in the Punjab there is almost no enforcement of labour laws. The shift lasts 12 hours in practice even if it is meant to be eight hours. There are extreme health and safety risks from hot metals and if there is an accident the worker is just paid off. These are listed companies. It's all in the open, nothing is hidden. These are all formal enterprises although not all the workers have social insurance. Many of the workforce are long-term but on fixed-term contracts. They might think they are permanent but they don't have permanent contracts. They go back to the village every year to take two months off. They get a new contract each time even if they don't realise it. (Labour economist interviewed in Delhi, 2013)

[80] IHD, *India Labour and Employment Report 2014*, above n 76.
[81] ibid.
[82] ibid.

Permanent contracts are highly valued and only permanent employees are able to form unions, undermining the effectiveness of unions:

> You might go to a registered factory. 10 per cent of the workers would be permanent, 20–30 per cent casual workers on the books, employed for three months at a time, then, 60 per cent employed through labour-only subcontractors, not on the books. Only the permanent workers are allowed to form unions. Of the 60 per cent, most are migrants. They don't return to the village each year, they may stay in Kolkata for four to five years, then move on to Kerala, for example. The moment they leave, to see their family, they lose their job. (Labour economist interviewed in Delhi, 2013)

C. A Closer Look at Informality in China

We find a number of similarities with this picture in China, although the study of informality is made more difficult there by the lack of a similar, official effort to map the extent of the informal labour force. The Chinese authorities, unlike their Indian counterparts, do not recognise 'informal work' as a relevant statistical category. There is, however, a widely shared belief among researchers that China has been undergoing increased informalisation since the implementation of market-orientated reforms which, as in India's case, began in the 1980s and have intensified over time:

> Within a generation, urban China has moved from a highly protected 'iron rice bowl' system that guaranteed workers in state-owned enterprises (SOEs) and collectively owned enterprises permanent employment, cradle-to-grave benefits, and a relatively high degree of equality to a market-dominated employment characterised by considerable variation in wages, welfare provisions, labour law enforcement, and job security ... the growth of informal employment is but the latest step in a downward slide of workers' employment security since the introduction of the labour contract system in 1986.[83]

How strong is the evidence for this view of the trajectory of employment in China? In the absence of official data on informality, evidence for the size of the informal sector has to be pieced together from a combination of government statistics using other categories, and independent surveys. Park and Cai use data from the China Labour Statistical Yearbooks and annual censuses to arrive at an estimate of an informal workforce of around 40 per cent of total urban employment in 2005.[84] They get to this figure by removing those recorded as employed in state or collective employment, which was just over 20 per cent in 2005, having been around

[83] Gallagher et al, 'Introduction and Argument', above n 63, 4–5.

[84] A Park and F Cai, 'The Informalisation of the Chinese Labour Market' in S Kuruvilla, C Lee and M Gallagher (eds), *From Iron Rice Bowl to Informalization: Managers, Workers and the State in a Changing China* (Ithaca, NY, Cornell University Press, 2011).

80 per cent in 1978; employment in a registered enterprise (co-operatives, partnerships and limited liability companies), which amounted for around 10 per cent of the total in 2005; private-sector self-employment, recorded as 20 per cent in that year; and foreign employment, which was then around 5 per cent. What is left is an 'other' category which was unrecorded in 1985, around 15 per cent of the total in 1990, and 36 per cent by 2005, although it had earlier peaked at 39 per cent in 2003.

Park and Cai suggest that this residual category, which they propose consists of 'unreported urban workers and unregistered informal employment, including undocumented work by migrants in urban areas', gives a good measure of China's informal sector.[85] Their working definition of informality is phrased in terms of the practice of employment rather than by reference to the intended coverage of legal rules. Their approach focuses on 'workers who lack formal labour contracts' and includes some 'who work full-time on a relatively long-term basis with high job security but have limited participation in social insurance programmes' as well as those working on a part-time and casual basis 'with no security or sense of control' as well as some of the self-employed.[86]

The suggested informality rate of 40 per cent for urban employment in 2005 is high by the standards of the global North but much lower than in India, and it appears to be falling, contrary to Gallagher, Lee and Kuruvilla's assessment. It is based on a broad understanding of informal work as it includes workers in full-time and secure positions who are treated as informal because they lack a formal contract or access to social insurance, whether or not they were entitled to receive them, as well as those in casual or insecure work.

Despite the overall reduction in the incidence of informal work suggested by the data that can be pieced together, important barriers to formality persist. Account must be taken of the role played by the regulation of migration in patterns of informalisation and formalisation in China. As part of the *hukou* system, social benefits in China have been linked to a person's place of origin (the English poor law was not dissimilar in this regard).[87] As a result, many Chinese migrant workers remained unprotected in practice even when they were working under formal labour contracts in urban areas. A national reform enacted in 2014 made it possible as a matter of law to register and receive benefits in one's place of residence regardless of origin. However, as Li puts it, this was but 'a small step in the right direction', with many city governments erecting new barriers to establishing permanent residency and benefit levels often remaining highly segmented.[88]

[85] ibid.
[86] ibid, 20.
[87] Deakin and Wilkinson, above n 14, ch 3.
[88] B Li, 'China's Hukou Reform a Small Step in the Right Direction' (*East Asia Forum*, 13 January 2015), http://www.eastasiaforum.org/2015/01/13/chinas-hukou-reform-a-small-step-in-the-right-direction/; B Li, 'China Going Nowhere on Hukou Reform' (*East Asia Forum*, 19 May 2017), http://www.eastasiaforum.org/2017/05/19/china-going-nowhere-on-hukou-reform/.

Yet at the same time, the major shift in labour regulation associated with the Labour Contract Law of 2007 has also positively affected formalisation. Fieldwork we conducted in the Yangtze and Pearl River Delta regions between 2013 and 2016 suggests that, at least in larger enterprises, both Chinese and foreign-owned, there was an acceptance of the 2008 law, and an adjustment to the more protective labour law regime which it introduced, around this time. Human resources managers in China, as elsewhere, are unlikely, even in a confidential interview, to admit to failing to comply with the law, but a notable feature of our interviews was the criticism of the law for being both too strict in its own terms and too rigidly enforced – a view which suggests that the system of labour inspection through regional and city-level offices is more than purely formal.

One interview with a CEO suggested that the law had led to widespread changes in workplace practices within the firm:

> The Labour Contract Law marked a critical change, from 2008. There was a lot of public debate about it. China is still not a country governed by law, by real regulation. I had many classmates in bio companies.[89] The view was that the courts would support any irrational claim by an employee. And many companies were having a hard time. So we spent a huge amount on changing our practices, checking many things. (CEO, Chinese subsidiary of foreign-owned multinational corporation, interviewed in 2013)

Another interviewee complained that the rules were inflexible, but commented that the local government provided detailed guidance:

> We have to comply with the 2008 law. The rules on dispatch work are very stupid. You need time to adjust to them. The local government gives us detailed guidance. Law-making like this is rather inflexible. Foxconn said, 'we will replace workers with equipment when this law comes in'. We didn't do that. (Human resources director, Chinese subsidiary of foreign-owned multinational corporation, interviewed in 2013)

The human resources director of a Chinese-owned multinational corporation raised concerns that the laws placed a burden for a 'harmonious society' on private enterprises, rather than spreading risk through the development of a welfare system.

> We want to strictly follow the laws, all of them, not just those affecting workers. These new laws will make Chinese companies lose their competitiveness. The aim of building a harmonious society has a cost. From this company's point of view the new labour law is good and we should protect our employees. But the country's welfare system must be further developed. Some of these costs should be met by the welfare system. (Human resources director, Chinese-owned multinational corporation, interviewed in 2013)

The argument for including those without formal labour contracts within the category of informal employment is that without a written agreement they are

[89] The term 'bio companies' in this quote refers to biotechnology firms which explore the use of micro-organisms, such as bacteria or yeasts, or biological substances, such as enzymes, to perform specific industrial or manufacturing processes. Applications include production of certain drugs, synthetic hormones, and bulk foodstuffs.

likely to find it more difficult in practice to access social insurance protections and other employment-related benefits.[90] However, under the Labour Law of 1994, which was in force prior to the changes made by the Labour Contract Law from 2008, the legal rights attached to the employment relationship were in any case restricted. There were some working time protections and a right to notice and redundancy pay, but minimal controls over the dismissal decision. Not all employers during this earlier period were under a duty to provide social insurance which largely operated through regional or city-wide programmes. The transition from the 'iron rice bowl' model was one from a protected, if highly state-directed, version of the labour relationship, to one that was increasingly mediated by contract, with a substantial share of the workforce working informally. However, the share of the informal labour force in China remains significantly smaller than that in India, and seems to be falling as a result of the enactment of the Labour Contract Law and its implementation in the fast-growing coastal regions.

VI. Conclusion

Researching trajectories of formalisation and informalisation is not straightforward in light of the multiple meanings accorded to the term 'informality', the lack of consistency in the statistical categories used to describe informal employment, and the rapid pace of change in many emerging markets. Some preliminary conclusions may be suggested.

First, clarity is needed on the statistical categories used to describe informal labour, which currently elide some important distinctions between traditional sectors to which the concept of labour market risks is largely irrelevant; own-account work and household-based enterprises in which the distinction between labour and capital is unclear; and segments of the waged labour force characterised by precariousness and insecurity, which have a relationship to informality but are by no means beyond the scope of labour law rules. In relation to the latter category, a further distinction is relevant, namely that between workers who should be protected by labour laws but are not because of enforcement problems, and those who are not covered because of incomplete de jure coverage. The expansion of the definition of informality to include all workers who do not enjoy de facto labour law protection is in danger of depriving the concept of its usefulness.

Second, we need to arrive at a better understanding of the relationship of informality to long-run capitalist dynamics. The emergence of formal labour markets in the global North, while compatible with the long-run development

[90] Park and Cai, 'The Informalisation of the Chinese Labour Market', above n 84.

of capitalism, also required active social states. Industrialisation was a necessary but not sufficient condition for formalisation. In the global South, the persistence of the informal labour market is not only or even principally related to the phenomenon of late or recent industrialisation; it is also the consequence of policies which have encouraged casualisation and undermined labour market institutions. India's example shows the risks of this route. Whether China's different developmental path will lead to a different outcome remains to be seen, but the experiment initiated by the Labour Contract Law of 2007 is one with global ramifications.

Not unlike England at the point of its rapid industrialisation in the decades after 1750, China has seen its state undertake a set of actions designed to regulate and stabilise labour supply. As was the case with industrialising England, it is important not to overstate the worker-protective and socially progressive dimensions of the contemporary Chinese government's approach. For one, big gaps remain in the living standards and life chances of established urban residents versus those from rural areas, including internal migrant workers – some 260 million strong – who make up an outsized share of China's informally employed population. However, a set of policies aimed at promoting stability in both housing and employment, coupled with very high rates of economic growth, are contributing to the steady growth of formal work in China, particularly in contrast to the much slower formalisation of Indian labour markets.

Unlike China, India's employment structure today is much as it was in the late 1970s: an island of formality surrounded by a sea of informality. India's economic growth, though significant, has fallen well short of China's – and, being the 'office of the world' to China's 'factory of the world', has been less apt to absorb large numbers of working people from rural areas. Political dynamics in the Indian context have also been less conducive than in China to the development of an urban infrastructure that supports formalisation. In particular, local government has not been charged with such a clear mandate to drive economic growth and has not exerted as much control over revenues and key institutional levers.

The recent small decline in the relative size of the informal sector in India has occurred at the same time as informalisation or 'casualisation' has been accelerating within the formal sector, even in the heart of the industrial economy. As a result, India's industrial trade union movement, representing not just a small fraction of India's employed population but a declining segment of the industrial workforce that, in the post-colonial imagination, was meant to become an ever-expanding population of social rights-bearing citizens, is facing an ever-growing challenge. As this trend unfolds, it has become easier for critics of labour regulation to cast industrial unions as an 'aristocracy of labour' out of synch with the interests of most working people. However, some of India's poverty alleviation programmes, most notably the Mahatma Gandhi National Rural Employment Guarantee Scheme, have been successful in stabilising work and incomes.

With around 34 per cent of the world population and nearly 40 per cent of its employed population, India and China, despite their differences, confront a common challenge: how to extend the realisation of social citizenship rights more widely and in ways that soften rather than harden the distinctions between urban and rural, 'advanced' and 'backward', privileged and marginalised. How the issue of labour informality is perceived will be a critical part of the debates to come in both countries.

INDEX

www.ingramcontent.com/pod-product-compliance
Ingram Content Group UK Ltd.
Pitfield, Milton Keynes, MK11 3LW, UK
UKHW021909150926
475560UK00003B/267